THE HANDY
WESTERN
PHILOSOPHY
ANSWER
BOOK

About the Author

Ed D'Angelo earned a Ph.D. in philosophy from the State University of New York at Stony Brook, where he studied continental philosophy and developed a philosophical theory of human consciousness. He also holds a master's degree in library science from the State University of New York at Albany. Currently an independent scholar, until his retirement in 2014 Dr. D'Angelo was a supervising librarian at the Brooklyn Public Library, where for the last eleven years of his career he led a philosophy discussion group for the public. Additionally, Dr. D'Angelo taught philosophy at Stony Brook, Rensselaer, SUNY Albany, Sienna College, and Empire State College. He lives in Brooklyn, New York, with his wife, Lisa.

THE HANDY
WESTERN
PHILOSOPHY
ANSWER
BOOK

The Ancient Greek Influence on Modern Understanding

Ed D'Angelo, Ph.D.

VISIBLE
INK
PRESS

Detroit

ALSO FROM VISIBLE INK PRESS

The Handy Law Answer Book
by David L. Hudson, Jr., J.D.
ISBN: 978-1-57859-217-3

The Handy Literature Answer Book: An Engaging Guide to Unraveling Symbols, Signs, and Meanings in Great Works
by Daniel S. Burt, Ph.D., and Deborah G. Felder
ISBN: 978-1-57859-635-5

The Handy Math Answer Book, 2nd edition
by Patricia Barnes-Svarney and Thomas E. Svarney
ISBN: 978-1-57859-373-6

The Handy Military History Answer Book
by Samuel Willard Crompton
ISBN: 978-1-57859-509-9

The Handy Mythology Answer Book
by David A. Leeming, Ph.D.
ISBN: 978-1-57859-475-7

The Handy New York City Answer Book
by Chris Barsanti
ISBN: 978-1-57859-586-0

The Handy Nutrition Answer Book
by Patricia Barnes-Svarney and Thomas E. Svarney
ISBN: 978-1-57859-484-9

The Handy Ocean Answer Book
by Patricia Barnes-Svarney and Thomas E. Svarney
ISBN: 978-1-57859-063-6

The Handy Personal Finance Answer Book
by Paul A. Tucci
ISBN: 978-1-57859-322-4

The Handy Philosophy Answer Book
by Naomi Zack, Ph.D.
ISBN: 978-1-57859-226-5

The Handy Physics Answer Book, 3rd edition
by Charles Liu, Ph.D.
ISBN: 978-1-57859-695-9

The Handy Presidents Answer Book, 2nd edition
by David L. Hudson
ISB N: 978-1-57859-317-0

The Handy Psychology Answer Book, 2nd edition
by Lisa J. Cohen, Ph.D.
ISBN: 978-1-57859-508-2

The Handy Religion Answer Book, 2nd edition
by John Renard, Ph.D.
ISBN: 978-1-57859-379-8

The Handy Science Answer Book, 5th edition
by The Carnegie Library of Pittsburgh
ISBN: 978-1-57859-691-1

The Handy State-by-State Answer Book: Faces, Places, and Famous Dates for All Fifty States
by Samuel Willard Crompton
ISBN: 978-1-57859-565-5

The Handy Supreme Court Answer Book
by David L Hudson, Jr.
ISBN: 978-1-57859-196-1

The Handy Technology Answer Book
by Naomi E. Balaban and James Bobick
ISBN: 978-1-57859-563-1

The Handy Texas Answer Book
by James L. Haley
ISBN: 978-1-57859-634-8

The Handy Western Philosophy Answer Book: The Ancient Greek Influence on Modern Understanding
by Ed D'Angelo, Ph.D.
ISBN: 978-1-57859-556-3

The Handy Weather Answer Book, 2nd edition
by Kevin S. Hile
ISBN: 978-1-57859-221-0

PLEASE VISIT THE "HANDY ANSWERS" SERIES
WEBSITE AT WWW.HANDYANSWERS.COM.

THE HANDY WESTERN PHILOSOPHY ANSWER BOOK

Visible Ink Press®
43311 Joy Rd., #414
Canton, MI 48187–2075

Visible Ink Press is a registered trademark of Visible Ink Press LLC.

Most Visible Ink Press books are available at special quantity discounts when purchased in bulk by corporations, organizations, or groups. Customized printings, special imprints, messages, and excerpts can be produced to meet your needs. For more information, contact Special Markets Director, Visible Ink Press, www.visibleink.com, or 734–667–3211.

Managing Editor: Kevin S. Hile
Art Director: Mary Claire Krzewinski
Typesetting: Marco Divita
Proofreaders: Larry Baker and Christa Brelin
Indexer: Shoshana Hurwitz

Cover images: *The School of Athens* fresco (Vatican Museum), *Aristotle and His Disciples* (National and Kapodistrian University of Athens); all other images, Shutterstock.

ISBN: 978–1–57859–556–3

Cataloging-in-Publication Data is on file at the Library of Congress.

Printed in the United States of America.

10 9 8 7 6 5 4 3 2 1

Table of Contents

Acknowledgments

Since ancient times philosophy has been practiced in dialogue with one's friends, and this book is no exception. I would like to thank each of my following friends for reading my manuscript, for talking with me about it, and for giving me the emotional support I needed to make it through the most difficult times: Rolando Perez, Sharin N. Elkholy, John M. Koller, Naomi Zack, Roger Smith, Michael Spataro, and Scott E. Weiner. Most of all I would like to thank my wife, Lisa J. Cohen, for her enduring love and for our dinnertime conversations that contributed in no small way to the writing of this book. Finally, I would like to thank Roger Janecke and Visible Ink Press for conceiving of the "Handy Answer" Series and giving me the opportunity to publish this book. A special thanks goes out to Kevin Hile for his professionalism in editing the book.

Photo Sources

Introduction

I was first drawn to philosophy in high school. Though my high school, like most high schools in the United States, did not offer classes in philosophy, they did offer advanced classes in science and mathematics that provoked in me philosophical questions about the nature of space, time, and logic. For example, I wondered about the mysterious notion that space itself is curved and that time travel might be possible. So called "black holes," whose gravitational field is so strong that even light cannot escape from them, are like funnels in space that suck anything that crosses the "event horizon" into oblivion—or through a "wormhole" to another point in space or time.

There are many reasons that people are drawn to philosophy, and my own interests soon expanded beyond my early questions about the foundations of math and science. For several generations now, our culture has been rapidly changing, and some of us have been questioning older beliefs and ways of life. There have been intractable political differences and endless culture wars. Many of us on both sides of the cultural divide have lost trust in government and organized religion. Seeking an alternative, some have experimented with new forms of politics, social organization, and spirituality. All of these developments have led to a great deal of confusion and puzzlement. Who and what can we believe, and how can we know it? Philosophy offers answers to questions like these, and some people are drawn to philosophy for that reason.

Yet another reason that people are drawn to philosophy is that they enjoy solving a good puzzle. Philosophy is a lot like detective work. There is a mystery to be solved. You collect clues. You make connections. Suddenly you enjoy a flash of insight and all the pieces fit together. Like Archimedes (c. 287–c. 212 B.C.E.), who suddenly discovered how water is displaced by submerged bodies while he was taking a bath, you shout, "Eureka!" (I have found it!)

Philosophy in general is the attempt to use the reasoning powers of our own minds to answer our own questions. It is the pursuit of answers to questions about the universe and our place in it, the nature of justice and the good society, the purpose of life, and our own powers of reasoning themselves that enable us to answer these questions. However, because philosophy is just as much about learning how to use your own mind as it is about the answers, you cannot learn philosophy by just memorizing the answers. You must also learn the reasons behind those answers so that you can learn how to use your own mind to find the answers for yourself.

This book can be used as a ready reference to answer specific questions that you may have about philosophy. There are a particularly large number of answers to questions about ancient Greek philosophy and philosophy since the twentieth century. To find answers to your questions, just search the index for the topics that interest you or browse through the relevant chapter. But if you want to learn the reasons behind the answers and improve your own powers of reasoning in doing so, it is best to read this book in sequential order from the first page to the last.

The history of philosophy itself did not develop in a haphazard fashion but in a logical order such that each successive philosophy built upon the ones that came before it. Thus, to completely understand philosophy as it is done today, it is necessary to trace the entire history of philosophy back to its beginning in ancient Greece. Unfortunately, it is not possible to adequately cover the entire history of philosophy in one volume. Instead, I focus on the beginning and the end of that history. The end of that history is of interest because it includes our own time. The beginning is of interest because that is when some of the best philosophy was done and when the foundations for all that came after were laid.

Once the reader has mastered ancient Greek philosophy, they will be well positioned to study medieval philosophy, the Renaissance, and the modern philosophy of the seventeenth and eighteenth centuries. Medieval philosophy was the application of Neoplatonism and the Greek philosophers Plato and Aristotle to questions in Christian, Jewish, and Islamic theology. The Renaissance was inspired by the discovery of new texts by Plato and other classic authors and their translation into Latin. And modern philosophy was based in large part on a renewed interest in the ancient Greek philosophy of the Hellenistic period and its application to philosophical problems in modern science.

Because so much philosophy is written in a technical language for a specialized audience, it can appear to be intimidating to the general reader. A glossary at the back of this book can assist the reader with some of these important terms. It is my firm belief, however, that philosophy at its best aims for clarity, not obfuscation, and that it is based in ordinary language and common sense. In any case, that is what I have tried to achieve in this book. I hope you have as much fun reading it as I did in writing it.

THE BASICS

What is philosophy?

Philosophy is a disciplined practice of thinking about the most fundamental or original concepts—the "first principles"—that we use to make sense of ourselves and our world. These are concepts that we usually take for granted in our daily lives and even in scientific inquiry. We use them all the time, but we don't think about them. In that respect, philosophers are like young children who ask questions about things that older children and adults don't question or even give much thought to. Philosophy requires what is known in Zen Buddhism as a "beginner's mind" (*shoshin*), which is a mind that is open and empty of preconceptions. Philosophy lies at the end of any inquiry. If you keep asking questions long enough, you will eventually end up doing philosophy. Philosophy is about the ultimate questions and the answers to those questions—the first principles, where our beliefs begin.

Is philosophy always written?

No, philosophy is not always written. It is not necessarily even spoken. Philosophy is a type of thinking. However, writing is a powerful tool for thinking, and a written record of philosophical thinking has been kept for thousands of years in Europe, parts of the Middle East and North Africa, and most parts of Asia. Because we only possess written records of philosophical thinking in these parts of the world, the historical study of philosophy is usually limited to them.

Is philosophy only found in colleges and universities?

No, philosophical thinking is our birthright. Philosophical thinking is part of human nature and is found in all human societies to some degree or another, in all age groups, and at all levels of education. Children sometimes demonstrate a greater interest in philosophical questions than their parents, including those who have been college educated. Except during times of social change or personal crisis, adults often find no need to question their fundamental conceptions about themselves, the meaning of life, or the nature of reality. It is also a fact that many famous philosophers throughout history did not hold academic positions and that academic philosophy as it exists today dates only to the late nineteenth and early twentieth centuries.

What are some of the methods used by philosophers?

Philosophers have sought answers to their questions by means of logical reasoning, carefully inspecting first-person experience, studying the history of ideas and how those ideas came to be, interpreting historical texts, organizing their ideas into grand integrated systems, and creatively coining new concepts. Some philosophers emphasize some of these methods more than others. Analytic philosophers emphasize logical reasoning (especially deductive logic and logical analysis) above all else and are expert in its use. Phenomenologists have developed the method of carefully inspecting first-person experience to a very high level of sophistication. Georg Wilhelm Friedrich Hegel and (1770–1831) Aristotle (c. 384–c. 322 B.C.E.) organized knowledge into comprehensive systems. Systematic philosophers don't think you can understand the universe piecemeal. They think you need to understand the big picture before you can really understand the details, because the details are related to one another by the structure of the whole system. Some Continental philosophers believe that philosophy requires the use of imagination to coin new words and concepts. However, almost all serious students of philosophy have studied the history of philosophy to better understand philosophical ideas. Philosophers have never worked in complete isolation from one another. They have always developed their own philosophical ideas in response to what others before them thought. Therefore, to understand their philosophical ideas it is necessary to trace the history of their ideas. This is notably different from science. The scientific method is based on the most recent theories and on contemporary observations and measurements of the world, not on the history of science.

What are the historical roots of the written traditions in philosophy?

The historical roots of European, Middle Eastern, North African, and West Asian philosophy lie in ancient Greece. The traditions of India and East Asia developed independent of Greece. Most of the major philosophical traditions of India and East Asia, with the notable exception of Jainism in India and Confucianism in China, can be traced back to the Rig Veda, which was written in the second millennium B.C.E. in the Punjab region of northwestern India. The traditions rooted in the Rig Veda include Hinduism and Buddhism in all their varieties. An important distinguishing feature of ancient Greek philosophy is that it was secular. All philosophical traditions of India and East Asia were religious. However, Greek philosophy provided the foundations for philosophical thinking in Judaism, Christianity, and Islam.

MAJOR SUBDIVISIONS OF PHILOSOPHY

What are the major content areas of philosophy?

No matter what the tradition, philosophy must answer certain basic questions: What is? What is reality? What is knowledge? What is the purpose of life? Consequently, philosophy may be divided into three major areas: *metaphysics*, which is the study of reality or of what is; *epistemology*, which is the study of knowledge; and *value theory*, which may be divided into *ethics* and *aesthetics*.

What is metaphysics?

Metaphysics is the theory of reality. What is real? What is illusion? What's the difference between reality and dreams or imagination? Is reality one or is it many? Is the world composed of atoms? What kinds of things are real? What is mind? What is matter? Is mind real? Is matter real? How are mind and matter related to one another? What is space? What is time? Is time real? Does change really exist or is reality ultimately unchanging? Is space real? What do universal terms like "blue" or "good" or "beautiful" refer to? Does anything exist other than particular blue things or particular good things or particular beautiful things? Do universals exist? If not, then what makes them real?

What is epistemology?

Epistemology is the theory of knowledge. Epistemology asks questions such as these: What is knowledge? Is knowledge a true proposition, such as the proposition "Socrates is a man"? Or is knowledge more like "seeing"—in other words, a direct apprehension of what is real? Or is knowledge an idea in our minds that accurately represents what is real? Or is knowledge knowing how to do something, like knowing how to ride a bicycle? Or is knowledge whatever a given community agrees is knowledge? Is knowledge dependent on social context, so that what is knowledge in one society may not be knowledge in another society, or must knowledge be universally true in order to count as knowledge at all? Does the language we speak condition what we know, or can we know independent of language? How do we know if we really know, or if we're mistaken? Are there any reliable criteria we can use to determine the authenticity of our knowledge? Are there any reliable methods we can use to acquire knowledge? What are the sources of knowledge?

Metaphysics is the quest for a theory of the ultimate nature of reality. People seek it through philosophy, spirituality, religion, dreams, and the sciences. According to some modern thinkers, the science of quantum mechanics offers a key to the nature of reality.

3

What is empiricism?

Empiricism is the theory that perception is our only source of knowledge. According to empiricists, the mind can only rearrange knowledge obtained through the senses. It cannot create knowledge. The mind is capable of logical reasoning, but logic is not a source of new knowledge. Logic only draws out the implications of what we already know.

What is rationalism?

Rationalism is the theory that the mind has other sources of knowledge besides the senses. Rationalists have supposed that mathematical truths and ethical truths, for example, are grasped by the mind alone, without the aid of the senses.

What is philosophy of science?

Philosophy of science is a subfield of epistemology that studies science as a type of knowledge. It asks questions such as these: What is the scientific method? Do different sciences use different methods? Are scientific methods a reliable source of knowledge? How do we know that science is reliable? What makes it reliable? Does science accumulate facts over time so that it is always gradually increasing its store of knowledge? Does science periodically go through periods of revolutionary upheaval when its basic models of reality are challenged by anomalous facts? During periods of revolutionary upheaval, are there rational standards for determining which way science will proceed, or is the course of science determined only by power struggles between competing groups of people? Does science discover knowledge or construct it?

What is logic?

Logic is a subfield of epistemology that studies arguments that are composed of propositions that make knowledge claims. Logic is the study of what we can infer from a given set of propositions. For example, given the propositions "Socrates is a man" and "All men are mortal," we can infer that "Socrates is mortal." If the given propositions are true, and we follow the rules of logic, then the inferred proposition will also be true. Thus, logic gives us rules for reliably making inferences from what we know to what we didn't explicitly know before those inferences were made.

What is symbolic logic?

The rules of logic depend only on the form of our propositions, not their content. Be-

Mention the word "logic" and an image of the character Spock from *Star Trek* might come to mind. But logic is not about lacking emotions; it is really the art of inferring conclusions given a set of true propositions. It is a structured way of thinking and solving problems.

cause logic depends only on the form of our propositions, not their content, the study of logic can be carried out entirely with abstract symbols that have no meaning and don't refer to anything. For example, given the propositions "Bobo is a clown" and "All clowns are funny," we can infer that "Bobo is funny." This is so because all arguments of the form "A is a B" and "All Bs are C," therefore "A is C" are "valid," regardless of what A or B or C mean or refer to. A "valid" argument is one that must be true if the given propositions are true. Logic can determine the validity of arguments based only on their form, without knowing anything about their component propositions or terms. Thus, symbolic logic dispenses with real words that have meaning and uses only abstract symbols like A, B, and C or P, Q, and R. Even "logical operators" such as "and," "or," "therefore," "not," and "all" are represented by symbols.

What is deductive logic?

Deductive logic is the study of arguments whose conclusions must be true if their premises or given propositions are true. The conclusion of a deductive argument follows necessarily from its premises with mathematical certainty. Indeed, mathematics uses deductive logic to derive theorems from axioms, which are the fundamental premises of a mathematical system. For example, deductive logic is used to construct proofs in geometry. Given the truth of its premises, the conclusion of a valid deductive argument is not merely likely to be true but is necessarily and with absolute certainty true.

What is inductive logic?

Unlike deductive arguments, the conclusion of an inductive argument may be false even if its premises are true. The conclusion of a valid inductive argument is probably true but may not be. Many arguments based on observations of real events in the world are inductive arguments. For example, if you observe a series of white swans, you may inductively argue that the next swan you observe will also be white. But of course, the next swan might not be white. It might be black.

What is dialectical logic?

Dialectical logic is the logic of disputation between opposing speakers. Rather than proceeding in a straight course from premise to conclusion, as in either deductive or inductive logic, dialectical reasoning proceeds by way of negation. One speaker makes a claim, then the other contradicts that claim, and the original speaker makes a counter claim, which in turn is countered. Back and forth the dispute continues, with each speaker revising his or her claims on each round. It is presumed by practitioners of dialectics that the speakers spiral closer to agreement and truth with each round. Unlike deductive logic and inductive logic, it is not possible to separate the form of dialectical arguments from their content, and there are no rules for determining the truth of dialectical arguments based only on their form. In that sense, dialectical logic isn't really a logic at all but rather a style of conversation.

What is ethics?

Ethics is the study of what is good or right, and its opposite, what is bad or wrong. There are many different ethical theories about what is good or right, bad or wrong. According to some, our actions themselves are good or bad, right or wrong. According to others, our actions can be judged only according to their consequences. According to yet others, only the will or intention to act is good or bad, right or wrong. Yet others assert that it is only our character or disposition to act that is good or bad. Some ethical theories hold only the individual morally accountable, whereas others make moral judgments about entire communities, collectively. Ethics is not only about social behavior. The ancient Greeks believed that how you care for yourself is also a matter of ethical concern.

What is political philosophy?

Political philosophy is a subfield of ethics because it is concerned with good and bad, right and wrong, in political matters. Is government good, or would anarchy be better? Why should we or why should we not have a government? What is a good government? What is the best form of government? What is justice? What is injustice?

What is social philosophy?

Social philosophy is the ethics of social institutions, customs, and cultures. Insofar as social philosophy is distinguished from political philosophy, it is concerned primarily with nonpolitical social institutions, customs, and cultures. However, since it is often impossible to separate the political from the nonpolitical, social and political philosophy are often combined into one field of study.

Political philosophy is the subfield of ethics that asks in what ways governments are good or bad, right or wrong. What is the best, most ethical form of government? What makes a good and just political leader? What, for that matter, is justice?

How is ethics different from morality?

Philosophers often use the terms "ethics" and "morality" interchangeably. However, sometimes "morality" is used to refer to a specific set of beliefs about what is good or right, whereas "ethics" refers to the philosophical reasons for those beliefs.

What is aesthetics?

Aesthetics is the philosophical study of beauty and art. Since beauty is found in nature as well as in art, aesthetics is not only the study of art. And since not all art is beautiful, aesthetics is not only the study of beauty. In fact, one question asked in aesthetics is whether the value of art derives only from its beauty or if its value might derive from some other purpose, such as to express or evoke an idea or an emotion. A related question in aesthetics is whether the meaning of a work of art is due only to its own form or if it depends on something referred by the work of art outside itself. The theory that the meaning of a work of art is due only to its own form is known as formalism.

PHILOSOPHY BEFORE SOCRATES

Who were the Pre-Socratics?

The Pre-Socratics lived in ancient Greece and its colonies in the sixth and fifth centuries B.C.E. and were the first philosophers in the Western tradition. As their name suggests, nearly all Pre-Socratics were actively engaged in philosophy before Socrates (c. 470–399 B.C.E.), and none were influenced by him. No original writings by the Pre-Socratics survive. We know of them only through a few brief quotations and accounts of their ideas found in the works of philosophers who wrote after the time of Socrates. The Pre-Socratics include the schools of the Milesians, the Eleatics, the Pythagoreans, the Atomists, and the Sophists, as well as Xenophanes, Heraclitus, Empedocles, and Anaxagoras.

Why were the Pre-Socratics called the "Pre-Socratics"?

The Pre-Socratics were called "Pre-Socratics" because they wrote before and without any influence from Socrates, but also because they have traditionally been understood as precursors to Socrates and to his students Plato and Aristotle. Most Western philosophy is based on Plato and Aristotle and only indirectly on the Pre-Socratics.

How did Pre-Socratic philosophy get started?

The first philosopher recognized as such in the Western tradition was Thales (c. 624–c. 547 B.C.E.), who was a resident of the Ionian Greek settlement of Miletus, a busy trading port on the southwest coast of Asia Minor, which comprises most of present-day Turkey. Situated at the crossroads in the Eastern Mediterranean, the city of Miletus exposed its residents to a wide variety of different ideas, tales, and customs. This provoked a few exceptional individuals to question their own beliefs and to search for what would be true not only for a particular people but for all.

Were the Pre-Socratics influenced by any earlier traditions?

While they introduced their own unique innovations, the Pre-Socratics were influenced by earlier scientific and religious ideas from the Eastern Mediterranean, ancient Egypt, and India.

What is Pre-Socratic philosophy?

There were many different individuals and schools of Pre-Socratic philosophy, but what they share in common is a search for the *arche* of all things. *Arche* is an ancient Greek word (ἀρχή) meaning "source," "origin," or "beginning," and in the writings of the first philosophers, "element" or "first principle." It is the root of the word "archetype." The arche is the one underlying principle that explains the many things that appear in the world. The concept of the arche, therefore, presupposes a binary opposition between the one and the many and between being and appearance. Thus, Pre-Socratic philosophy can also be characterized by the search for the one true reality behind the appearances and the attempt to reconstruct or explain how those appearances come to be out of their source in the arche.

THALES

Who was Thales?

Thales of Miletus (c. 624–c. 547 B.C.E.) was an engineer by trade, a mathematician, and an astute observer of the natural world. But he is most famous for being the first philosopher in the Western philosophical tradition and the founder of the Milesian school of Pre-Socratic philosophy.

What were some of Thales's achievements in mathematics, science, and engineering?

Thales traveled to Egypt where he studied surveying, astronomy, and engineering, but he is given credit for several discoveries of his own. He devised a crude telescope and measured the diameter of the Sun and the moon and determined the exact dates of the solstices and equinoxes. He was the first to advise the use of the Little Dipper, which contains the North Star, as an aid to navigation. He is said to have predicted a solar eclipse that occurred during a his-

Thales of Miletus was regarded by Aristotle to have been the first Greek philosopher to establish the tradition that he, Plato, and Socrates would later follow.

toric battle. Using his knowledge of geometry, he was able to measure the height of ships at sea. According to a tradition that originates with the third-century C.E. biographer Diogenes Laërtius and the fifth-century C.E. philosopher Proclus, Thales devised proofs for five mathematical theorems, one of which still bears his name.

What makes Thales a philosopher?

The ancient Egyptians possessed a great deal of mathematical know-how, which they used in building the pyramids, in surveying the land, in astronomy, and in other practical endeavors, but they had no theoretical knowledge and showed no evidence of abstract thought. They knew *how* to do things based on rules of thumb, but they didn't ask *why* those rules of thumb worked. For example, they lacked logical proofs for mathematical theorems. Whether it is true or not (as tradition reports) that Thales devised proofs for five mathematical theorems, there is ample evidence that Thales was interested in theoretical knowledge. Thales persistently asked "why?" about everything until he reached the first principle. It is this that made him a philosopher.

What was Thales's first principle?

Pneuma was the ancient Greek word for "breath," but it could also connote "spirit" or "soul" because breath, like spirit or soul, is what gives things life. According to a tradition that dates to Aristotle (c. 384–c. 322 B.C.E.), Thales believed that all things are full of "spirit" (Latin *dæmon,* Greek *daimōn,* English *demon*) or "soul" (Greek *psyche*), but everything else we know about Thales indicates that he tried to explain everything in terms of nature (Greek *physis*). Therefore, it is more likely that Thales believed that everything was alive in some sense rather than that everything was full of demons. But, Thales observed, all life contains water. If everything is alive in some sense, and if all life contains water, then, Thales concluded, water is the first principle of everything. Water is that which explains the coming to be and perishing of everything. It is that out of which everything comes and that to which everything returns.

How did Thales explain earthquakes?

According to Thales, the earth floats upon a vast ocean of water. Earthquakes were caused by waves on that ocean. Although his theory was wrong, it demonstrates how he used theoretical reasoning to explain things in terms of nature, rather than appealing to hidden or unknown forces or supernatural beings.

ANAXIMANDER

Who was Anaximander?

Anaximander (610–546 B.C.E.) was a student or associate of Thales and also his friend and successor in the Milesian School of Philosophy. Like Thales, he had a keen interest in geometry and the natural sciences. He made original contributions to geography, astronomy, biology, cosmogony, and philosophy. His attempt to provide a rational explanation of the world influenced the entire course of Western philosophy and science that came after him. His theory of the first principle reappeared in Neoplatonism nearly a thousand years later and influenced Western mysticism thereafter.

What were Anaximander's achievements in natural science?

Anaximander developed a primitive theory of evolution. He reasoned that humans could not have developed suddenly because infants are unable to feed themselves. Therefore, humans must have developed

A third-century Roman mosaic of Anaximander can be seen in Trier, Germany. With a keen interest in astronomy, geography, and biology, Anaximander sought rational explanations for how the world functions.

from other species who can feed themselves immediately after birth. Anaximander said that humans first developed from fish and that only later, after they were cast ashore, did they learn how to live on land. Anaximander was the first to use a gnomon, or shadow stick, to measure the time of day and the dates of the solstices and equinoxes. And he was the first to build a celestial globe with a chart of the stars. Contrary to Thales, he postulated that the earth is suspended in air and stays in place because it is surrounded equally on all sides by the stars. In geography, he drew the first map of the known world.

What is Anaximander's *apeiron*?

The ancient Greek word *apeiron* means "without end, limit, or boundary." The *apeiron* may therefore be understood as an undivided space without limits or boundaries. How-

What was Anaximander's first principle?

Anaximander's first principle (*arche*) was the unlimited, the *apeiron*. Anaximander observed that the world as we experience it is an ever-changing flux of alternating and opposed qualities. Light turns to dark and dark turns to light. Heat turns to cold and cold turns to heat. Wetness becomes dryness and dryness becomes wetness. Since the world consists of opposite qualities, it is not possible that everything arose from the same quality, such as Thales's water. An *arche* is not merely a source or first principle but a dominating or ruling one. If water or some other quality were the first principle, then it would have annihilated all opposite qualities. The *apeiron* is not any one form or quality but the source of them all.

What is the sole surviving quotation from Anaximander's writings?

"The Unlimited is the first principle of things that are. It is that from which the coming-to-be [of things and qualities] takes place, and it is that into which they return when they perish, by moral necessity, giving satisfaction to one another and making reparations for their injustice, according to the order of time."

ever, space refers to logical space as well as to geometric space. Limits or boundaries divide geometric space into shapes, but they also divide logical space into binary pairs of opposite concepts or qualities. Without limits or boundaries, then, there is only formless chaos. The apeiron as it rests within itself is formless chaos, but it is also a reservoir of potential forms and gives birth to them when limits or boundaries are imposed upon it. Thus, according to Anaximander, forms are created when they separate off from the primordial chaos in an alternating sequence of opposites, one after the other, in a perpetual cycle of birth and death that has a moral order and purpose.

What were the historical predecessors to Anaximander's apeiron?

The ancient Greek poet Hesiod believed that the world was formed out of a primordial chaos. In the creation stories of the ancient Near East, the primordial substance is a watery chaos. In the Rig Veda, the oldest sacred text of ancient India, the primordial substance is the dragon Vritra, which is formless chaos. The ordered cosmos is created by the heroic Indo-Aryan storm god Indra, who slays the dragon with a thunderbolt and releases the Seven Rivers from its belly. According to the late music professor Ernest Mc-Clain, Vritra represents the undifferentiated spectrum of sound frequencies. The Seven Rivers represent the seven basic tones that divide the spectrum of sound frequencies into a musical scale. Thus, ordered sound or music—the epic poetry of the Rig Veda itself that sustains the social order and the cosmos—is created by imposing limits or boundaries on the unlimited spectrum of sound frequencies.

How has Anaximander's concept of the apeiron been used in quantum physics?

In the Copenhagen interpretation of quantum physics, matter and energy do not exist until they are measured. Prior to measurement, we have only a probability distribution for what may occur given by the Schrödinger wave equation. Therefore, the primordial reality in quantum physics resembles Anaximander's apeiron. Like Anaximander's *apeiron*, the primordial reality in quantum physics is a reservoir of potential but still-to-be-determined forms. For this reason, the physicist Max Born called the primordial reality of quantum physics the *apeiron*.

13

ANAXIMENES

Who was Anaximenes?

Anaximenes (c. 585–c. 528 B.C.E.) was the third and final member of the Milesian School of Philosophy, following Anaximander, who was his older associate. Like his predecessors, Anaximenes proposed a first principle or primary substance that would provide a rational explanation for everything. Anaximenes believed that the first principle and primary substance of all things was air. According to Hippolytus, Anaximenes believed that all things, even gods and demons, come to be as products of air. Anaximenes improved upon Anaximander and Thales insofar as his theory not only identified the primary element but also provided a plausible explanation as to how the primary element changes into all the other elements. Everything comes to be, according to Anaximenes, through a process of condensation or rarefaction. For example, when air is cooled or exposed to a cold object, it appears to condense into liquid. When a liquid is cooled further, it turns into a solid. On the other hand, when liquid is heated, it evaporates into air. When heated further, according to Anaximenes, it bursts into flame. Anaximenes was the first to delineate the exact sequence of transformations from one element to the next: air condenses successively into wind, cloud, water, mud, earth, and stone. Air rarefies into ether and then fire.

In what way did Anaximenes and Thales think alike?

The Greek word for air, *aer,* is related to the Greek word for breath, *pneuma*, which can also mean "spirit" or "soul." Just as breath gives things life, just as our spirit or soul holds us together, giving us our identity and making us one person, so too did Anaximenes believe that air is in all things and makes them what they are. Thus, Anaximenes and Thales employed similar reasoning, though they arrived at slightly different conclusions. Whereas Thales supposed that because all living things are made of water, then water must be the primary substance, Anaximenes supposed that because all living things breathe, then air must be the primary substance.

HERACLITUS

Who was Heraclitus?

Heraclitus (c. 535–c. 475 B.C.E.) was a philosophical sage from the Ionian Greek city of Ephesus, located on the western coast of Asia Minor about forty-eight miles north of Miletus by road in modern Turkey. A total of 139 short fragments of his writings survive. They are pithy, often enigmatic statements full of ambiguity and paradox that seem to condense great wisdom into only a few words. He was born into an aristocratic family that came with a hereditary office that carried religious and political duties, but according to Diogenes Laërtius he withdrew from public life and eventually retired to the mountains where he lived on grass and roots, causing him to become ill of dropsy (edema), an excess of water, and die at the age of sixty. The story of Heraclitus's death may derive from one of his fragments in which he says that it is "death for souls to become water," perhaps intending to make the point that the soul is fire.

In spite of Heraclitus's stated disdain for most other philosophers, there is evidence of influence from the Milesian school of philosophy. Like the Milesians, he proposed a primary substance. In his case, he proposed fire as the primary element of the universe. And like Anaximenes, he believed that the elements change into one another by way of condensation and rar-

Building on Anaximenes's ideas about states of matter, Heraclitus believed that change was a natural state of existence and that everything was in a process of becoming something else.

efaction. In fact, he took Anaximenes's focus on change itself one step further and developed the theory that nature (*physis*) is essentially nothing but change, or "becoming." What we take to be permanent or even stable substances are really processes of continual change, like fire. But change is not chaotic or arbitrary. Change occurs according to a rule of law, which Heraclitus called the *Logos*, an ancient Greek word meaning a "reasoned account." Although everything changes, it changes in accordance with the *Logos*, which does not change, and which is true in all times and places. The *Logos* is one, common to all, and universal. Most men live, however, "as if they had a private intelligence of their own." Only a few are capable of grasping the *Logos*, and it was for these few that he wrote.

Why did Heraclitus often write in riddles and paradoxes?

Some ancient authors believed that Heraclitus wrote in riddles and paradoxes because he wanted to make sure that only the worthy few would understand what he was saying. But according to Heraclitus, it is not he himself who is paradoxical and hard to understand but rather reality. As he says in one of his fragments, "nature loves to hide." A similar sentiment is found in this fragment, which may explain why he used so many metaphors and other figures of speech: "the lord whose oracle is at Delphi neither speaks nor conceals, but gives signs." Nature does not reveal itself in straightforward or unequivocal terms because nature is a play of opposites that is itself contradictory or paradoxical. Nature is a fire that is forever kindling itself and then extinguishing itself, again and again, in exact measures, in accordance with the *Logos*. The elements transform into one another and then return back again, in an endless circle. But, he said, "in the

15

circumference of the circle the beginning and the end are common." Therefore, "the way up and the way down are one and the same." What appear to be opposites are actually the same: "Opposition brings concord. Out of discord comes the fairest harmony." The many become one. "That which is at variance with itself agrees with itself. There is a harmony in the bending back, as in the cases of the bow and the lyre." But equally so, concord brings opposition. Out of harmony comes discord. "The name of the bow is life, but its work is death." War, Heraclitus tells us, is "the father and king of all." War is the "common condition," "strife is justice," and "all things come to pass through the compulsion of strife." (Quotations of Heraclitus are from Philip Wheelwright, *The Presocratics*.) Out of strife the many are born. The one becomes many.

What did Hegel say about Heraclitus?

The German philosopher Georg Wilhelm Friedrich Hegel (1770–1831) has been one of the most influential philosophers of the modern age. He was the first to study philosophy historically and is famous for his dynamic and dialectical logic. In his *Lectures on the History of Philosophy*, Hegel said that "there is no proposition of Heraclitus that I have not adopted in my Logic." Hegel believed that Heraclitus was the first to discover the dynamic and dialectical logic by which paradoxes or contradictions are resolved and opposites are united as one, from which come new contradictions and opposites, in a repeating cycle.

EMPEDOCLES

Who was Empedocles?

Empedocles (c. 495–c. 435 B.C.E.) was a prophet, a philosopher, and a physician, and he was active in democratic politics in his native city of Akragas on the southern coast of what is today Sicily. Akragas was one of the richest and largest of the ancient Greek colonies. Empedocles was the author of two poems, *On Nature* and *Purifications*, both written in hexameter verse. *Purifications* was an autobiography of his life as a "spirit" (Latin *dæmon*, Greek *daimōn*, English *demon*) who was exiled from the spirit world for shedding blood and putting his trust in strife. He was subsequently incarnated as a prophet who warned that love and abstention from bloodshed are morally imperative. Empedocles forbade the eating of flesh, even the flesh of animals sacrificed in religious ceremonies. Like the Pythagoreans, he believed that humans could be reincarnated as animals, so eating the flesh of animals was equivalent to cannibalism. Aristotle writes about Empedocles in his works on biology and physics, and as a result more attention has traditionally been given to his philosophy of nature. However, recently discovered fragments of his writings found on an Egyptian papyrus scroll suggest that *On Nature* and *Purifications* may have been parts of one poem and that their two themes are more closely related than previously suspected.

Empedocles was the philosopher who defined the four primary elements of fire, earth, air, and water. This concept of matter survived for centuries.

What were the four primary elements according to Empedocles?

Empedocles is most famous for his discovery of the four primary elements: air, water, earth, and fire. Aristotle added a fifth primary element, ether, which fills the atmosphere that the celestial bodies reside in. According to Empedocles, everything is composed of mixtures of the four primary elements. Hippocrates, the founder of Western medicine and the probable author of the "Hippocratic Oath," related the four primary elements to the four basic humors of the human body: blood, phlegm, black bile, and yellow bile. The theory of the four temperaments—sanguine, phlegmatic, melancholic, and choleric—was also based on the four elements. The theory of the primary elements remained an integral part of West-

The idea that the universe is composed of four elements or combinations of those elements was basic to philosophy and science from the time of the ancient Greeks through the Middle Ages.

17

ern scientific and philosophical thought for two thousand years until the dawn of modern chemistry. Even modern chemistry retains a vestige of the four elements in its theory of the four states of matter: gas, liquid, solid, and plasma.

How, according to Empedocles, did the four primary elements form all the things of our world?

Empedocles believed that the primary elements combine with one another in different proportions to form the many things of our world due to the power of love. On the other hand, he believed that they separated from one another due to the power of hate or strife. Love and strife may therefore be compared to the forces of attraction and repulsion in modern physics, except that love and strife are not only material forces. Empedocles called the four elements the four "roots" (Greek *rhizōmata*). They don't merely combine with one another in a mechanical fashion; they grow into one another to form complex organisms.

What was Empedocles's theory of cosmogony?

Empedocles believed in something like a cyclical big bang theory, except that his theory is not only about the material universe but also about a spiritual process. According to Empedocles, the universe explodes due to the power of strife into a spinning vortex of many different things. At some point, it reverses course and begins to contract due to the growing power of love. The many things combine to form larger wholes until the universe becomes one undifferentiated sphere. Then the process is repeated when strife tears the sphere apart once again.

What was Empedocles's theory of evolution?

Empedocles picked up where Anaximander's theory of evolution left off. Like Anaximander, whose theory was inspired by fish fossils found at inland quarries, Empedocles believed that humans evolved from fish. But Empedocles added an explanation for how humans evolved that comes close to Darwin's theory of natural selection. Empedocles

---

How did Empedocles solve the problem of change presented by Parmenides?

Empedocles agreed with Parmenides that it is impossible for anything to come to be from what is not, and it is impossible that what is should ever cease to be. How then is change possible? Empedocles answered that the primary elements are never created or destroyed. In that sense, nothing ever comes to be or ceases to be. However, there is a mingling and interchange of parts in different proportions and shapes that form the many things of nature.

18

believed that in an earlier stage of cosmic history, organic parts were randomly combined (or not) in different ways. There were heads without necks, isolated arms and legs wandering about, and oxen with the faces of men. Some of these were successful at reproducing. Others were sterile and did not survive. Thus, Empedocles's theory contained the rudiments of the modern theory of natural selection, according to which random mutations produce a variety of different life forms, some of which survive and reproduce, and others that do not.

ANAXAGORAS AND ARCHELAUS

Who was Anaxagoras?

Anaxagoras (c. 500–c. 428 B.C.E.) was born in the Ionian Greek port of Clazomenae in Asia Minor, not far from Ephesus, where Heraclitus lived, on the western coast of present-day Turkey. According to Cicero, he was at one time a student of Anaximenes. According to the third-century C.E. biographer Diogenes Laërtius, he came from a wealthy family of high standing and was the first to teach philosophy in Athens, where he lived for thirty years. Among his students was Pericles, the great democratic statesman. According to one ancient report, Anaxagoras was charged with atheism and impiety for his materialistic theory that the Sun is a fiery rock instead of a god, and he received a sentence of banishment. According to another report, he was also charged with treasonable dealings with Persia and

sentenced to death. In either case, Diogenes Laërtius reports that his persecution was carried out by political enemies of Pericles, who persuaded the public to save Anaxagoras. He fled to Lampsacus, where he died and was buried with highest honors.

What were the primary elements according to Anaxagoras?

The primary elements according to Anaxagoras were the *homoeomerias*, or "seeds" of things. Like Empedocles, Anaxagoras believed that it is impossible for anything to come to be from what is not or for what is to cease to be. Therefore, he believed that everything is composed of elements that always were and always would be. However, Anaxagoras did not think that the many different qualities that we experience could be explained by a mixture of only four primary elements. Instead, he

Anaxagoras got in trouble with authorities for asserting that the Sun is a fiery rock and not a god; he also correctly deduced what causes eclipses.

believed that there is an unlimited number of different primary elements each with their own special quality. When we eat bread and olives, for example, the bread and olives do not cease to exist or turn into hair and flesh. Rather, the bread and olives contain parts or seeds of hair and flesh as well as seeds of bread and olives and an unlimited number of other seeds with other qualities. Our bodies separate out more seeds of hair and flesh from the bread and olives and less of the others. Hair contains more hair seeds than other kinds of seeds and that is what makes it appear to be hair. Whatever there is most of in a thing is what determines its manifest nature. But according to Anaxagoras, everything contains seeds, of everything else, because no matter how many times seeds are diluted with other seeds or divided into smaller parts, they can always be divided further, without limit. It is impossible to completely separate one kind of seed from any of the others. Thus, everything contains a portion of everything else.

What is Mind, according to Anaxagoras?

Mind (Greek *nous*) is intellect or cognition. Mind is that which knows. Mind has knowledge of all that is, and it is this knowledge that gives mind its power and command over everything. Mind is not one's own personal mind or consciousness, which would be different from other personal minds. Mind is not a thing. All Mind is alike, Anaxagoras says, whereas all things are different. Mind is cognition itself, apart from any particular person who engages in cognition or any particular object of knowledge. Mind is "unlimited, autonomous, and unmixed with anything, standing entirely by itself." If it were not pure and unmixed with anything, it could not, according to Anaxagoras, have command over everything.

How was the cosmos created, according to Anaxagoras?

In the beginning, according to Anaxagoras, before any separation occurred, all things and qualities were mixed up together to such an extent that no distinct thing or quality could be discerned. Mind then took charge and the original mixture began to rotate, and the force of rotation caused the elements to separate. Mind established the revolving movements of the stars, sun, moon, and planets, and of the air and ether. Mind separated dense from rare, hot from cold, bright from dark, and moist from dry. Mind thus established the order of all that was, is, and ever will be.

How did Anaxagoras explain rainbows?

Anaxagoras said that rainbows were not the goddess Iris but a glimmer of the Sun reflected on clouds. He thereby replaced a mythological explanation with a materialistic one.

Who was Archelaus?

Archelaus was a student of Anaxogoras. Socrates may have studied with Archelaus and at least knew of him. He was a philosopher of nature like the Milesians, and according to some reports he was born in Miletus. But according to Diogenes Laërtius, he also taught ethics and believed that what is good and just depends not upon nature but convention. He modified Anaxagoras's theory by claiming that mind is air. He was also the first to claim that sound is produced by a movement of air.

THE ATOMISTS: LEUCIPPUS AND DEMOCRITUS

Who was Leucippus?

Leucippus (fifth century B.C.E.) founded the school of atomists in Abdera between 540 B.C.E. and 530 B.C.E. Abdera was located on the Mediterranean coast of Thrace, in Greece. Simplicius says that he was born either in Elea or Miletus. Diogenes Laërtius says he may have been born in Abdera. In any case, his philosophy exhibits the influence of both the Eleatic philosophers and the Milesians.

What was Leucippus's philosophy?

There is only one original fragment of Leucippus that survived. Everything else we know about Leucippus comes second hand from later sources. The sole surviving fragment is a statement of determinism. In it, Leucippus says that nothing is random, and everything happens for a necessary reason. From later sources, we know of Leucippus as the founder of the theory of atomism. The theory of atomism was the theory that everything is composed of tiny, indivisible, microscopic particles of different shapes that move about in empty space. Leucippus therefore anticipated the modern atomic theory of matter.

How did atomism solve the philosophical problems posed by the Eleatic school of philosophy?

The Eleatic school of philosophy argued on logical grounds that it is impossible for what is ("being") to come from what is not, and that it is impossible for what is to cease to be, that is, to not be. Therefore, Eleatics denied the possibility of change. According to the Eleatics, reality is an indivisible plenum, meaning it is completely full, it is one, and it is unchanging. The world that we experience of sensory qualities, change, and multiplicity is all an illusion. The atomists agreed with the Eleatics

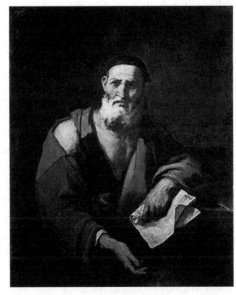

Leucippus is credited as the first philosopher to propose that all matter is made up of tiny, indivisible atoms.

21

about the nature of being. Each atom is in itself an indivisible plenum—unchanging, impenetrable, and without sensory qualities. However, according to the atomists, there are many plenums, not just one. Atoms, they say, are suspended in empty space. They do not have sensory qualities like hot, cold, blue, or loud. But they do have shape, location, and velocity. How can they say that atoms are suspended in empty space if the only thing that is, is the plenum? By a logical sleight of hand, they say that there is nothing but plenum because empty space is not. Empty space is not being. Therefore, being remains a plenum. And by placing atoms in empty space, they make it possible for atoms to move. Change can then be explained by the movement of atoms, just as it is in modern physics and chemistry.

Who was Democritus?

Democritus (c. 460.–c. 370 B.C.E.) of Abdera was an associate or student of Leucippus and the second Pre-Socratic atomist. He may have also studied with Anaxagoras and may have been influenced by the Milesians through him. In any case, his philosophy demonstrates a strong interest in mathematics and the study of nature, although according to ancient reports he was the first to study aesthetics, and over two hundred ethical maxims that he wrote also survive. He came from a wealthy noble family in Abdera and exhausted his inheritance on travel. According to Diogenes Laërtius, he studied geometry with Egyptian priests. According to ancient reports, he also studied in Ethiopia, with Chaldean (Babylonian) magi in Persia, with gymnosophists in India, and with Pythagoreans.

What did Democritus say about knowledge?

Democritus distinguished between obscure knowledge and genuine knowledge. Obscure knowledge is knowledge that we obtain through our sense organs. This type of knowledge, according to Democritus, is not reliable and so is not really knowledge at all. Obscure knowledge is not reliable because it tells us more about how reality affects our sense organs than it does about reality itself. That is why Democritus says that sense qualities such as hot and cold, and blue and green, exist only by convention—in other words, they are social constructions like language. Reality itself contains none of the qualities we experience with our sense organs because reality consists only of the void (empty space) and atoms. But atoms are colorless, tasteless, and soundless. Atoms are defined in strictly quantitative or mathematical terms by their extension, location, and velocity in space. To obtain genuine knowledge, it is necessary to employ a finer faculty than our sense organs. It is necessary to employ the intellect (Greek *nous*). In this respect, Democritus anticipated Descartes and the scientific revolution by two thousand years.

What was Democritus's ethics?

Democritus's ethics anticipated the later ethical theory of Epicurus, known as Epicureanism. Democritus believed that the good is happiness (Greek *euthymia*) and that happiness is a mood of cheerfulness and serenity. The good can be achieved by exercising moderation and proportion in all of life's affairs. But moderation and proportion can be determined only by rational thought (Greek *noesis*), not by pleasant sensation alone (Greek *aesthesis*). What is pleasant, Democritus said, is different for everyone, but the good, like the true, is the same for all. Life, he said, is short, fragile, and fraught with difficulties, so it is necessary to possess in moderation and measure hardship by real need in order to achieve happiness. Greed, envy, and even excessive admiration lead to unhappiness. But greed is not only about money. Democritus said, "It is greed to do all the talking and not want to listen at all."

Democritus was sometimes called the "Laughing Philosopher" for his tendency to mock those with whom he disagreed. Many portraits of Democritus, such as this one by Hendrick ter Brugghen, show him grinning or laughing.

Why was Democritus known as the laughing philosopher?

The Romans Seneca and Juvenal and the philosophers of the Renaissance referred to Democritus as the "laughing philosopher" because Democritus valued cheerfulness and because they believed that he must have found the lack of moderation with which most people pursue their aspirations to be ridiculous and absurd. The terms "Abderitan laughter" and "Abderite," which means "scoffer," derive from Democritus, who was from Abdera.

What were some of Democritus's mathematical achievements?

Democritus was the first to discover that the volume of a cone is equal to one third of the volume of a cylinder of the same base and height. Democritus may also be given credit for highlighting the problems associated with the concept of a continuum and proposing atomism as a solution. In one of his surviving fragments, Democritus asks whether the two planes above and below a cut parallel to the base of a cone are of equal diameter. If they are equal, then the cone would be a cylinder, not a cone, because the diameter of each cut parallel to the base would not be different. On the other hand, if they are not equal, then the cone would have a step-like structure.

Arguments like these that draw out the paradoxes inherent in our intuition of continuous change or difference were originally constructed by the Eleatics to prove that there is no continuous change or difference and that therefore reality is One and unchanging. Change and multiplicity, they believed, are illusions. The atomists agreed that there is no continuous change or difference, but instead of concluding that reality is One and unchanging, they concluded that there is discrete change and difference. Change and multiplicity can be saved either by abandoning our intuition of continuous change or difference, so we acknowledge that conical objects are really discrete, step-like structures, or by solving the very difficult problems related to the concept of a continuum. The atomists chose to abandon the continuum. They believed that all the real things in the universe are composed of atoms that have a finite size and cannot be further divided. It was not until the late nineteenth century that the mathematicians Georg Cantor and Richard Dedekind solved the problems associated with the concept of a continuum. A "Dedekind cut" of the cone would result in two planes that are unequal without the cone having a step-like structure because although the two planes would have different diameters, the difference would be infinitely small.

THE ELEATIC SCHOOL: PARMENIDES, ZENO, AND MELISSUS

Who was Parmenides?

Parmenides was born in about 515 B.C.E. to a wealthy family of high standing in the Greek colony of Elea in southern Italy. In the mid-fifth century B.C.E., he founded the Eleatic school of philosophy. According to Plato, Parmenides was a venerable sixty-five-year-old man when he visited Athens and made a powerful impression upon Socrates, who must have been about nineteen years old at the time. Consequently, Parmenides appeared as an important philosophical figure in several of Plato's dialogues. Parmenides was the first metaphysical monist in Western philosophy, which means that he believed that reality is One. He was also the first rationalist insofar as his metaphysics was based on rational thinking about the concept of "being" or of the verb "is," not on observations or speculations about nature. He distinguished between a changing flux of illusory appearances, which are the subject of "common opinions" (Greek *doxa*), and true reality, which can be known only by means of reason or "logos." By introducing these ideas, he prepared the way for Platonism and certain strands of Western mysticism.

What did Parmenides write?

Parmenides wrote only one work, an epic poem written in dactylic hexameter verse titled *On Nature*. Only fragments of the poem survive. The poem tells the story of the author's mystical journey, in a chariot led by the maiden daughters of Helios, the sun god, through the gates of Day and Night, to the Underworld, where he meets the Goddess of Truth. The Goddess distinguishes between the way of truth and the way of opinion and begins in the first part of the poem by explaining the principles of truth. In the second part of the poem, the Goddess explains that it is necessary to become acquainted with common opinions as well so that the philosopher can recognize mere appearances for what they are and not be taken in by them.

24

What was Parmenides's philosophy?

Parmenides's philosophy was diametrically opposed to the philosophy of Heraclitus, who believed that reality is a world of "becoming" or "coming-to-be," an ever-changing war of opposites. Parmenides believed that reality is One, undifferentiated, and unchanging: a full, uniform sphere, equal on all sides and surrounded by nothing, for it is all that is. Not even thought about the One can be differentiated from the One: "Thought and being are the same." Reality "neither was nor will be, it simply is—now, altogether, one, continuous." The appearance of a world of many things in flux is mere illusion, what he calls the "way of opinion." Opinions (Greek *doxa*) are common beliefs derived from experience and

Considered the founder of ontology—the study of being and the concepts related to being—Parmenides established the Eleatic school that included such philosophers as Zeno of Elea and Melissus of Samos.

tradition. They are not, according to Parmenides, reliable. *Logos,* which is rational thinking, is the only "way of truth." Listening to logos, we learn that it is impossible for anything to come to be from what is not or for anything to come to not be, because what is not does not exist. What is not is absolutely nothing. Only what is, is. Common opinions "that mortals accept and rely on as if true—coming-to-be and perishing, being and not-being, change of place, and variegated shades of color—these are nothing more than names." Reality is one continuous whole. Only arbitrary conventions—common opinions—divide that continuum into multiple discrete objects by giving them names.

Who was Zeno of Elea?

Zeno of Elea (c. 490–c. 430 B.C.E.) was a student and associate of Parmenides, who was twenty-five years Zeno's senior. According to Plato, Zeno was tall, handsome, and beloved by Parmenides. An apocryphal story originally told by Diogenes Laërtius reports that Zeno was part of a conspiracy to overthrow a local tyrant. When captured by the tyrant, he refused to reveal the names of his accomplices, bit the tyrant, and refused to let go until he was stabbed. The story, whether accurate or not, testifies to the character of Zeno's argumentative style, which is tenacious. Zeno is most famous for his paradoxes, which were intended to provide logical arguments in defense of Parmenides's claim that Being is One, Unchanging, and Unmoving, and that Not-Being is not and cannot be thought or spoken about.

What type of logical argument did Zeno employ?

Zeno was the first to develop a type of logical argument called by Aristotle the "dialectical syllogism" and known among medieval logicians by the Latin phrase *reductio ad*

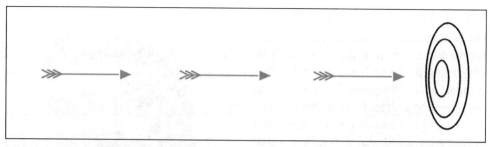

Zeno's arrow paradox asserts that motion is actually impossible because at any particular moment of time the arrow is fixed at a particular point.

absurdum, which means, in English, to reduce to the absurd. Zeno's method was to start with his opponent's claim and then show how absurd conclusions logically follow from it. Instead of constructing an argument to show how one's own claim is true, the *reductio ad absurdum* shows how the opposite claim is false. If the opposite of one's own claim is false, then one's own claim must be true.

What is the arrow paradox?

The arrow paradox relies on our common-sense notion that time consists of an infinite series of instant moments. But if time is an infinite series of instant moments, then a moving arrow occupies a space equal to itself at any one instant in time. In other words, during any instant, a moving arrow is just where it is, and nowhere else. Therefore, during any and all instants, the arrow is not moving. Therefore motion is impossible.

What is Zeno's racetrack paradox?

In the racetrack paradox, Zeno argues that a runner will never complete a race because before he completes the race, he must traverse the first half of the racetrack. But after he traverses the first half of the racetrack, he must traverse the first half of the remainder of the racetrack, which is equal to one quarter the length of the racetrack. And in order to traverse the one quarter of the racetrack that remains, he must complete the first half of that, which is equal to one eighth the length of the racetrack. And so on ad infinitum. This can be formulated mathematically as the infinite series $\frac{1}{2}^n$ as n goes from 1 to infinity ($\frac{1}{2} + \frac{1}{4} + \frac{1}{8} + \frac{1}{16} + \ldots$). The series adds up to 1 (the completion of the race) only when n actually reaches infinity. Zeno argued that it is impossible to traverse an infinite series of finite lengths of space in a finite amount of time. Therefore, the runner will never complete the race. In another version of the racetrack paradox, the runner never even gets started. For the runner to complete the race, he must first complete the first half of the race. But for the runner to complete the first half of the race, he must first complete the first quarter of the race. And so on. Just as in the first version of the paradox, we have an infinite series. The runner can never get started because the end of the series can never be reached in a finite amount of time. Therefore, motion is impossible.

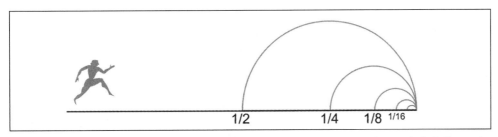

In the racetrack paradox, a runner can never reach the finish line because they must first reach the halfway point to the finish, then they must travel halfway down the rest of the distance, and so on, and so on, always halving the distance but never finishing.

Have Zeno's paradoxes ever been solved?

The solution to Zeno's paradoxes was a long time coming. All of Zeno's paradoxes rely on the contradictions implicit in our common-sense notions of space and time, or, more generally, our common-sense notions about the continuum and the related concept of infinity. To solve Zeno's paradoxes, one must formulate a theory of the continuum that is both mathematically sound and free of logical contradictions. Aristotle thought that Zeno's paradoxes were a result of the false belief that a continuum is an *actual* as opposed to merely a *potential* infinite series. For example, according to Zeno's racetrack paradox, it is impossible to traverse a racetrack because an infinite series would have to be traversed in a finite amount of time. But according to Aristotle, a racetrack does not consist of an *actual* infinite series. A racetrack can only be *potentially* divided into an infinite series. An actual racetrack is a finite series of finite units. Therefore, the racetrack *can* be completed in a finite amount of time.

The Roman Catholic Church agreed with Aristotle that the racetrack is not an actual infinite series because, according to the Church, nothing is infinite except God. Aristotle's solution to Zeno's paradoxes was accepted for two thousand years. But the problem with Aristotle's solution is that it is not mathematically sound. A continuum *is* an actual infinite series. Zeno was wrong to think that an infinite series can't converge on a finite number, but he was right that a continuum is an actual infinite series. Aristotle's mistake was of no consequence for him because he didn't use mathematics to understand the world. His view of the world was qualitative, not mathematical. But the view of the world that emerged in the scientific revolution of the seventeenth century was mathematical. In particular, Newtonian mechanics requires the mathematical theory of calculus. In calculus, an infinite series converges on a finite number because each successive number in the series decreases in quantity at a fast-enough rate that the sum of all numbers in the series converges on a finite number. The infinite series $1/2 + 1/4 + 1/8 + 1/16 + \ldots$ adds up to the number 1 even though there are an infinite number of fractions in the series because, although there are an infinite number of fractions in the series, they become infinitely small. The concept of an infinite series that is used in calculus provides a solution to Zeno's paradoxes. But calculus doesn't explain why the concepts of the continuum and of infinity as they are used in calculus are sound. It merely assumes they are. A demonstration of the soundness of these concepts had to wait for the development of set theory in the late nineteenth and twentieth centuries. Hence Zeno's paradoxes were not fully solved until quite recently.

Who was Melissus of Samos?

Melissus of Samos (fifth century B.C.E.) was the third and final figure in the Eleatic school of philosophy founded by Parmenides. Born on the island of Samos in the eastern Aegean Sea, off the coast of modern-day Turkey, Melissus was not only a philosopher but the admiral of the Samian navy and the commander of the fleet that defeated Pericles and the Athenians in 441 B.C.E. Samos was a rich and powerful Ionian Greek city state and a rival of nearby Miletus. The Samians opened up trade and alliances with states around the Mediterranean, including Egypt, which protected it from the Persians. Like Parmenides and Zeno, Melissus believed that reality is One, undifferentiated, undividable, unchanging, and unmoving. His only disagreement with his predecessors was that he believed that the One is unlimited in extension, not a sphere, since if it were a sphere, there would be something outside of it that was not itself, which is impossible because then there would be two.

What was Melissus's argument against motion?

Melissus argued that there can be no motion without empty space because a body cannot move into a space that is occupied by another body. However, there cannot be any emptiness because what is empty is nothing and what is nothing cannot be. Therefore, there is no empty space and, therefore, there can be no motion. The atomists agreed with Melissus that empty space was necessary for motion, but they believed that empty space existed and that therefore, although the atoms like the One are undifferentiated and unchanging, they do move.

What is time according to Melissus?

Time is only the way that things appear to us—the "way of opinion"—not how they really are. The real, says Melissus, cannot come to be or perish. The real is now, always was, and always will be. Therefore, the real is unlimited in time as well as space. It has neither beginning nor end. Consider a historical event. D-Day occurred on June 6, 1944. It was true before June 6, 1944, on June 6, 1944, and after June 6, 1944, that D-Day occurred on June 6, 1944. Regardless of whether anyone knew it or not, it was always true and always will be true that D-Day would occur or did occur on June 6, 1944. In this sense reality does not change; only the way that it appears to us changes, depending on our vantage point in time. In modern philosophy, this is known as "eternalism" or "block time" or the "block universe," because reality is viewed as a four-dimensional "block" rather than a three-dimensional space moving through time. Time is likewise viewed as a fourth dimension in Einstein's general theory of relativity.

What were some of Melissus's arguments against change?

If there is no motion, then the world cannot be changed by rearranging its parts, because the parts would have to move for them to be rearranged. Nor is qualitative change possible. Blue cannot become green. Fire cannot become water. Blue is blue. Green is green. Fire is fire, and water is water. If a quality did change, it would cease to be because it is what it is, and if it changed, it would cease to be what it is. It would become nothing. But if there were nothing, then it would be impossible for anything to come to be, because nothing can arise out of nothing.

PYTHAGORAS

Who was Pythagoras?

Pythagoras (c. 570–c. 495 B.C.E.) was the mysterious and legendary founder of a monastic religious community in the Greek colony of Croton in southern Italy and the creator of a unique mathematical and musical view of the world whose influence extends down to the present day. Members of the community that Pythagoras established were sworn

to secrecy, and no original writings by Pythagoras himself survive. What we know about Pythagoras is derived from what others wrote about him, and much of what was said about him was fanciful and fantastic. For example, he was said to have a golden thigh and to be seen in two places at the same time. Therefore, there is little known for certain about him. We do know, however, that Pythagoras was born on the island of Samos not far from Miletus, the birthplace of Western philosophy. Thales ignited his interest in mathematics and astronomy and advised him to visit Egypt, and he studied geometry and astronomy with Anaximander. Like the Milesians, Pythagoras understood the world in terms of binary pairs of opposites, including the principal pair of opposites, the unlimited and the limited. However, he also studied mathematics, astronomy, religion, and mysticism with Egyptian priests, with the Arabs, with the Chaldaeans of Babylon, and with the Persian prophet Zoroaster.

Pythagoras was one of the most influential Pre-Socratic philosophers. Famous for such things as the Pythagorean theorem (the sum of the squares of the two adjacent sides of a right triangle is equal to the square of the hypoteneuse), he also wrote on other mathematical and music theories and, spiritually, about the transmigration of souls (metempsychosis).

29

How did the Pythagorean community in Croton come to an end?

In the early part of the fifth century B.C.E., the Pythagoreans entered public life in the Greek city states of southern Italy and occupied important political positions, but the residents of Croton distrusted them and resented their political influence. They feared that Pythagoras possessed dangerous magical powers. In about 508 B.C.E., when Pythagoras was an old man, there was a popular uprising against the Pythagorean community led by Cylon, a local noble, in which their buildings were burned, many were killed, and others, including Pythagoras himself, fled into exile. The community was never rebuilt, but Pythagorean philosophy survived, and some of the Pythagoreans were even elected to high political office again.

What way of life did the Pythagoreans practice in their community in Croton?

The Pythagorean way of life followed a pattern of ritual purification followed by a revelation of divine wisdom that had already been established in ancient Greece by the Eleusinian mysteries. The Pythagoreans believed that the purpose of life is to bring harmony to one's soul and cleanse it of its impurities. This goal could not be achieved in one lifetime. Upon death, the soul is reborn into another animal or human body, in which it has another opportunity to harmonize and cleanse itself. Ultimately, the soul is released from the body (Greek *sôma*), which was equated with a tomb (Greek *sêma*). To achieve this goal, members of the Pythagorean community in Croton followed an ascetic and communal way of life in which all property was shared in common. Admission to the community was tightly restricted. Newly admitted members of the community listened to Pythagoras through a linen curtain for five years. Only after their trial period ended were they permitted to see Pythagoras in person. They wore white clothing. Sex was discouraged in all seasons except winter, when it was permitted only between married couples for the purposes of procreation. Thus, the restriction of sex to married couples for the purposes of procreation that later became the rule in Judaism and Christianity originates with the Pythagoreans.

What was the status of women in the Pythagorean community?

Women were admitted to the Pythagorean community as equals to men. There is a tradition that attributes Pythagorean writings to Theano, who was either the wife, daughter, or student of Pythagoras, and to Perictione, who was Plato's mother. Although those writings were probably written under false pseudonyms and their true authors are unknown, the attribution of these valued writings to Theano and to Perictione illustrates the high esteem in which women were held in the Pythagorean community. The attribution of Pythagorean writings to Perictione also demonstrates the close affinity that was felt between Pythagorean and Platonic philosophy.

According to the biographer Iamblichus (c. 250–c. 330 C.E.), the Pythagoreans began each day with a solitary walk in a quiet place because they believed their minds should be calm and harmonious before conversing with others. They strengthened their memory by recalling the events of the previous day, and of the day before that, and perhaps of their previous lives. Then they gathered together to discuss their studies and walk to sacred places such as temples. They sang hymns to Apollo. Afterward they engaged in a variety of physical exercises. This was followed by a spare lunch of bread and honey in which they ate in groups of ten, the perfect number. Then came more studies and walks followed by baths and dinner preceded by the appropriate libations and sacrifices. There were strict dietary regulations, and they were said to be vegetarians, but there are conflicting reports about which meats if any were permitted.

What did Pythagoras learn from the ancient civilizations he studied?

Pythagoras learned ancient arithmetic, geometry, and astronomy, and he probably also studied religious theories having to do with the celestial bodies, which were identified with gods or spirits. Ancient mathematics and astronomy developed out of the need to construct a reliable calendar that guided the production of crops. In agricultural civilizations, what happens in the heavens determines what happens on earth because the growth of crops depends on the position of the sun in the sky. This mundane observation may have inspired the much more general philosophical saying "As above, so below," which is common to Hermeticism, alchemy, and astrology. Ancient astronomy, which was not distinguished from astrology, was a way to divine the future on earth as well as in the heavens, because it was believed that what happens in the heavens determines what happens on earth. But if the movement of the celestial bodies is essentially mathematical, then that means that everything on earth is also mathematical.

What did Pythagoras discover about music and mathematics?

According to legend, Pythagoras discovered the numerical properties of musical harmony while passing by a blacksmith's shop. He noticed that hammers of different weights produced harmonious sounds when struck on an anvil if the weights were in certain proportions to one another. If one hammer weighs twice as much as another, then the two hammers will produce harmonious tones that are exactly one octave apart from one another. If one hammer weighs half more than the other in the proportion 3:2, then another harmonious musical interval will be heard, that of the fifth. If one hammer weighs one third more than the other in the proportion 4:3, then the harmonious interval of the fourth will be heard. The same correspondence between musical intervals and mathematical proportions can be demonstrated by blowing through holes in a cylindrical pipe that are spaced apart at appropriate intervals and by plucking strings of different lengths. Harmonious tones will be heard if the distance between the holes or the lengths of the strings are in the proportions 2:1, 3:2, or 4:3. Thus, Pythagoras concluded that music has a mathematical structure and that mathematical structure is musical.

What was the tetractys?

The Pythagoreans represented numbers with dots placed in geometric configurations. The tetractys was a triangular configuration of ten dots with four dots on each side, one dot at the top, two in the next row, three in the next, and four at the bottom. It was believed to contain all the secrets of the universe.

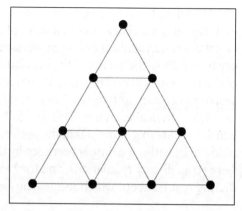

Pythagoras's tetractys was considered a mystical symbol that contains the secrets of the universe.

Each row represents different types of geometric forms. The first row, containing a single dot, represents a single point in space. The second row, containing two dots, represents a line, because a line is determined by two points. The third row, containing three dots, represents a plane, because a plane is determined by three points. The fourth row, containing four dots, represents a tetrahedron, because a tetrahedron is determined by four points. The ratio of the first row to the second row, 1:2, is the octave. The ratio of the second row to the third row, 2:3, is the fifth. The ratio of the third row to the fourth row, 3:4, is the fourth. The four dots on each side of the triangle represent wholeness and justice. The total number of dots is ten, the perfect number, known as the decad.

What was the Pythagorean view of the world?

From the ancient agricultural civilizations, Pythagoras learned that the world both above in the heavens and below on earth is mathematical. To this insight he added his discovery that music is mathematical, and that mathematics is musical. Thus, the heavenly bodies studied by the ancient civilizations were not only mathematical but also musical, and the supreme mystical experience for the Pythagoreans was to hear the "Music of the Spheres," which is the music of the ten revolving globes that contain all the heavenly bodies. According to the Pythagoreans, there is a fire at the center of the universe that cannot be seen from earth because the inhabited part of the earth always faces away from the central fire. The earth, the moon, the sun, the five known planets, and the fixed stars each rotate in their own sphere around the cosmic fire. The Pythagoreans considered the number ten (the decad) to be a perfect number. To arrive at ten spheres, they postulated a counter-earth situated on the opposite side of the central fire that also revolves around the central fire in its own sphere.

What was the Pythagorean quadrivium?

The Pythagorean quadrivium was the combined study of arithmetic, geometry, music, and astronomy, together as one unit. Plato included the quadrivium in his ideal educational system, and it was an important component of the liberal arts curriculum throughout the European Middle Ages.

How did Pythagorean philosophy shape Western civilization?

The Pythagoreans anticipated so many aspects of Plato's philosophy that Plato was often believed to have been a Pythagorean himself. The revival of Platonic philosophy during the early Christian era known as Neoplatonism recognized no difference between Platonic and Pythagorean philosophy. Neoplatonism in turn exerted a powerful influence on the foundations of Christian theology and mysticism. Pythagorean philosophy also lies behind alternative spiritual traditions, including numerology and number mysticism, Gnosticism, Hermeticism, Rosicrucianism, and alchemy. Lastly, modern science would not have been possible without the Pythagorean conviction that the universe is a well ordered, rational, and indeed mathematical system that can be known by the human mind.

THE SOPHISTS

Who were the Sophists?

The Sophists were the first professional teachers in ancient Greece. For a price, they taught free citizens what they needed to know to succeed in the public realm and preserve or enhance their social status. Greek society during the time of the Sophists changed from a traditional society ruled by established families to a more open, commercial, and democratic society in which free citizens negotiated the terms of social relationships with one another in the law courts and public assemblies. Since social relationships were negotiable, rather than fixed, there was an increase in social mobility, at least for free citizens. Social status became more dependent on one's words and actions instead of being determined solely by the family to which one was born. *Arête* is the ancient Greek term for virtue or excellence, meaning what a thing is good for. Those with greater *arête* enjoyed higher social status. Originally *arête* referred to military virtues such as courage and fortitude in battle. Later, it referred to the ability to win in the courts and public assemblies. In traditional Greek society, it was believed that men were born with *arête*, but the Sophists claimed that *arête* was something that could be taught and learned, and that therefore social status was something that could be acquired through education. During the time of the Sophists, a free citizen's *arête* was the ability to win in the courts and public assemblies. The Sophists taught free citizens the art of persuasive speech, which gave them the ability to win in the courts and public assemblies. In this sense, the Sophists were the first lawyers and professional politicians.

What was Plato's complaint about the Sophists?

Very few original writings by the Greek Sophists survive. Most of what we know about the Sophists is derived from Plato's unsympathetic portrayal of them in his dialogues. Plato's complaint about the Sophists was that they were not interested in truth or righteousness

33

but in social power. For a price, the Sophists taught people how to persuade others and thereby gain power, wealth, and social status. They taught people how to make the weaker argument appear to be the stronger argument—in other words, how to make what is false appear to be true, in order to win social favors.

Who was Protagoras?

Protagoras (490–c. 420 B.C.E.) was the first and the most famous of the Greek Sophists. Plato devoted an entire dialogue to Protagoras and cites him as the founder of the Sophists. Protagoras is most famous for one of his few surviving fragments in which he says that "man is the measure of all things." This fragment is usually interpreted to mean that there is no absolute truth and that all knowledge is relative to man. It is not clear, however, whether Protagoras meant that all knowledge is rela-

A 1662 painting by Salvator Rosa shows Protagoras at right and Democritus at center. Protagoras was considered to be the founder of the Sophists.

tive to individual men or if all knowledge is relative to particular societies or cultures. In Plato's dialogue the *Theaetetus*, Socrates interprets Protagoras's fragment to mean that knowledge is relative to the individual. Socrates says that different people often perceive the same things differently. For example, one person may feel cold while another feels warm, even though both are blown by the same wind. However, shortly later in the *Theaetetus*, Plato has Protagoras say that the purpose of sophistic education is not to replace false beliefs with true beliefs, because it is not possible to think anything other than what one experiences, but to replace unhealthy beliefs with healthy ones. The role of the Sophist in any given society, then, is not to replace false beliefs with true beliefs, because according to Protagoras "whatever seems right and admirable to a particular city-state (polis) is right and admirable—during the period of time in which that opinion continues to be held" but to replace unhealthy beliefs with healthy ones by making the healthy ones *seem* to be true and therefore actually *be* true insofar as truth is whatever one can be persuaded is true.

Who was Gorgias?

Gorgias (c. 485–c. 390 B.C.E.) denied that it was possible to teach *arête,* but like the other Sophists he accepted a fee for his services and taught rhetoric and the art of persuasion in public affairs. Gorgias was a student of the great philosophical tradition that began in Miletus. He studied with Empedocles and mastered the techniques of dialectical argument that had been developed by Zeno in the Eleatic school. He wrote books about nature. However, the absurd conclusions of the Eleatic school—that reality is One and unchanging and that the world of change and multiplicity that we experience is an illusion—ultimately led him to believe that knowledge of the world is impossible. Using the logical techniques he learned from the Eleatics, Gorgias argued that nothing is real; that if anything were real, it could not be known by us; and even if it could be known, it could not be communicated. Gorgias was therefore one of the first skeptics, which is a philosophical position that holds we cannot know anything. Although we cannot know anything, least of all about the natural world, we can still master rhetoric and the art of persuasion, and it is this that Gorgias taught, for a fee.

Who was Thrasymachus?

Thrasymachus (c. 459–c. 400 B.C.E.) was a Sophist who flourished around the time of Socrates and Plato. He is most famous for his role in *The Republic,* where in the opening chapter of Plato's dialogue he argues that justice is the advantage of the stronger— in other words, that might makes right. The remainder of Plato's *Republic* can be read as an attempt to establish the possibility of moral knowledge and to refute the claim that justice is nothing more than the advantage of the stronger.

Who was Callicles?

Callicles (c. 484–late 5th century B.C.E.) was a key figure in Plato's dialogue the *Gorgias,* according to which Callicles was a Sophist who learned his trade directly from Gorgias. Like Thrasymachus, Callicles rejects the possibility of moral knowledge or truth. He claims that justice is the advantage of the stronger and that it is unnatural and wrong for the weak to resist the domination of the strong. Callicles particularly disliked democracy and the rule of law because he thought they were merely devices by which the many who are weak subvert nature and dominate a few strong individuals. But whereas Thrasymachus believed that power is its own reward, Callicles was a hedonist who believed that pleasure and happiness are the rewards of power. There is no higher moral standard than what brings the greatest pleasure or happiness to those who have the power to obtain it. Like Thrasymachus, Callicles serves primarily as a foil for Plato's arguments that there must necessarily be moral truth.

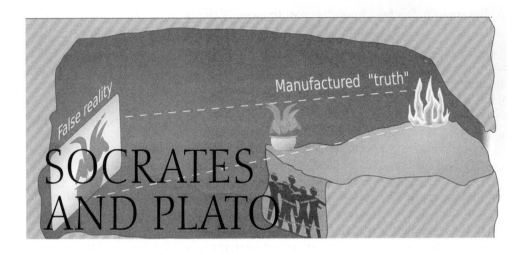

Who was the founder of Western philosophy?

Plato (c. 427 B.C.E.–c. 347 B.C.E.) was the founder of Western philosophy. His work was so influential that the philosopher Alfred North Whitehead (1861–1947) claimed that the entire history of Western philosophy consists of a series of footnotes to Plato. Although the Pre-Socratics were practicing philosophy in the Western world for generations before Plato, only a few fragments of their work survived, and what little survived was later subsumed by Plato's philosophy or by his student Aristotle's philosophy. In addition to founding Western philosophy, Plato also had a profound influence on Christian theology and Western mysticism more broadly. Both Friedrich Nietzsche (1844–1900) and Martin Heidegger (1889–1976) would have agreed with Whitehead that Western philosophy has been a series of footnotes to Plato, but each bemoaned that fact instead of celebrating it. Both believed that Western philosophy took the wrong path starting with Plato and found more to like in the Pre-Socratics, although classicists do not believe that Heidegger's interpretation of the Pre-Socratics was historically accurate.

Why is the history of philosophy important to students of philosophy?

The history of philosophy is important to students of philosophy because it is generally not possible to fully understand a philosophical work without also studying works that came before it. Philosophy is different from science in this way. When we study science, we study the contemporary state of scientific knowledge, not its history. There are several reasons for that. First, philosophers write in response to their predecessors and build upon their work. Second, philosophers usually wrote for an audience that was familiar with their predecessors and so they didn't feel a need to repeat what their predecessors said. For example, philosophers did not always define technical terms if those terms were used by their predecessors. Third, there is no generally agreed-upon method in philosophy to falsify or invalidate past theories. There is even debate about what historical figures meant to say. The scientific method is quite different. Contemporary scientific theories stand on their own and can be understood without studying their history. Each new generation of scientists must clearly define the terms they use, state assumptions and premises, and confirm the validity of their theories for themselves. Some philosophers have claimed that they were building a new philosophy from scratch—from the ground up—that didn't require their readers to study their predecessors. But in fact, none of them ever succeeded in doing that.

Who was Plato?

Plato (c. 427–c. 347 B.C.E.) was an ancient Greek philosopher and the founder of the Western philosophical tradition. The son of Ariston and Perictione, he was born into one of the wealthiest aristocratic families in Athens. In his youth, Plato was one of a number of young people who circled around Socrates (c. 470–399 B.C.E.). He was so affected by the execution of Socrates by the democratic state of Athens on charges of impiety and corrupting the youth that he wrote several dramatic dialogues featuring Socrates as the moral hero of the story. All told, thirty-five dialogues and thirteen letters or Epistles that have been attributed to Plato have survived.

Plato's uncle Charmides, on his mother Perictione's side of the family, and Charmides's uncle Critias were said to have been among the "Thirty Tyrants" who overthrew the Athenian democracy in 404 B.C.E. Whether this is historically accurate or not, it is true that Plato did not favor democracy. Plato's vision of the ideal state is presented in his greatest dialogue, *The Republic*. There, he argues that the ideal state is one that is ruled by an elite class of "philosopher-kings" who are appointed to their positions based on merit and education. *The Republic* outlines the course of education required to prepare students to become philosopher-kings.

Plato attempted to establish an ideal society in the Greek colony of Syracuse in ancient Sicily. At that time Syracuse was ruled by the tyrant Dionysius I. Plato believed that the ideal society could be created if philosophers became kings or if kings became philosophers. He thought he might be able to educate Dionysius I to become a philosopher-king, perhaps because Dionysius I's brother-in-law and trusted advisor, Dion, was already a disciple of Plato's. But he failed, and Dionysius nearly assassinated him when Plato spoke out against tyranny.

Plato established the Academy in Athens in 387 B.C.E. and established the Platonist school of thought.

Following the death of Dionysius I, his young and ill-prepared son Dionysius II assumed power. Dion invited Plato back to Syracuse to educate his nephew Dionysius II to become a philosopher-king. However, that plan also failed. Both Plato and Dion were forced to flee Syracuse, though Dion later returned to Syracuse and overthrew Dionysius II. Dion ruled Syracuse for a short time before Calippus, another student of Plato's, assassinated him and seized power. Calippus ruled for about a year before he was forced into exile. Plato was discouraged by the failure of his attempts in Syracuse and never got involved in politics again. He returned to the "Academy," the school in Athens that he had established, to teach philosophy. Plato's greatest student there was Aristotle, who nearly equaled Plato as an important founder of the Western philosophical tradition. Aristotle tutored Alexander the Great (356–323 B.C.E.), who conquered most of the known world in his day. But Alexander's empire did not achieve Plato's ideal either.

How do we know who Socrates was?

Socrates did not write anything. History has preserved his memory only because he appears as a character in the writings of other ancient Greeks. Most of what we know about Socrates comes from Plato's dialogues, in which he appears as the heroic protagonist, and it is the Platonic Socrates that has had the greatest impact on Western civilization. But he also appears in Aristophanes's comic play *The Clouds* and in several dialogues written by the historian Xenophon. Plato's portrayal of Socrates differs only slightly from Xenophon's. They were both students of Socrates and greatly admired him for his intelligence and his character. Xenophon portrays a Socrates who presented a poor defense at his trial because he believed that it was better to die before the indignities of old age set in (Socrates was executed when he was seventy or seventy-one years old) than to defend oneself against unjust charges. Plato portrays a Socrates who refused to com-

promise with the prosecution at his trial in exchange for a lighter sentence to make the moral point that it is better to suffer injustice than to implicate oneself in an injustice by cooperating with the prosecution. Aristophanes portrays Socrates as a materialistic scientist and an impious atheist with his head literally in the clouds. Plato's portrayal of Socrates is generally considered to be the most reliable, and it is Plato's Socrates that philosophers are referring to when they talk about Socrates.

Who was Socrates?

Socrates (c. 470–399 B.C.E.) was born into a family of workers and artisans in ancient Athens. He was remarkably ugly. His eyes

Socrates was Plato's teacher and established the "Socratic method" of questioning and answering ethical problems.

39

were crossed and bulged. He had a pug nose and a pot belly, and he dressed poorly. His father, Sophroniscus, was a stonemason, and his mother, Phaenarete, was a midwife. Socrates himself practiced his father's trade, though he spent most of his time in the marketplace , or *agora*, questioning whoever would engage with him about their moral beliefs. But in a metaphorical sense, Socrates also practiced midwifery. The Socratic method of questioning, known as *elenchus*, is a form of midwifery because Socrates used it to assist his interlocutors in "giving birth" to their latent understanding of moral ideas.

In spite of his poverty, Socrates married twice and had several children. His philosophical conversations, or "dialogues," in the agora attracted a circle of young aristocratic men including Plato and Xenophon. He served bravely in the Athenian army as an armored infantryman, or *hoplite*, and saved the life of the notorious general Alcibiades. Socrates was also associated with Critias, the leader of the "Thirty Tyrants" who were installed in power by Sparta in 404 B.C.E. after it defeated Athens in battle. Due to his association with Alcibiades, Critias, and other antidemocratic aristocrats, Socrates was early on suspected of being disloyal to Athenian democracy. These suspicions grew until his enemies, lacking any evidence of treason, prosecuted him on drummed-up charges of not respecting the patron gods of Athens and of corrupting the youth. He was sentenced to death and forced to drink hemlock, a poison. Both Xenophon and Plato wrote accounts of Socrates's trial and execution. On the basis of their accounts, Socrates became known as a martyr and the founder of Western philosophy. His moral reputation in Western civilization is perhaps second only to Jesus Christ.

SOCRATIC ETHICS

What is *arête*?

The word *arête* (ἀρετή) is usually translated into English as "virtue," but it had additional meanings in ancient Greece. Whereas the English word *virtue* means only moral goodness, the ancient Greek word *arête* also referred to the fitness of a thing to achieve its purpose or potential. A strong, courageous soldier possessed *arête* because he could fight well in battle. A skillful orator possessed *arête* because he could persuade his audience. Even a strong horse could possess *arête* if it served its purpose well. Thus, the word *arête* is sometimes better translated as "excellence." The word *arête* was related to the words *araomai,* which meant "to pray," and *aristos,* which meant "the best." The word *aristocracy* was composed of the root terms *aristos,* "the best," and *kratos,* which meant "rule or power." The word *aristocracy,* therefore, meant a society ruled by the best, that is, a society ruled by those who possessed *arête*. In Plato's philosophy, *arête* takes on the additional meanings of being true and beautiful. Thus, in Plato's philosophy, *arête* combines moral goodness with functionality or effectiveness, truth, and beauty.

How did Socrates differ from the Sophists?

For a fee, the Sophists promised to teach young men virtue or excellence (*arête*) and hence prepare them for high public office. In traditional Greek society, it was believed that *arête* could not be taught because it was inherited from one's family. If you were born into an aristocratic family of high standing, you possessed *arête*. If not, you didn't. The Sophists challenged this by putting *arête* up for sale. The Sophists reflected the rise of democracy and commercial activity in Athens and the decline of the traditional feudal social order. Socrates did not believe that *arête* could be taught, nor did he charge a fee for his services. Instead, he thought of himself as a midwife, helping students to remember what they already knew and realize their innate moral potential. As such, he set himself apart from the commercial, democratic social order. However, he was also critical of the traditional aristocratic elites, including the Thirty Tyrants. He believed that *arête* is innate to the individual soul and is not something that can be imported into the soul from either a teacher or one's ancestors. His moral individualism set him apart from the traditionalists, while his belief that *arête* cannot be taught, let alone taught for a fee, set him apart from the Sophists and the new democratic, commercial social order.

How was Socrates's understanding of *arête* different from the Sophists'?

According to Socrates, *arête* is truth and the moral excellence of the soul. According to the Sophists, *arête* is the ability to persuade others in the law courts and public assemblies regardless of the truth or moral excellence of what one is persuading others to believe. The Sophists taught rhetoric because rhetoric is the art of persuasion, and by persuading others, one could obtain wealth, honor, and power. Therefore, *arête* as conceived by the Sophists was an outward social attribute, whereas according to Socrates, *arête* is an inner quality of the soul.

Why does Socrates believe that it is better to suffer injustice than to commit injustice?

Because to commit injustice is to harm your soul, whereas to suffer injustice is to suffer harm to your body. The body is only a passing illusion. True happiness depends on the peace and harmony of the soul, which is shattered by committing injustices.

What moral problem does the Ring of Gyges demonstrate in Plato's *Republic*?

According to ancient Greek myth, anyone who wears the Ring of Gyges becomes invisible. Today, the internet allows people to become invisible by speaking anonymously or under false identities. In the second chapter of Plato's greatest dialogue, *The Republic*, Socrates argues that it is always better to do what is right, even if you are never punished for doing wrong. Doing what is right is not a means to an end or the price you have to pay to get what you want, according to Socrates, but is worth doing for its own sake. Glaucon (Plato's brother and a frequent character in *The Republic*) disagrees. To prove his point, he asks Socrates to perform a thought experiment. Imagine, he says, that you possessed the Ring of Gyges and could make yourself invisible. You would be able to steal anything you wanted, rape whoever you wanted, or even commit murder—all without being detected or punished. Who wouldn't commit those crimes if they could get away with them? Socrates claims that committing crimes damages the peace and harmony of your soul, which causes unhappiness regardless of whether you are ever identified or punished.

THE SOCRATIC METHOD

Why did Plato write in the form of dialogues?

Plato lived long before the invention of the printing press. Philosophers in the ancient world communicated with one another through live conversation or handwritten documents. Since written documents were in relatively short supply, it was always better to talk directly with a philosopher. Both Plato and Aristotle established schools for this purpose. Plato believed that a live conversation with a philosopher is better than reading anything a philosopher wrote because a live philosopher can talk back, answer your questions, and correct misunderstandings. Plato viewed writing in general as inferior to live speech. He believed that writing is merely a mnemonic aid—a crutch to help us remember what had previously been spoken—and is a pale shadow of the original spoken word. That's one reason that Plato wrote in the form of dialogues or dramatic conversations. He didn't think of writing as a different form of communication with its own style or conventions but rather as an inferior imitation of live speech, which normally takes place in the form of dialogues. Socrates did not write anything at all.

What is the Socratic method of dialectics, or *elenchus*?

According to the Oracle of Delphi, no one in Greece was wiser than Socrates. But Socrates knew that he did not know anything. What then could the Oracle have meant? According to Socrates, the answer to the riddle is that he was wiser than anyone else in Greece because he alone knew that he did not know. Everyone else thought they knew something when they did not. It was the knowledge of his ignorance that made him wiser than everyone else. To test the Oracle's prophecy, Socrates questioned everyone, trying to find one person whose claim to knowledge could hold up to his barrage of questions. Socrates did not state what he knew, because he didn't claim to know anything; instead, he asked others to tell him what they thought they knew.

The Socratic method or, in ancient Greek, the method of *elenchus* (ἔλεγχοζ), starts with a question—generally a moral question, since it is moral knowledge that is required for wisdom—such as "What is justice?" or "What is piety?" or "What is courage?" The person being questioned by Socrates answers by offering a definition of the moral concept being investigated. Socrates then questions his interlocutor about the proposed definition in such a way as to draw out its logical implications. For example, if courage

What is the meaning of the Greek word *aporia*?

The Greek word *aporia* (ἀπορία) is derived from the word *áporos* (ἄπορος), which is composed of the root terms *a-* (ἀ-), meaning "no" or "not," and *póros* (πόρος), meaning "passage." Thus, the meaning of the Greek word *aporia* was "impasse," an impassable situation from which there is no way out. In philosophy, the word *aporia* refers to a state of perplexity, confusion, or puzzlement brought about by a logical contradiction, paradox, or other absurdity encountered in the course of an inquiry. In Plato's philosophy, the concept of *aporia* is closely related to the concept of the labyrinth. A labyrinth is a maze from which there is no easy escape. According to ancient Greek myth, the Minotaur, who was a man with the head of a bull, resided at the center of the labyrinth, where he devoured all who entered. In Plato's dialogue the *Euthydemus*, Socrates says that an impasse reached in their inquiry was like being in a labyrinth: "and then we got into a labyrinth, and when we thought we were at the end, came out again at the beginning, having still to seek as much as ever."

is acting without fear, then how is courage different from recklessness? After a series of questions like this, the person being questioned by Socrates finds themselves contradicting their original claim or other strongly held opinions and not knowing what to believe. The word in ancient Greek for this state of confusion was *aporia* (ἀπορία).

What is the Euthyphro dilemma?

The *Euthyphro* was one of Plato's early Socratic dialogues that ends in an impasse, or *aporia*. In the dialogue, Socrates challenges Euthyphro to define piety. Euthyphro responds with a series of proposed definitions, but none of them survive Socrates's criticisms. In one of his proposals, Euthyphro defines the pious to be what the gods love. Socrates asks whether the gods love the pious because it is pious, or if it is pious only because it is what the gods love. Socrates argues that they both can't be true without engaging in circular reasoning. If the gods love the pious because it is pious, then what is pious? If the pious is only what the gods love, then the pious is what the gods love. But what do the gods love? The gods love the pious. But what is pious? What the gods love.

An *aporia* is an impassable problem, which according to Plato is like a labyrinth that you enter and manage to emerge from without finding what you sought.

Thus, the dilemma. One or the other must be true but not both. Socrates and Euthyphro conclude that the gods love the pious because it is pious. The pious is not pious because the gods love it. But they fail to define what is pious.

How was the Euthyphro dilemma discussed in monotheistic religion?

Jewish, Christian, and Islamic religious thinkers discussed the Euthyphro dilemma in a slightly modified form. The form of the dilemma that they discussed concerned the moral good rather than piety: Is the good commanded by God because it is good, or is it good because it is commanded by God? Some religious thinkers have argued that the good is good because it is commanded by God. This is known as the divine command theory of morality, or voluntarism. Other religious thinkers have tried to resolve the dilemma by arguing that in the case of God, both horns of the dilemma are true. The good is good because God commands it. But God commands it because he is good, and it is his nature to command what is good.

PLATO'S ACADEMY

What was Plato's Academy?

The Academy was a philosophical community established by Plato in the early fourth century B.C.E. that resided at a site named Akademia, after the ancient Greek hero Akademos, in the northern suburbs of ancient Athens. Admission to the community was selective, but there was no fee. Like the Pythagorean community, the Academy admitted both men and women. The site of the Academy was sacked by the Romans about three hundred years after its founding, but members of the community continued their work at other locations in Athens. In the early fifth century C.E., a group of Neoplatonists reestablished the Academy at its original site. The Christian Emperor Justinian finally closed the Academy in 529 C.E. during his campaign against pagan heresies. However, members of the community fled the Western Empire to Constantinople and the Middle East, where many Platonic texts survived at least until the fifteenth century when they were recovered and translated into Latin. These texts helped bring about a revival of ancient Greek culture in Western Europe known as the Renaissance.

Why did Plato establish the Academy?

The Socratic method of *elenchus* is found in Plato's early dialogues, which were written before Plato established the Academy. Socrates practiced the method of *elenchus* because he conversed with Sophists and with strangers in public places who did not argue in good faith or with a sincere desire to acquire knowledge. Since there was no possibility of finding common ground with these conversation partners, conversations with them could only end in a state of *aporia*, that is, confusion or contradiction. In

44

Artist Raphael's fresco depicting Plato's Academy near Athens. Plato and Aristotle are shown debating at the center of the scene.

order to arrive at positive conclusions, it is necessary to converse with friendly conversation partners who share a sincere desire to acquire knowledge. Plato established the Academy to foster these kinds of conversations among friends. These "friends of wisdom" are the true "philosophers."

PLATO'S THEORY OF KNOWLEDGE

Do Plato's written dialogues arrive at final positive conclusions?

That is debatable. Certainly, many of the early dialogues do not. They end in confusion or contradiction. But even the later dialogues do not end conclusively in a way that forestalls further questioning. Even one of Plato's most central theories—the theory of forms—is subjected to the Socratic method in his late dialogue *Parmenides*. Plato does not present his beliefs in straightforward language. His dialogues are rich with metaphor, symbolic imagery, allegory, and parable. Nowhere in his dialogues does Plato speak in his own voice or appear as one of the characters.

45

Why do Plato's written dialogues not arrive at final positive conclusions?

Plato may not have believed that it is possible to transmit knowledge through written language. Written works, to Plato, are like orphans separated from their origin in the living mind of their authors. Authors and their readers are strangers to one another. All that written works can do is undermine your false beliefs and point you in the right direction. Live conversation with sympathetic partners is a better way to acquire knowledge. But ultimately, knowledge according to Plato is not even transmitted by live speech because knowledge is not a matter of *saying* the right thing but is a kind of *seeing* with the mind. A sighted person can talk about beautiful scenery all day with a blind man, but if the man can't open up his eyes and see for himself, he will never know what you're talking about.

What is Plato's theory of knowledge and the soul in his dialogue the *Meno*?

The *Meno* starts out like the early Socratic dialogues that end in a state of *aporia*. Meno arrives in Athens from another Greek city with a large entourage of slaves. Socrates asks him to define virtue or *arête*. Meno thinks he knows what virtue is, but after several questions from Socrates he is left dumbfounded. Socrates considers this an improvement over his initial condition since now at least he no longer thinks he knows what virtue is when he does not. But that is not how the *Meno* ends. Socrates goes on to make a positive claim about knowledge. Socrates says that we already know everything there is to know (including the most important knowledge of all, which is wisdom, the knowledge of virtue). But we have forgotten it. To acquire knowledge, then, all we need to do is remember what we already knew. But if we already knew it, when did we know it? Since you can go all the way back to birth and still not find a time when we knew it, we must have known it prior to birth. But if we knew it prior to birth, then the soul must have existed before we were born. It is in that disembodied state between births that we glimpse knowledge. We acquire knowledge by remembering what we knew prior to birth.

How does Socrates demonstrate the existence of innate knowledge in Plato's dialogue the *Meno*?

Socrates demonstrates the existence of innate knowledge by showing how one of Meno's slaves can solve a problem in geometry without being given the answer. Meno's slave is an uneducated boy. When initially questioned by Socrates about how to double the area of a square, the slave boy gives the wrong answer. He thinks that to double the area of a square it is necessary to double the length of one of its sides. When he realizes his error, he finds himself in a state of *aporia*. But after further questions, the slave boy is able to see that a square with a side drawn along the diagonal of the original square would be twice as large. Socrates claims that this demonstrates that the slave boy must have remembered what he already knew since Socrates did not give him the answer but merely asked him questions. Skeptics may argue that Socrates asked leading questions. But the demonstration has convinced many students of mathematics since the time of Socrates that knowledge of mathematics is innate because the feeling of recognition or déjà vu when learning mathematics is common among students of mathematics.

How does Plato's concept of innate knowledge differ from empirical knowledge?

Empirical knowledge is acquired through our sense organs. For example, I know that the rose is red because I can see it with my eyes. Without eyes, I would have no way of knowing that the rose is red unless someone who did have eyes told me that it was red. Empirical knowledge is therefore acquired after birth, because only after birth do we have bodies equipped with sense organs. Innate knowledge, on the other hand, is acquired by the mind and does not require the use of the sense organs. Whether we acquired innate knowledge prior to birth in a disembodied state, as Plato seems to have believed, or were merely born with innate knowledge, all the "rationalists" in the history of Western philosophy believed that at least some of our knowledge is innate.

Why did the sign over the entrance to Plato's Academy warn, "Let no one enter here who is ignorant of geometry"?

The purpose of the Academy is to study philosophy, which is the study of innate, abstract ideas, independent of physical or sensible objects. According to Plato, mathematical knowledge is at a lower level than philosophical knowledge because mathematical knowledge is usually acquired with the assistance of visual aids, such as drawings of geometrical forms on a blackboard. For example, it was with the assistance of such drawings that Meno's slave boy was able to grasp the Pythagorean theorem, which is an innate, abstract mathematical idea. Philosophy is the act of thinking about innate, abstract ideas *without* the aid of visual or other sensory images. But by providing examples of innate, abstract ideas, mathematics prepares students to do philosophy. Mathematics introduces students to innate, abstract ideas before they are able to think about them without the assistance of visual or other physical aids.

PLATO'S THEORY OF FORMS

Which ancient Greek words did Plato use to refer to the forms, and what did they mean in ancient Greek?

Plato used two words to refer to the forms: εἶδος, which when transliterated is spelled *eidos*, and ἰδέα, which is transliterated as *idea*. Both ancient Greek words come from an Indo-European root meaning "see." They both mean that which is seen, a look, or an appearance, particularly of a form or shape. Plato used these words metaphorically, since he didn't mean that we see the forms with our eyes but that the way we "see" the forms with our minds is somehow similar to the way we see visual forms or shapes with our eyes. The ancient Greek words for "appearance" and "form" are related to εἶδος and ἰδέα. The word for form or shape in ancient Greek was μορφή, which is transliterated as *morphē*. The word for appearance in ancient Greek was φαινόμενα, transliterated as *phainomena* or *phenomena*. The root φαίνω, transliterated as *phainō*, meant "shine." Thus,

47

an *idea* or *eidos*—a Platonic form—is an ideal form or shape (*morphē*) that "shines" (*phainō*) or "appears" (*phainomena*).

How does an ideal form—a Platonic form—differ from a physical form or shape?

An ideal form is not located at any point in space or time. It does not have a size. It does not have duration, that is, it does not span any length of time. A physical form can be perceived with the senses: you can see it and touch it. An ideal form can only be known by the mind. For example, consider the difference between a triangle drawn on a blackboard with a piece of chalk and the ideal form of a triangle. The drawing on the blackboard is in space and has a certain size. It has a certain duration in time. The chalk lines that represent the sides of the triangle have a certain length and thickness. On the other hand, the ideal triangle has a shape or a form (of a triangle) but no size. You can't see the ideal triangle with your eyes or touch it. You can only conceive it with your mind. The ideal triangle has no beginning or ending in time, nor is it found at any particular location in space. The ideal triangle is an abstract idea that may be conceived by anyone, anywhere, and at any time. It is, in a sense, both everywhere and nowhere.

What are some examples of Platonic forms?

Geometrical forms such as a square, a circle, and a triangle are Platonic forms. Numbers and other mathematical concepts are Platonic forms. Moral concepts like truthfulness, courage, temperance, justice, and the good are Platonic forms. Aesthetic concepts such as beauty in all its variations, as well as beauty itself, are forms. Physical things are not forms, but many physical things imitate or represent forms. However, not all physical things imitate forms. In the *Parmenides* Socrates says that vile and worthless things that lack *arête,* such as hair, mud, and dirt, are not only not forms but also do not even imitate forms in the way that a chalk drawing of a triangle imitates the form of a triangle.

What are the qualities of a Platonic form?

A Platonic form is whole and complete, pure and uncorrupted by anything that it is not. It cannot become something that it is not or be destroyed. A form is perfectly what it is. It is one, true, good, and beautiful. It is the ideal against which all physical things are measured and toward which everything strives. The forms possess *arête* (excellence). Thus, to know the forms is to acquire *arête*.

What is *mimesis*?

In ancient Greek theater, *mimesis* referred to the reenactment of dramatic events on the stage. In Plato, mimesis referred to the imitation or representation of the forms by physical things or events in nature. It is a key term in Plato's philosophy because it was used to describe the relationship between the forms and physical things or events. According to Plato, the forms are the archetypes or models that physical things imitate or represent. The form of a physical thing is also its *arête* or excellence. The better physical things imitate their forms, the better they are what they can be because the forms are the best that they can be. For example, the form of a statesman is pure and perfect statesmanship. Living statesmen can only approximate the statesmanship of the form itself, but the closer they approximate it, the better statesmen they are.

How did Plato reconcile the philosophical theories of Heraclitus and Parmenides?

According to Heraclitus, the world is a continuous process of change or "becoming" driven by a conflict or "war" of opposites. Heraclitus famously said, "No man ever steps into the same river twice, for it's not the same river and he's not the same man." Parmenides, on the other hand, believed that reality or "Being" is One and unchanging. His student Zeno constructed arguments to prove that a world of many changing things results in logical contradictions. Plato reconciled these two contradictory philosophies by postulating three degrees or levels of reality or "Being." At the top, according to Plato's theory of reality, were the forms, which are most real—indeed, absolutely real. Plato's forms had most of the properties of Parmenides's concept of Being. Like Parmenides's Being,

What is *methexis*?

In ancient Greek theater, *methexis* (μέθεξις) referred to a type of theater in which the audience participated in the dramatic events being performed. Plato used *methexis* to refer to the participation of physical things in the forms. Like *mimesis*, it is a key term in Plato's philosophy because it was used as a metaphor to describe the relationship between physical things and the forms.

Plato's forms are unchanging. Although there are many forms, they are logically inter-connected with one another in such a way as to form a united, harmonious system.

The highest form of all, the form of the Good, is a principle of harmony that allows many to act as One. At the bottom, according to Plato's theory of reality, was Non-Being or nothingness—the absolutely unreal. Plato imagined nothingness to be empty space, which he called the "receptacle." It is in this empty space that the world of Becoming appears. The receptacle can be metaphorically described as a womb in which things come to be and as a stage on which imitations of the forms appear as reenactments.

The world of Appearance and Becoming, according to Plato, stands midway between Being and Non-Being. It is neither fully real nor fully unreal. It is not One and un-changing like the forms. But it is not absolutely nothing either. The world of Appearance and Becoming is a mixture of Being and Non-Being, of the real and the unreal. In fact, it is exactly what Heraclitus said it was, a world of continuous change driven by a war of opposites. Nothing is ever what it appears to be because as soon as it appears, it be-comes something else. As soon as it is (Being), it is not (Non-Being). Thus, Plato rec-onciled the philosophies of Heraclitus and Parmenides. They were both correct, in Plato's view, but were about different levels of reality. Parmenides was correct about the forms, and Heraclitus was correct about the world of Appearance and Becoming.

THE ANALOGIES OF THE SUN AND THE DIVIDED LINE

What is Plato's analogy of the Sun?

In Plato's dialogue *The Republic,* the character Glaucon, who happens to have been Plato's brother, asks Socrates what the Good is. Unable to say directly what the Good is, Socrates responds by offering an analogy. He says that the Good is like the Sun. Just as the light of the Sun makes it possible to see physical things by shedding light on them, the Good makes it possible for us to know the forms by bringing them to our attention. Plato is suggesting here that cognition depends upon a value judgment. We cannot know something unless we recognize that it has value and is worth attending to. Being smart is not enough to acquire knowledge. You also need to have the right values. Because the Good is required for knowledge, Socrates says that the Good is not the same as knowl-edge but is superior to knowledge in power and dignity. But, paradoxically, Socrates also says that the Good is the highest form of knowledge and that it can be known, just like the Sun can be seen.

What is Plato's analogy of the divided line?

The analogy of the divided line follows immediately after the analogy of the Sun in Plato's *Republic* and expands upon Plato's theory of knowledge. The analogy of the divided line presents the theory that there are four different types of cognition that achieve lesser or greater degrees of knowledge about reality. Plato has Socrates speak for him. Socrates begins his discussion of the divided line by instructing Glaucon to divide a line into two unequal segments and then to divide each of those segments again in the same unequal proportion, resulting in four line segments, *a*, *b*, *c*, and *d*, as in the diagram below.

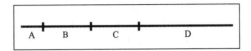

For example, if the line is 9 units long and it is divided by a proportion of 1 to 2, then the first division of the line will result in two line segments. The first line segment, equal to the length of *a* + *b*, would be 3 units long. The second line segment, equal to the length of *c* + *d*, would be 6 units long. If each of those line segments is then divided again by the same 1-to-2 proportion, segment *a* would be 1 unit long, segment *b* would be 2 units long, segment *c* would be 2 units long, and segment *d* would be 4 units long. The lengths of the four line segments, then, are proportional to one another, according to the mathematical formula $(a + b)/(c + d) = a/b = c/d$. Socrates is suggesting by this mathematical analogy that the relationship between the upper two segments of the divided line, *c* + *d*, to the lower two segments, *a* + *b*, is analogous to the relationship between *b* and *a* and to the relationship between *d* and *c*. Since each segment of the line represents a different type of cognition and degree of knowledge, Socrates is saying that the respective relationships between the different types of cognition and degrees of knowledge are analogous to one another.

What does the lowest segment of the divided line represent?

Each segment of the divided line represents a different type of cognition and degree or level of knowledge. The lowest level of cognition, represented by segment *a*, is mere guesswork or conjecture based upon nothing more than imagination, which is the capacity to entertain images. Conjecture is translated from the Greek word εἰκασία, which is transliterated as *eikasía*. The word "imagination" is translated from the Greek word φαντασία, which is transliterated as *phantasia* and is the etymological root of the English word "fantasy." The word "image" is translated from the Greek words *phantasmata*, which means "apparition" or "ghost," and *eikona*, which means "picture."

Imagination is limited to knowledge of shadows, reflections, and other images of physical things. It does not extend to knowledge of the things themselves because an image is a representation of a thing, not the thing itself. For example, a photograph of an elephant, a reflection of an elephant in a pool of water, or a shadow of an elephant is an image of the elephant, not the elephant itself. In general, one object can be represented by many different images with varying degrees of accuracy. Imagination is the type of cognition that enables us to have knowledge of images but only indirect and imperfect knowledge of the thing that those images represent. For example, a photograph of an elephant provides a

51

lesser degree of knowledge about that elephant than would the actual elephant. The photograph resembles the elephant in some respects, but it leaves out a lot. In fact, images are so far removed from reality that according to Plato, imagination doesn't provide us with genuine knowledge at all but only with opinion (Greek *doxa*).

What does the second-lowest segment of the divided line represent?

The second-lowest segment of the divided line, segment *b*, represents belief (in Greek, πίστιζ, transliterated as *pistis*) based upon sensation (αίσθηση, transliterated as *aísthisi*). Sensation gets us closer to reality than imagination because sensation is an immediate experience of physical things that produces firm convictions or beliefs. Seeing, as they say, is believing. Belief is the type of cognition that you have when you stand before an actual elephant and see it directly with your own eyes. Whereas imagination dwells primarily upon the images of objects, sensation grasps the objects themselves. Sensation seems to provide knowledge of the one (τοένα, *to éna*) true reality behind the many (τοπολλά, *to pollá*) images of a thing. But because physical things are themselves an imitation (*mimesis*) of an even deeper reality, Plato does not believe that sensation provides a genuine form of knowledge either, but like imagination, only another type of opinion (*doxa*).

How are the different parts of the divided line related to one another?

Segment *a* is related to segment *b* in the same way as segment *c* is related to segment *d*, and both are related in the same the way that segments *a* and *b* taken together are related to segments *c* and *d* taken together. So, once we understand any of one of these relationships, we can understand the others. The easiest of these relationships to understand is the one between segment *a* and segment *b*. Segment *a* represents opinions about images such as shadows, reflections, and pictures of physical things. Segment *b* represents opinions about physical things. Therefore, the relationship between segment *a* and segment *b* is based upon the relationship between a thing and its image, such as the relationship between a woman and her shadow, or between a man and his reflection, or between an elephant and a picture of that elephant. Plato's preferred metaphor in describing this relationship is that of a shadow. The objects of knowledge in the two upper segments of the divided line are the forms—the ultimate reality. The objects of opinion in the two lower segments of the divided line are physical things and their images, which are both sensible. Sensible things, according to Plato, are mere shadows of the forms. They resemble the forms, but they are imperfect imitations of them, and they aren't fully real. They have no independent reality apart from the forms. They fall midway between Being and Non-Being in the world of Appearance and Becoming that is described so well by Heraclitus.

What do the two upper segments of the divided line, *c* and *d*, represent?

The upper two segments of the divided line, *c* and *d*, represent knowledge of the intelligible forms, which can only be known by the mind. This is true knowledge.

> ## Are there two worlds or realities according to Plato, a world of forms and a world of sensible things?
>
> No, there is only one reality according to Plato. Sensible things have no independent reality apart from the forms. They are mere shadows or imitations of the forms. Whatever reality they have is derived from the forms. Sensible things are just forms that are dimly conceived. Plato suggests that sensible things are forms that are combined with some degree of Non-Being or nothingness. So there literally is nothing separating the forms from sensible things except the limitations of our own minds.

What is the lower of the two types of knowledge of the intelligible forms?

The lower of the two types of knowledge of the intelligible forms is διάνοια, which is transliterated as *dianoia* and usually translated as "discursive thought." Διάνοια is derived from the root words διά or *dia* and νοέω or *noéo*. *Dia* is a preposition meaning "to go through or across to the other side," as in "diameter," to measure across a circle. *Noéo* is a verb meaning "to conceive" or "to think out." The word *noéo* is itself derived from the word νοῦς or *nous*, meaning "mind." *Dianoia,* therefore, means "to think through or across with the mind."

Dianoia in Plato's philosophy means "to think through from premises or hypotheses, with the aid of sensible images, to conclusions." For example, *dianoia* is the kind of reasoning we use in geometry when we use visual images such as chalk drawings of triangles to demonstrate a theorem. More generally, *dianoia* is sequential reasoning from premises to conclusions assisted by using visual images in any field of mathematics. The objects of knowledge obtained by dianoia are the mathematical forms, that is, mathematical knowledge.

What does the highest segment of the divided line, segment *d*, represent?

The highest segment of the divided line represents dialectics (διαλεκτική), which is the type of cognition we must use to obtain the truest form of knowledge, which Plato calls *epistēmē* (ἐπιστήμη). Epistemic knowledge is knowledge of first principles, but according to Plato the first principles are the forms of what is best and most excellent. The forms of excellence are the ideal against which everything is measured and toward which everything strives. They are not only what things are in their deepest, truest nature but also their purpose or reason for being. The forms of excellence include the forms of moral goodness, justice, and beauty. Dialectics is therefore the type of cognition by which we obtain epistemic knowledge of the forms of moral goodness, justice, and beauty.

53

PLATO'S THEORY OF THE COSMOS

What is Plato's dialogue the *Timaeus* about?

Plato's late dialogue the *Timaeus* is about nature (Greek *physis*) and the cosmos. The *Timaeus* is about sensible things—physical things and their images—which are the objects of opinion in the two lower segments of the divided line. The *Timaeus* was one of the few works of ancient Greek philosophy to survive the fall of the Roman Empire and the most important Platonic dialogue in the development of early medieval philosophy. Unlike most of Plato's earlier dialogues, there is very little dialogue in the *Timaeus*. It consists almost entirely of a long speech given by the title character. Timaeus is presented in Plato's dialogue as a Pythagorean philosopher from the Greek colony of Locri in modern-day Calabria at the tip of the Italian peninsula. It is not surprising, then, that the theory of the cosmos that Timaeus presents is Pythagorean. Timaeus claims that the fundamental structure of the cosmos is mathematical. Indeed, the basic building blocks of the physical world, he says, are triangles. The physical world is a shadow of the mathematical forms, and therefore the study of the physical world requires the use of *dianoia* or mathematical reasoning (segment *c* of the divided line). However, in spite of the use of mathematical reasoning, belief about sensible objects remains at most a "likely story" because the physical world consists of mere shadows of the forms, and it is not possible to have certain or genuine knowledge about something that isn't fully real.

"Cosmos" in the Greek sense means "ordered world," and the opposite of cosmos is chaos. In Plato's *Timaeus* the title character explains that the cosmos is based on mathematics, but the physical world is made up only of shadows of the true forms underlying reality.

What is a cosmos?

The Greek word *cosmos* (κόσμος) means "ordered world." The opposite of a cosmos isn't nothingness or the absence of a world, but *chaos* (χάος).

How was the cosmos made according to Timaeus?

According to Timaeus, the cosmos was made by the Demiurge (*dēmiourgos*, δημιουργός), who is a divine craftsman. The Demiurge did not create the world out of nothing, *ex nihilo*, but instead constructed the cosmos by imposing order upon a pre-existing chaos of discordant and disordered motion. Just like a craftsman uses a blueprint or model to build a house by imposing order on wood, the Demiurge used the forms as a blueprint or model to construct the cosmos by imposing order upon chaos. That's why physical things and the cosmos itself are images of the forms. But they are imperfect images of the forms, as are all images, and for that reason they are subject to change and destruction. Parmenides believed that the cosmos had the form of a sphere because he believed that a sphere is the most perfect form, reducible to a single principle: equal distance from a central point.

Timaeus agrees with Parmenides that the world has the form of a sphere. But unlike Parmenides, who believed that the sphere was never created because it is eternal and always existed, Timaeus believes that the cosmos was constructed by the Demiurge and will be destroyed again and again in a never-ending cyclical process. Likewise, Parmenides believed that the cosmos is unmoved and unchanging, whereas Timaeus believes that the cosmos has an intelligent soul and spins round and round on its own axis, performing a choral dance in concert with the stars and other celestial bodies. The cosmos is not eternal because it is not a perfect image of the forms. But since the cosmos was constructed as an image of the forms, which *are* unchanging and eternal, the cosmos, according to Timaeus, is a "moving image of eternity."

What makes the stars and other celestial bodies circle the heavens and do so in such an orderly fashion?

According to Timaeus, animals can move themselves because they possess a soul that causes them to move. Inanimate objects are not capable of moving themselves but are always moved by a force they receive from other objects. Because the stars and other celestial bodies appear to move themselves, they must possess a soul, and because they move together in harmony with one another and with the cosmos, they must be moved by the soul of the world. Furthermore, since orderly motion is better than disorderly motion, and since order is impossible without reason, the Demiurge gave the world soul an intelligent mind capable of reason. Hence, the stars and other celestial bodies circle the heavens in an orderly fashion because they are moved by a rational world soul.

Why did the Demiurge give the world an intelligent soul?

The Demiurge is good, and since whoever is good is without jealousy, he made the world to be as good and as much like himself as possible. Since nothing that is lacking intelligence can ever be better than what has intelligence, and since intelligence cannot exist in anything other than the soul, the Demiurge gave the world a soul (*psyche*, ψυχή) and implanted intelligence or mind (*nous*, νουζ) in it. Hence, the Demiurge made the cosmos an intelligent living being composed of body, soul, and mind.

PLATO'S MATHEMATICAL AND MUSICAL THEORY OF THE COSMOS

What are the four basic elements of the world according to Timaeus, and what are they made of?

The four basic elements are air, water, fire, and earth. Everything else in the world is composed of these four basic elements. The elements themselves are composed of triangles, which are the simplest two-dimensional geometric shapes. The two primary types of triangles that the elements are composed of are the isosceles triangle, whose angles are 90°, 45°, and 45°, and the scalene triangle, whose angles are 90°, 60°, and 30°. Two isosceles triangles joined together form a square, whereas two scalene triangles joined together form an equilateral triangle. Each element is a convex regular polyhedron constructed out of a combination of the two primary types of triangles. A polyhedron is a three-dimensional shape with flat polygonal faces. A regular polyhedron is a polyhedron whose faces are identical regular polygons. A regular polygon is a polygon with equal sides and angles. Fire is a tetrahedron (a pyramid). Air is an octahedron. Water is an icosahedron. Earth is a hexahedron (a cube).

What are the Platonic solids?

The Platonic solids are convex regular polyhedrons. They are perfectly symmetrical and mathematically beautiful. There are only five convex three-dimensional shapes that can be constructed out of identical regular polygons: the tetrahedron (four equilateral triangles), cube or hexahedron (six squares), octahedron (eight equilateral triangles), icosahedron (twenty equilateral triangles), and dodecahedron (twelve pentagons). The

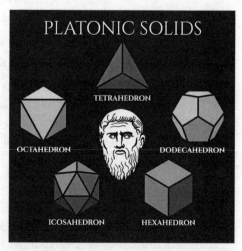

These five solids are the only forms that can be made with identical regular polygons.

first four are elements according to Plato. Of the last, the dodecahedron, Plato only says that the Demiurge used it to construct the heavens.

What is a geometric sequence or progression?

A geometric sequence or progression is a sequence of numbers in which the ratio of every two successive numbers is equal. For example, the sequence of numbers 3, 9, and 27 is a geometric sequence because 3/9 = 9/27. The ratio of 3 to 9 is the same as the ratio of 9 to 27.

What is a logarithmic spiral?

A logarithmic spiral is a spiral with a constant curvature. The angle between the radial and tangent lines through any point on the spiral is constant. The mathematical formula for a logarithmic spiral is $r = ae^{b\theta}$, where r is the radius or distance from the center of the spiral, θ is the angle of rotation, and a and b are constants or fixed numbers. The distances between each turn of the spiral and between each turn of the spiral and its center is a geometric sequence or progression. Logarithmic spirals are found throughout nature, from seashells and plants to hurricanes and the arms of the Milky Way galaxy. The rationalist philosopher and mathematician René Descartes was the first to discover the mathematical properties of logarithmic spirals in 1638. But the concept of a geometric progression, without which the mathematical properties of a logarithmic spiral could not be understood, dates back to Plato, the founder of the rationalist tradition in philosophy.

What is a Sierpiński triangle?

A Sierpiński triangle is a triangle that contains an infinite number of triangles similar to itself in a recurring pattern. A Sierpiński triangle is constructed by connecting the midpoints of the sides of an equilateral triangle to form another equilateral triangle half the size of the first and then repeating the process in the remaining uninscribed areas an infinite number of times. A Sierpiński triangle is a type of fractal known as an iterated function system (IFS) fractal because it is constructed by means of an iterative process. IFS fractals have the property of self-similarity, which means that the same form or pattern is repeated at all scales. Not only is the pattern of the whole repeated in every part, but it is repeated in every part of every part, and so on, to infinity. A Sierpiński

This diagram illustrates the construction of a Sierpiński triangle using an iterative process that can be repeated an infinite number of times.

triangle contains many geometric sequences, including the number of triangles, the length of the sides of the triangles, and the area of the triangles. For example, the number of black triangles in each iteration is 1, 3, 9, 27, 81 ... or 3^p, where p is every integer from 0 to infinity. IFS fractals are found throughout nature and in art.

What is geometric proportion?

A sequence of numbers are in geometric proportion to one another when the ratio of every two successive numbers is equal. For example, the sequence of numbers 3, 9, and 27 are in geometric proportion to one another because 3/9 = 9/27. The equal ratio of every two successive numbers in a geometric sequence is its geometric proportion. In our example, the geometric proportion is 1/3 from left to right or 3/1 from right to left. The concept of geometric proportion can also be understood in terms of geometric forms. For example, a rectangle with one side that is 3 units long and another side that is 9 units long would have the same form, shape, or proportion as a rectangle with one side that is 9 units long and another that is 27 units long. Only their size would differ.

What is the geometric mean of a sequence of numbers?

In general, the geometric mean of any sequence of n numbers is equal to the nth root of the product of those numbers. For example, the geometric mean of the sequence 3, 9, and 27, is 9, because the cube root of $3 \times 9 \times 27$ (= 729) is 9. This principle can also be illustrated geometrically: a rectangular box that is 3 units wide by 9 units deep and 27 units long has the same geometric mean (9) and consequently the same volume as a cube that is 9 units long on all sides ($3 \times 9 \times 27 = 9 \times 9 \times 9$). The geometric mean of a geometric sequence that contains an odd number of numbers is always the central number in the sequence. For example, the geometric mean of the geometric sequence 1, 3, 9, 27, and 81, which contains five numbers, is the central number 9. Applying this rule to any geometric sequence that contains an odd number of numbers is a quick way to compute the nth root of the product of the numbers in that sequence. The fifth root of $1 \times 3 \times 9 \times 27 \times 81$ (= 59,049) is 9.

What is the arithmetic mean?

The arithmetic mean (also known as average) of any sequence of numbers is the sum of those numbers divided by the number of numbers in that sequence. For example, the arithmetic mean of 2, 4, 8, and 14 is calculated by adding together 2, 4, 8, and 14 to get

---

What is the harmonic mean of two numbers?

The harmonic mean of two numbers, a and b, is twice the product of the two numbers divided by their sum, that is, $2ab / (a + b)$.

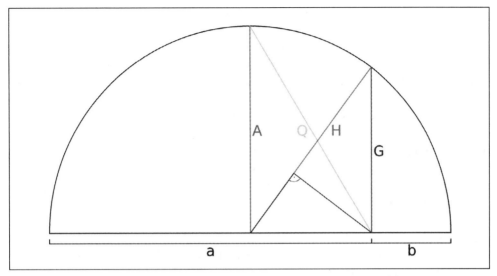

The different types of means between two numbers, *a* and *b*, can be illustrated geometrically using the diagram provided above. In this diagram *A* is the arithmetical mean or average of *a* and *b*. *G* is the geometric mean of *a* and *b*. *H* is the harmonic mean of *a* and *b*. And *Q* is the quadratic mean of *a* and *b*.

the sum, which is equal to 28, and then dividing that sum by 4, to get 7, the arithmetic mean or average.

What is a harmonic sequence?

A harmonic sequence is one in which each number of the sequence is the harmonic mean of the number that came before it in the sequence and the one that followed it.

What is a harmonic sequence in music?

If a string or a monochord of length L is plucked, it will emit a fundamental note that has a wavelength equal to $2L$ plus a sequence of harmonious overtones whose wavelength is an integer fraction of $2L$: $2L/2, 2L/3, 2L/4, 2L/5, 2L/6....$ This sequence of wavelengths is a harmonic sequence because each number in the sequence is the harmonic mean of the number that came before it in the sequence and the one that followed it. The frequency of a sound wave is inversely proportional to its wavelength. Inverting the numbers in the harmonic sequence of wavelengths yields a sequence of frequencies in which each frequency is equal to an integer multiple of the frequency of the fundamental note, $1/2L$: $2/2L, 3/2L, 4/2L, 5/L, 6/2L....$

How did the Demiurge divide the world soul and construct the circles upon which the stars and other celestial bodies rotate?

According to Timaeus, the Demiurge divided the world soul by separating portions in quantities proportionate to the numbers 1, 2, 3, 4, 8, 9, and 27. This sequence of numbers is composed of two geometric sequences: one of the form 2^m (1, 2, 4, 8) and another of the form 3^p (1, 3, 9, 27), where m and p are integers. Numbers of the form $2^m 3^p$ were used in the Pythagorean musical tuning system, so the Demiurge divided the world soul in the same way that the Pythagoreans divided the musical scale. Next, the Demiurge inserted the arithmetic and harmonic means between the numbers in each of the two geometric sequences. The result is a sequence of numbers that if interpreted as tone numbers defines a musical scale in the Greek Dorian mode of four octaves and a major sixth in length. The Demiurge then divided this sequence of numbers into two lengthwise, separating numbers in the sequence 2^m, which is a sequence of octaves, from numbers in the sequence 3^p, which is a sequence of perfect fifths, and made the two sequences cross each other at their centers to form the letter X. Next, the Demiurge bent both sequences around into circles. The circle of fifths was further divided into seven unequal circles, while the circle of octaves was left undivided. To the circle of fifths, the Demiurge attached the sun, the moon, and the five planets known in the ancient world (Mercury, Venus, Mars, Jupiter, and Saturn). To the circle of octaves the Demiurge attached the stars.

How are the elements united together in the body of the cosmos?

According to Timaeus, two elements cannot be united together without a third element acting as a bond between them. Air is the common bond between fire and water that unites them together. Thus, fire is united to air in the same way as air is united to water. Both fire and water are united to air. The same relationship holds between air, water, and earth. Water is the common bond between air and earth that unites them together. Thus, air is united to water in the same way as water is united to earth. The relationship between each of these three elements has the form of an analogy: a is to b as b is to c. The middle term, b, of the analogy, is the bond that unites the two extreme terms, a and c, together. But since the elements according to Timaeus are numbers, the relationship between them can also be expressed as equal ratios: fire/air = air/water

How does beauty manifest itself in the Platonic cosmos?

Beauty manifests itself in the Platonic cosmos as geometric proportion. Beauty in this view is not a subjective judgment, "in the eye of the beholder," but is an objective structure of reality. In fact, most people recognize beauty in geometric proportion, and it is found in many works of art. The principle of geometric proportion is also common in sacred art and architecture, where it is believed that geometric proportion represents the ultimate nature of reality. For example, Islamic, Gothic, and Renaissance architects constructed buildings according to geometric proportions because they, like Timaeus, believed that God created the world according to the principle of geometric proportion.

and air/water = water/earth. But this is the form of a geometric sequence where air would be the geometric mean between fire and water and water would be the geometric mean between air and earth.

Timaeus says that a continued geometric proportion is the best bond and unites the terms in a sequence most perfectly. To illustrate how the elements are related to one another according to Timaeus, let's assign the number 3 to the first term in our sequence and assume that the sequence has a geometric proportion of 1/3 from left to right. In that case, fire would be 3, air would be 9, water would be 27, and earth would be 81. According to Timaeus, prior to the construction of the cosmos, the four elements existed in a disordered, chaotic relationship to one another, but afterward they were united with one another in geometric proportions by the geometric mean between them. The number 9 is the geometric mean that unites the numbers 3 and 27 to one another by a common rule, the geometric proportion or ratio of 1/3. The number 27 is the geometric mean that unites the numbers 9 and 81 to one another by the same proportion, 1/3. Thus, 3/9 = 9/27 = 27/81, or stated as an analogy, fire is to air as air is to water, and air is to water as water is to earth. All four elements are united in harmony by a common proportion or ratio. According to Timaeus, the body of the cosmos was therefore constructed by the Demiurge as a unified whole using the principle of geometric proportion.

How are analogies and proportions related in Plato's philosophy?

The Greek word for analogy, ἀναλογία, means both analogy and proportion. In general an analogy has the form "a is to b as c is to d," or, using symbolic notation, a:b::c:d. Equal proportion is a type of analogy because the mathematical equation $a/b = c/d$ has the form "a is to b as c is to d." Because they share a common form, proportion is analogous to analogy. Plato employs many analogies in his philosophy because the structure of reality, according to Plato, is proportional, and proportion is analogical.

Why did Plato believe that the structure of the cosmos is that of geometric proportion?

The ancient agricultural civilizations of the Nile River Valley and of the Tigris-Euphrates River Valley had already known thousands of years before Plato that the movement of celestial bodies across the sky could be understood mathematically. Astronomy was of vital importance to them because the rhythm of agricultural life depended on the change of seasons that followed upon the movement of the sun and other celestial bodies. In a very real sense, their lives here on earth depended on what happened up above in the heavens. "As above, so below," said Hermes Trismegistus, who inspired Western magic, astrology, and alchemy. Hence astronomy to the ancients was not just the study of celestial bodies up above but also of events here on earth.

It was not until Pythagoras, however, that it became known that music could also be understood mathematically. Pythagoras discovered that music has the mathematical structure of geometric proportion. This led the Pythagoreans to conclude that the move- **61** ment of celestial bodies produced a kind of music, the "music of the spheres," perhaps not detectable by the human ear but knowable by the mind. The Pythagoreans discovered that each note in the musical scale corresponds to the length of a monochord (a single stringed instrument) that is used to produce that note. Further experiments with monochords revealed that the note produced by a monochord that is one unit long sounds like the note produced by a monochord that is two units long. The note produced by a monochord that is two units long sounds like the note produced by a monochord that is four units long. In general, the same notes repeat every time the length of the monochord is halved or doubled in the geometric sequence ... ⅛, ¼, ½, 1, 2, 4, 8 ... or 2^n, where n is equal to any integer. This property of the musical scale is known as octave invariance because the same notes repeat in every octave. The discovery of octave invariance added further conviction to the belief that the cosmos and everything in it could be understood mathematically and, moreover, to the belief that the cosmos could be understood as music, which possesses the structure of geometric proportion.

Why did Plato believe that number theory, geometry, music, and astronomy were kindred forms of knowledge?

In section 530d of Plato's dialogue *The Republic*, Socrates says that a kinship exists between music and astronomy. We hear music with our ears, and we see the movement of celestial bodies with our eyes. But according to the Pythagoreans, with whom Socrates agrees, the same numbers that are used to construct the Dorian (Greek) musical scale can also be used to construct a calendar and predict the movement of celestial bodies. There is a kinship between music and astronomy because both are based in Pythagorean number theory. But Pythagorean number theory, in turn, has a kinship with geometry, because the Pythagoreans understood numbers in terms of geometric forms. The Pythagorean theorem, for example, states that the square of the hypotenuse of a right triangle is equal to the sum of the square of each of its other two sides. It can be understood numerically in terms of the algebraic formula $c^2 = a^2 + b^2$, where c is the length of the hypotenuse. It can also be understood in terms of geometric forms by drawing three squares along each of the three sides of a right triangle. The area of the square whose side is c units long equals the sum of the area of the other two squares.

Thus, Plato believed that number theory, geometry, music, and astronomy are kindred sciences that study the same thing, the ideal geometric forms. After

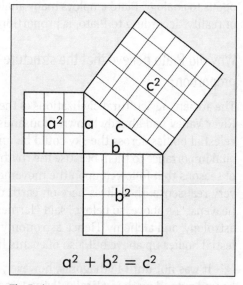

The Pythagorean theorem can be expressed through the use of geometric forms, as this drawing shows.

Plato, and throughout the European Middle Ages, astronomy (which was closely associated with astrology) and music were regarded as special areas of mathematics alongside arithmetic and geometry. Beginning in the sixth century C.E., the four together constituted a course of study known as the "quadrivium," which was a prerequisite to the study of philosophy proper. Throughout the Middle Ages, philosophy proper was considered to be the practice of dialectics, which is the mode of cognition represented by the topmost segment, segment *d*, of Plato's divided line.

How are physical things related to mathematical forms?

The lowest level of cognition in the analogy of the divided line is conjecture about mere images or shadows of physical things. The next highest level of cognition is belief based on direct perception of physical things themselves. For every one physical thing, there can be many images that represent it. But what holds those many images together as one is the physical thing from which they all originate. A physical thing is a deeper reality than its images because it is the origin or first principle (*arche*, ἀρχή) that gives meaning (*énnoia*, ἔνοια) to the many different images in which it dimly appears. I'm not sure what to make of several photographs until I realize that they are all photographs of the Taj Mahal. Each photo captures only one aspect of the original Taj Mahal, which, of course, embodies all aspects of itself. Physical things like the Taj Mahal are in turn, according to Timaeus, mere shadows or images of mathematical form. All physical things, according to Timaeus, are combinations of the four elements: fire, air, water, and earth. But fire is made of many tiny particles, each of which is in the shape of a convex regular polyhedron with four sides. Particles of air are in the shape of a convex regular polyhedron with eight sides. Particles of water are in the shape of a convex regular polyhedron with twenty sides. Particles of earth are in the shape of a convex regular polyhedron with six sides.

All the perceived qualities of the elements are reducible to these geometric forms. Fire, for example, burns because a polyhedron with four sides has sharp points that cut up whatever it comes in contact with. Each of these four polyhedrons can themselves be broken down into a combination of isosceles and scalene triangles. Therefore, the fundamental nature or first principle (*arche*, ἀρχή) of physical things is geometric form. There are many particles of fire, all in the shape of a convex regular polyhedron with four sides. But there is only one form of a convex regular polyhedron with four sides.

The mathematical structure of the physical world is a deeper reality than perceptual objects because it is the origin or first principle—indeed, the archetype—that gives meaning (*énnoia*, ἔνοια) to the many different perceptual objects in which it dimly appears. The mode of cognition by which we know mathematical form directly and most lucidly is *dianoia* (διάνοια), represented by the third segment, segment *c*, of Plato's divided line.

How did Plato's account of the physical world contribute to the development of modern physics and astronomy?

Most of what Timaeus says about the physical world strikes the modern reader as complete nonsense, and indeed, taken at face value, most of it is. But without the

63

The Taj Mahal is a masterpiece of geometric proportion, an artistic expression of the ultimate nature of reality.

Pythagorean-Platonic faith in the mathematical structure of the physical world, modern physics and astronomy might not have developed in the way that they did. In fact, modern physics and astronomy did not develop until after Plato and Pythagoras were reintroduced into Western culture during the Renaissance. The faith in the mathematical structure of the physical world was not enough by itself to enable the development of modern physics and astronomy. Indeed, astronomy was stymied for thousands of years by Ptolemy's assumption that the movement of all celestial bodies could be explained by circular movements because the circle is the most perfect geometric form. Modern physics and astronomy could not develop until scientists tried to fit mathematics to the empirical facts rather than fitting the empirical facts to their metaphysical assumptions about mathematics.

Johannes Kepler (1571–1630), for example, rejected the Ptolemaic theory, but he did not abandon his faith that the movement of the planets could be explained mathematically. He simply substituted one mathematical theory based upon metaphysical assumptions for another based on the empirical observations of his predecessor, Tycho Brahe (1546–1601). He discovered that the planets moved in elliptical orbits instead of circular ones. Newton (1643–1727) formulated mathematical equations to explain the motion of material bodies in space, such as an apple falling from a tree. And today physics does the same for subatomic particles and energy.

PLATO'S ETHICS

What are the four cardinal virtues?

The four cardinal virtues are temperance, prudence, fortitude, and justice. To these four virtues the fathers of the Church added three theological virtues: faith, hope, and charity. Together they constitute the seven Christian virtues. The three theological virtues derive from the letters of St. Paul. The four cardinal virtues derive from the four components of the good mentioned by Socrates in Plato's *Republic*.

How do the Christian virtues differ from Plato's concept of the good?

The Christian virtues differ in three key respects from Plato's concept of the good. First, Plato did not believe that the will is a separate faculty apart from intellect. He believed that anyone with knowledge of what is right would want to do what is right. Christians, on the other hand, believe that the will is a separate faculty apart from intellect and that it can be tempted by the desires of the flesh. They believe that it is possible to do wrong even when you know what is right because you may lack the will to do right. Second, Plato did not believe that what is good is good because God wills it but that God is good because he wills what is good. In Plato's theory, nothing, not even God, exists prior to the forms, including the forms of the good. Third, for Plato, the forms of the good are beautiful because all forms are harmonious proportions, and harmonious proportions are beautiful. For Christians, on the other hand, a moral act can be good without also being beautiful. Christian virtue is a moral concept divorced from aesthetics. The Greek concept of excellence is both moral and aesthetic. Because the Platonic conception of the good unites beauty with moral goodness, it is closer to the Greek concept of excellence (*arête*) than it is to the Christian concept of virtue.

How does the Christian concept of prudence differ from Plato's?

Both Plato's concept of prudence (Greek *phronēsis*, φρόνησιζ) and the Christian concept of prudence (Latin *prudentia*) meant practical wisdom. Both concepts of prudence meant knowing how to make the right judgments in particular situations. But what makes a judgment right according to Plato is that it is true, and what makes it true is that it has the proper form or proportion. On the other hand, what ul-

The concept of "good" differs in Christian versus Greek philosophy. Christians separate will from intellect and good from beauty, and they believe that God wills what is good (rather than good existing before God).

timately makes a judgment right according to the Christian concept of prudence is that it is in obeisance to God's will, since God creates moral truth by command.

How does the Christian concept of fortitude differ from Plato's?

The Christian concept of fortitude (Latin *fortitude*) meant having the will to suppress fear and attack evil. It is closely related to the Christian virtue of patience, which also requires a resolute will. The Christian concept of fortitude is derived from Plato's concept of courage (Greek *andreia*, ἀνδρεία), which, by contrast, meant knowing what warrants fear and in what proportion.

How does the Christian concept of temperance differ from Plato's?

The Christian concept of temperance (Latin *temperantia*) meant having the will to suppress sinful desires of the flesh. Desires of the flesh are sinful when they are unnatural and contradict God's law regarding how we should use our bodies. Gluttony is sinful because it is a desire for food in excess of the natural appetites that God gave us to sustain our bodies. Lust is sinful because it is a desire for unnatural sex. God created our sexual organs for the purpose of reproduction. Any other use of our sexual organs is unnatural and therefore sinful. Plato's concept of temperance (Greek *sōphrosynē*, σωφροσύνη), on the other hand, is not about having the will to suppress sinful desire but about knowing the proper proportions of our desires. Platonic temperance is analogous to tuning a musical instrument so that the notes played on the instrument will be in proper proportion to one another and sound best.

What is dialectics?

Dialectics (διαλεκτική), represented by the highest segment of the divided line, is a philosophical conversation or dialogue (διάλογος) by questions and answers that seeks a mental or intellectual intuition (*noesis*, νόησις) of excellence (*arête*) that can be expressed in a verbal account (*logos*, λογος). Unlike the Socratic method of refutation or *elenchus* that is displayed in Plato's early Socratic dialogues and in Book I of *The Republic*, Platonic dialectics is not negative or destructive. It does not end in *aporia*

How Is Justice Viewed Differently by Plato?

The Christian virtue of justice (Latin *justitia*) means having the will to give God and our neighbors their due. But what is owed to God and our neighbors is determined by God's will and his law. Thus, justice is obeying God's law. According to Plato, on the other hand, justice as a moral capacity of the soul is knowing the duties of one's station in a just society. But a just society is one in which the parts of society are brought into harmony by being placed in proper proportion to one another. A just society is one patterned upon the forms. Thus, justice as a moral capacity of the soul is knowing the form of social justice (Greek *dikē*, δίκη).

(ἀπορία) or puzzlement but in a mental or intellectual intuition (noesis) of first principles (ideas, archetypes). Whereas dianoia proceeds from first principles to their logical consequences, dialectics proceeds in the opposite direction, from ideas as they are immediately given to the mind (νοῦζ), to their logical presuppositions, the first principles.

Dialectics makes manifest the excellence of an idea and what it is in its essential nature. A typical dialectical dialogue begins with a question about what a particular moral concept means. For example, what is courage? A definition of the moral concept is proposed. For example, courage is acting without fear. The logical consequences of the proposed answer are deduced. For example, recklessness is acting without fear; therefore, recklessness is courage. Typically, the logical consequences of a proposed answer lead to contradictions or other absurdities that cause those engaged in the dialogue to abandon or revise their initial answer and to propose another. The process is repeated until a satisfactory answer is found that is both intuitively correct and does not lead to absurdities. For example, courage is knowing what warrants fear and in what proportion.

How are the forms of goodness and beauty related to the mathematical forms?

According to the analogy of the divided line, the mathematical forms (segment *c* of the divided line) are images of the forms of goodness and beauty (segment *d*). The mathematical forms are related to the forms of goodness and beauty in the same way that shadows, reflections, and pictures (segment *a*) are related to physical things (segment *b*) and as sensible things in general (segments *a* and *b*) are related to the intelligible forms in general (segments *c* and *d*). But the image of a thing and the thing itself share some qualities in common. A photo of a red balloon is red just like the red balloon. Similarly, the mathematical forms and the forms of goodness and beauty share an important quality in common, that of geometric proportion. The mathematical forms "imitate" (*mimesis*) or "participate" (*methexis*) in the forms of goodness and beauty because they share the common quality of geometric proportion. And it is because they share this quality that the mathematical forms remind us of the forms of goodness and beauty. But they are not those forms themselves. The forms of goodness and beauty are geometric proportions, but they are something more than just geometric proportions.

PLATONIC LOVE

Was pederasty condoned in ancient Greece?

Sex between aristocratic men and adolescent boys was condoned under strict conditions. The boy had to be physically mature and of the age at which military training normally began. The relationship had to be approved by the boy's father. The boy could not be too eager to yield to the older man's sexual desire. The older man was not the object of the boy's sexual desire. The boy was the object of the older man's sexual desire. In return for granting sexual favors to older men, boys from ambitious aristocratic families could build lifelong relationships with well-connected older men. The boy's interest in the relationship was pedagogical. The older man served as the boy's mentor and teacher. In return for sex, the boy received a political education from the older man. He acquired *arête*.

Pederasty, under very specific conditions, was condoned in ancient Greek society. The younger man benefitted by having an older mentor who would train him in politics.

What is Platonic love?

Platonic love is the love of progressively higher levels of beauty. At its lowest level, Platonic love is the love of beautiful physical things, in particular the bodies of beautiful adolescent boys. The word that Plato used for the love of beauty was *eros* (ἔρως), the root of our word "erotic." Platonic love is analogous to sexual desire insofar as they both entail a desire to become one with beauty. But Platonic love is not a desire for sex. In *The Republic,* Socrates says that nothing is more exciting than sex. He warns that the extreme pleasures of sex will drive a person out of their mind no less than extreme pain. The problem with sexual pleasure is that it is not bound by any limit or proportion. It is unmeasured. But true love is temperate and harmonious because true love is a love of beauty, and beauty is order and proportion. Boys may be beautiful, but sex is not. It is better, then, to love the soul of your beloved than his body.

Socrates tells us that the best love of all is a love for someone who has both a beautiful body and a beautiful soul. But if our beloved's body is blemished, we will not love him any less, so long as his soul is beautiful. The love of a beautiful soul is higher than the love of a beautiful body. Higher still than the love of beautiful souls is the love of the forms reflected in those souls. The forms are models of harmony and proportion. They are more beautiful by far than physical things, which are merely their shadows, and even more beautiful than their reflections in the souls that know them. Finally, Platonic love reaches its apex with the love of the form of beauty itself. Going back down the hierarchy of beauty, we find that the forms are beautiful because they all share in the form of beauty itself. Souls are beautiful because the forms are reflected in their thoughts. Bodies are beautiful because they reflect their beautiful souls. Physical things in general are beautiful because they are images of the forms.

According to Plato, how is philosophy like making love?

The word "philosophy" means "love of wisdom" and is derived from the Greek word *philosophia* (φιλοσοφία). The Greek word *philosophia* was probably coined by Pythagoras and is composed of the root words *philos* (φίλος), which meant love in the

68

sense of friendship, and *sophia* (σοφία), which meant wisdom. But in Plato's philosophy, *eros* is substituted for *philos*. Plato believed that the love of wisdom, though far superior to the erotic love of beautiful bodies, was analogous to it. Since the Platonic forms are the source of wisdom, and the highest form of Platonic love (*eros*) is the love of the forms, the highest form of Platonic love is philosophy, the love of wisdom.

In the act of cognition, the soul receives knowledge of a form just as in the act of lovemaking the beloved receives the lover's seed. Knowledge of a form, when implanted in the soul, gives birth to a stream of words (*logos*, λόγοζ) that can be transmitted from teacher to student. Words that are not just meaningless sounds but that convey knowledge of a

Michelangelo's David represents the ancient Greek ideal of youthful male strength and beauty. It was completed during the Florentine Renaissance in 1504 after Plato was translated into Latin.

form (an idea) are fertile. When a receptive student hears meaningful words, the student acquires knowledge of the form being conveyed. The student is then able to produce a new stream of words based on their understanding of the form and convey knowledge of the form to another student. The stream of words produced by each generation of students is not necessarily the same stream of words because different words can convey knowledge of the same form or meaning. Each generation of words is analogous to the one that preceded it because each generation of words shares the same form, but they are not necessarily identical. Knowledge is not a mere parroting of words but a genuine understanding that can be expressed with different words that express the same meaning.

In Plato's dialogue *The Symposium*, Socrates recalls that in his youth the philosopher and priestess Diotima taught him that love is not only love of beauty but also love of reproduction and procreation in beauty. Lovers seek to achieve immortality by reproducing and procreating in beauty. Analogously, teachers seek to achieve immortality by transmitting their ideas to their students, who in turn transmit them to their students. In Plato's dialogue the *Phaedrus*, Socrates says that in a dialectical dialogue the speaker "finds a congenial soul and then proceeds to plant and sow in it words which are able to help themselves and help him who planted them; words which will not be unproductive, for they can transmit their seed to other natures and cause the growth of fresh words in them, providing an eternal existence for their seed; words which bring their possessor to the highest degree of happiness possible for a human being to attain." The bodies of lovers aren't immortal, but their ideas are.

PLATO'S THEORY OF JUSTICE

What is the principal problem discussed in Plato's *The Republic* and how does Socrates solve it?

The principal problem discussed in Plato's greatest dialogue, *The Republic*, is the problem of justice. Thrasymachus sets up the problem by claiming that justice is the interest of the stronger. Socrates responds by reversing his claim. To the contrary, Socrates says, it is in our interest to be just. Only justice sets the parts of the soul in harmony with one another. An unjust soul is divided against itself and can never be happy. Glaucon and Adeimantus agree with Socrates, but they are unsatisfied with his answer. They want him to show them in much greater detail why a just soul is strong and happy and an unjust soul is not. Socrates proposes that to do so we should first examine the nature of justice in society. He says that justice can be found in both the individual soul and in society since the structure of the soul is analogous to the structure of society. But it would be easier to see justice in society because society is on a larger scale than the individual soul.

The character of the individual members of society are made manifest in the character of the whole society. Therefore, we should examine the nature of justice in society first. To do so, Socrates constructs a model of a perfectly just society and of an educational system that would prepare its members for positions of authority. He says that the educational system of a perfectly just society would implant knowledge of the form of justice into the souls of its students, and he uses a series of famous analogies and allegories to help us to see what knowledge and education are: the analogy of the Sun, the analogy of the divided line, and the allegory of the cave.

Having completed his model of a perfectly just society, Socrates constructs models of progressively more unjust societies. A comparison of the most perfectly just society with the most unjust shows that the just society is strong and happy while the unjust society is not. Then the analogy is made to the soul. If the unjust society is unhappy, then the unjust soul must be unhappy too. And if that is not enough to convince his interlocutors that it is better to be just than to be unjust, Socrates concludes with the myth of Er, the tale of a soldier who dies in battle and returns to tell a story about the afterlife. According to Er, the gods give the departed an opportunity to choose their next life. The wise choose a good life that brings them happiness. They make good life choices. The unwise choose to become tyrants and suffer all the torments that tyrants suffer. They make poor life choices. Finally, justice is done, and it is self-administered. If only they had studied philosophy. Philosophy teaches people to make wise choices, chief among them the choice of the life to which they will be reborn after death. In that sense, philosophy is preparation for death.

How does Plato's dialogue *The Republic* begin?

Plato's dialogue *The Republic* begins with a conversation between Socrates, Cephalus, his son Polemarchus, and Thrasymachus. The conversation proceeds in the usual style of the early Socratic dialogues in which Socrates practices the dialectical method of *elenchus*, refuting all answers to a moral question until everyone is left in a state of puzzlement or *aporia*. In this case, the question is, "What is justice?" Cephalus, a wealthy, retired businessman, is the first to speak. Looking back on his long life, Cephalus says that the greatest benefit of wealth is that it enables you to pay your debts and face death and the afterlife with a clear conscience. Justice, he says, is paying your debts. Socrates refutes his claim by citing a case in which it would be wrong to pay your debts (returning borrowed weapons to a man who has gone mad). Polemarchus is the next to speak. He proposes that justice is to benefit your friends and harm your enemies. Socrates refutes that, too, by saying that since justice is good, it never harms anyone, friend or foe. In Plato's dialogue *Gorgias*, Socrates says that a just punishment does not harm the soul of the wrongdoer and may, in fact, improve it. Finally, Thrasymachus, a rhetorician and a Sophist whose name means "fierce fighter," proposes that justice is the interest of the stronger. In other words, might makes right. The ruling class makes laws to suit its interests. They call that "justice," and that is the only justice that exists. Socrates says that Thrasymachus has it backward. It is in one's interest to be just. Justice is the excellence (*arête*) of the soul. Only by being just can one be strong and happy.

Socrates draws an analogy between the art of living and the art of tuning a musical instrument, the seven-stringed lyre. He says that a just person is like a musician whose excellence or *arête* is demonstrated by adjusting the pitch of each string of the lyre to the correct measure. If a string is tightened too much or too little, it will be off-pitch. Similarly, to live well one must know how to act with the correct measure. But only those who are just act according to measure. The unjust seek as much as they can for themselves at everyone else's expense, without limit or measure. But there must be honor even among thieves, otherwise they will be weak and unable to harmonize their actions for a common purpose. Similarly, the various desires in a person's soul will conflict and cause that person to be unhappy if each is allowed unlimited expression. But in spite of these preliminary arguments, Socrates concludes the conversation by admitting that he has not spoken with the correct measure. He admits that he has been like a glutton eating in such haste that he has not enjoyed any one dish before rushing off to eat another. He admits that he has gone off on tangents before completing any single line of inquiry and that the outcome of their conversation is that he knows nothing. Thus, the conversation ends in puzzlement or *aporia*, with the account of justice still not complete.

A passage from Plato's *Republic* is preserved on this parchment fragment from the third century C.E.

How does the dialectical method and tone of conversation change in Book II of *The Republic*?

The tone of conversation in Book I of Plato's *Republic* is ironic, sarcastic, and even belligerent. The dialectical method that Socrates employs in Book I, the method of *elenchus*, is negative and critical. Its primary purpose is to refute the claims made by his interlocutors, not to establish what is true. Socrates employs this method in Book I of *The Republic* because he doesn't feel that he is on common ground with any of his interlocutors. None of his interlocutors acknowledges that there is a universal truth about justice that is greater than their desires. Thrasymachus baldly asserts that there is no such thing as justice at all. Lacking any common ground, all that Socrates can do is react as if to an enemy, attempting to stop them in their tracks by paralyzing them in a state of *aporia*.

In Book II of *The Republic,* Socrates engages in conversation with Glaucon and Adeimantus, two very different souls. Glaucon and Adeimantus are Plato's older brothers. Like Plato himself in his youth, they sit with modest, open minds at Socrates's feet listening to what he has to say because they are confident that he has something to teach them. Thus, beginning in Book II of *The Republic,* Socrates adopts a didactic tone and a pedagogical method of dialectics. The conversation continues in a dialectical manner, by question and answer. But Socrates is no longer interested in refuting his interlocutors, nor does the conversation end in a state of *aporia*. Instead, he constructs a grand model of justice using a rich tapestry of symbols, metaphors, analogies, myths, and allegories.

What is the problem posed to Socrates by Glaucon and Adeimantus at the end of Book I of *The Republic*?

Glaucon and Adeimantus, who are Plato's older brothers, are much more sympathetic conversation partners than Thrasymachus. They are not interested in arguing for its own sake but are genuinely interested in acquiring knowledge. Nor are they immoralists like Thrasymachus. They agree with Socrates that justice is something that is good for its own sake, not something that is good only for the rewards that a good reputation brings. Thus, with them Socrates employs a more constructive style of dialectics whose purpose is to acquire knowledge of justice. But Glaucon and Adeimantus are disappointed with the way that Socrates concluded his conversation with Thrasymachus. They do not agree with Thrasymachus that the life of an unjust person is better than the life of a just person, but they don't think that Socrates has given them a complete account of why it is better to be just than to be unjust.

So Glaucon picks up the conversation where Thrasymachus left off. He plays the devil's advocate and says that no one is just for its own sake but only as a means to an end. Citizens obey the law only because they are afraid of being punished and because the law protects them from becoming a victim of injustice, not because they believe it is the right thing to do. In a society without government, no one would be just. There

> ## How does Socrates demonstrate that it is better to be just than to be unjust?
>
> He constructs a model of a just society and compares it with a model of an unjust society. He shows how an unjust society will fall apart into warring factions whereas a just society will enjoy peace and harmony. He draws an analogy between a just soul and a just society, and between an unjust soul and an unjust society. He concludes that a just soul will be happier than an unjust soul for the same reason that a just society is happier than an unjust society. A just soul will be harmonious and "well-tuned," whereas an unjust soul will be marked by discord.

would be no restraint on injustice, and everyone would do whatever they wanted. To drive home his point, Glaucon asks Socrates to imagine how anyone would act if they possessed the Ring of Gyges. A person who wears the Ring of Gyges becomes invisible, so they can commit any crime and take whatever they want without being found out and punished. Why, Glaucon asks, would someone wearing the Ring of Gyges choose to be just? How would their lives be better than the lives of those who use the ring's powers to commit crimes and get away with them?

PLATO'S MODEL OF AN IDEAL SOCIETY

How does Socrates begin the construction of his model of a just society?

Socrates begins by noting that no individual human being is self-sufficient and can satisfy all their own needs. We need each other. Fortunately, people possess a variety of different talents that suit them for different occupations. Therefore, we can satisfy all our needs by coming together in organized communities and producing different goods and services for one another. Our most basic needs are for food, shelter, and clothing. Therefore, at a minimum, a community will require farmers, builders, shoemakers, and weavers. But if these skilled workers are to focus on what they know best, we will need smiths and carpenters to manufacture their tools and equipment. Herdsmen will be needed to supply leather, wool, and work animals. But even these will not be able to supply all the needs of our community. We will need merchants to import goods from other communities as well as to export goods in return. We will need sailors to ship goods abroad. As the economy grows, we will need markets where traders exchange goods for money. There will be unskilled workers who perform hard physical labor for a wage. And so on. Socrates refers to the entire class of workers whose task is to satisfy our bodily needs or "appetites" as "farmers and craftsmen." In this case, Socrates is using "farmers and craftsmen" as a synecdoche. This means a figure of speech in which the part represents the whole. This is because farmers and craftsmen are only a part of the entire class of workers that he is referencing.

What would life be like in the simple community of farmers and craftsmen described by Socrates?

After Socrates completes his account of the occupations that would be necessary to supply our basic bodily needs, Glaucon asks him what life would be like in such a community. Socrates says that members of such a community would enjoy simple pleasures. They would recline on beds of yew and myrtle and eat on clean leaves. For dessert they would enjoy figs, chick peas, and beans. They would wear clothing in the winter, but not in the summer when clothing is not needed. They would sing hymns to the gods and enjoy one another's company. But to avoid the risks of hunger and war, they would take care not to have too many children.

What is Glaucon's complaint about the simple community of farmers and craftsmen described by Socrates?

Glaucon complains that the simple community of farmers and craftsmen described by Socrates is fit only for pigs. It satisfies all of a person's basic bodily needs but provides

The society that Plato describes is a fairly simple one consisting of farmers and craftsmen surviving on the basics of food, clothing, and shelter. Having more than this, such as enjoying luxuries, would inevitably lead to crime and war.

no luxuries. Socrates responds to Glaucon by telling him that the community he has described is sound, but that if its members fail to temper their appetites and seek out luxuries beyond the limits set by their natural needs, it would be necessary to add additional occupations to the community. The land that had been sufficient to feed the community would no longer be sufficient. The community would covet its neighbor's land in order to expand production. If its neighbor did the same, there would be war. In order to prepare for war, it would be necessary to raise an army, the so called "guardians."

Is the luxurious community a just community?

Temperance is moderation and proportion. The luxurious community is excessive. Therefore, the luxurious community is not temperate. According to Socrates, temperance is one of the four components of goodness. The others are courage, wisdom, and justice. Temperance is not the same as justice, but it is necessary for there to be justice. Therefore, the luxurious community is not a just community. But Socrates is not finished constructing his model of a just community. Once the guardians are properly educated, they will restrain the appetites and restore temperance to the community.

Who are the guardians, and how do they change the nature and class structure of the community?

The guardians are the soldiers first introduced by Socrates into his account of the just community to fight wars for the luxurious community of farmers and craftsmen. But according to Socrates, intemperance is the root cause of a host of vices in public and private life as well as war. Therefore, the guardians are needed to regulate and temper the appetites of the farmers and craftsmen as well as to fight wars. In addition to serving as soldiers, the guardians are also needed to serve as police and judges. The best of the guardians are needed to serve as rulers. Therefore, once the guardians are introduced by Socrates into his account of the just community, the state becomes ruled by a government. And because the appetites of the just state are tempered by the guardians, it is no longer luxurious or intemperate. A just state must have the proper proportions. It must not be too small or too large. If it is too small, it will not be able to satisfy all its needs. If it is too large, it will fall apart into factions. A just state is just the right size so that it is united and self-sufficient. In fact, the proper size of the just state is that of an ancient Greek city, the *polis*, from which we get our word "politics." The just state is therefore a city-state, and it is composed of three main social classes: the farmers and craftsmen, the guardians, and the rulers.

Who is permitted to tell lies and for what purpose?

Only the rulers may tell lies and only if they are in the public interest. It is wrong for a private citizen to lie to a ruler just as it would be wrong for a patient to lie to their doctor or for a sailor to lie to the captain of a ship. A doctor cannot heal a patient if the patient reports false symptoms. A captain cannot run a ship based on false information. A lie is useful only as a sort of medicine. It inflicts a small harm for the larger good of the

What is the noble lie?

The noble lie is a myth or fable that the rulers of the just city-state tell to promote peace and harmony between the three social classes: the farmers and craftsmen, the guardians, and the rulers. According to the first part of the myth, citizens of all social classes were given form deep within the ground, beneath the land occupied by the city-state, and then delivered up to the surface by their mother earth. This part of the myth is intended to make all citizens feel like brothers and sisters and to care for their land as if it were their mother and to defend it from any attack. According to the second part of the myth, God mixed gold into the souls of the rulers, silver into the souls of the guardians, and iron or bronze into the souls of farmers and craftsmen. It is because the souls of citizens contain either gold, silver, bronze, or iron that they are destined to become, respectively, either rulers, guardians, skilled workers, or laborers.

patient. But only a doctor knows how to administer medicine. Analogously, only the rulers know how to lie for the larger good of the city-state, because only the rulers know what the larger good of the city-state is.

How are citizens really assigned to a social class in the just city-state?

In reality, the just city-state is a meritocracy in which citizens are assigned to a social class based on merit. The just city-state is an equal opportunity employer. Men and women have an equal opportunity to become farmers, craftsmen, guardians, or rulers. Although children and their parents usually belong to the same social class, it is possible for the children of farmers and craftsmen to become guardians or rulers, and it is possible for the children of rulers to become guardians or farmers and craftsmen. To become a guardian of the just city-state, citizens must demonstrate an aptitude to fight, since their role is to guard the city-state from its enemies. In order to fight, they must be strong, brave, and high spirited. But they must also learn what is worth fighting for. If they don't, they might become mercenaries willing to fight for anyone, or worse, they might turn on their fellow citizens or on each other. Therefore, to become a guardian, citizens must also have a strong love for wisdom that will sustain them through the difficult process of education that is required to learn what is worth fighting for.

To become a ruler, a guardian must demonstrate the highest degree of wisdom and prudence in guarding the city-state. Candidates for the ruling class must love the just city-state so much that their conviction to serve its best interest is not shaken even when they are put through the most severe tests and trials. They must not flinch in the face of danger or hardships, nor must they be easily deceived or tempted by pleasures. To make doubly sure that they place the public interest above their private concerns, the rulers and guardians are not permitted to have families or to own private property. They eat their meals in common. Men and women are mated according to eugenic principles to produce the finest offspring. But children are raised in communal nurseries so that every guardian feels like a brother or sister to one another.

PLATO'S PHILOSOPHY OF EDUCATION

What is the purpose of educating the guardians?

Besides making them better fighters, the purpose of educating the guardians is to edify them and develop the excellence (*arête*) of their souls. This is accomplished by exposing children to works of art, music, and literature that reflect the highest values of goodness, truth, and beauty. Before they know why, children who are educated in this way will develop a love for things that are good, true, and beautiful, and come to resemble them. By the time they are capable of reason, they will recognize the good, the true, and the beautiful, as if they were old friends. It is their love for the good, the true, and the beautiful that will hold them firm in their conviction to guard the just city-state.

What do the guardians study during their childhood education?

The education of the guardians starts with the study of music, which includes poetic stories about the gods. After their souls have been formed by the study of music, they practice gymnastics to form their bodies.

What kind of poetic stories are told to the guardians during their childhood education?

The poetic stories told to the guardians during their childhood education are examples of useful lies administered as medicine because they are not literally true but are allegories that contain a mixture of truth and falsehood. Since these stories provide role models for young children, they are censored to omit any reference to conduct that is immoral or unbecoming of a guardian. Contrary to traditional Greek myths, the gods described in these stories are always truthful, good, and temperate. They do not lie. They never do real harm to anyone, only good. Their appetites are well tempered. They never display an excessive appetite for food or sex. They do not lose their temper or fight with one another. Because excessive laughter can be insulting and cause fights, the gods are never described as being overcome by laughter. Children are never told horror stories about the underworld or life after death because if they are going to become brave warriors, they must not fear death. For the same reason, they are not told stories in which there is wailing and lamentation over fallen heroes.

Warriors in Plato's ideal state would not only be soldiers but would also be well educated in literature, music, and the arts.

77

What kinds of harmony, melody, and rhythm should the guardians be exposed to during their childhood education?

The harmonies, melodies, and rhythms that the guardians are exposed to during their childhood education should conform to the moral intention of the stories they are told. Children should not be exposed to harmonies and melodies that are appropriate to dirges and songs of sorrow because those would provoke fear of death and make the guardians cowardly. Nor should they be exposed to harmonies and melodies that are appropriate to drinking songs or laxity because those would make the guardians intemperate. Socrates prohibits the use of certain Lydian and Ionic modes because they are modes used for dirges and drinking songs (a mode is a type of musical scale). Socrates permits the Dorian and Phrygian modes to be used in the education of the guardians because they are appropriate for the words of a brave warrior facing death or hardship with steadfast resolve. They are also appropriate for prayers, for teaching, and for learning, because all of these require modesty and moderation.

There are restrictions on instruments as well. Flutes, harps, and lutes should not be used because they span too many harmonies. They are luxurious and intemperate. Only the simple seven-stringed lyre or cithara should be used. In ancient Greek mythology, the flute was associated with Dionysus, the god of wine, ecstasy, and intoxication. The lyre was associated with Apollo, the god of light, form, and order. Similarly, rhythms of great complexity or diversity should not be used. Instead, only simple rhythms that are graceful and express the character of a brave and orderly life should be used. To sum up, the only music that the guardians should be exposed to during their childhood education should be music that instills in them a love of beauty, truth, order, temperance, and courage.

What other kinds of art and craftsmanship should the guardians be exposed to during their childhood education?

Children being educated to become guardians should be exposed to excellence in all forms of art and craftsmanship, including painting, sculpture, weaving, furniture, and architecture. A child who is constantly exposed to excellence in art and craftsmanship will learn to love what is beautiful and good and come to resemble them. The same principle applies to all forms of art as it does to music. Excellence in art expresses or reenacts the excellence of the soul of the artist. By constantly exposing children to excellence in art, their souls too become excellent.

What kind of physical training should the guardians receive, and when should it begin?

According to Socrates, physical training should begin after the guardians have received an education in music because, contrary to popular belief, a sound mind is required to develop a sound body, not the reverse. The physical training of the guardians includes moderate diet, exercise, and medical care. Just as moderation in music brings temperance to the soul, moderation in diet, exercise, and medical care brings health to the body. The guardians are fed a simple diet without luxury or excess. Meats are roasted over an open fire, since soldiers in the field are unable to carry pots and pans. No sweets of any kind, or any of the rich and heavily spiced foods of Sicily, are included in their diet. Other indulgences are frowned upon as well. Asked if he would approve of a Corinthian winch for any man trying to stay in shape, Socrates replies, definitely not. The exercise routine prescribed for the guardians is limited to simple gymnastics without weight training. The purpose of gymnastics is not only to build bodies but also to instill courage in the soul. Muscle building develops pride and confidence in one's body, high spirits, and courage. But too much muscle building in proportion to music would make the guardians excessively fierce, cruel, and stupid. Too little muscle building in proportion to music would make the guardians soft and effeminate. Just the right amount of muscle building is needed to give the guardians courage.

PLATO'S THEORY OF THE JUST CITY–STATE

Would the guardians need many doctors, lawyers, and judges?

No; if they are well educated, they would not. If the guardians follow a simple diet and engage in moderate exercise, they would rarely need a doctor to treat illness in their bodies because most illness is caused by intemperance in eating and exercise. Similarly, if the guardians study simple and temperate forms of music, they would rarely need a judge to treat injustice in their souls because crime and vice are caused by excessive variety and complexity in musical education. A free and well-educated person is autonomous and self-directing. She is master and judge of herself and would rarely need to surrender care of her body—and never her soul—to others. It is shameful, Socrates says, to need a doctor to treat an illness caused by sloth, gluttony, or lust. Equally shameful is to waste your time in courts of law, either as plaintiff or defendant. It is not shameful to need a doctor to treat a wound or an occasional acute illness. But Socrates does not believe that life should be prolonged at any cost. When chronic illness and constant doctoring prevent you from taking care of yourself and performing your social duties, it is time, he thinks, to pull the plug.

Would the constitution of the just city-state contain many laws regulating contracts, civil lawsuits, taxes, tariffs, and criminal justice?

No, it would not be necessary to have many laws of this type in the constitution of the just city-state because its system of moral education would ensure that its governors administer these affairs wisely. If the rulers of a city-state are not wise, then no constitution would protect them. The ultimate foundation of the just city-state lies not in its constitution but in the moral character of its governors. Attempting to cure corrupt governors by expanding the constitution is like attempting to cure a glutton with medicine. Laws, like medicine, cannot correct the root cause of the problem, which is bad character. Only education can do that.

Is there any place for frivolous entertainment or recreation in the just city-state?

No, culture is a serious business in the just city-state because its moral character depends upon it, and once that's lost, its very existence would be threatened. Music and

Music and poetry are a necessity for any stable city-state, according to Socrates.

poetry, Socrates says, cannot be disturbed without shaking the foundations of the city-state. That's why there are strictly enforced regulations controlling all forms of education and culture, including gymnastics. Consuming frivolous entertainment is like eating pastries. It provides immediate short-term pleasure at the expense of long-term health and happiness.

How will the just city-state be able to defend itself against wealthy cities?

The just city-state will be able to defend itself against wealthy cities because it is stronger than they are. The just city-state is temperate. Wealthy cities are not. Intemperance causes crime and vice as well as civil strife. Rich men are fat and make poor soldiers. They are no match against the highly educated and well-trained warrior athletes of the just city-state. Wealthy cities are also weakened by internal divisions between the wealthy and the poor. The just city-state may not enjoy the same luxuries as wealthy cities, but it is happier than they are because it is harmonious and united. The citizens of the just city-state know their appropriate role and cooperate with one another to achieve a common goal. In a war, the citizens of the just city-state would unite together against their enemy, while the citizens of a wealthy city would fight among themselves.

PLATO'S THEORY OF THE SOUL

What does Plato's Chariot Allegory tell us about the nature of the soul?

In Plato's dialogue *Phaedrus,* Socrates says that the soul is like a chariot steered by a charioteer and pulled by two winged horses. All charioteers and horses of the gods are good and noble. But one of the horses that pull human chariots is not. One of the horses that pull human chariots is white and handsome, but the other is dark and ugly. One is

In the chariot allegory, a charioteer—representing the intellect and reason—must guide a chariot that is pulled by one winged horse representing the spirited part of the soul, and a second winged horse representing lusts and appetites. The horse representing the spirited part of the soul is willing to follow the commands of the charioteer (i.e., reason) while the second horse is not.

noble and of good breeding, but the other is the opposite. The white horse willingly flies up towards the heavens, while the dark horse is drawn back down to earth. The charioteer represents the rational part of the soul, whereas the horses represent the irrational, passionate parts. The white horse represents the spirited part of the soul, which harbors a desire for honor, whereas the dark horse represents the appetites, which are desires for material things and the pleasures they bring.

According to the allegory, the human charioteer tries to steer the chariot up towards the heavens, but he has a difficult time of it because the dark horse is always struggling to fly back down to earth to enjoy earthly pleasures. The white horse is honorable and follows the commands of the charioteer. But the dark horse will only obey if it is beaten because all it knows is pain and pleasure. If the charioteer can succeed in restraining the dark horse and steer the chariot up towards the heavens, the soul will enjoy a vision of the eternal forms of goodness, truth, and beauty. This will enable the chariot to circle the heavens with the gods. But to the degree that the charioteer fails, the chariot will be driven back down to earth, and the soul will be reborn into a body with a lower form of intelligence. Parmenides had used similar imagery to describe the philosopher's ascent towards truth, and by repeating that imagery Plato is affirming his affinity with Parmenides.

81

How can temperance be understood in terms of Plato's Chariot Allegory?

To be temperate is to exercise self-control. It is to be master of oneself. But to be master of oneself implies that there is a better and a worse part of oneself and that the better part can rule the worse. According to Socrates, the better part of the soul is the rational part, which is represented in the Chariot Allegory by the charioteer, and the worse part of the soul is the irrational, which is represented in the Chariot Allegory by the winged horses. A temperate soul is one in which the rational part of the soul, represented by the charioteer, orders and controls the irrational parts, bringing them into harmony with one another so they all pursue the common goal of flying upwards.

How does Plato's Chariot Allegory compare with psychoanalyst Sigmund Freud's theory of the id, ego and superego?

The id in Sigmund Freud's (1856–1939) psychoanalytic theory is composed of irrational and amoral desires, primarily libido or lust, and it compares well with Plato's dark horse. The ego is the rational part of consciousness that orients us in the real world and serves to restrain our irrational desires. It compares with Plato's charioteer. The superego consists of moral standards internalized from one's parents during childhood and serves to restrain our immoral desires. The superego doesn't have a very close analogue in Plato's Chariot Allegory. But insofar as both the white horse and the charioteer serve to restrain immoral desires, it compares with them. What Freud and Plato have in common is the belief that bodily desires and instincts are not inherently moral but that they can be restrained by a higher form of consciousness and "sublimated" to serve a moral purpose.

Where are wisdom, courage, temperance, and justice located in the just city-state?

In order to plan for the future and make good executive decisions for the sake of the whole city, its rulers must be wise. Therefore wisdom, or prudence, is found in the rulers who govern the just city-state. The rulers are selected from among those guardians who have passed the most severe tests and proven that they are most wise. Courage is found in the guardians whose role it is to defend the just city-state in times of war. Temperance is not found within any one social class but is a harmony between all three social classes, like the harmony between the three primary notes of the musical scale. Temperance is a voluntary, consensual agreement between all three social classes that the rulers ought to rule and everyone else ought to obey because the rulers are the most wise and rational. Temperance integrates the social classes into a harmonious whole that can work together to achieve a common goal. Like temperance, justice is not found within any single part of society but rather refers to the way in which the parts of society are related to one another. Whereas temperance unites the different parts of society into a harmonious whole, justice divides society into different social functions. Justice is an appropriate division of labor.

In a just society, each social class and each member of society has a different role to play, a unique social duty. It would be an act of injustice to deny your duty and play a social role that was not appropriate for you. For example, it would be unjust if someone who had a natural talent for making shoes became a ruler, or if someone who demonstrated a talent to rule wisely became a farmer. Justice is doing your own duty and no one else's. A just city-state is therefore a well-ordered community in which each social class and each member of society plays their appropriate role.

What are the three parts of the soul?

We examined the just city-state first because it is larger than the soul and it is easier to discern its parts and structure. But the city-state is merely an analogy of the soul, which is the original form or pattern upon which the city-state is constructed. For example, all virtues of the city-state exist in their original form and originate in the souls of its citizens. A city is courageous because there is courage in the souls of its soldiers. It is wise because there is wisdom in the souls of its rulers. Each part and structure of a city-state corresponds to a part and structure of the soul. The rulers of the just city-state correspond to the reasoning part of the soul. The guardians correspond to the spirited part of the soul. And the farmers and craftsmen correspond to the appetites. The reasoning part of the soul is the part that plans for the future and makes decisions for the benefit of the whole person. Its virtue is wisdom. The spirited part of the soul causes us to become angry or indignant. Its virtue is courage.

The appetites are our desires to seek pleasure and avoid pain from physical things. We can distinguish reason from the appetites because reason often conflicts with the appetites. For example, we may have an appetite for a large amount of food, but our reason counsels us to moderate our consumption to stay healthy. The fact that children are capable of anger and indignation from an early age but may never develop the capacity for reason demonstrates that the spirited part of the soul is different from the reasoning part. To illustrate the difference between the spirited part of the soul and the appetites, Socrates offers the example of a man who passes by an execution. He wishes to see the bodies of the executed, but he feels that it is wrong to indulge his morbid curiosity and holds his eyes closed. As he walks by the corpses, he opens his eyes and yells out to himself with indignant anger, "There, damn you, feast on this banquet for sordid appetites." Socrates claims that the spirited part of the soul will always ally with reason against the appetites and that no examples can be found in which the spirited part of the soul sides with the appetites against reason. A soul is temperate when reason with the assistance of the spirited part of the soul tempers and restrains the appetites. A just soul is a well-ordered soul in which each part of the soul fulfills its appropriate function.

How is the soul related to the body?

Although the perpetually changing appearances found in the realm of becoming are not separate entities apart from the eternal Platonic forms, because the appearances are nothing more than a moving image of the forms, Plato often speaks about the soul as if it were a separate entity capable of existing apart from the body. For example, in the *Phaedo,* Plato adopts the Pythagorean-Orphic religious belief that the soul is imprisoned in the body as in a tomb. The body is the cause of ignorance and of everything that is bad and base. Every pain and pleasure and accompanying passion, fear, or desire that we experience while our souls are imprisoned in our bodies is only another nail in our coffin or tomb. These powerful feelings produced by the things that appear to us through our bodily sense organs persuade us to believe that the appearances are real and bind us to them when in fact they are only phantasms, mere ghosts or shadows of the eternal forms. True life and liberation begin only when

As with later Christian thought, Plato believed that the soul was something separate from the body. The body prevents the soul from seeing what reality truly is, and only after death, when the soul is liberated, do we truly see.

the body dies and the soul is released from its prison. Philosophy prepares us for this ultimate liberation from the body by training us to use the reasoning part of our soul to contemplate the eternal forms and to not be misled by our bodily sense organs or seduced by the powerful passions and desires they produce in us.

Why is a just soul happy and an unjust soul unhappy?

Socrates uses a medical analogy to explain why a just soul is happy and an unjust soul is unhappy. He says that a healthy body depends on the natural order of its parts. The parts of a healthy body each perform their appropriate function and work harmoniously and in proper proportion with one another. A healthy body is beautiful because its parts are organized in a harmonious pattern, and it is strong because its parts are unified behind a common purpose. In an unhealthy body, one or more of its parts fails to perform its appropriate function and may interfere with the performance of other parts. Similarly, a just soul, like a well-tuned lyre, is one in which each of its parts performs its appropriate function and works together harmoniously with other parts to achieve a common purpose. A just soul is a happy soul because it is strong, healthy, and beautiful. A just soul possesses *arête*. By contrast, an unjust soul is fraught with internal conflict and disorder, making it sick, ugly, and weak. Thus, Socrates concludes that it is better to live for justice and beauty regardless of whether your reputation is improved by doing so because justice and beauty are intrinsic goods that bring happiness to your soul. Injustice can never be preferable to justice even if you are never punished for your misdeeds because injustice brings disorder to your soul and makes you unhappy. Thus, Socrates inverts the claim made by Thrasymachus at the beginning of *The Republic* that justice is the interest of the strong. It is in your interest to be just, and only the just can be strong.

THE ALLEGORY OF THE CAVE

What is necessary for the ideal city-state to actually exist?

The just city-state outlined in Plato's *Republic* is an ideal model against which we can measure any actually existing city, but it is possible that no actually existing city measures up to the ideal. According to Socrates, for a city-state to measure up to the ideal, either philosophers must become kings (rulers) or kings must become philosophers, because only philosophers possess knowledge of the ideal form of the just city-state. By "philosopher" Socrates does not mean anyone who appears to be a philosopher or anyone who is widely believed to be one, such as the Sophists in his day or philosophy professors in our day, but rather anyone who really possesses knowledge of the ideal forms.

It is in the nature of being a philosopher to know the forms or essences of things rather than only particular examples of them. For example, knowledge of beautiful things is not, according to Socrates, philosophical knowledge. In fact, it is not knowledge at all but rather mere opinion (*doxa*). Particular things exist in the intermediate realm of mere appearances and becoming, between Being and Non-Being. They are neither eternal forms nor are they nothing at all. They are moving shadows or imitations of the forms. As soon as you glimpse them, they disappear or turn into their opposite. Young becomes old. Life becomes death. Beautiful things appear ugly in another perspective. Appearances (phenomena) possess no substantial or enduring reality, and therefore knowledge of them is not possible. Only the forms themselves, such as the ideal form of the just city-state, can be known. Unless the rulers of a city are philosophers and possess this knowledge, they cannot possibly rule wisely because they would not possess the blueprint or model they need to construct an ideal city.

What must the guardians who are chosen to become the future rulers of the just city-state do to complete their education?

Because a city-state can be just only if it is ruled by philosophers, and because a philosopher is someone who possesses knowledge of the forms, the future rulers of the just city-state must receive an education in the forms. Music, poetry, art, and gymnastics instill a love of beauty, truth, order, temperance, and courage in the guardians. And by exposing the guardians to sensible objects that reflect the eternal forms, they prepare the guardians for knowledge of the forms. But music, poetry, art, and gymnastics do not themselves provide knowledge of the forms because their objects of study are sensible. Only mathematics and dialectics whose objects of study are the eternal forms can provide knowledge of the forms. Therefore, to complete their education to become rulers of the just city-state, it is necessary for the guardians to study mathematics and dialectics.

Mathematics stands midway between opinion about sensible objects and dialectical knowledge of the forms. The objects of mathematical knowledge are eternal forms, but the act of mathematical knowledge employs visual aids such as drawings of geometric figures and temporal processes such as deductive reasoning. Because it relies on visual aids and temporal processes, Socrates believes that mathematics is less demanding than dialectics, and so he places its study before dialectics in the course of education prescribed for the future rulers of the city-state. However, once the soul has become accustomed to abstract reasoning in mathematics, it can then move on to the study of dialectics where both the act of knowing and its object transcend the sensible world of time and space.

What is the setting of Plato's allegory of the cave?

Imagine an underground cave connected to the surface of the earth by a long, steep passageway. Inside the cave is a group of prisoners who since birth have been chained to one of the walls of the cave in such a way that they can only see the wall in front of them, but nothing behind. On a ledge behind the prisoners there is a stage for puppets. Behind the stage is a fire whose light casts shadows of the puppets onto the wall of the cave that the prisoners can see. A parapet hides the puppeteers, so the prisoners do not see shadows of the puppeteers. Since the shadows on the wall of the cave are the only things the prisoners have ever seen, they believe that they are real. They compete with one another

Why is Plato's allegory of the cave so famous and important?

The allegory of the cave is so famous and important because it provides a compelling portrait of Plato's philosophy that has inspired readers ever since it was written. In dramatic and colorful fashion, it tells the story of the perils and rewards of the human pursuit of enlightenment and liberation. It contains in condensed symbolic form the key principles of Plato's philosophy of the forms and of knowledge, education, and politics. Socrates recites the allegory of the cave at the climax of Plato's most historically influential dialogue *The Republic,* immediately after presenting the analogies of the Sun and the divided line. The analogies of the Sun and the divided line convey crucial information about Plato's theory of knowledge but serve in Plato's *Republic* only to prepare the reader for the even greater and more comprehensive philosophical vision represented by the allegory of the cave.

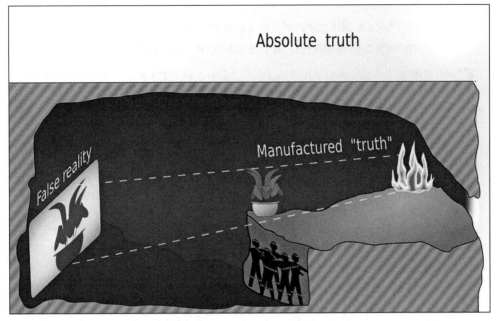

Plato's allegory of the cave from his *Republic* compares a world in which people kept in ignorance believe that shadows on a wall are reality, but the enlightened philosopher, escaping his prison, discovers what the real world, illuminated by the Sun, actually is.

to identify the shadows and remember the sequence and arrangements in which they appear. They have no idea that the things they see are only shadows of puppets.

What happens when one of the prisoners in the cave is freed from her chains?

She turns to face the fire but is dazzled by the bright light. Her eyes hurt and she has difficulty seeing the puppets in front of the fire. By comparison, the shadows seemed much more real to her than the puppets because she and her fellow prisoners were able to see them clearly and without pain. Wanting to turn back to the shadows, she is instead dragged by force up the long, steep passageway that leads out of the cave. The light of the sun is even brighter and more painful than the light of the fire in the cave. At first, all she can bear to look at are shadows and reflections of objects in pools of water. As her eyes adjust to the bright light, she is able to look at objects themselves, such as plants and animals. Finally, she can see the sun itself. She realizes that the sun is the source of light and the cause of the seasons and of all life on earth.

What happens when the freed prisoner returns to the cave?

She has difficulty seeing in the dark after having been out in the bright sunlight. She can't compete with the other prisoners at identifying the shadows and remembering

How does Plato's allegory of the cave represent the different levels of knowledge depicted in the analogy of the divided line?

Each step in the prisoner's journey out of the cave represents a higher level of knowledge as depicted in the analogy of the divided line. The shadows on the wall of the cave represent images such as shadows and reflections of physical objects. Seeing the shadows on the wall of the cave represents imagination, which is the basis for mere conjecture and guesswork, the lowest level of knowledge. The puppets represent physical objects themselves. Seeing the puppets represents perception, the second lowest level of knowledge. The fire in the cave represents the sun in the physical world. The cave represents the realm of sensible objects. The world outside the cave represents the realm of intelligible objects, the forms. The shadows of objects in the world outside the cave represent the mathematical forms. The objects themselves represent the moral and aesthetic forms. The sun in the world outside the cave represents the Good.

their sequence and arrangements. They laugh at her and think she has ruined her eyesight by leaving the cave. They resolve to kill anyone who tries to release another prisoner and guide them out of the cave.

What does the freed prisoner's journey out of the cave and her return into the cave represent?

The prisoner's journey out of the cave represents the course of education that the guardians must traverse to become philosophers and, therefore, qualified to rule the just city-state. The cave may also symbolize a womb or a tomb, and in that case the journey out of the cave would represent the birth of a new life or rebirth. The steep incline of the passageway out of the cave represents the difficulty of the course of education required to become a philosopher. The community of prisoners represents a society of unenlightened citizens who think that philosophy is dangerous and will kill anyone who questions their beliefs. Plato is alluding here to the historical Socrates who was convicted by the people of Athens and executed on charges of corrupting the youth. The freed prisoner's return into the cave represents the obligation of guardians who receive a philosophical education at state expense to return to civic life and serve the just city-state as its wise and prudent rulers. Although the guardians who receive a philosophical education would prefer to spend their lives in philosophical contemplation, since they are much happier in the world outside the cave than they are inside the cave, Socrates would like to remind them that the purpose of leaving the cave and obtaining a philosophical education is to obtain knowledge for the benefit of the whole society, not only for themselves. The highest knowledge obtained is knowledge of the Good, which is the principle of unity and social harmony.

THE INEVITABLE DEGENERATION OF THE JUST CITY–STATE

Why must the just city-state inevitably degenerate into progressively more corrupt forms of government?

The just city-state is not an ideal form but rather an imitation of an ideal form in the physical world of space and time. Although the forms are timeless, the city-state and its citizens are not. To maintain the city-state's population, its citizens must replicate themselves by means of sexual reproduction. Unfortunately, according to Plato, replication errors occur in sexual reproduction. Because space and time are irrational and unknowable, our calendars will always be at least slightly inaccurate, and births will occur at the wrong times. Children will be born under the wrong configuration of stars and planets, "under a bad sign," producing inferior offspring who corrupt the state and cause it to degenerate.

Why does Socrates refer to the just city-state as an aristocracy?

The Greek word *aristokratia* is composed of the root terms *aristos*, meaning "best," and *kratia*, from *kratein*, meaning "to be strong, to rule." Therefore an "aristocracy" is a society ruled by the best. According to Socrates, the just city-state is an "aristocracy" because it is ruled by reason, which is the best (or most excellent) part of the soul. What

---

Why are space and time irrational and unknowable according to Plato?

Unlike Aristotle, Plato does not employ the concept of matter. What makes something physical for Plato is not that it contains matter but that it is extended in space and subject to change. Space is a passive "receptacle" or womb that receives images of the forms, whose ultimate source is the Good. The forms are rational and knowable, and insofar as physical things imitate the forms, they are too. But space is irrational and unknowable. Much to their dismay, the Pythagoreans discovered that certain geometric proportions, such as the ratio of the hypotenuse of a right triangle to one of its legs or the area of a circle to the square of its radius, are equal to irrational numbers like $\sqrt{2}$ and π (pi). An irrational number is a number that cannot be expressed as the ratio or proportion of two integers or by a finite or repeating series of digits. An irrational number is therefore incalculable and unknowable. We can approximate an irrational number, but we can never get it completely right. Since time is measured by movement in space, it too cannot be measured with complete accuracy. Our calendars will always be wrong by some small fraction of time.

gives the philosopher-kings the authority to rule the just city-state is that reason rules the spirited part of their souls and their appetites.

What types of government does aristocracy degenerate into, and in what order?

According to Socrates, aristocracy degenerates into timocracy; timocracy degenerates into oligarchy; oligarchy degenerates into democracy; and democracy degenerates into tyranny. Tyranny is the worst form of government because it is not ruled by reason at all but by the tyrant's appetites.

How does aristocracy degenerate into timocracy?

Aristocracy degenerates into timocracy when the children of aristocrats are born out of time with a lesser share of reason than their parents possessed and a greater share of the spirited part of their souls. The spirited part of the soul is the ambitious and aggressive part of the soul that desires status, power, and success. Timocrats retain their parents' military virtues but are less interested in education and do not trust philosophers in positions of power. A timocracy is a society ruled by soldiers. Timocrats seek to obtain status, power, and success by means of military conquest and, in their later years, by means of the acquisition and ostentatious display of wealth.

How does timocracy degenerate into oligarchy?

Timocracy degenerates into oligarchy when the children of timocrats are born out of time with a lesser share of spirit than their parents possessed and a greater share of appetite. Seeing that honor and glory don't necessarily put food on the table, they devote themselves to making money instead. But they are not completely ruled by their appetites. They make reason their slave and employ it to count their money. But oligarchs are not interested in money only as a means of fulfilling their appetites. Oligarchs are more interested in money as a means of securing their economic status. Oligarchs value money above pleasure. They believe in hard work and thrift. They spend money only on their most necessary appetites, and they suppress the others in order to become wealthier. An oligarchy is a society ruled by the wealthy whose only qualification to rule is their wealth. Consequently, oligarchies are not managed wisely. Because they concentrate wealth in the hands of a few, oligarchies are discordant societies, marked by class conflict and weakened by internal divisions between the rich and the poor.

How does oligarchy degenerate into democracy?

Oligarchy degenerates into democracy when the children of oligarchs are born out of time with greater appetites than their parents possessed, but without reason or honor to restrain them. Frustrated by their parents' austerity, the children of oligarchs become spendthrifts and hedonists. Many are driven into poverty by their wasteful expenditures on unnecessary pleasures, causing the ranks of the poor to grow. The oligarchs do nothing to stop this trend, since they profit from other people's wasteful expenditures. In fact, they lend the spendthrifts money so that when they default on their loans, they can purchase their property at bargain prices. This only causes the number of poor people and their resentment towards the rich to grow even more until, finally, the poor rise up and seize control of the state. Thus, democracy is born.

A democratic society is one that is ruled by many poor and undistinguished people just as the democratic soul is ruled by many common appetites. Reason is capable of distinguishing between good and bad pains and between good and bad pleasures. For example, a medical procedure may be painful, but if the patient is rational, they know that it is good for them. A sweet pastry may taste very good to a diabetic, but if they are rational, they know that it is not good for them. Lacking the capacity to reason, the democratic soul cannot distinguish between good and bad pain or between good and bad pleasure. Pain and pleasure become the only standards of value. Something is good if it is pleasurable and bad if it is painful. Since it is pleasurable to fulfill an appetite, it is good to fulfill an appetite. Since it is painful to deprive an appetite, it is bad to deprive it. Since everyone has appetites, and it is always pleasurable to fulfill an appetite, it is good to fulfill any and every appetite that anyone might have. In a democracy, everyone is equal and is equally entitled to fulfill their appetites because all appetites are equal. The greatest good in a democracy is liberty because there is no legitimate reason to deprive anyone of anything they want. Taken to its logical extreme, democrats ignore all laws and recognize no legitimate coercive authority. Taken to its logical extreme, democracy is anarchy.

How does democracy degenerate into tyranny?

Without laws to protect the few remaining wealthy property owners, the poor rally around a populist leader who promises to seize their wealth and distribute it to them. However, once in power, the populist leader becomes a tyrant, only interested in fulfilling his own most depraved appetites. Lacking restraint of any kind, the tyrant sleeps with his mother and murders his father. He becomes a creature of drunkenness, lust, and utter madness, letting loose in the light of day what most people experience only in their darkest dreams.

IT IS BETTER TO BE
JUST THAN UNJUST

Why is the tyrant unhappy?

Without reason to harmonize the different parts of his soul, the tyrant is always at war with himself and is unable to act with consistent or focused intent. The tyrant is a slave to his own appetites, which are many and without limit. It is impossible for the tyrant to completely fulfill all his appetites because they conflict with one another and are unquenchable. The tyrant's relationships with those around him are also fraught with conflict. The tyrant is only interested in satisfying his own appetites, not those of anyone else. He gets what he wants from other people by threatening them with violence or by bribing them. His closest advisors are flatterers and liars. His bodyguards are mercenaries. He lives in constant fear of betrayal or assassination. He trusts no one, and no one trusts him.

Socrates asserted that tyrants are never happy because they are too worried about maintaining power while surrounded by people they cannot trust.

How does Socrates calculate how much more pleasure the philosopher-king enjoys than the tyrant?

Socrates uses Pythagorean number theory to calculate how much more pleasure the philosopher-king enjoys than the tyrant. He says that the tyrant is third removed from the oligarch, because between the tyrant and the oligarch is the democrat. He says that if we can agree that the philosopher-king and the aristocrat are one and the same, then the oligarch in turn is third removed from the philosopher-king, because between the aristocrat and the oligarch is the timocrat. Therefore, he says, the philosopher-king must be separated from the tyrant by a number that is three times three (3×3), which equals nine (9). The tyrant's pleasure is represented by a plane number, i.e., a square. The philosopher-king's pleasure is represented by a cube. If the length of each side of the tyrant's square is one (1) unit long, then the length of each side of the cube would be equal to three times three or nine (9) units. The area of the tyrant's square measures the tyrant's pleasure. Therefore, the tyrant's pleasure equals $1 \times 1 = 1$. The area of the philosopher-king's cube measures the philosopher-king's pleasure. Therefore, the philosopher-king's pleasure equals $9 \times 9 \times 9 = 729$.

How can Socrates's calculation of the tyrant's displeasure be understood in terms of Pythagorean music theory?

Socrates presents the five types of government in an ordered, geometric sequence. First comes aristocracy, followed by oligarchy, timocracy, democracy, and tyranny, in that order. It is a geometric sequence because the relationship between each two successive elements of the sequence is the same. Aristocracy stands in the same relationship to timocracy as timocracy does to oligarchy, and so on. If each element in a geometric sequence is a number, then the ratio or proportion of each two successive numbers in the sequence is equal ($a/b = b/c = c/d$, and so on).

How much happier is the philosopher-king than the tyrant?

According to Socrates, the philosopher-king enjoys precisely 729 times more true pleasure than the tyrant and is therefore 729 times happier.

If we consider that an aristocracy is composed of three classes or parts all acting as one and in harmony with one another—the philosopher-king, the guardians, and the farmers and craftsmen—then we obtain the following geometric sequence: philosopher-king, guardians, farmers and craftsmen, timocrats, oligarchs, democrats, and tyrants. Socrates says that the philosopher-king enjoys 729 times more pleasure than the tyrant and, inversely, the tyrant suffers 729 times more displeasure than the philosopher-king. If the philosopher-king enjoys 729 units of pleasure and the geometric proportion of our sequence is 1/3, then the guardians enjoy 729/3 = 243 units of pleasure, the farmers and craftsmen enjoy 81, the timocrats 27, the oligarchs 9, the democrats 3, and the tyrant 1. Thus, we obtain the geometric sequence 729, 243, 81, 27, 9, 3, and 1. If the philosopher-king suffers one unit of displeasure and the geometric proportion of our sequence is 3, then we get the reverse, which measures the relative amount of displeasure suffered by each element in the sequence 1, 3, 9, 27, 81, 243, and 792. If we divide each element of the first sequence by 792, we get the sequence 1, 1/3, 1/9, 1/27, 1/81, 1/243, and 1/792.

These sequences appear in the Pythagorean musical tuning system because Pythagorean tuning multiplies the frequency of the base note by a ratio of either 3/2 or 2/3 and then adjusts each note to fit into the same octave by multiplying or dividing by a multiple of 2. Pythagorean musical tuning is based on a geometric sequence of musical intervals known as perfect fifths, each tuned in the ratio 3/2 in ascending order or 2/3 in descending order. There are thirteen notes and twelve intervals in the Pythagorean tuning system. If the sequence of notes is arranged vertically, the base note is in the middle and there is a tritone at the bottom and at the top. If the base note is 1, then the tritone in ascending order from the base note is 729 divided by a multiple of 2, and the tritone in descending order is 1/729 multiplied by a multiple of 2. The tritone is known as the "devil's interval" because it sounds dissonant and unpleasant. The heavy metal band Black Sabbath uses the tritone in its eponymous song.

In Pythagorean tuning, if the base note is D, then the frequency ratio of the D note to the base is 1/1, the frequency ratio of the A note to the base is 3/2, of the E 9/8, of the B 27/16, of F♯ 81/64, of C♯ 243/128, and of G♯ 729/512. In descending order from the base note, we have the sequence 1/1, 4/3 for the G note, 16/9 for the C, 32/27 for the F, 128/81 for B♭, 256/243 for E♭, and 1024/729 for A♭. In Socrates's calculation, the D note (= 1) is the philosopher-king, and the tritones G♯ and A♭ (729/512 and 1024/729) are tyrants. Frequency ratios that are multiples of 2 sound the same due to octave invariance, and so multiples of 2 or 1/2 can be ignored. The philosopher-king (1) is therefore equal to 729 times

93

the tyrant represented by the tritone A♭ (1/729) and only 1/729 times the tyrant repre-sented by the tritone G♯ (729). Perhaps this is why Socrates says that the philosopher-king enjoys 729 times as much pleasure as the tyrant and suffers 1/729 as much displeasure.

Now, the A note and the G are guardians. The E note and the C are farmers and crafts-men. Aristocracy is a pentatonic musical scale consisting of two ascending and two de-scending fifths. The B note and the F are timocrats. Timocracy is a diatonic musical scale consisting of three ascending and three descending fifths. F♯ and B♭ are oligarchs. Oli-garchy is a musical scale consisting of four ascending and four descending fifths. C♯ and E♭ are democrats. Democracy is a musical scale consisting of five ascending and five de-scending fifths. The tritones G♯ and A♭ are tyrants. Tyranny is a chromatic musical scale consisting of six ascending and six descending fifths.

Any musical scale composed of fifths will suffer some degree of dissonance because fifths and octaves do not perfectly coincide. The modern chromatic scale resolves this problem by tuning each fifth in the ratio $2^{7/12}$, which is approximately 1.498—not exactly 3/2, but close enough for the human ear. However, the Pythagorean tuning system makes each note further above or below the base note slightly more out of tune, until one tritone is out of tune by 11.73 cents and the other by −11.73 cents. Although both tritones should sound like the same note, they don't because their frequency ratios dif-fer by 23.46 cents, nearly a quarter semitone, which is known as the Pythagorean comma. In order to avoid the severe dissonance that playing both tritones would pro-duce, Pythagorean tuning requires musicians to omit one tritone from their repertoire, leaving only twelve playable notes and eleven fifths. Thus, tyranny is the most disso-nant and unpleasant musical scale.

How does Socrates use his calculation of the philosopher-king's pleasure to argue that it is better to be just than unjust?

At the beginning of *The Republic,* Socrates is challenged to explain why it is better to be just than unjust. If you could wear a ring that made you invisible, so that you could commit any crime you wished without being caught and punished, why wouldn't you commit those crimes? Thrasymachus said that only a fool would not take advantage of the ring and commit crimes that benefit them. The surest way to happiness is to com-mit injustices while enjoying a reputation for justice. The surest way to misery is to be just while appearing to be unjust, because it is the appearance of injustice that is pun-ished, not the reality. Socrates's response was that you should not take advantage of the ring because injustice is harmful to your soul. Justice is good for the soul, and only a good soul is genuinely happy. Centuries later, the Gospels echoed Socrates: "For what shall it profit a man, if he shall gain the whole world, and lose his own soul?" (Mark 8:36 King James Version; also Matthew 16:26 and Luke 9:25).

After a few cursory arguments defending his claim that only a just soul is happy, Socrates draws an analogy between the soul and the city-state. He says the city-state is like the soul writ large. If we can show that a just city-state is happier than an unjust city-state, we will have shown that a just soul is happier than an unjust soul. Then he constructs a model of the just city-state. The just city-state is composed of three social classes: the philosopher-kings, the guardians, and the farmers and craftsmen. Analogously, the just soul is composed of reason, the spirited part, and the appetites. In the just city-state, the philosopher-kings rule the farmers and craftsmen with the assistance of the guardians. In the just soul, reason rules the appetites with the assistance of the spirited part of the soul. Both the just city-state and the just soul are unified and harmonious. The most unjust city-state is ruled by a tyrant who is a creature of chaotic impulses and drives. The most unjust soul is ruled by appetite. Both the unjust city-state and the unjust soul are fraught with dissonance and conflict. Using Pythagorean number theory and music theory, Socrates calculates that the philosopher-king enjoys 729 times more pleasure than the tyrant. Therefore, by analogy, the just soul is 729 times happier than the unjust soul. Therefore, even if you gain the whole world by unjust means, it is better to be just than unjust.

ARISTOTLE AND THE AGE OF ALEXANDER THE GREAT

How important and influential was Aristotle?

Aristotle was the second most important and influential philosopher in the history of philosophy. In fact, Aristotle could easily be regarded as *the* most important and influential philosopher in the history of philosophy were it not for the fact that Aristotle was himself influenced by his beloved teacher, Plato. With good reason, the Platonists of the Roman period (the "Neo-Platonists") regarded Aristotle to be a Platonist like themselves. On the other hand, their interpretation of Plato was not strictly true to Plato but was influenced by their reading of Aristotle, and it was this Aristotelian-influenced version of Platonism that was passed on to the medieval Christian world after the fall of the Roman Empire. All of Plato's own works except the *Timaeus* were lost to the Latin West after the fall of the Roman Empire. Likewise, all of Aristotle's works except for two of his works on logic—the *Categories* and *On Interpretation*—were lost to the Latin West after the fall of the Roman Empire, leaving Neo-Platonism to dominate Western philosophy in the early medieval period. But Aristotle's works were preserved in the Greek-speaking Byzantine Empire and in the Middle East, where together with the works of Plato and the Platonists they were translated into Arabic and exerted great influence on medieval Islamic philosophy from the Iberian Peninsula to parts of India and Central Asia. Jewish scholars working under Muslim rule in the Iberian Peninsula were also greatly influenced by Aristotle; the most notable of these was Maimonides.

By the mid-twelfth century, Aristotle's works were recovered in the West and began to be translated into Latin, with the result that the "schoolmen" or "scholastics" of the thirteenth century became increasingly influenced by Aristotle. By the beginning of the modern period, Aristotle dominated higher education to such a degree that those wanting to create a new system of learning based on the new science were compelled to reject Aristotle and scholastic philosophy. However, Aristotle continued to dominate philosophical education in the universities of Western Europe well into the eighteenth century and beyond. Perhaps the greatest philosopher of the Enlightenment, Immanuel Kant (1724–1804), based his categories of the understanding, the foundation of his philosophical system, on Aristotle's metaphysical categories and declared that no progress had been made in logic since Aristotle. Today, Aristotle is still studied with great interest, and his "virtue ethics" has enjoyed renewed attention not only in philosophy but also in education.

Founder of the Lyceum and the Peripatetic school of philosophy, Aristotle was a student of Plato and would go on to teach Alexander the Great.

What was the course of Aristotle's life up to his departure from Plato's Academy?

Aristotle was not born in Athens, so throughout his life, whenever he lived in Athens, he did so as a resident alien, not as a citizen. Aristotle was born in 384 B.C.E. to a wealthy, landowning family in the northern Greek kingdom of Macedonia. His father, Nicomachus, was well connected with the royal house of Macedonia and served as court physician to Amyntas III, king of Macedonia, in 393 B.C.E. and again from 392 B.C.E. until 370 B.C.E. Nicomachus died when Aristotle was a young boy, leaving Aristotle to be raised by his uncle Proxenus.

In 367 B.C.E., when Aristotle was seventeen years old, he was sent to Athens to study at Plato's Academy, the leading center of learning in the Greek world. Aristotle was probably Plato's best student and was destined to become his most famous. Though Aristotle's thinking remained essentially Platonic during his tenure at the Academy and for some time thereafter, there is evidence that Aristotle had already begun to question Plato's theory of the forms while he was at the Academy, because some of his arguments against the forms appear in Plato's later dialogue, the *Parmenides*. But the disagreement between Plato and Aristotle about the forms was a disagreement between friends who were engaged in a cooperative pursuit of knowledge. In the *Nicomachean Ethics* Aristotle said that he would prefer not to criticize the theory of the forms because "those who introduced the forms are friends of ours," but though he loved them both, he said, "piety bids us to honor truth before our friends." In the *Parmenides*, Plato presents Aristotle's arguments against the forms in a sympathetic light, and in his final work, the *Laws*, Plato makes no mention of his theory of the forms at all. Thus, Aristotle may have influenced the later Plato as much as Plato influenced Aristotle.

Aristotle's love for Plato and loyalty to him are testified by the fact that he remained at Plato's Academy for twenty years until Plato died in 347 B.C.E. Aristotle did not leave the Academy until leadership of the Academy passed to Plato's nephew, Speusippus. Aristotle may have been disappointed that he was not appointed to be the Academy's new leader, and he certainly objected to the direction that Speusippus was taking the Academy, because contrary to Aristotle's own philosophical interests and inclinations, Speusippus focused work at the Academy on Pythagorean mathematics. There was also a resurgence of anti-Macedonian sentiment in Athens that may have made Aristotle uncomfortable living there. In 349 B.C.E., Philip II of Macedonia attacked Olynthus, the head of a federation of city-states known as the Chalcidian League and a key ally of Athens. Demosthenes roused his fellow Athenians to action, but Olynthus fell to the Macedonians the following year. In 347 B.C.E., the Athenians, led by Demosthenes, were forced to negotiate a peace settlement on unfavorable terms with Philip II. Hence, anti-Macedonian sentiment was running high in Athens when Aristotle departed.

GREEK HISTORY IN THE AGE OF ARISTOTLE AND ALEXANDER THE GREAT

Who was Demosthenes?

Demosthenes (384–322 B.C.E.) was an Athenian statesman, diplomat, and orator who devoted his life to restoring Athenian supremacy in Greece and opposing the imperial ambitions of the Macedonian dynasty. Cicero, the great Roman orator, considered Demosthenes to have been one of the greatest orators that Greece ever produced. As Philip II of Macedonia expanded his control of Greece southward, Demosthenes helped the Athenians to organize a coalition of Greek city-states against him, including an alliance with the powerful city-state of Thebes. However, the Athenian coalition was defeated in 338 B.C.E. by Philip II and his son Alexander the Great at the historic Battle of Chaeronea. After the assassination of Philip II in 336 B.C.E., the Athenians saw an opportunity to rebel against Macedonian rule, but an uprising led by Demosthenes was defeated. In 335 B.C.E., Demosthenes was instrumental in

Orator, lawyer, and statesman Demosthenes worked to restore Athens's influence in Greece.

organizing another uprising of Athens and Thebes against Macedonia that was funded by the emperor of Persia, Darius III. This uprising, too, was defeated. After Alexander the Great's death in 323 B.C.E., Demosthenes once again urged the Athenians to rise up against Macedonian rule. But Antipater, who was the acting governor of Greece and the executor of Aristotle's will, put down the rebellion and demanded that the Athenians turn over Demosthenes and other leading anti-Macedonian agitators. Demosthenes fled to a sanctuary where he poisoned himself to death to avoid being arrested and executed.

Who ruled Macedonia during Aristotle's lifetime?

Archelaus I was king of Macedonia from 413 B.C.E. until his assassination in 399 B.C.E. His son Amyntas III ascended to the throne only after seven years of dynastic feuds and is considered by historians to be the founder of the unified Macedonian state. The final challenger to the throne was Pausanius, who ruled briefly in 393 B.C.E. until Amyntas III assassinated him. Amyntas III subsequently ruled Macedonia from 392 B.C.E. until 370 B.C.E., when he died of natural causes in his old age. Amyntas III had three sons with his wife Eurydice: Alexander II was the oldest, followed by Perdiccas III, and Philip II. Ptolemy of Aloros was a diplomatic envoy to Athens employed by Amyntas III. He may have been Amyntas II's nephew and therefore a member of the Argead dynastic family.

After Amyntas III died, Alexander II assumed the throne, and Ptolemy instigated an affair with Eurydice. According to the Roman historian Justin, but not confirmed by any other source, Ptolemy was also married to Eurydice's daughter Eurynoe, who foiled a plot by Ptolemy and her mother to assassinate her father, Amyntas III, by revealing the plan to him. Alexander II faced an external threat from the Illyrians (in present-day Albania), as his father had, but it was an internal threat that ended his reign. He was assassinated in 368 B.C.E. by agents of Ptolemy.

Upon Alexander II's death, Ptolemy was appointed regent because Perdiccas III was too young to assume the throne. Ptolemy ruled as regent only a few years until he was assassinated by Perdiccas III in 365 B.C.E. Euphraeus of Orseus, a student of Plato's, served as a highly trusted advisor to Perdiccas III but opposed Philip II because of Philip II's imperial designs on Orseus. When Philip II's forces invaded Orseus, Euphraeus committed suicide. Perdiccas III was killed in a military expedition in 359 B.C.E., whereupon the throne fell to his infant son, Amyntas IV.

Philip II served briefly as the infant king's regent but quickly seized the throne for himself. According to the Roman historian Justin, Amyntas III also had three younger children with a second wife, Gygaea, whom Philip II had killed to prevent them from ever challenging his claim to the throne. Philip II expanded the domain of his father's kingdom to include most of mainland Greece and formed alliances with other parts of Greece that he did not conquer. In the winter of 338–337 B.C.E., following the defeat in the battle of Chaeronea of an alliance of Greek states led by Athens and Thebes, Philip

II united most of Greece except Sparta in a federation known either as the Hellenic League or the League of Corinth. Philip II had plans to invade and conquer the Persian Empire in Asia Minor, but he was assassinated in 336 B.C.E. before he could execute his plans. At age twenty, his son Alexander III ascended to the throne and ruled until his death in 323 B.C.E. He not only unified all of Greece under his rule, but he also conquered the Persian Empire, Egypt, Babylon, and lands as far east as Central Asia and India. He is remembered as the greatest military commander of all time. He was Alexander the Great.

Who assassinated Philip II?

Philip II was assassinated in 336 B.C.E. by Pausanias of Orestis, one of his bodyguards and, according to a story alluded to by Aristotle and elaborated upon by Diodorus Siculus, a former lover. Pausanias publicly embarrassed Philip II's new lover, who was a friend of Attalus, one of Philip II's generals. When Philip II's new lover committed suicide by acting recklessly in battle to retrieve his honor, Attalus punished Pausanias by getting him drunk and raping him. Philip II declined to punish Attalus for the rape, provoking Pausanias to assassinate him. The assassination took place at the wedding of Philip II's daughter, Cleopatra of Macedon (or Epirus), and her mother Olympias's brother, Alexander I of Epirus. Philip II gave Alexander I his daughter Cleopatra to marry in an attempt to repair his alliance with Epirus, which had been strained by Philip II's divorce from Olympias. Philip II had a practice of using marriage to form political alliances.

Like the Persians, but unlike most other Greeks of the classical era, the Molossians of Epirus and the Macedonians permitted their kings to have more than one wife. The Molossians and Macedonians identified with the older Homeric traditions of Greece, which permitted polygyny. Philip II married seven women, nearly all for the purpose of forming alliances with other kingdoms. Olympias of Epirus was Philip II's fourth wife. The family of Olympias claimed to be descendants of Achilles, the hero of the Trojan War and of Homer's *Iliad*, but they were not Macedonians, and therefore her son Alexander III was not a full-blooded member of the Argead dynasty.

After Pausanias was captured and killed, his corpse was crucified by Alexander I of Epirus. But as soon as her brother Alexander left Macedonia, Olympias had a memorial erected in honor of Pausanius. Olympias was angered by Philip II's marriage to a young Macedonian woman named Cleopatra Eurydice, who was the niece of general Attalus, because this marriage jeopardized her son Alexander III's inheritance of the throne. Attalus and his niece were Macedonians and members of the Argead dynasty, so any children that Philip II had with Cleopatra Eurydice would have a stronger claim to the throne than Alexander III. After Philip II's assassination, Olympias murdered both of Cleopatra Eurydice's children—daughter Europa and son Caranus—whereupon Cleopatra committed suicide. According to another story by a second-century Greek historian named Pausanius, Olympias had both Europa and Cleopatra burned alive. For these reasons and others, ancient historians believed that Olympias may have had something to do with the plot to assassinate Philip II.

What is the legend about how Olympias conceived Alexander the Great?

According to Plutarch's *The Life of Alexander*, legend has it that Zeus in the form of a serpent seduced Olympias and fathered Alexander the Great. Olympias was a devoted follower of the cult of Dionysus and may have introduced the practice of handling snakes into the cult. When Philip II saw his wife Olympias cavorting with the serpent, he lost all desire for her. While visiting the Oracle at Delphi, he was told that he would lose sight in the eye that witnessed the event. One year after Alexander the Great was born, Philip II lost an eye in the siege of Methone. As a mature man, Alexander the Great identified himself as a god, and the legend of his divine conception spread throughout his empire. After he completed his conquests, Alexander became more insistent that he was a god, and, like the Persian rulers he overthrew but contrary to Greek tradition, he expected his subjects to defer to him as such. Alexander alternately identified himself with Achilles, the founding ancestor of his mother's bloodline; Heracles (or in Latin, Hercules), the founding ancestor of his father's bloodline; or Dionysus, whom his mother worshipped.

Who was Dionysus?

Dionysus was the ancient Greek god of wine, ecstasy, and fertility. According to the most popular variation of the myth, he was the son of Zeus, the supreme god of the Greeks, and Semele, a mortal woman and the daughter of the King of Thebes. Ancient Greek theater was dedicated to Dionysus and featured three types of drama: tragedies, comedies, and satyr plays. According to Aristotle, tragedy developed out of the satyr dithyramb, which was a passionate choral song or chant that inspired wild dancing during religious ceremonies dedicated to Dionysus. Based on comparative anthropology, it is likely that the religion of Dionysus was originally a possession cult in which female followers of Dionysus, known as maenads, entered trance states by means of intoxication or frenzied dancing and became possessed by the spirit of Dionysus. Similarly, actors in Greek theater became possessed by characters who represented Dionysus. The ancient Greek word for tragedy meant "song of the goats," referring to the chorus of half-man, half-goat creatures known as satyrs, who sang the satyr dithyramb. Satyrs were the male com-

Heracles (Hercules) was the son of Zeus and ancestor of the Argead dynasty, the royal house that ruled Macedonia from about 700 to 310 B.C.E.

panions of Dionysus. Goats were sacrificed in Dionysian ceremonies and represented Dionysus himself.

Throughout the history of Western art, satyrs have been portrayed as intoxicated, lustful creatures who danced, played music, and chased maenads or nymphs. In ancient Greek art, they were depicted with permanent, elongated erections, and satyr plays were bawdy spectacles full of obscene jokes and lewd sexual behavior. The maenads were portrayed entering ecstatic trance states by means of intoxication and frenzied dancing to the accompaniment of music while wearing faun skins and, sometimes, handling snakes. Their ceremonies reached a climax when, with their bare hands, the maenads tore apart a goat or other sacrificial animal representing the god Dionysus and then ate its raw flesh. The maenads were literally out of their minds. The Greek word for ecstasy means "to stand outside oneself," and the word "maenad" is derived from Greek words meaning "raving," "frantic," and "furious."

But eating the flesh of Dionysus is not the end of the story, because according to all the different variations of the myth, Dionysus is reborn after his violent destruction. Thus, the myth of Dionysus fits the archetypal pattern of all the mystery religions of the ancient world in which the hero dies a violent death only to return once again to life, in an endless cycle that mirrors the fertility of mother earth herself. Ultimately, the destruction of the hero's life was not, therefore, a cause for pessimism about life but, on the contrary, was an affirmation of life as an eternal cycle of regeneration.

How did Olympias shape Alexander the Great's character and education?

Alexander III of Macedonia, or "Alexander the Great," was born in 356 B.C.E. to King Philip II of Macedonia and his wife, Olympias, who was not a Macedonian but the daugh-

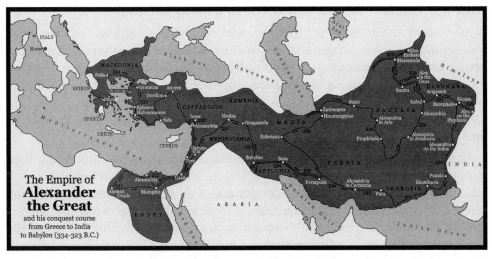

From 334 to 323 B.C.E. Alexander the Great carved out a huge empire that spanned Greece, northeast Africa, and much of what is now Iran, Iraq, and Pakistan. His territory disintegrated after his death, however.

ter of the king of the Molossians in Epirus. Alexander's father was an ambitious military commander who succeeded in unifying most of Greece under the umbrella of the Hellenic League. But Alexander's mother, Olympias, may have been an even more influential person in Alexander's life than his father. Olympias was a beautiful but violent woman with a fiery temperament and a strong will, and she passed these qualities on to Alexander. She was ruthless in her pursuit of power and was determined to make her son Alexander the next king of Macedonia, by any means necessary, including murder.

But Olympias also had a love of learning, and she passed this on to Alexander. She taught him the story of their noble descent from Achilles, the hero of Homer's tales about the Trojan War and the founding ancestor of the Molossian royalty in Epirus. One of Alexander's childhood tutors, Lysimachus of Acarnania, nicknamed Alexander "Achilles," and the name stuck. Olympias made sure that Alexander received the best possible education. She recruited a kinsman from Epirus, Leonidas, to tutor and mentor Alexander in his early childhood. Leonidas was a stern teacher who exercised the strictest military discipline on the young Alexander and taught him to hold every luxury in contempt.

Philip II called for the great philosopher Aristotle to tutor Alexander between the ages of thirteen and sixteen. It was during this time that Homer's *Iliad* became Alexander's favorite book. Alexander had Aristotle prepare a special annotated copy of the *Iliad* for him, which he kept with him at all times, even sleeping with it and a dagger under his pillow. Aristotle taught Alexander that bodily pleasure is not the greatest good. Like Plato before him, Aristotle taught that a virtuous or excellent soul is more desirable than physical beauty. When the adult Alexander was offered beautiful boys for his pleasure, he took offense, objecting that he had never done anything so shameful as to lead anyone to think that he would want to be offered mere hedonistic pleasures.

What was Alexander the Great's relationship with Hephaestion?

Some modern historians believe that Alexander may have had at least one male lover, his dear friend Hephaestion, in addition to three wives. But if they were lovers, Hephaestion was no mere sex object. Both products of the Macedonian aristocracy and born the same year, they grew up like brothers. Together they studied with Aristotle, who taught them that the truest and best form of friendship is based on a love for one another's ethical character and a shared understanding of the purpose or goal of life, its final good.

Aristotle himself recognized that the friendship between Alexander and Hephaestion was of this kind. He said that they were so close as to be of one soul in two bodies. Several ancient historians record Alexander expressing the same sentiment. Hephaestion served as Alexander's second in command and commander of the elite Macedonian cavalry, the best in the ancient world. Hephaestion was not only Alexander's closest friend but throughout his military campaigns also his most trusted advisor and confidante. When, in 327 B.C.E., Alexander married his second wife, Stateira II, the daughter of Darius III, the last king of the Achaemenid Empire of Persia, he arranged for Hephaestion to marry her sister Drypetis, so that they would become brothers-in-law and they and their sons could rule an integrated Persian and Greek Empire. When Hephaestion died in 324 B.C.E., Alexander was inconsolable. He arranged an elaborate funeral for Hephaestion in Babylon, where a year later he himself died.

What is the history of Alexander the Great's military campaigns?

At age sixteen, Alexander's formal education ended and his military career began. His father, Philip II, went abroad to wage war on Byzantium, an ancient Greek colony that later became Constantinople and, later still, Istanbul, leaving Alexander behind to serve as regent of Macedonia. At once, a Thracian tribe revolted. Alexander put down the revolt, colonized the region with Macedonians, and founded a city that he named Alexandropolis. When his father returned, Alexander was dispatched to Thrace to put down other revolts and also successfully defended Macedonia from the Illyrians, who had invaded from the north.

In 338 B.C.E., Alexander joined his father on a march south, culminating in the Battle of Chaeronea, where together they defeated an alliance of Greek states led by Athens and Thebes. Alexander is credited with defeating the Sacred Band of Thebes, the most elite unit of Theban warriors, which was composed of 150 pairs of male lovers. Modern excavations confirmed that this event occurred as recorded by ancient historians when the bodies of 254 soldiers were discovered at the site of the battle beneath an ancient monument known as the Lion of Chaeronea.

An illustration showing the Macedonians battling the Thracians at the Battle of the Carts in 335 B.C.E. The battles with Thrace became Alexander the Great's first military victories.

In the winter of 338–337 B.C.E., Philip II established the Hellenic League or League of Corinth, effectively uniting most of Greece under his rule. In spite of Alexander's military successes, there was pressure on Philip II to produce an heir to the throne who was Macedonian on both sides of his family. In 338 or 337 B.C.E., Philip II divorced Olympias and married Cleopatra-Eurydice, the niece of his general Attalus. At the wedding banquet, Attalus outraged Alexander by questioning his legitimacy as an heir to the throne. Philip II not only failed to defend Alexander but in a drunken rage drew a sword on him. Olympias fled to Epirus with Alexander. Philip II later reconciled with his son, but in 336 B.C.E. he was assassinated by his bodyguard Pausanias. Upon his father's death, Alexander the Great became king of Macedonia.

Like most of his predecessors, the first thing Alexander did as king was to eliminate all possible rivals to the throne by killing them. Among his victims was Attalus. In 335 B.C.E., Alexander protected his northern flank by waging military campaigns as far north as the Danube River and defeated several tribes, including the Thracians and the Illyrians. Then, as hegemon (supreme commander) of the Hellenic League, he successfully executed his father's plan and conquered all of the Persian Empire. Over a ten-year period beginning in 334 B.C.E., he marched across the Persian Empire and fought a series of battles that established his rule over the entire region. In 326 B.C.E., he invaded the Indian subcontinent, reaching the southernmost tip of the subcontinent and the island of Sri Lanka before his exhausted troops forced him to turn back. In 323 B.C.E., at the age of thirty-two, he died after a fever lasting several days in Babylon, which he intended to make the capital of his empire. At the time of his death, Alexander's empire extended from the Danube River north of Greece to Egypt in the south and the Indus River in the east. It included lands formerly occupied by the world's three oldest urban-agricultural civilizations: the Nile River Valley in Egypt, the Tigris-Euphrates River Valley of Mesopotamia, and the largest land area of them all, the Indus River Valley.

Who were the Kurgans?

The Kurgans were a people who lived in the Pontic-Caspian steppe from the fifth to the third millennium B.C.E. The Pontic-Caspian steppe extends from lands north of the Black Sea to the Caspian Sea. According to the "Kurgan hypothesis," the Kurgan people of the Pontic-Caspian steppe spoke the Proto-Indo-European (PIE) language that was the root source of all Indo-European languages, including the Sanskrit language of the ancient ruling class of India; ancient Greek; Persian; Latin; and various northern European languages, including Slavic, Celtic, German, and English. The hypothesis further holds that the Kurgans were the first to domesticate the horse and invent the chariot, and that they were a warlike people, patriarchal and hierarchically organized. They worshipped patriarchal sky gods such as Zeus. Originally pastoral nomads, they always engaged in animal husbandry.

The "Kurgan hypothesis" was first put forth by Lithuanian American archaeologist Marija Gimbutas (1921–1994) in the 1950s based on comparative mythology, archaeology, and linguistics, and recently genetic research has provided significant evidence for the hypothesis. It is the prevailing theory about the origin of Indo-European languages and cultures. According to the hypothesis, in successive waves over thousands of years, the Kurgan people invaded and conquered all the areas where Indo-European languages were later spoken, including the Indus River Valley, Persia (Iran), and Greece. According to Gimbutas, prior to the invasion of the Kurgans, the Neolithic people who lived along the Danube River in what she called "Old Europe" were a peaceful, egalitarian, and matrilineal people who worshipped an earth or moon goddess. Here and elsewhere, the Kurgans replaced indigenous cultures with a patriarchal, patrilineal, hierarchical caste system ruled by military chiefs.

Who was Bucephalus?

Bucephalus was Alexander the Great's horse. The name "Bucephalus" means "ox-head," and Bucephalus was said to have a head as large as an ox's. According to Plutarch, Bucephalus was a wild horse that no one could tame. Alexander surprised his father when at the young age of twelve or thirteen, he succeeded in taming the horse. Philip II was so impressed that he told his son to look for a kingdom larger than Macedonia, because Macedonia was too small for him. Alexander rode Bucephalus from then on, until in 326 B.C.E. the horse died in a battle in the Indus River Valley. Alexander buried Bucephalus and established a city named after him in the vicinity of where he died. Bucephalus represented the power of Alexander's cavalry and his skill as a military commander. Alexander's cavalry was in fact so effective that after the cavalry delivered its crushing blow, he rarely had to rely on his infantry to finish the job.

What was the relationship between Greeks and Persians?

Greeks and Persians had fought one another for centuries prior to Alexander the Great. They were perpetual enemies, and there were some notable differences between their cultures. But Greek city states such as Sparta also allied themselves with Persia in return for material support in their wars with other Greek city states. And independent Greek mercenaries were often employed by the Persians in battles against Greeks. Moreover, the Greek and Persian ruling classes shared common ancestors and some common cultural traits. They were all descendants of the Kurgan invaders. Greeks, Persians, and Indians all spoke Indo-European languages with a common root in the Proto-Indo-European language of the Kurgan people. Like the Kurgans, they were hierarchically organized, patriarchal, and ruled by war chiefs. Comparative analysis of their religious and mythological beliefs reveals similarities as well due to their common ancestry. They all worshipped patriarchal sky gods. Mother earth goddesses and the mystery religions associated with them probably predated the Kurgan invasions.

What was Zoroastrianism?

Zoroastrianism was the official religion of the Persian Empire at the time of Alexander's conquests. The Zoroastrians were the first to introduce the concept of free will, long before the concept became a cornerstone of Christian morality and religion. The Zoroastrians also introduced other moral and religious concepts prior to their adoption by Christians or Muslims, such as the belief in a divine savior or messiah, the notion of a final judgment, a dualistic morality of good and evil, belief in heaven and hell, and belief in the Devil. The Zoroastrians believed in a universal brotherhood of mankind united under one loving and forgiving supreme God.

How did Alexander the Great plan to unite the Greek and Persian Empires?

Alexander could be brutal on the battlefield and toward those he distrusted or who betrayed him. He responded to uprisings and resistance from Persians with the utmost violence. But when possible, he much preferred to act in partnership with the Persians to achieve his goals. That was not only the humane thing to do but was better strategically because the Greeks were greatly outnumbered. It was much easier for Alexander to rule his empire with the cooperation of the Persians than

Zoroaster (or Zarathustra) was a prophet who lived sometime in the second millenium B.C.E. and founded what became the official religion of Persia. Many Zoroastrian concepts and beliefs were adopted by Christianity.

without their cooperation. So when the local Persian officials were amenable to his demands, he was happy to appoint them to positions of authority. For example, in Babylon, Alexander rewarded the Persian Mazaeus for surrendering the city by making him the satrap (local governor). He also granted Mazaeus the unusual privilege of minting silver coins. However, Alexander appointed a Macedonian to command the local armed forces. Thus, Mazaeus ruled Babylon in partnership with a Macedonian.

Persia was by no means an uncivilized society. It hosted numerous centers of learning, including Babylon, where the study of ancient mathematics and astronomy had been revived. Alexander had no desire to destroy Persian culture. In Egypt and Babylon, he permitted the Persian priesthood to continue to practice their religion, which in Alexander's day was the religion of Zoroastrianism. In some cases, the local people welcomed Alexander because he freed them from oppressive rulers. In Western Asia Minor, for example, Alexander removed the Persian tyrants and replaced them with democratic governments. Alexander settled large numbers of Greek soldiers in Persian territory and encouraged them to intermarry with local Persian nobility. He retained much of the Persian administrative bureaucracy while introducing Greek political institutions.

Bessus was the Persian governor of Bactria in Central Asia until he killed his close relative, Persian emperor Darius III, and for a brief time designated himself the king of kings of Persia. Alexander the Great had Bessus executed for regicide in the Persian manner in 329 B.C.E. for killing Darius III and established Oxyartes as governor of Bactria. Oxyartes was a Bactrian nobleman who had joined Bessus in his resistance against Alexander. After the death of Bessus, Oxyartes resumed the fight against Alexander. He deposited his wife and children in a fortress. But Alexander seized the fortress and married his daughter Roxana. Upon hearing this, Oxyartes surrendered to Alexander and became his loyal subject.

Alexander married three times, and all his wives were Persian royalty. In addition to Roxana, Alexander married Stateira II, the daughter of Darius III, on the same day in 324 B.C.E. that he married Parysatis II, the daughter of Persian king Artaxerxes III. The marriage celebration in the Persian capital of Susa lasted five days, during which time eighty Persian noblewomen were married to the highest ranking Greek soldiers, including Alexander's friend Hephaestion, Seleucus, Ptolemy I Soter, Perdiccas, Eumenes, and Craterus. These marriages were followed by the official registration of ten thousand others between Persian women and Macedonian soldiers that Alexander rewarded with generous gifts. The children of all these marriages would be both Greek and Persian. Thus, Alexander planned to unite the Greek and Persian empires by intermarrying their ruling classes and creating one united ruling class.

What did the Macedonians think about Alexander's plans to unite the Greeks and the Persians?

Judging from the fact that nearly all the Macedonians who married Persian women divorced them as soon as Alexander died in 323 B.C.E., they were not happy at all with the prospect of sharing their empire on an equal basis with the Persians. The only Macedonian elites who did not divorce their Persian wives were Hephaestion, who died before Alexander, and Seleucus, who founded the Seleucid Empire. In addition to their dislike of Alexander's plan to intermarry Greeks and Persians, Macedonian troops attempted a mutiny at Opis, because so many non-Greeks had been incorporated on an equal basis into Alexander's army and administration that it threatened their own privileged position.

What did the Athenians think about Alexander's empire?

Athens was the largest and most intellectually advanced city-state in ancient Greece. The Persians had invaded Athens and waged war against it for generations, so the Athenians could not have been displeased that a coalition of Greek forces had finally vanquished their perennial foe. However, the Athenians were a proud people and cherished their independence. They resented and hated Macedonian imperialism. They allied with Thebes and lost a war against Philip II and his son Alexander in a last-ditch effort to stop Macedonian imperialism. Thus, when Alexander the Great died, the Athenians cheered.

Did Alexander spread Greek culture or preserve Persian customs and traditions?

Both. Alexander preserved many local customs and traditions of the lands he conquered. He even adopted some of these customs himself. He fashioned himself to be an emperor in the Persian style, and in accordance with Persian custom, he required even his Macedonian generals to treat him like a god. The mass weddings at Susa, too, were conducted according to Persian custom. But by preserving and adopting these and other customs, Alexander was able to coopt the Persian administrative infrastructure and use it to spread Greek culture throughout his empire. He required all public officials throughout his empire to speak Greek. He centralized the treasury and tax collection system and standardized the coinage of money. He confiscated the enormous hordes of silver in the Persian treasury and spent the newly minted coins on his soldiers, public officials, and public works. The expansion of the money supply caused the economy to grow. He built over seventy new cities with Greek markets, temples, theaters, laws, and architecture. He populated these cities with Greek colonists. He built many new cities named after himself, and even one named after his horse. He established the city of Alexandria in Egypt with a Greek university and gymnasium. The Great Library of Alexandria was founded after Alexander's death by his general, Ptolemy I Soter. By 100 B.C.E., Alexandria was the largest city in the eastern Mediterranean and its most important center of Greek learning. Alexander the Great ushered in the Hellenistic Age, during which time Greek culture spread across southwestern Asia.

Though his empire was short-lived, Alexander's campaigns had the effect of spreading Greek culture across much of the civilized world.

ARISTOTLE'S POLITICAL VIEWS

What was the meaning of the word *polis* in ancient Greece?

The ancient Greek word *polis* is the etymological root of the English word "politics." But the concept of the *polis* in ancient Greece was not limited to politics or government in the modern sense. The *polis* was a politically and socially organized group of people who shared a common language, common customs, and a common historical tradition. The Greek *polis* was a sovereign and independent political unit like the modern nation-state. It answered to no higher political authority. It possessed an army. It waged war, collected taxes, made laws, and performed all the basic functions of a national government. But it was much smaller than a nation-state. The typical Greek *polis* was about the size of a modern county, with an urban center and perhaps a few villages scattered about the countryside. It was a "city-state." During Alexander's day, the city-state of Athens was the largest in Greece. Its total population may have exceeded 300,000. But only about 10 percent of that total were citizens. The rest were women and children, slaves, resident aliens, or peasants living in the countryside.

But the *polis* was not just a state in the modern sense, because the word also referred to civil society. The *polis* was not just a political association of people; it included all the other ways in which people associated with one another: the family and the household; the marketplace where products and services were exchanged; the temples where the gods were worshipped; and the theater and the gymnasium. Nor was the *polis* defined by the territory it happened to occupy. The *polis* was the people insofar as they were socially and politically organized. The people could pack up and leave (as many Greek colonists did), and they would still be the *polis* so long as they continued to associate with one another in their customary manner.

What would Aristotle have thought about Alexander's plans to build an empire?

According to Aristotle, an empire is too large to be well governed. Aristotle argues that "law is order, and good law is good order; but a very great multitude cannot be orderly." The state that combines right size with good order is beautiful, and states that are too big or too small are dysfunctional, just as a plant or animal that is just the right size is beautiful, and ones that are too big or too small lose their nature or are spoiled. Aristotle's model of the state is based on the ancient Greek *polis* and his study of the constitutions of 158 city-states. A state that is too large is incapable of constitutional government. For that reason, an empire is incapable of constitutional government.

In his *Politics,* Aristotle says that a state must be just the right size, not too big or too small. It must have not only the right number of inhabitants but more importantly the right number of citizens to function well, because the power of a state comes from the number and character of its citizens, and only a small percentage of a state's inhabitants are citizens. It must be large enough not only to be self-sufficient and to satisfy the appetites of its inhabitants but also to enable its citizens to live well, which according to

111

Aristotle required the development of moral and intellectual excellence. But it must not be too large. Part of moral excellence is governing well, since it is the duty of citizens to govern. Among the civic duties of citizens is to judge lawsuits and distribute offices according to merit. If the population is too large, it is impossible for citizens to know one another's characters, and "where they do not possess this knowledge, both the election to offices and the decision of lawsuits will go wrong." In fact, if the population is too large, Aristotle worries that foreigners will usurp the offices of citizens.

Finally, Aristotle argues that the land area occupied by the state must be large enough for the state to be self-sufficing. But it should not be too large, because it should be possible to "take it in at a single view, for a country which is easily seen can be easily protected," and it is the duty of citizens to protect their country. Since, then, an empire is too large to govern well, its citizens cannot develop moral excellence, and therefore they do not live well. But the purpose of a state is to enable its citizens to live well. An empire is therefore a failed state.

Why did Aristotle think that non-Greeks had not achieved their full human potential?

Aristotle believed that humans are by nature political animals. He says in the *Politics* that a person who is incapable of living in a state, or who is so self-sufficing that they do not need to live in a state, must be either a beast or a god—either less than human or more than human. Animals can make sounds that indicate pain or pleasure, but only humans can speak and engage in rational deliberation with one another about what is right and wrong or just and unjust. But humans can realize their political nature and deliberate with one another about justice only within a constitutional political order such as the Greek *polis*. A person who does not live in a constitutional political order has no opportunity to exercise and develop their political nature and consequently cannot achieve their full human potential. But only the Greeks were ruled by laws created by free men who engaged in rational deliberation with one another about the nature of justice. Barbarians to the north of Greece lived in families and tribes that were arbitrarily ruled by men, not by laws, while Persians lived in a despotic empire. Therefore, both lacked the opportunity to develop their civic nature and achieve their full human potential. Thus, Aristotle makes the apparently shocking claim in the *Politics* that "among barbarians no distinction is made between women and slaves, because there is no natural ruler among them: they are a community of slaves, male and female. Wherefore the poets say, 'It is meet that Hellenes should rule over barbarians'; as if they thought that the barbarian and the slave were by nature one." Aristotle does not believe that all barbarians are by nature slaves. But he does believe that barbarians live like slaves because they have not developed their civic capacity for self-governance.

Why does Aristotle think that non-Greeks have not developed their civic capacity for self-governance?

Aristotle relies on a theory first developed by Hippocrates, the founder of Western medicine. In his book *On Airs, Waters, and Places*, Hippocrates says that the quality of a land's water and climate determines the character of its inhabitants. In the *Politics*, Aristotle says:

> Those who live in a cold climate and in Europe are full of spirit, but wanting in intelligence and skill; and therefore they retain comparative freedom, but have no political organization, and are incapable of ruling over others. Whereas the natives of Asia are intelligent and inventive, but they are wanting in spirit, and therefore they are always in a state of subjection and slavery. But the Hellenic race, which is situated between them, is likewise intermediate in character, being high-spirited and also intelligent. Hence it continues free, and is the best-governed of any nation, and, if it could be formed into one state, would be able to rule the world.

Those who live in cold, northern climates such as the Thracians, Celts, and Scythians of Europe are full of spirit (Greek *thumos*) but lack intelligence, according to Aristotle, whereas those who live in hot, southern climates, such as the inhabitants of the Persian Empire, are intelligent but lack spirit. Aristotle believed that good governance requires both spirit (the character trait of warriors) and intelligence (the character trait of philosophers). Only the Greeks, who live in an intermediate climate, possess both of these civic virtues, so only they are capable of good governance, though to varying degrees because there are differences between Greeks, too.

What did Aristotle think about Alexander's plan to unite the Greeks and Persians?

Aristotle does not directly address this question in any of his works that we currently possess. However, an answer to this question can be gleaned from the few comments that Aristotle made in the *Politics* about the proper size of the state and about the character traits of non-Greeks or barbarians. Aristotle would probably not have approved of Alexander's plan to unite the Greeks and Persians because he believed that an empire is too large to be well governed and because he did not believe that non-Greeks possessed the character traits necessary for self-governance in a constitutional polity or *polis*. Aristotle says in his *Politics* that the inhabitants of the Persian Empire are always in a state of subjection and slavery because they lack spirit (*thumos*). They lack spirit because of the effects of their environment on their character and because they have become habituated to a condition of subjection after living for long years under a despotic regime.

Aristotle does not believe that foreigners should be treated badly just because they are foreigners. He refutes those who say that the guardians of the state should be friendly towards those they know and fierce towards those they don't know. He says in the *Politics* that it is not "right to say that the guardians should be fierce towards those whom they do not know, for we ought not to be out of temper with any one; and a lofty spirit is not fierce by nature, but only when excited against evil-doers." Aristotle is not xenophobic. But neither does Aristotle believe that all people everywhere are morally equal regardless of their particular circumstances. Though Aristotle recognizes that all human beings have the *potential* to develop their character, like an acorn that requires the appropriate soil and climate to grow into an oak tree, they require the appropriate environmental and historical conditions to realize their full potential. Character is not something like the Christian or Platonic soul that resides in an eternal heaven. As the particular environmental and historical circumstances of Greeks differ from those of non-Greeks, so does their character.

PLUTARCH, ARRIAN, AND ERATOSTHENES

Who was Plutarch?

Plutarch (46–120 C.E.) was an ancient Greek philosopher who acquired Roman citizenship and became one of the most widely read authors of the Roman and Byzantine empires. His works were revived in the Latin West during the Renaissance and influenced major figures in Western intellectual history, including Francis Bacon, Michel de Montaigne, and William Shakespeare. He wrote moral essays and biographies of noble Greek and Roman characters. Among his biographies were *On the Fortune or the Virtue of Alexander* and *The Life of Julius Caesar*. The purpose of his biographies was to encourage mutual respect between Greeks and Romans and to provide models of virtue. The purpose of his biographies was not to provide his readers with historical knowledge. In fact, his writings contain numerous historical inaccuracies. He was skeptical about the human capacity to acquire knowledge and instead concentrated his efforts on morally improving his readers.

Plutarch retained lifelong ties with Plato's Academy, but he was also influenced by Aristotle and by Zeno of Citium, the founder of Stoicism. He established a school of moral philosophy in the Greek town of Chaeronea, where he also served as the mayor. He was a pagan and a priest at Delphi. But his moral and religious beliefs are very similar to those of Christianity. He believed in free will and the immortality of the soul. He believed in a universal moral law and that we are all brothers and sisters under one God. He believed that the many different gods of different peoples are only different names for one and the same God.

Plutarch's writings about morality would later influence such writers and philosophers as William Shakespeare and Francis Bacon.

Who was Arrian of Nicomedia?

Arrian of Nicomedia (c. 86–c. 160 C.E.) was a Greek philosopher and historian who wrote about Alexander the Great and became one of the most respected writers of the Roman Empire. He had a distinguished political career in Rome. Emperor Hadrian appointed him governor of Cappadocia, and Emperor Antoninus Pius gave him the honorary title of consul of the Roman Empire.

Arrian was born in Nicomedia, which was the capital of the ancient kingdom of Bithynia in Asia Minor and one of the early centers of Christianity. He was a student of the Stoic philosopher Epictetus. Arrian's most famous work is his *Anabasis,* which chronicles Alexander the Great's military campaigns. Besides Plutarch, he claimed that his sources included Eratosthenes, a Hellenistic philosopher and the chief librarian of the library of Alexandria; Ptolemy I Soter, Alexander's general and the founder of the Ptolemaic Empire of Egypt; and Aristobulus, a friend of Philip II's, who accompanied Alexander on his military campaigns. But Arrian is also known for the *Enchiridion of Epictetus*, a short summary of Stoic ethical principles as applied to everyday life, which resembles Reinhold Niebuhr's "Serenity Prayer": The key to a happy life is to accept the things you can't change, the courage to change what you can, and the wisdom to know the difference. Arrian's *Enchiridion* was a common school textbook in Scotland during the Scottish Enlightenment and was read by several key figures of that time, including moral philosopher Frances Hutchinson and classic liberal economist Adam Smith.

Who was Eratosthenes?

Eratosthenes (c. 276–c. 194 B.C.E.) was a Greek citizen of the Ptolemaic Kingdom whose thirst for knowledge in a wide range of fields led him to significant achievements in philosophy, mathematics, geography, astronomy, and music theory. He was a skilled poet and the chief librarian of the Library of Alexandria, the greatest library in the ancient world. He is best known for being the first person to measure the circumference of the earth based upon the principles of geometry and sound assumptions about the sun's distance from the earth. But he is also famous for inventing the "sieve of Eratosthenes," a method for identifying prime numbers.

Eratosthenes studied philosophy in Athens with Zeno of Citium, the founder of Stoicism, and studied ethics with Zeno's colleague, Aristo of Chio. According to Roman historian Strabo (c. 64 B.C.E.–c. 24 C.E.), Eratosthenes disagreed with Aristotle's belief that Greeks were morally and intellectually superior to non-Greeks or barbarians. According to Strabo (*Geography*, Book I, Chapter 4), Eratosthenes believed that there are good and bad people among both Greeks and barbarians, "for not only are many of the Greeks bad, but many of the Barbarians are refined—Indians and Arians, for example, and, further, Romans and Carthaginians, who carry on their governments so admirably." And this is the reason that Alexander the Great judged Persians according to their character and honored them if they exhibited "law-abiding and political instincts, and qualities associated with education and powers of speech." Eratosthenes also studied under Arcesilaus, the skeptical Platonist who founded the Second or Middle Academy of Plato.

Bernardo Strozzi's 1635 painting, *Erastosthenes Teaching in Alexandria*. Erastothenes believed that there were good and bad people among both Greeks and barbarians (non-Greeks).

Eratosthenes wrote *Platonikos*, a book about the mathematical foundations of Plato's philosophy. In his old age, Eratosthenes became blind. Out of despair over his inability to read or observe nature, he committed suicide by starving himself to death.

What happened at Opis according to Arrian?

In 324 B.C.E., Alexander the Great was forced to return from his campaign into the Indian peninsula by his exhausted troops. At Susa, the capital of the Persian Empire, he married Roxana and Stateira II. He also conducted a mass marriage of eighty Persian noblewomen with the highest-ranking Macedonian soldiers and the official registration of ten thousand other marriages between Persian women and Macedonian soldiers. According to Arrian's account, which is generally considered to be the most reliable, when Alexander stopped at Opis, an ancient administrative center of Babylonia, he declared to his troops that he was discharging those who were unfit for service and sending them back home to Macedonia with gifts. Although Alexander spoke these words with the intention of pleasing his troops, they were offended and thought that Alexander regarded all of his Macedonian troops as unfit for service. According to Arrian, though some modern scholars question Arrian's reliability on this point, they were also annoyed by Alexander's Persian dress and by his pretensions to be a god and an emperor in the Persian style, and because he trained Persian troops in the Macedonian style of warfare and introduced them into Macedonian units. When the Macedonian troops threatened mutiny, Alexander rose up in anger and had thirteen leaders of the mutiny rounded up and executed. He then made a speech in which he recounted the many ways that he and his father had benefitted their Macedonian soldiers, and how they had benefitted him, and concluded that he and his father had reaped few rewards for their efforts compared to the riches gained by their troops.

Three days after his speech, Alexander appointed the elite of the Persians "to the command of all the squadrons, and only allowed those who received the title of 'kinsmen' from him to kiss him." Upon hearing this, the Macedonian soldiers were filled with grief and implored Alexander to take pity on them. A spokesperson said: "Sire, what grieves the Macedonians is that you have already made some Persians your 'kinsmen,' and the Persians are called 'kinsmen' of Alexander and are allowed to kiss you, while not one of the Macedonians has been granted this honor." Whereupon Alexander responded: "I make you all my 'kinsmen' and henceforward that shall be your title." According to Arrian, the troops then kissed Alexander and returned to their camps with songs of triumph. Alexander celebrated by holding a banquet for 9,000 guests. He seated the Macedonians next to him, the Persians next to them, and "then any of the other peoples who enjoyed precedence for their reputation." Then Alexander "and those around him drew wine from the same bowl and poured the same libations," beginning with the Greek seers and the Zoroastrian priests, the Magians. Alexander "prayed for other blessings and for harmony and partnership in rule between Macedonians and Persians," and all 9,000 guests "poured the same libation."

The implication of Arrian's account of what happened at Opis is that Alexander made the Greeks and the Persians and other peoples brothers under the same God, to whom they poured the same libations. The resemblance to Christianity is obvious, for in their holy rite of communion, Christians also draw wine and pour libations to the same God.

According to Plutarch, what was Aristotle's advice to Alexander the Great regarding the Persians?

Plutarch claimed in his book *On the Fortune or the Virtue of Alexander*, I.6, that Aristotle urged Alexander to "treat the Greeks as a leader would but the barbarians as a master," and to "care for the Greeks as friends and kinsmen, while treating the others as animals or plants." Plutarch's claim is shocking to the modern ear. But there is no evidence in Aristotle's extant writings that he ever said any such thing. What Aristotle believed was that the Persians had not fully developed their human capacity for political excellence and were therefore unable to govern themselves well. However, Aristotle would not have advised Alexander to rule the Persians because Aristotle was opposed to imperialism. Nor did Aristotle believe that the Persians should be treated badly because they were strangers or foreigners. Aristotle believed that all people should be judged according to their character. He just didn't happen to believe that the character of non-Greeks or barbarians enabled them to govern themselves well, as Greeks did in the *polis*. So in that respect, Plutarch was correct that Aristotle would not have approved plans to unite the Greeks and Persians as equals under one government.

Was Aristotle a cosmopolitan?

No, Aristotle was not a cosmopolitan. Aristotle believed that the city-state was the largest unit of government that could function well.

Why were Arrian and Plutarch cosmopolitans?

As Greeks living in the Roman Empire, both Arrian and Plutarch had a personal interest in promoting cosmopolitanism because cosmopolitanism justifies the notion that non-Romans can and should live as equals with Romans under one state. They lionized Alexander the Great because he demonstrated that a Greek could build and manage an empire as well as a Roman. They constructed a moral tale about Alexander as a benevolent leader who united all the world's peoples into one loving, universal brotherhood because that tale promoted the idea that different peoples could and indeed *should* live as equals under one empire. They found support for their opinion in Eratosthenes and in his teacher Zeno of Citium, the founder of Stoicism, because they were cosmopolitans. Thus, Plutarch (*On the Fortune or the Virtue of Alexander*, I.6) explains that Zeno's Stoicism "may be summed up in this one main principle: that all the inhabitants of this world of ours should not live differentiated by their respective rules of justice into separate cities and communities, but that we should consider all men to be of one com-

The idea that all people in the world could live together under one common set of laws and one government is called "cosmopolitanism."

118

munity and one polity, and that we should have a common life and an order common to us all." Using the Christian imagery of a shepherd and his flock, Plutarch adds, "even as a herd that feeds together and shares the pasturage of a common field." Plutarch reserves even higher praise for Alexander than for Zeno, because whereas Zeno merely espoused the idea of cosmopolitanism, contrary to Aristotle's advice, Alexander implemented it. For Alexander "brought together into one body all men everywhere, uniting and mixing in one great loving-cup, as it were, men's lives, their characters, their marriages, their very habits of life."

ALEXANDER THE GREAT AND GREEK PHILOSOPHY

Who was Callisthenes of Olynthus?

Callisthenes (c. 360–c. 327 B.C.E.) was Aristotle's great-nephew. He wrote a ten-volume history of Greece and a history of Alexander's military campaigns, *The Deeds of Alexander*. In collaboration with Aristotle, he compiled a complete list of the victors of the Pythian Games, which was important for Greek chronology. However, his writings survive only in fragments. On Aristotle's recommendation, he served Alexander the Great as historian of his military campaigns in Asia. Even though Callisthenes was the first to refer to Alexander's divine birth, he offended Alexander in 327 B.C.E. by refusing to prostrate himself before him as if he were a god, as was the Persian custom but not the Greek. Other Macedonians followed suit and refused to prostrate themselves, causing Alexander to abandon the custom. Shortly thereafter, Callisthenes was falsely implicated in a conspiracy to assassinate Alexander. Callisthenes was thrown into prison where, according to different accounts, he died either of torture or disease. Aristotle and his Peripatetic school of philosophers never forgave Alexander. In memory of Callisthenes, Aristotle's student and successor, Theophrastus, wrote *Callisthenes; or, a Treatise on Grief*.

What did Alexander think about philosophers?

Alexander the Great was tutored by Aristotle and retained a lifelong respect for philosophers and for learning in general. He donated a large sum of money to Aristotle's school for philosophy in the Lyceum, and he established gymnasiums in towns across his empire where Greek-speaking men learned to read and write and could discuss philosophy as well as train for athletic contests. He took philosophers, scientists, engineers, and historians with him on his military excursions and collected biological specimens for Aristotle. Many of his friends and generals, such as Hephaestion, were fellow students of Aristotle. Among the philosophers who accompanied Alexander were Pyrrho and Anaxarchus. Most modern historians believe that Alexander read Xenophon's *Anabasis* and used it as a guide to his own military campaigns in Persia. Xenophon was a philosopher, a student of Socrates, an historian, and a mercenary who wrote about what he had learned about the Persian Empire during his military service there.

How did their travels in India with Alexander the Great influence the Greek philosophers Pyrrho and Anaxarchus?

According to Diogenes Laërtius, the Greek philosophers Pyrrho of Elis (c. 360–c. 270 B.C.E.) and Anaxarchus (c. 380–c. 320 B.C.E.) accompanied Alexander the Great on his expedition to India where they studied with Indian philosophers whom the Greeks called "gymnosophists." The Indian philosophers were called gymnosophists because they were naked (like Greek athletes in a gymnasium) Sophists or teachers (gurus). The Indian gymnosophists were ascetics who lived a life of solitude, wore no clothing, and subsisted on a meager diet. Pyrrho and Anaxarchus were so impressed by them that they adopted their ascetic lifestyle. According to Diogenes Laërtius, they also adopted their attitude of suspending judgment or withholding assent, which the Greeks called epoché (ἐποχή). The attitude of epoché makes knowledge of things as they are in themselves beyond their fleeting appearance to us impossible, since such objective knowledge requires us to judge whether the appearance of things truly represents their objects or not. This holds true for our moral judgments as well as our judgments about matters of fact. According to Pyrrho, moral judgments are merely social conventions or customs that vary from one community to the next and are not necessarily true or true by nature.

The purpose of the attitude of *epoché* was to relieve suffering by inducing a tranquil state of consciousness free of anxiety, which the Greeks called *ataraxia* (αταραξζα). According to modern research by Adrian Kuzminski and Christopher Beckwith, the gymnosophists that Pyrrho and Anaxarchus studied with were probably early Buddhists. Indeed, the Buddha refused to answer questions about the ultimate nature of reality, stating that possible answers to these questions were neither true nor false, not both true and false, and not neither true nor false. Like Pyrrho's philosophy, the purpose of Buddhism was to relieve suffering by inducing a tranquil state of consciousness free of clinging and grasping, not to acquire knowledge of ultimate reality. In that sense, both Pyrrho and the early Buddhists were perhaps the world's first agnostics because they suspended judgment about the nature of ultimate reality.

Was Aristotle a skeptic?

Aristotle was the furthest thing from a skeptic. Aristotle could not have imagined giving up knowledge to relieve suffering because, according to Aristotle in *Metaphysics*, "all men by nature desire to know," and there is nothing that makes us happier than the pursuit and contemplation of knowledge. Aristotle believed that it is human nature to wonder and ask questions: "wondering in the first place at obvious perplexities, and then by gradual progression raising questions about the greater matters too." It would be a cruel joke if there were no answers to our questions. But Aristotle was not only confident that there were answers to our questions; he was confident that we were fully capable of obtaining those answers. According to Aristotle, human beings possess all the powers necessary to obtain knowledge, including the power to reason and to speak.

Contrary to what many philosophers since Kant have believed, Aristotle did not believe that language or human cognition prevents us from obtaining knowledge of things as they are in themselves. Aristotle believed that our sense organs are well suited to providing us with experiences from which we abstract knowledge of the true nature of things, as they are in themselves, and not merely as they appear to us. Similarly, he believed that human cognition and language are powerful tools in our pursuit of knowledge, not obstacles in the way of it. When it came to human knowledge, Aristotle was an enthusiastic optimist. Although his theories about the natural world were largely superseded by modern science, it is hard to imagine how modern science would have developed without the enthusiasm and confidence in the pursuit of knowledge that Aristotle bequeathed to Western civilization.

What was the fate of Alexander's empire after he died?

At the time of Alexander the Great's death in 323 B.C.E., neither of the two remaining heirs of Philip II were fit to rule. Philip III Arrhidaeus was Alexander's half-brother by a different mother. According to a story told by Plutarch, Philip III was poisoned with a magic potion and rendered mentally disabled by Alexander's mother, Olympias. Modern historians doubt the veracity of Plutarch's story, but we do know that Philip III Arrhidaeus was mentally impaired.

There was a struggle between two of Alexander's generals—Perdiccas and Meleager—over who should be recognized as heir to the throne. Alexander's third wife, Roxana, was pregnant with the future Alexander IV. Perdiccas favored Alexander IV because recognizing Alexander IV as heir to the throne would make Perdiccas the regent (acting emperor). With the help of Perdiccas, Roxana had Alexander's wife Stateira II, her sister Drypteis (who had married Hephaestion), and Alexander's wife Parysatis II all killed to eliminate rivals to Alexander IV. Meleager favored Philip III as heir to the throne. Meleager ordered the execution of Perdiccas, but instead Meleager and 300 of his troops were killed by Perdiccas. The remaining generals compromised on an agreement to recognize both Philip III and Alexander IV as heirs to the throne. But since neither was fit to rule, Perdiccas became regent anyhow. However, his rule didn't last long.

A series of wars quickly broke out in 322 B.C.E. between contenders to the throne known as the Wars of the Diadochi, or Wars of Successors to Alexander. Perdiccas was killed by his colonels, Seleucus I Nicator, Peithon, and Antigenes, during a civil war with Ptolemy in 320 B.C.E. Philip III was killed by Olympias in 317 B.C.E. Olympias was killed in 316 B.C.E. And Cassander, king of Macedonia, killed Roxana and Alexander IV in 310 B.C.E.

When the dust finally settled in 275 B.C.E., the Hellenic world had been chopped up into a changing number of kingdoms with shifting borders. Cassander was the son of Antipater, Alexander the Great's regent in Macedonia, and studied with Aristotle alongside Alexander the Great. Cassander ruled Macedonia and most of Greece from 305 B.C.E. until his death in 297 B.C.E. The Antigonid Dynasty, founded by one of Alexander the Great's generals and Diadochi, Antigonus I Monophthalmus, ruled Macedonia and most of Greece between 276 B.C.E. and its defeat by Rome in 168 B.C.E. The Seleucid Dynasty was founded by another of Alexander the Great's generals and Diadochi, Seleucus I Nicator. The Seleucid Empire stretched from parts of Asia Minor and the Levant in the west to parts of modern-day Pakistan and Turkmenistan in the east. The Seleucid dynasty did not end until its defeat by Rome in 63 B.C.E.

The Kingdom of Pergamon at the western end of Asia Minor was established by Alexander's general and another Diadochi, Lysimachus, who had been educated with Alexander at the royal court in Pella. In 282 B.C.E., Philetaerus, who was one of Lysimachus's lieutenants, betrayed Lsyimachus and founded the Attalid dynasty, which ruled until its final defeat by Rome in 129 B.C.E. Following Alexander's death in 323 B.C.E., Ptolemy I Soter was made governor of Egypt. Ptolemy I Soter was one of Alexander's best generals. He was a childhood friend of Alexander's, and together they had studied with Aristotle. Over a series of years Ptolemy consolidated power and in 305 B.C.E. declared himself pharaoh. The Ptolemaic Empire included most of the southeastern Mediterranean region, stretching from Libya to southern Syria and from Cyprus, Crete, and parts of Greece and Turkey to Egypt and Sudan. In its final 150 years, it survived threats from Macedonia and the Seleucid Empire by forming an alliance with Rome. The last

Ptolemy was Cleopatra IV, who attempted to preserve her dynasty by bearing the Roman emperor Julius Caesar a child. After Caesar's murder, Rome was divided between Mark Antony and Octavian. Again seeking to preserve her dynasty, Cleopatra bore Mark Antony three children. Octavian declared war on Mark Antony and Cleopatra. With their defeat, the Ptolemaic dynasty came to an end in 30 B.C.E.

How did Alexander the Great change the course of the history of philosophy?

The death of Alexander the Great marks the end of the classical age of Greece and the beginning of the Hellenistic. Modern historians have debated whether the culture of the classical age was superior to that of the Hellenistic, but most Hellenistic Greeks themselves looked back at classical Greece as a golden age. Hellenistic Greeks devoted a great deal of energy to the preservation of texts from the classical age, and the dissemination of these texts may have been their greatest contribution to humanity. Besides the great public library founded by the Ptolemies in Alexandria and the one modeled on it in Pergamon, many smaller private collections of books were assembled by wealthy individuals. According to ancient historians, books from Aristotle's private library formed part of the original collection in Alexandria.

There were also libraries associated with the schools of philosophy in Athens, which remained the leading center of philosophy. The Seleucids constructed libraries in Antioch and Nysa, both in Asia Minor. However, in spite of their attempts to preserve the culture and philosophy of classical Greece, the culture and philosophy of the Hellenistic period was markedly different from that of classical Greece. Some historians speculate that this change was due to the change in the political structure of Greek society. Whereas during the classical age the prevailing political form was that of the *polis,* or city-state, in the Hellenistic period the prevailing political form was that of an empire, albeit smaller empires than Alexander's.

Contrary to Plutarch's idealistic vision of a universal cosmopolitan brotherhood, the typical Hellenistic empire was also rigidly class stratified. The ruling class was composed of Greeks and a very small number of local elites, while nearly all the local people occupied the lower classes. Although there was cultural influence running both ways between Greeks and locals, and there was some intermarriage between Greek colonists and locals, the Greeks jealously guarded their own culture because it made them feel superior to locals and justified their rule. For example, the gymnasiums and theaters found in

Knowledge from the early Greek civilization was housed in a number of libraries during the Hellenistic era, including the famous Library of Alexandria, which was, in its day, the greatest repository of scrolls in the world.

123

many Hellenistic cities were built for Greeks, not locals. Koine Greek (a dialect of the Greek language) was the lingua franca of the entire Hellenistic world (and later, of the Christian New Testament), but it was spoken only by Greeks and local elites who served as administrators, not by local commoners.

The conditions of life in an empire caused Hellenistic Greek culture and philosophy to develop differently than classical Greek culture and philosophy. For one thing, the Hellenistic Greek elite did not only rule local cultures; they were also influenced by them. For example, in the Greco-Bactrian Kingdom and in the Indo-Greek Kingdoms that were carved out of the eastern end of the Seleucid Empire, some Greeks became Buddhists, and a syncretic Greco-Buddhist culture developed. The Ptolemaic emperors adopted Egyptian customs such as deifying themselves and marrying within their families, and they established the worship of syncretic Greco-Egyptian gods. For another thing, life in an empire, even if it was a relatively small kingdom, was different from life in a classical Greek *polis*. Although only a small percentage of the population of a classical Greek *polis* were citizens, those who were citizens enjoyed a sense of fellowship with one another and collectively governed themselves. The citizens of a classical *polis* enjoyed freedom and autonomy that even the ruling class of Hellenistic empires did not. Although some Hellenistic philosophers idealized the values of a cosmopolitan world order, others felt alienated and disempowered by it. Thus, there resulted a pessimistic undertone to most Hellenistic philosophy.

The purpose of philosophy in the Hellenistic period was no longer knowledge per se, as it was for Aristotle and the other philosophers of the classical age, but rather relief from suffering. It is as if they had become sick of living and required a remedy. Indeed, philosophy in the Hellenistic age became a form of psychotherapy. Thus, today, practices such as cognitive behavioral therapy, Albert Ellis's rational-emotive therapy, and even Alcoholics Anonymous all draw upon Hellenistic philosophy.

ARISTOTLE'S LIFE AFTER HIS DEPARTURE FROM PLATO'S ACADEMY

Who was Eubulus?

Eubulus was a wealthy fourth-century B.C.E. banker from Bithynia on the southern coast of the Black Sea in the north of Asia Minor. Eubulus loaned money to an official of the Persian Empire who put up the towns of Assos and Atarneus as collateral for the loan. Assos and Atarneus were two wealthy commercial towns in northwestern Asia Minor on the shore of the Aegean Sea. When the Persian official defaulted on the loan, Eubulus became the despotic ruler of Assos and Atarneus. The Persian Empire controlled most of Asia Minor. But because of internal feuds and incompetent administration of their empire, some parts of Asia Minor, including Assos and Atarneus during the time when Eubulus ruled them, were able to secede from the empire.

124

Who was Hermias of Atarneus?

Hermias was an extremely close and loyal friend of Aristotle's dating from their days together at Plato's Academy. But he had humble origins as a Bithynian slave belonging to Eubulus. Hermias was so valued by Eubulus that he sent Hermias to Plato's Academy to receive the best possible education, just as Aristotle had been sent there by his uncle Proxenus. When Hermias returned from Plato's Academy, he was freed from slavery and became a despotic ruler of Assos and Atarneus in partnership with Eubulus, his former master. When Eubulus died in about 351 B.C.E., Hermias became the sole ruler of Assos and Atarneus. He continued to rule in a despotic manner until Aristotle's arrival in 347 B.C.E., at which time he ruled according to Platonic principles. As a consequence, he won support from the surrounding countryside for his more tolerant and enlightened rule and further consolidated his power.

Perhaps through his ties with Aristotle, Hermias forged an alliance with Philip II, king of Macedonia, who had plans to invade and conquer the Persian Empire in Asia Minor. But later, Philip II withdrew military support from Hermias because of threats he received from the Athenians, who didn't want the Macedonians to expand into Asia Minor. The Persians took advantage of Hermias's weakened position, and in 341 B.C.E. they hired a Greek mercenary to capture him. Aristotle wrote letters to the mercenary urging him to change sides, to no avail. Hermias was taken in chains to Susa, where he was tortured to death for information about the Macedonian plan to invade the Persian Empire. But he refused to give them any information. His last dying words were "tell my friends that I have done nothing shameful or unworthy of philosophy." Aristotle erected a monument to Hermias at Delphi commemorating Hermias's courage and loyalty, and there are frequent references to Hermias in Aristotle's surviving works.

What did Aristotle do after his departure from Plato's Academy?

Perhaps at the request of Philip II, who wished to forge an alliance with Hermias, Aristotle set sail with the philosopher Xenocrates and a few other friends for Atarneus, where Aristotle also had family ties. Once there, Hermias offered to provide him and his colleagues with everything they needed to pursue scientific research in Assos. Aristotle accepted the offer and relocated to Assos, where he pursued zoological and other biological research. After a couple of years in Assos, Aristotle relocated again to the city of Mytilene on the island of Lesbos, which was so close to Assos that the two cities could be seen from one another. At Mytilene he was joined by another friend from Plato's Academy, Theophrastus (c. 371–c. 287), who was a native of Lesbos. The two developed such a close and lasting relationship that some twenty years later, Theophrastus became Aristotle's successor as head of the Lyceum, the school of philosophy that Aristotle was to establish in Athens. Theophrastus's research in botany was of such high quality that he is often cited as the founder of the field.

In general, the work of Aristotle and his team of researchers during this period of time was of such high quality that much of their research in biology was not improved upon until well into the modern era, and in some cases not even then. For example, as late as the nineteenth century, scientists dismissed Aristotle's hypothesis about the hectocotyl arm of an octopus until it was finally discovered that the hectocotyl arm of an octopus is in fact used to transfer sperm to a female octopus. Aristotle's speculation about the function of the hectocotyl arm was probably based on anatomical considerations, not on observation of an octopus in the act, since Aristotle put the idea forth as a hypothesis, not as a known fact.

Besides his own direct observation of living things, Aristotle's research also relied on reports he received from fishermen, shepherds, beekeepers, and others who worked with animals. Aristotle wrote extensively on biology, and his book on anatomy, the *Dissections*, was richly illustrated with drawings of many different

Theophrastus of the island of Lesbos became friends with Aristotle and would eventually succeed Aristotle to head the Lyceum.

species of animals. Unfortunately, in the age before the printing press, it was even more difficult to reproduce anatomical drawings than it was to reproduce words, so Aristotle's *Dissections* has been lost. But we know enough about this period of Aristotle's life and work to know that it formed the basis of his later philosophical development. Unlike the early modern philosophers who took mechanical physics to be the foundation of the sciences, Aristotle took biology to be the model science.

What did Aristotle say about the social nature of human beings?

Aristotle believed that human beings are social not for utilitarian reasons (as a means to an end) or by accident, but by nature. Human beings, he said, are by nature social animals. An individual human being is in its essence a part of society and is defined by its social function. In that sense, Aristotle believed that society precedes the individual and that the essence of an individual presupposes society. After making these points in his book the *Politics*, Aristotle famously wrote, "Anyone who either cannot lead the common life or is so self-sufficient as not to need to, and therefore does not partake of society, is either a beast or a god."

What did Aristotle think was divine in human beings?

Reflecting Aristotle's reverence for human intelligence and the pursuit of knowledge, he believed that when we engage in intellectual contemplation, we come as close to becoming gods as is humanly possible. In the *Nicomachean Ethics*, he wrote, "If then the intellect is

Did Aristotle live a socially active lifestyle?

In keeping with his philosophy, Aristotle led a very socially active lifestyle. He maintained a large circle of family and friends, was fully engaged in the politics of his day at the highest levels, and established a school of philosophy in the Lyceum, where he taught and engaged in collaborative research with his fellows. He did not live the life of a reclusive, ascetic sage. That said, however, Aristotle did not believe that intellectual contemplation is dependent on society. The wise man, Aristotle said in his *Nicomachean Ethics*, can "contemplate by himself, and the more so the wiser he is; no doubt he will study better with the aid of fellow-workers, but still he is the most self-sufficient of men."

something divine in comparison with man, so is the life of the intellect divine in comparison with human life. Nor ought we to obey those who enjoin that a man should have man's thoughts and a mortal the thoughts of mortality, but we ought so far as possible to achieve immortality, and do all that man may to live in accordance with the highest thing in him; for though this be small in bulk, in power and value it far surpasses all the rest."

Did Aristotle marry and have children?

During his time in Mytilene, on the island of Lesbos, Aristotle married Pythias, the niece or adopted daughter (or both) of his friend and host, Hermias. They had a daughter who was also named Pythias. Pythias the Elder engaged in collaborative biological research with her husband, Aristotle. In 335 B.C.E., when Aristotle returned to Athens to open his school in the Lyceum, his wife Pythias died.

Aristotle subsequently established a relationship with one of his wife's maids, a woman named Herpyllis, who like him was a native of Stagira. Given that Herpyllis was a servant in Aristotle's household, she was probably a slave. Although we know from his will that Aristotle must have freed Herpyllis, he still could not marry her because of her relatively low social status. Nonetheless, they remained dedicated companions to one another until Aristotle's death, and together they had a son, Nicomachus. Aristotle provided generously for Herpyllis in his will, leaving her a house of her choice at his family's estates in either Chalcis or Stagira, numerous slaves, money, and furniture, and he instructed his executors to ensure that she be given to a worthy husband, if she chose to remarry. Aristotle appointed Antipater, the governor of Greece, to be the chief executor of his will. After Aristotle's death, Nicomachus edited some of Aristotle's notes on ethics, which have been known ever since as the *Nicomachean Ethics*.

Why did Aristotle leave Mytilene?

In 343 B.C.E., Philip II invited Aristotle to tutor his son, Alexander the Great, and offered him use of the Temple of the Nymphs at Mieza as a boarding school. In return, Philip

II rebuilt Aristotle's hometown of Stagira, which he had destroyed when he defeated Olynthus, the head of the Chalcidian League, and annexed the entire Chalcidice peninsula, including Stagira, in 348 B.C.E. Philip II promised to repopulate Stagira by pardoning those of its citizens who were in exile and freeing those who had been enslaved.

Aristotle also tutored other children of Macedonian aristocrats in Mieza. Among the most famous were Ptolemy, the founder of the Ptolemaic Kingdom of Egypt; Cassander, the son of Antipater and the future king of Macedonia; and Hephaestion. There is evidence that Aristotle's students retained a lifelong interest in philosophy as a result of their tutelage under Aristotle. Ptolemy founded the library at Alexandria. And Hephaestion carried on a correspondence with both Aristotle and Xenocrates, a Pythagorean Platonist who succeeded Speusippus as head of the Academy from 339/338 B.C.E. to 314/313 B.C.E.

Ptolemy I Soter (c. 367–282 B.C.E.) was a historian of Alexander the Great and a student of Aristotle and went on to establish the Ptolemaic Kingdom of Egypt.

Aristotle remained at Mieza for about three years until Alexander the Great completed his studies and joined his father on military campaigns. We know comparatively less about the subsequent five years of Aristotle's life between 340 B.C.E. and 335 B.C.E. other than that he remained in Macedonia either at the king's court in Pella or in his hometown of Stagira, where he continued his scientific and philosophical studies.

What were the political circumstances that allowed Aristotle to return to Athens in 335 B.C.E. and open his own school of philosophy in the Lyceum?

In the years prior to 335 B.C.E., Aristotle had won the respect of Alexander the Great and had become a friend of Antipater's. By the time Alexander the Great succeeded his father as king in 336 B.C.E., the Macedonians had already won the Battle of Chaeronea and become the hegemonic leader of the Hellenic League. But in 335 B.C.E., Alexander cemented his rule over Greece by brutally crushing a rebellion against Macedonian rule in Thebes, which was instigated by Demosthenes, the anti-Macedonian, Athenian statesman. Thus, by 335 B.C.E., anti-Macedonian elements in Athens had been decisively defeated, allowing Aristotle to return.

When Alexander launched his campaign to conquer the Persian Empire, he left Antipater behind to serve as regent of Macedonia in his absence. According to ancient historians, both Alexander the Great and Antipater supported Aristotle in several ways during his second period in Athens. They funded Aristotle's school, providing money for both scientific research and books. According to Roman historian Pliny, Alexander had thousands of men collect biological specimens from across his empire for Aristotle's study. Though that claim may have been exaggerated, we can take the essence of the claim to be true, that Alexander provided Aristotle with substantial assistance in his scientific and philosophical research. Alexander even erected a statue in honor of Aristotle in Athens.

What did Aristotle do during his second period in Athens?

Aristotle lived in Athens again from 335 B.C.E. until 323 B.C.E. when the death of Alexander the Great reignited anti-Macedonian sentiment in Athens. During this time, he lectured and carried on conversations with his fellow philosophers, pursued scientific research, and developed his mature philosophy. Most of Aristotle's works that have survived date from this period of his life. We can be sure that he remained politically active as well, and it is recorded that he used his friendship with Antipater and Alexander the Great to protect Athens and the school he established there. Because Aristotle was not an Athenian citizen and could not own property, his school was conducted in a public gymnasium known as the Lyceum. Aristotle's school came to be known as "peripatetic," from the Greek word meaning "to walk about," because there were covered walkways ("peripatoi") in the Lyceum where members of Aristotle's school would walk while they talked about philosophy. The Peripatetic school is best understood as a fellowship of philosophers and scientists rather than a school in the modern sense of the word, because there was no tuition, prescribed curriculum, exams, or degrees.

Why did Aristotle flee Athens for a second time in 323 B.C.E.?

Aristotle fled Athens in 323 B.C.E. because the death of Alexander the Great unleashed anti-Macedonian forces there. Although Aristotle had appealed to Alexander the Great

---

How did Aristotle's mature philosophy differ from his earlier work?

Although Aristotle had already begun to question Plato's theory of the forms when he was a member of the Academy, his mature philosophy represented a departure from his earlier work and was shaped by his intervening years of biological research. Aristotle's mature philosophy is systematic, highly structured, and logical, but it is based on biology rather than mathematics as Plato's philosophy was. Aristotle took the living organism to be the model or paradigm for what it means to "be" in general, whereas for Plato the model or paradigm for what it means to "be" is the object of an abstract idea, such as a number. For Aristotle, all "things" or "beings" are like living organisms at least insofar as they are to be understood or explained in the same way that living organisms are understood or explained.

Aristotle was a teacher to Alexander the Great, but even though he didn't condone the Macedonian's imperialistic endeavors, Aristotle was compelled to flee Athens after Alexander's death for fear of Macedonia's enemies.

and Antipater on behalf of Athens, and although Aristotle's political philosophy did not condone Alexander's imperialism or his domination of other Greeks, he was still disliked by anti-Macedonian parties in Athens. Alluding to the execution of Socrates, Aristotle said that he fled Athens so that Athens would not sin twice against philosophy.

Where did Aristotle die?

In 323 B.C.E., Aristotle fled Athens for Chalcis, a town on the island of Euboea in what was then the kingdom of Macedonia, where his mother, Phaestis, had once lived and her family still owned property. He died there one year later, in 322 B.C.E., of natural causes.

ARISTOTLE'S THEORY OF KNOWLEDGE

According to Aristotle, what is knowledge?

It is a special kind of belief. The Greek word for the type of belief that Aristotle understood to be knowledge was *episteme* (ἐπιστήμη). What makes epistemic knowledge special is that it is self-reflective. In order for our beliefs to count as knowledge, they must not only be true, but we must know *why* they are true. We must have reasons or evidence for our beliefs. And because we cannot have an infinite regress of reasons for our reasons, and reasons for those reasons, ad infinitum, at some point we must have reasons that are either true by definition or self-evident. According to Aristotle, it is human nature to seek such knowledge, though, of course, not all humans may realize their potential to achieve such knowledge.

According to Aristotle, what are the three types of knowledge?

The three types of knowledge are theoretical knowledge, practical knowledge, and productive knowledge.

What is theoretical knowledge?

Theoretical knowledge is the contemplation of eternal and unchanging objects by the mind or intellect. The Greek word for mind or intellect was *nous* (νοῦζ). The Greek word for thinking or for the mental activity of contemplation was *theoria* (θεωρία). The Greeks understood *theoria* as a kind of seeing or vision. Thus, theoretical knowledge was something seen as in a vision. Because the object of *theoria* is unchanging and eternal, some ancient and medieval philosophers believed that there is only one *nous* and that *Nous* is God. In that case, *theoria* is seeing through God's eye. According to Aristotle, *theoria* is an activity that is its own goal; in other words, theoretical knowledge is something that we seek for its own sake, not as a means to a greater good. In fact, there is no greater good, nor any greater happiness, than the life of the mind. Theoretical knowledge may be divided into theology, ontology, physics (which for Aristotle included biology and psychology), and mathematics.

What is practical knowledge?

Practical knowledge is knowledge about how to act with excellence (*arête*). Unlike theoretical knowledge, we seek practical knowledge not for its own sake but for the sake of acting with excellence. The Greek word for acting or doing was *praxis* (πρᾶξιζ), which is etymologically related to our words "practice" and "practical"; and the Greek word for practical knowledge was *phronesis* (φρόνησῐζ). Practical knowledge may be subdivided into ethics (the study of moral virtue or excellence in personal character and action), economics (how to best manage a household, which was the basic unit of production in the ancient world), and political science (Aristotle and his team of researchers studied the constitutions of 158 city-states to determine the best form of government).

What is productive knowledge?

Productive knowledge is the knowledge of how to make something. We do not seek productive knowledge for its own sake but for the sake of making something. The Greek word for making was *poiesis* (ποίησιζ), and the Greek word for productive knowledge was *techne* (τέχνη). Aristotle divided productive knowledge into crafts and mimetic arts. Crafts enable us to produce useful objects. For example, the craft of making armor produces armor that protects soldiers in battle. The craft of housebuilding produces homes that provide shelter. Statecraft produces the state. What Aristotle called the mimetic arts are what we call the fine arts. This is knowledge of how to produce beautiful objects that do not necessarily have any use besides the pleasure given by their beauty. Examples would be painting, sculpture, music, poetry, and theater.

ARISTOTLE'S WRITINGS

Was Aristotle a systematic thinker?

Yes, Aristotle was probably the greatest systematic thinker in the history of Western philosophy. His writings are encyclopedic in the sense that they cover almost every topic imaginable, but they were not a random collection of facts and theories. Everything fit together according to a rigorous logic. The overall structure of his work is architectonic with a vertical series of levels like the floors of a building. His theory of logic parallels his theory of beings (his "ontology"), and together these two theories form the foundation of his system. At the level above ontology and logic is physics, which is the study of a special class of beings, the beings of nature that are subject to change. At the level above physics is psychology, which is the study of the soul. The soul is that which animates living beings. At the level above psychology is ethics, which is about the excellent or virtuous activity of human beings. And finally, the level above ethics is politics, which Aristotle regards as a branch of ethics having to do with statesmanship. None of these fields of study can be understood without first understanding the level below it. Each level is logically dependent upon the one below it.

How much did Aristotle write?

In his *Lives of Eminent Philosophers,* the ancient biographer Diogenes Laërtius lists about 150 books written by Aristotle, containing a total, he says, of 445,270 lines. Aristotle's work was encyclopedic. He wrote books on nearly everything: biology, psychology, biographies of famous persons, the history of Greece, the history of philosophy, ethics, political science, economics, education, meteorology, astronomy, mathematics, theology, ontology, logic, and the philosophy of science. Also included are several books of his correspondence with Philip II, Alexander the Great, and Antipater. Of this enormous body of work, only about one fifth has survived. But even that small fraction of Aristotle's work runs to 2,465 pages in *The Revised Oxford Translation.*

Why is Aristotle so difficult to read?

Plato's writings are works of art as well as philosophy. They employ literary devices that capture the reader's imagination. They are replete with vivid portrayals of compelling characters. There is no use of technical or arcane language. There is no missing information. There are no sentences with awkward grammatical constructions. In short, they are beautifully written. Unfortunately, this cannot be said of Aristotle's extant writings. They are written in awkward, stilted prose with no literary or aesthetic grace. It is often necessary to read sentences in Aristotle's writings several times to untangle them. And even then, the reader often has the sense that they missed something. Indeed, they have. They missed Aristotle's lectures.

Aristotle's extant writings were merely lecture notes. They were never intended for public consumption. Aristotle's extant writings were notes he jotted down to re-

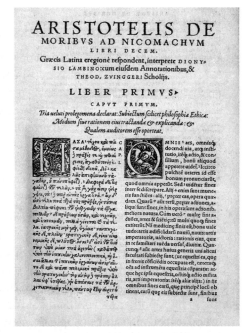

The first page of a 1566 edition of Aristotle's *Nicomachean Ehtics*. In addition to philosophy, Aristotle wrote histories, and books on biology, psychology, political science, education, economics, astronomy, mathematics, and more.

mind himself what he wanted to say when he lectured (some of the writings attributed to Aristotle may also have been compiled from notes taken by his students). When he delivered his lectures, he most likely would have elaborated upon his notes by providing the necessary background information, adding examples, and answering his students' questions. We have none of that when we read Aristotle, which is why he is so difficult to read. The irony is that, according to Cicero, who was one of the greatest orators and rhetoricians who ever lived, Aristotle's writings were of great beauty and fluency, a "golden flow of speech," he said. Was Cicero reading the same Aristotle that we are reading? No, not at all. Aristotle wrote dialogues like Plato did, but except for a few fragments, those have not survived. It is probably from these dialogues that Cicero acquired his admiration for Aristotle's writing style.

What happened to Aristotle's writings after his death?

In his *Geography,* the Roman philosopher and historian Strabo says that Aristotle left his library and his own writings to Theophrastus, to whom he also left his Peripatetic school in Athens. Theophrastus in turn, Strabo says, left Aristotle's writings to Neleus of Scepsis, whose heirs in Asia Minor hid them in an underground trench to prevent them from being seized by the kings of Pergamon for their own library. Much later, Neleus's heirs sold Aristotle's writings for a large sum of money to a book collector who

How many of Aristotle's books survive, and what are they about?

Only about thirty-one of Aristotle's books survive, excluding spurious works falsely attributed to him. Since the first century B.C.E., when Andronicus compiled Aristotle's works, they have been placed into four categories. The first is logic and epistemology. The following three correspond to the three areas of knowledge: theoretical, practical, and productive. Aristotle did not believe that logic and epistemology could be placed in any of the three areas of knowledge because they were tools employed in all three. For this reason, Aristotle's medieval editors placed his books on logic and epistemology in a category titled the *Organon*, a Greek word meaning "tool." There are six books in the *Organon*.

There are nineteen books of theoretical knowledge. Of these, eighteen are about "physics" or the "philosophy of nature" (our word "physics" comes from the Greek word *physis*, which meant "nature"). Since, according to Aristotle, all natural things change, physics is the study of things that change. There are five books on animals; one on youth, old age, life and death, and respiration; one on longevity and shortness of life; another on youth and old age; six on psychology; one on meteorology; one on astronomy; and a couple on nature and change in general. The nineteenth book of theoretical knowledge, following those on physics, is titled *Metaphysics*, which literally means "that which follows physics," because Aristotle's editors filed it after the books on physics. *Metaphysics* is about ontology (the study of beings *qua* being, or being itself) and things that do not change. Following the book on metaphysics are the books on practical knowledge: three books on ethics and one on politics. Finally, there are two books on productive knowledge: the *Rhetoric* (how to speak and write persuasively and with style) and the *Poetics* (about tragic plays). In addition to these, in 1879, papyrus rolls containing Aristotle's study of the constitution of Athens were found buried under the sands of Egypt.

returned them to Athens. When Roman general Sulla sacked Athens in 86 B.C.E., he confiscated Aristotle's writings and brought them to Rome where Andronicus of Rhodes, the last head of the Peripatetic school, compiled the definitive edition of Aristotle's works that is still the basis for modern editions today.

Strabo presumably received this story from a Peripatetic philosopher with whom he studied named Boethius of Sidon, who was a student of Andronicus of Rhodes. Plutarch repeated Strabo's story, and for centuries it was believed. Modern historians, however, provide a less colorful account of what happened to Aristotle's writings. According to them, the Peripatetic school fell into decline in the mid-third century B.C.E., overshadowed by Academic Skepticism and other schools of philosophy that were more popular in the Hellenistic period. There is evidence that Aristotle's writings were copied and preserved during this time, but they were not much studied until the Andronicus edition was published in Rome sometime late in the first century B.C.E. The Andronicus edition provoked a revival of the Peripatetic school of philosophy, and it thrived for another three centuries. After the fall of Rome, most of Aristotle's writings, except for two of his works on logic—the *Categories* and *On Interpretation*—were lost to the West. However, copies were preserved in the Byzantine or Eastern Roman Empire and in Arab translations. The first Latin translations of Aristotle were not completed in the West until the thirteenth century.

ARISTOTLE'S REVISION OF PLATO'S THEORY OF FORMS

What is the third man argument?

In his late dialogue *Parmenides,* Plato presents an argument that has come to be known as the "third man argument" against his own theory of forms. Because Aristotle repeats the same argument in his *Metaphysics* and *Sophistic Refutations,* it is possible that Plato obtained the argument from Aristotle when they were working together at the Academy. The argument is based on several presuppositions, each of which can itself be questioned, and it is possible that in presenting the argument, Plato only meant to call into question one or more of these presuppositions.

Among the questionable presuppositions is Aristotle's conception of forms as universals. But it is clear that Aristotle's intention in using the third man argument was to call into question Plato's theory of forms itself. Aristotle argues that if a particular thing such as a man is a man because it "participates" in the form of man, then there must be a second form of man, form of man #2 (which is the third "man" in the argument) that explains why both the particular man and the form of man are both man. The argument treats the form of man as if it were the same kind of thing (the same form) as the particular man. The argument further assumes that if there are two things of the same kind, then there must be a form or kind that contains them both as particular examples of that form or kind. Thus, if the particular man and the form of man are both kinds of man, then there must be a second form of man, form of man #2, that contains both the particular man and form of man #1 as particular examples. But if that is the case, then the same argument applies to the particular man, form of man #1, and form of man #2. Thus, there must be a form of man #3. The argument can be repeated indefinitely. So, there must be a form of man #4, and a form of man #5, and so on, ad infinitum. Since this result is absurd, Plato's theory of forms must not be true.

How did Aristotle revise Plato's concept of a "form"?

The ancient Greek words that Plato used for our word "form" were *eidos* (εἶδος) and *idea* (ἰδέα). Both words were derived from an Indo-European root meaning "to see." For Plato, a "form" was an ideal shape or geometric proportion (*morphē*) that "shines" (*phainō*) or "appears" (*phainomena*). What makes the forms ideal is that they are "seen" or known not by our body's eye but by the mind's eye, by *nous*. Thus, for Plato, a form was a pattern analogous to a geometric shape that could be copied to reproduce many analogous replicas that preserve the same proportions but may alter the absolute size of the pattern.

Aristotle's concept of form was quite different. Whereas Plato's concept of form was based on geometric concepts, Aristotle's concept of form was based on his use of the logical concepts of genus and species, universal and particular, in biology. A form, in Aristotle's conception, is a kind or species of thing, a category or class of things. In the case of plants and animals, Aristotle used the Greek word for form, *eidos*, to mean the visible characteristics of a species that uniquely define it. Since all particular examples of a given kind or species of thing have the same form, Aristotle referred to the forms as "universals." For example, all particular horses such as Black Beauty and Bucephalus are members of the species of horse. "Horse" is a universal term that applies to all particular horses. Black Beauty is a horse. But so is Bucephalus. According to Aristotle's conception of forms, there is a logical hierarchy of forms. At the bottom of the hierarchy are particular things like Black Beauty and Bucephalus. Above those are species like "horse."

"Horse" is an example of a first-order species because it is at the bottom on the hierarchy of species, just above particulars. The Greek words that Aristotle used for first-order species was *atomon eidos*, which meant indivisible (*atomon*) forms (*eidos*) because they could not be further subdivided into more specific species. Higher order species are "kinds" that can be further subdivided into more specific species. For example, living organisms can be further subdivided into plants and animals. Animals can be further subdivided into the first-order species horses and dogs. The Greek word that Aristotle used for "kind" was *génos* (γένοζ), which we translate as *genus*. A genus is a species, too, but not an indivisible one because it can be subdivided into more specific species.

How Similar are Plato's and Aristotle's Theories of Knowledge

Both Aristotle and Plato believed that true knowledge—what they called epistemic knowledge—is not just a matter of holding true beliefs but also of knowing with certainty *why* those beliefs are *necessarily* true. Aristotle's term for epistemic certainty and necessity was *apodicticity*. Knowledge that is certain and necessary is *apodictic* (ἀποδεικτικόζ). Both Aristotle and Plato agreed that it is not possible to have apodictic knowledge of particular things that are subject to change because the existence and attributes of a thing that is subject to change are not necessary. They could be otherwise or not exist at all. Things and their attributes that are subject to change are "contingent," that is, they depend upon other things. According to both Plato and Aristotle, the only things that we can have apodictic and, therefore, epistemic knowledge of are the forms. Plato and Aristotle differ only in how they conceive of the forms and in how we can have knowledge of them.

ARISTOTLE'S LOGIC

How does Aristotle believe that we can have epistemic knowledge of a form or species?

According to Aristotle, to have epistemic knowledge of a form or species, we must explain the essential attributes of that form or species or category of things, and our explanation must take the form of a valid, deductive argument whose premises are necessarily true. Since valid, deductive arguments preserve the truth of their premises, such an argument proves that the conclusion of the argument is necessarily true. Aristotle called an argument of this type a *demonstration*, or in Greek, an *apodeixis* (ἀπόδειξιζ), because its conclusion is *apodictic*. Thus, in order to have epistemic knowledge of a form or species, we must construct a *demonstration*.

What is a declarative sentence?

Declarative sentences assert a judgment or belief about something that may be true or false. According to Aristotle's logic, the general form of a declarative sentence was "*S* is *P*," where *S* is the subject of the sentence and *P* is the predicate. If *P* is an attribute possessed by *S*, then the sentence "*S* is *P*" is true. If *P* is not an attribute possessed by *S*, then "*S* is *P*" is false. For example, the sentence "Diamonds are hard" is true because diamonds *are* hard. Declarative sentences are the only types of utterance that are true or false. Imperative sentences, exclamations, and questions are neither true nor false. Declarative sentences are also the smallest unit of language that convey knowledge, which is why they are the only type of sentence considered in Aristotle's logic, whose purpose is to teach us how to construct a demonstration of knowledge.

Declarative sentences were the subject of Aristotle's *On Interpretation*, one of the books in the *Organon*. Single words by themselves are meaningful, but they are neither true nor false, and they cannot convey knowledge. Only when words are combined with other words by the "copula"—the little word "is," the verb "to be," or another copular verb—do you get a declarative sentence that may be true or false and that may convey knowledge.

What are the terms of a declarative sentence?

Words are the smallest unit of language that convey meaning. Terms are words used in declarative sentences other than logical operators and the copula. The terms of the declarative sentence "*S* is *P*" are the terms *S* and *P*. By themselves, the terms of a declarative sentence are neither true nor false. But when joined together by the copula, they form declarative sentences that are either true or false. Aristotle identified ten categories of terms in his book the *Categories*: substance, quantity, quality, relation, place, time, position or posture, state or condition, acting, and being acted upon.

What are the ten categories of being or ways something can "be," according to Aristotle?

Because Aristotle was an epistemological optimist and did not believe that language comes between us and objective reality, he believed that the ten categories of terms used in declarative sentences are also the ten types of being or ways something can "be": substance, quantity, quality, relation, place, time, position or posture, state or condition, acting, and being acted upon. Primary substance is the fundamental form of being that serves as the ultimate subject underlying all other types of being. It includes things like my friend Jane and my cat Cordelia. In general, primary substances are particular things that can be referred to as this or that. Primary substances cannot be predicated of any subject. They are always the *subjects* of predication in declarative sentences. Aristotle's word for the subject of a declarative sentence was *hypokeimonon* (ὑποκείμενον), which means "the underlying thing." The Greek word *hypokeimonon* was translated into the Latin word *subiectum*, from which we get our word "subject." Aristotle says that first-order forms or species (*atomon eidos*) are substances too but only in a secondary sense, because they define the essence or "what-ness" of primary substances. He calls these secondary substances.

According to Aristotle, we cannot have knowledge of primary substances *as particular things*. We can only have knowledge of the forms or species to which they belong. I cannot know Cordelia as a particular thing. There is no specific form that makes her this particular cat. But I can know her as a member of the species cat who possesses the essential attributes of a cat and also has green eyes, weighs 5.6 pounds, and purrs in my lap. Aristotle calls these latter attributes "accidental" because they are not common to all members of Cordelia's species by virtue of their being members of her species. But they are also forms and can be known.

What is the Greek word that we translate as "substance"?

The Greek word that we translate as "substance" is *ousia* (οὐσία) (pronounced OO-zee-uh). But it is misleading to translate *ousia* as "substance," because we think of substance as homogeneous matter or amorphous "stuff," and that is not what *ousia* meant in ancient Greek; it simply meant "being," that which *is*. *Ousia* was the present participle of the verb *eimí* (εἰμί), which meant "to be." The medieval Aristotelians translated the Greek word *ousia* into the Latin words *substantia*, from which we get our word "substance," and *essentia*, from which we get our word "essence," because, according to Aristotle, it is the first category of being that is primarily being. The other categories derive their being from the first category of being. They are beings only because they can be predicated of beings in the first category. Thus, "being" primarily refers to the first category of being, which includes primary beings ("primary substances") and secondary beings ("secondary substances" or "essences"). The Latin medieval philosophers translated "being" as "substance" because primary substance serves as the underlying subject (the *hypokeimonon*) of declarative sentences, and the Latin word *substantia* is derived from a Latin word meaning "stand under, exist." They translated being as *essentia* because secondary substance is essence.

The remaining nine categories of being are ways in which a subject can be predicated in a declarative sentence. Since they can be predicated of a subject, they are not primary substances. But as terms in declarative sentences, they can be known. For example, in the sentence "Cordelia has green eyes," the color green belongs to the category of quality. Since green is a kind of color, color also belongs to the category of quality. In the sentence "Cordelia weighs 5.6 pounds," the number 5.6 belongs to the category of quantity. In the sentence "Cordelia purrs in my lap," the word "purrs" belongs to the category of acting and the phrase "in my lap" belongs to the category of place. In the sentence "Jane is my friend," "my friend" belongs to the category of relation.

What are the components of a logical argument?

A logical argument is composed of a series of declarative statements known as premises and a conclusion. The premises provide evidence or reasons to believe that the conclusion is true.

What is an inductive argument?

An inductive argument is an argument that proceeds from the particular to the universal. For example, from the observation of many solid objects, we may conclude that all solid objects fall to the earth when there is no countervailing force to stop them. In an inductive argument, each particular case by itself provides only partial support for the conclusion. Even adding up the evidence provided by each particular case only increases the likelihood that the conclusion is true, but it does not prove that the conclusion must be true as a matter of logical necessity. However, according to Aristotle, there is more to inductive reasoning than adding up the partial evidence provided by each particular case and calculating the probability that the conclusion is true. According to Aristotle, our minds are capable of recognizing a pattern in the particular cases that is greater than the sum of its parts. Thus, in Aristotle's view, inductive reasoning *can* yield necessary and universal truths.

What is a deductive argument?

A deductive argument is an argument in which the conclusion is necessarily true if its premises are true. The success of a deductive argument is not a matter of degree or likelihood. Either the argument succeeds in establishing that the conclusion must be true if the premises are true, or it fails. A successful deductive argument is known as a *valid* argument. An unsuccessful deductive argument is known as an *invalid* argument. An invalid argument is one in which the conclusion might be false even if its premises are true. The following argument is an example of a valid argument:

Premise: All house cats are feline.
Premise: Socrates is a house cat.
Conclusion: Socrates is feline.

Note that a valid argument can have false premises. All that validity means is that *if* the premises are true, then the conclusion *must* be true. If the premises of a valid ar-

An example of an invalid argument would be: 1) All men are animals; 2) Zebras are animals; therefore 3) All men are zebras.

gument are true, then in addition to being valid, it is also *sound*. If an argument is sound, then its conclusion must be true. The following argument is the most famous example of a sound argument:

Premise: All men are mortal.
Premise: Socrates is a man.
Conclusion: Socrates is mortal.

This argument is sound because it is a valid argument whose premises are true. The following argument is invalid:

Premise: All men are animals.
Premise: Zebras are animals.
Conclusion: All men are zebras.

Even though the premises of this argument are true, the conclusion is false, because the conclusion does not follow necessarily from the premises.

What is formal logic?

Formal logic is the study of the form of arguments. As we saw, deductive arguments can be valid even if their premises are false. That's because what makes a deductive argument valid is the form of the argument, not its content. It doesn't matter what the declarative statements of an argument are about. If you can show that the form of a deductive argument is valid, then you will know that its conclusion follows from its premises, even without knowing anything about the subject of the argument. Aristotle was the first philosopher to develop a theory of formal logic and identify valid forms of argument. Medieval philosophers made some relatively minor additions and modifications to Aristotle's logic, but it was not superseded until the development of mathematical logic in the nineteenth century.

What is a categorical statement?

A categorical statement is a statement that asserts or denies that all or some members of one category are members of another category. In Aristotle's view, categorical statements are not only a type of statement, but they also reflect the structure of reality, since, according to Aristotle, all things (beings) in the world are arranged in nested hierarchies of categories (forms, kinds or species) in which each category contains the categories immediately below it, which in turn contain the categories below them. Aristotle identified four types of categorical statement:

- Type A, Universal Affirmation: All S are P.
- Type E, Universal Negation: No S are P.
- Type I, Particular Affirmation: Some S are P.
- Type O, Particular Negation: Some S are not P.

Categorical statements contain two terms, the subject S and the predicate P; the copula "is" or "are"; and some combination of the logical operators "all," "some," "no" or "none," and "not."

What was Aristotle's theory of formal logic?

According to Aristotle, deductive arguments have the form of a syllogism. A syllogism is an argument containing three categorical statements: a major premise, a minor premise, and a conclusion. The categorical statements of a syllogism contain three categorical terms: the major term, the minor term, and the middle term. The major term is found in both the major premise and the conclusion. The minor term is found in both the minor premise and the conclusion. The middle term is found in both the major premise and the minor premise. It is the term that connects the subject of the conclusion with its predicate. For example, in the following syllogism, whose form was given the name BARBARA by medieval logicians because it contains three Type A categorical statements, the major term is "animals," the minor term is "humans," and the middle term is "primates."

- Minor Premise: All humans are primates.
- Major Premise: All primates are animals.
- Conclusion: All humans are animals.

If we substitute the symbol P for the major term "animals," S for the minor term "humans," and M for the middle term "primates," we get the following form of a syllogism:

- Minor Premise: All S are M.
- Major Premise: All M are P.
- Conclusion: All S are P.

Without knowing what S, P, or M represent, we know from the form of the syllogism alone that it is a valid deductive argument. That doesn't mean that its conclusion is necessarily true. Nor does it mean that its premises are true. Indeed, the claim that humans are primates is controversial in some quarters. All that validity means is that the conclusion must be true *if* both premises are true. Aristotle did a complete study of all the possible forms of a syllogism. Out of the 256 unique ways that the four types of categorical statements can be combined to form a syllogism, only twenty-four are valid arguments. Aristotle correctly identified all twenty-four.

Can any terms in a syllogism refer to particular individuals instead of classes or kinds of things?

According to Aristotle, only the minor term of a syllogism can refer to particular individuals because particular things are always the subject of predication and can never be predicated of other subjects. The following argument is an example of the BARBARA syllogism in which the minor term is the particular individual Socrates:

- Minor Premise: Socrates is human.
- Major Premise: All humans are mortal.
- Conclusion: Socrates is mortal.

Although at first sight this argument doesn't look like BARBARA because the minor premise and the conclusion do not appear to be universal affirmations (statements of the

All Men Are Mortals

And All Greeks Are Men

Then All Greeks Are Mortals

An example of a syllogism.

form "All *S* are *P*"), in fact they are because statements of the form "*S* is *P*," where *S* is a particular individual, are logically equivalent to statements of the form "All things that are *S* are *P*," which can be shortened to "All *S* are *P*."

How does a syllogism explain the essential attributes of a form or species?

We have already seen that, according to Aristotle, in order to acquire epistemic knowledge of a form or species, we must explain the essential attributes of that form or species, and our explanation must take the form of a valid, deductive argument whose premises are necessarily true. Such an explanation is called a *demonstration*, or in Greek, an *apodeixis*, because its conclusion is *apodictic*, which means that it is not only true but that it *must* be true for the reasons given in the demonstration. Now we have learned that, according to Aristotle, a valid, deductive argument has the form of a syllogism and that a syllogism explains why the conclusion of the argument is true by connecting its predicate to its subject. An example will illustrate how a syllogism explains the essential attributes of a form or species. Consider the following syllogism, which explains why lemon juice turns blue litmus paper red:

Minor Premise: All lemon juice is acidic.
Major Premise: All acidic liquids turn blue litmus paper red.
Conclusion: All lemon juice turns blue litmus paper red.

In this syllogism, the fact that all lemon juice turns blue litmus paper red is explained by the fact that lemon juice is acidic and that all acidic liquids turn blue litmus paper red. It is the middle term "acidic liquids" that connects "lemon juice" to its predicate "turns blue litmus paper red." Lemon juice turns blue litmus paper red *because it is acidic*. Note that we are not making any claims about a particular lemon. We are mak-

How do we know that the premises of a syllogism are necessarily true?

If a syllogism is valid, then we know that if its premises are true, its conclusion must be true. But how do we know if its premises are true? One way to know that a premise is true is if it is true by definition. A premise is true by definition if the predicate of the premise is logically contained in its subject. A famous example of a categorical statement that is true by definition is "All bachelors are unmarried." We know this statement is true. In fact, we know that it is necessarily true, because bachelors are by definition unmarried men. Another way that we can know if the premises of a syllogism are necessarily true is if they are self-evident. For example, the axioms and common notions of Euclidean geometry are self-evident. These include principles such as the axiom that a straight line may be drawn between any two points and the common notion that the whole is greater than the part. These principles are so appealing to our *intellectual intuition* (in Greek, *nous*) that it is enough just to understand their meaning to be convinced of their truth. It is not possible to provide a logical deduction of these principles, but instead they serve as premises in logical deductions that demonstrate less intuitively obvious truths. In this respect, they serve as *first principles*, or in Greek, *archai* (ἀρχαί), the plural of *arche* (ἀρχή). But not all self-evident truths are mathematical. According to Aristotle, there are also self-evident truths about ontology, theology, and the changing things of the physical world.

ing a claim about lemon juice in general because we can only demonstrate attributes of a species or kind, not of particular things.

According to Aristotle, how can we discover self-evident truths?

In the *Topics*, one of the books in Aristotle's *Organon*, Aristotle provides several techniques and strategies of dialectical reasoning that we can use to discover the self-evident truths that we will need to construct demonstrations of necessary and universal truths. Unlike demonstrations, which must begin with necessary truths, dialectical reasoning begins with reputable opinions (*doxa,* δόξα). According to Aristotle, an opinion is reputable and worthy of serious consideration if it is held by everybody, most people, all of the wise, most of the wise, or the most wise. Though these opinions are reputable, they are not necessarily true, and they may be false. *Doxa* include perceptions and experiences of particular things—in other words, what we call in modern science "observations."

Dialectics may be either inductive or critical and deductive. Critical deductive reasoning draws out the logical consequences of our opinions and reveals the ambiguities, equivocations, and logical contradictions lurking within them. Critical deductive reasoning is a powerful tool for developing a more clear and consistent set of beliefs. Starting from a multitude of opinions and observations about particular things, inductive reasoning proceeds up towards self-evident first principles from which many facts or true statements may in turn be deduced. Thus, Aristotle generally began his studies by examining a multitude of opinions and observations on any given subject. He winnowed out the ambiguities, double meanings, and logical contradictions, and by way of inductive reasoning he discovered those self-evident first principles (*archai*) that are both intuitively appealing and have the greatest power to explain a multitude of facts. The first principles that Aristotle seeks to provide a foundation for his demonstrations generally take the form of a universal affirmation that defines a form or species.

According to Aristotle, how can a form or species be defined?

To define a form or species, one must identify the genus to which the species being defined belongs and those attributes that differentiate it (the *differentia*) from other species of that genus. For example, Aristotle defines humans as rational animals. "Animals" is the genus to which "humans" belong and "rational" is the attribute that differentiates them from other species of animals.

How can a valid syllogism be made into a demonstration?

Consider our earlier example of a valid syllogism that explained why lemon juice turns blue litmus paper red:

- Minor Premise: All lemon juice is acidic.
- Major Premise: All acidic liquids turn blue litmus paper red.
- Conclusion: All lemon juice turns blue litmus paper red.

This argument is not yet a demonstration because its premises are not necessarily true. To make this argument a demonstration, we can either show how one or both of its premises are self-evident, or we can treat one or both of its premises as conclusions and derive them from premises that are self-evident. If we define acidic liquids as liquids that turn blue litmus paper red, then the major premise would be true by definition. However, in that case, the minor premise would be the same as the conclusion, and we would have explained nothing we didn't already know. Instead, we can use a definition of acids provided by chemist Svante Arrhenius in 1884: an acid is a chemical (genus) that increases the concentration of H^+ ions in water (differentia). In that case, neither premise is true by definition. But each may be true by inductive reasoning, based on many observations of lemon juice in water and of acidic liquids that are exposed to blue litmus paper.

We may also be able to construct a valid syllogism or a series of valid syllogisms premised upon a definition of acids that explains why lemon juice is an acid and why acidic liquids turn blue litmus paper red. In choosing a definition of an acid, we must be careful to choose one that is intuitively appealing and that explains as many facts as possible. For example, Arrhenius's definition fails to explain certain facts about acids and bases, and for that reason in 1923, chemists Johannes Nicolaus Brønsted and Thomas Martin Lowry developed another definition of acids and bases. Brønsted and Lowry defined acids as chemicals that donate protons, and bases as chemicals that accept protons. This definition explained a broader range of facts about acids because some acids do not increase the concentration of H^+ in water but do donate protons. Thus, the Brønsted-Lowry definition of an acid has stronger explanatory power than the Arrhenius definition.

According to Aristotle, how do self-evident first principles emerge from inductive reasoning?

In Chapter 19, Book II, of the *Posterior Analytics*, another work in the *Organon*, Aristotle says that deductive reasoning cannot establish the self-evident first principles that are the ultimate foundations of deductive reasoning. For that we must employ inductive reasoning. But how can that be? According to the modern conception of inductive reasoning that dates back to eighteenth-century philosopher David Hume, inductive reasoning can provide us only with explanations that are more or less likely, not with necessary and universal truth. The answer is that Aristotle's conception of inductive reasoning is different from the modern one. According to Aristotle, humans have the capacity to remember a series of sense-perceptions, and out of frequently repeated memories of the same thing, a universal concept (a "form") emerges that unites those sense-perceptions and memories into one single experience.

Aristotle uses the allegory of a rout in battle to explain this process. He says that the emergence of a unifying concept out of the memories of many sense-perceptions is "like a rout in battle stopped by first one man making a stand and then another, until the original formation has been restored." Out of a chaotic multitude, a unified force emerges as each man makes a stand. Out of a cacophony of sense-perceptions, as each

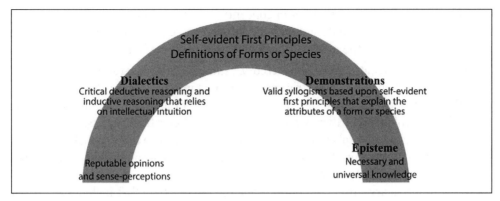

Self-evident First Principles
Definitions of Forms or Species

Dialectics
Critical deductive reasoning and
inductive reasoning that relies
on intellectual intuition

Demonstrations
Valid syllogisms based upon self-evident
first principles that explain the
attributes of a form or species

Episteme
Necessary and
universal knowledge

Reputable opinions
and sense-perceptions

Aristotle's Arc of Knowledge.

ARISTOTLE AND THE AGE OF ALEXANDER THE GREAT

sense-perception comes before us, a pattern emerges that unifies the chaotic multitude under a single form. The unifying form is not just a mental construct that is arbitrarily imposed upon the multitude of our sense-perceptions.

Aristotle is an epistemological optimist. He believes that the human soul has the capacity to grasp reality as it is. The unifying form is really there, in the world of things that we perceive with our senses. In fact, according to Aristotle, the forms exist only in particular things, not independently on their own as Plato believed, and it is only our perceptions of particular things that give us knowledge of them. "When one of a number of logically identical particulars has made a stand, the earliest universal is present in the soul: for though the act of sense-perception is of the particular, its content is universal— is man, for example, not the man Callias. A fresh stand is made among these rudimentary universals, and the process does not cease until the indivisible concepts, the true universals, are established: e.g. such and such a species of animal is a step towards the genus animal, which by the same process is a step towards a further generalization." "The soul," Aristotle says, "is so constituted as to be capable of this process." But it is not our soul's capacity for deductive or discursive reasoning that enables us to grasp the forms. It is our capacity for intellectual intuition (*nous*), which comes to us in a flash of insight.

ARISTOTLE'S THEORY OF THE COSMOS

What was Aristotle's cosmology?

Aristotle's cosmology was the generally accepted worldview until the sixteenth century when the Copernican revolution placed the sun at the center of the universe. According to Aristotle, the Earth is at the center of the universe and does not move. Surrounding the Earth are a series of concentric spheres that rotate around it. The atmosphere is sandwiched between the Earth and the innermost sphere, which is known as the lunar sphere because it is associated with the orbit of the Moon around the Earth.

Aristotle says that the exact number of concentric spheres is a problem for astronomy to solve, and he claims in different places that there are either forty-seven or fifty-five spheres responsible for the movement of the planets around the Earth.

The "planets" included the Moon, Mercury, Venus, the Sun, Mars, Jupiter, and Saturn, and they were attached to concentric spheres located in that order at greater distances from the Earth. More than one sphere was necessary to explain the irregular movement of the planets, which is why there were so many more spheres than planets. But only one sphere was necessary to explain the movement of the stars since they rotated around the Earth in perfect circular orbits. That sphere was the outermost sphere of the cosmos beyond which nothing exists—not even space or time—except the unmoved mover. Everything in the sublunary world (the world inside the lunar sphere that includes the Earth and its atmosphere) is composed of four elements: earth, air, fire, and water. Everything in the lunar sphere and beyond is composed of a special element called "ether." The four sublunary elements and everything that is composed of them are subject to change and destruction. Ether and everything that is composed of it is unchanging and eternal.

Each of the forty-seven or fifty-five planetary spheres and the stellar sphere are moved by a divine intellect that is associated with it. Beyond the outermost sphere is the prime and unmoved mover who is pure intellect and exists in neither space nor time. Aristotle calls the prime mover "the god" (*ho theos*). The prime mover is the first cause of all motion and change and the greatest good, the ultimate object of desire. But the prime mover does not itself move, because if it did, another mover would be required to explain its movement, leading to an infinite regress, which Aristotle says is impossible. Therefore, the prime mover cannot cause the celestial spheres and their divine intellects to rotate by mechanical force, because the use of mechanical force requires the causal agent to move. Instead, the prime mover causes the celestial spheres and their divine intellects to move as an object of love and desire, just as a lover is moved by their beloved's beauty.

The prime mover is what Aristotle calls the "final cause" of celestial motion. It is because they love the prime mover that the celestial spheres and their divine intellects imitate the prime mover by rotating eternally in perfect circles. Rotating in a circle around a fixed center is the closest thing to not moving at all since the same movement is eternally repeated. However, the rotation of the solar sphere around the Earth is what Aristotle calls the "efficient

The above figure from Peter Apian's Cosmographia (1524) is an illustration of the Ptolemaic system, which was based upon Aristotle's geocentric cosmology. Earth is at the center of the universe, surrounded by air and above air is fire. The innermost celestial sphere is the lunar sphere, followed by Mercury, Venus, the Sun, Mars, Jupiter, and Saturn. The outermost sphere is that of the stars.

cause" of the change of seasons, which in turn is the efficient cause of all change and motion in the sublunary world. But the movement of sublunary objects is irregular and finite, not eternal like the movement of the celestial spheres and bodies.

According to Aristotle, what are the elements of the universe?

To the four basic elements that the Pre-Socratic philosopher Empedocles identified, Aristotle added a fifth. Aristotle believed that the celestial bodies could not be composed of earth, water, air, or fire because those elements are subject to change. Since the celestial bodies are eternal, they must be composed of a different kind of element

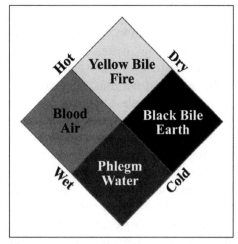

Aristotle associated the four elements of the universe with the four humors of black bile, yellow bile, phlegm, and blood.

that is not subject to change, which Aristotle called *ether*. Earth, water, air, and fire are the basic elements of the sublunary world only. Like Hippocrates before him and Galen long after, Aristotle associated the four humors of the body—black bile, phlegm, blood, and yellow bile—with the four elements. It is not possible to reduce any of these elements to more basic elements. However, each of the sublunary elements has two haptic qualities.

What are the haptic qualities of the elements?

Sublunary elements have haptic qualities (which can be sensed by touch) because they can be both seen and touched. Ether does not have haptic qualities because celestial bodies can be seen but not touched. According to Aristotle, there are two pairs of contradictory haptic qualities. Since it is not possible for anything to possess contradictory qualities at the same time and in the same way, each of the four sublunary elements has only one of each pair of haptic qualities. That results in four possible combinations of haptic qualities. Earth is dry and cold. Water is cold and wet. Air is wet and hot. Fire is hot and dry.

Are the basic sublunary elements immutable?

No, they are not. It is possible for each of the elements to be transformed into another element by changing one of its haptic qualities. Water can be changed into air by heating it up and replacing its haptic quality of cold with hot. Air can change into fire by drying it out so that its haptic quality of wet is replaced by dry. Fire can be changed into earth by cooling it down and replacing its haptic quality of hot with cold. Each of these transformations is reversible. For example, air can be changed into water. But only one haptic quality can be changed at a time, so it is not possible to directly transform water into fire or air into earth.

149

What are the basic elements made of?

According to Aristotle, each of the elements is made of prime matter. Aristotle postulated the existence of prime matter because he believed that nothing can change into something else unless there is something that stays the same across the change. If nothing stayed the same, we could not say that one element had changed into another but that one element perished and the other came into being out of nothing. And that, Aristotle believed, was impossible. When the sublunary elements change into one another by changing their haptic qualities, the prime matter of which they are made remains the same. The transforma-

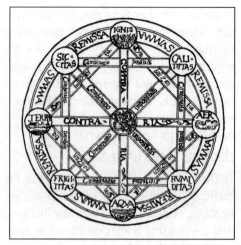

Leibniz represented the universe in this diagram as combinations of Aristotle's four elements.

tion of one element into another is therefore a process by which prime matter takes on different forms but does not itself change. However, prime matter is nothing besides the potential to take on form. By itself, it has no form and does not actually exist.

What are the three types of primary substances or beings in Aristotle's universe?

The three types of primary substances or beings are (1) sublunary things that can be both seen and touched; (2) celestial bodies that can be seen but not touched and the forty-eight or fifty-six divine intellects that animate them; and (3) the prime mover who is pure active intellect. Physics is the study of sublunary things. Astronomy is the study of celestial bodies. Theology is the study of the prime mover. The study of the divine intellects can be found in both astronomy and theology—in astronomy insofar as they animate the celestial bodies, and in theology insofar as they are divine. During the Middle Ages, Aristotle's divine intellects were believed to be angels and the prime mover was understood to be God. However, Aristotle's prime mover is an impersonal intellect and lacks many features of the God of the Abrahamic religions.

ARISTOTLE'S THEORY OF CHANGE
AND THE FOUR CAUSES

What types of change are there, according to Aristotle?

Aristotle says there are four types of change, but only sublunary things can change in all four ways. Sublunary things can change with respect to substance, quality, quantity, and place. Change with respect to substance is generation and destruction, as when something comes to be or ceases to be. Change with respect to quality is a change of attributes, such as the haptic qualities or colors. For example, when a tomato ripens, it changes color from green to red. Change with respect to quantity is a change in size, number, or duration, as when a man gains weight or his hair grows long. Change with respect to place is motion, as when a woman walks from one corner of the room to the other. Celestial bodies change only with respect to place. In other words, the only way that they can change is to move from one place to another. The celestial spheres, too, change only with respect to place. But they move only in the simplest way possible, which is to rotate in perfect circles around a fixed center. The prime mover does not change in any way at all.

What are Aristotle's four "causes" or types of explanation?

Although the Greek word *aitia* (αἰτία) is often translated as "cause," Aristotle's use of the word is better understood as "causal explanation," or simply as "explanation," because his conception of "causality" is closer to "explanation" than it is to the modern concept of causality. The modern concept of causality is that of a necessary temporal sequence of events. If I start to swing a bat at time t_1, at some later point in time, t_2, the bat will strike the ball, causing it to subsequently fly over the fence at time t_3. That is not what Aristotle meant by *aitia*.

Aristotle's four causes are four ways to explain physical substances and their attributes. Since physical substances are by their nature agents of change and subject to change, in order to explain physical substances and their attributes, the four causes must explain change. Hence, the four causes are designed to answer four questions about physical substances and change. The "formal cause" answers the question "What kind of thing is produced?" The "material cause" answers the question "What is it made of?" The "efficient cause" or "causal agent" answers the question "Who or what made it?" And the "final cause" answers the question "To what end or purpose?" These four causes are often explained using examples taken from the work of artisans and craftsmen and the things they produce.

For example, consider a carpenter who builds a house out of wood. The formal cause is what kind of thing the carpenter is building: a house. The material cause is what the house is made of: wood. In fact, the ancient Greek word for matter was *hyle* (ὕλη), which originally referred to wood, timber, trees, or forest. The efficient cause or causal agent is the carpenter. The end or purpose of the carpenter's work is the particular house that the carpenter has finished building. The carpenter builds the house by imposing the form of a house onto wood material. The carpenter begins with matter (the wood material) and ends with a composite of the original matter and the form of a house (the finished wood house). All physical substances are a composite of form and matter. It is the form of a house that makes the finished house a house, and the matter of the house that makes it this particular house.

Now consider a natural substance such as an acorn. The acorn is the seed of an oak tree that has what Aristotle calls the active potential or power to grow into an oak tree itself. Therefore, the acorn already has within itself the form of a fully grown oak tree and the power to impose that form upon itself. Whereas the agent cause of artificial processes such as building a house exist outside the thing being formed, the agent cause of natural processes such as the growth of an acorn into an oak tree exist within the thing being formed. According to Aristotle, all natural substances have within themselves an internal principle of change that is their "nature." An acorn grows into an oak tree but not a cedar because it is the nature of an acorn to grow into an oak tree. The acorn is the agent cause of the growth of the acorn into an oak tree. It contains within itself the form of an oak tree, but until it has imposed that form upon itself, it will not have grown into an oak tree. The acorn is also the material cause of the oak tree. It is the matter (the beginning of the process) that has what Aristotle calls the passive potential to be formed into a particular oak tree (the end of the process).

How must the four causes be used in demonstrations to explain the attributes of a form or species of physical things?

According to Aristotle, an explanation must have the logical form of a sound and valid syllogism. But in the case of physical substances and their changes, a complete and adequate explanation must also answer these four questions: "What kind of thing is pro-

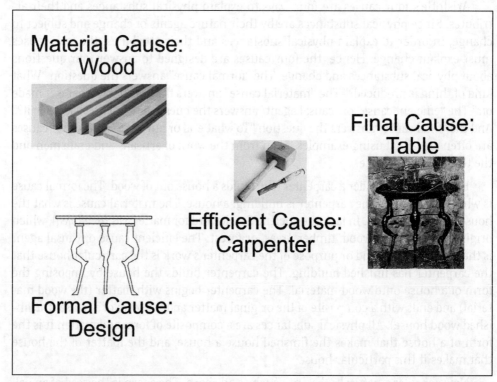

The above illustration shows how a table is the result of Aristotle's four causes: material cause, formal cause, efficient cause, and final cause.

duced?" (the "formal cause"); "What is it made of?" (the "material cause"); "Who or what made it?" (the "efficient cause" or "agent cause"); and "To what end or purpose?" (the "final cause"). This further requirement placed upon explanations is not based on logical considerations alone but on Aristotle's theory of physical substances and change, which is a part of his theory of things or beings (his "ontology"). Aristotle's discussion of physical things and change is not found in the *Organon*, the collection of his works devoted to logic, but in the *Physics* and in the *Metaphysics*. To see how the four causes can be used in a syllogism, let's look again at the following syllogism that explains why lemon juice turns blue litmus paper red:

- Minor Premise: All lemon juice is acidic.
- Major Premise: All acidic liquids turn blue litmus paper red.
- Conclusion: All lemon juice turns blue litmus paper red.

According to this argument, lemon juice turns blue litmus paper red because lemon juice is acidic, and all acidic liquids turn blue litmus paper red. All four causes are employed in this argument, making it a complete and adequate explanation. The material cause (the "matter") is litmus paper. The efficient cause (the agent of change) is lemon juice. The formal cause (the "form" imposed upon the matter) is the color red. The final cause (the end or result of the process) is red litmus paper (a composite of form and matter).

Why did Zeno of Elea believe that motion was impossible?

Zeno was a student and colleague of Parmenides who constructed the famous paradoxes that bear his name. The purpose of Zeno's paradoxes was to prove that Parmenides was

Why did Parmenides of Elea believe that change does not exist?

Parmenides points out that whenever we think, we are thinking about something that exists. We cannot think about what does not exist, because to think about what does not exist would be to think about nothing at all. But we cannot think about nothing at all, because to think about nothing at all would be to not think. Therefore, Parmenides concludes, "thought and being (what is, what exists) are the same." But to think about change would be to think about something that does not exist, since if something entirely new comes to be, then it did not exist before. And the same holds true if it is only an attribute of something that changes, for in that case, too, an attribute that now exists did not exist before, or an attribute that does not now exist, existed before. In either case, to think about change is to think about what does not exist, which is impossible. In making his case against change, Parmenides is relying on deductive reasoning, which he calls *logos*. He counsels us not to listen to common opinion (*doxa*) or even to what our senses appear to tell us, but to always listen to *logos* instead.

right that reality is one and unchanging. One typical paradox explains that it is impossible to even begin a race because in order to finish the race, it is necessary to reach half the distance to the finish; but in order to reach half the distance to the finish, it is necessary to reach one quarter of the distance; but in order to reach one quarter of the distance, it is necessary to reach one eighth of the distance; and so on, ad infinitum. Since it is impossible to traverse an infinite number of finite intervals in a finite amount of time, it is impossible to move.

How did Aristotle's theory of change solve the problems raised by Parmenides and Zeno?

Aristotle solved the problems raised by Parmenides and Zeno by conceiving of change in terms of the concepts of actuality (*energeia*, ἐνέργεια) and potentiality (*dunamis*, δύναμιζ). Whereas Parmenides and Zeno conceived of change as a series of actual events in time, Aristotle conceived of change as the actualization of what potentially existed before the change occurred. With this brilliant new way of conceiving of change, Aristotle undercut the logic of Parmenides and Zeno's arguments against change.

So, for example, whereas Parmenides argues that change is not possible because it requires us to think about something that does not exist, and we can only think about what actually exists, Aristotle argues that change does not require us to think about what does not exist, but about what potentially exists. Aristotle agrees with Parmenides and Zeno that something cannot come to be out of nothing. But Aristotle does not conclude that change is therefore impossible. Instead, he concludes that something comes to be out of something that has the potential to become that thing. Aristotle equated potential with the matter or material cause of the change, and he equated actuality with the formal cause or form of the change.

For example, consider a rough-hewn piece of marble recently taken from the quarry. A sculptor imposes the form of Zeus onto this piece of marble, changing it into a statue

What is the difference between active potential and passive potential?

Active potential is potency or power. It is the potential of something to take action upon and effect something else. *Passive potential* or receptivity is the potential to have something done to oneself: to receive something from or to be affected by an active causal agent. For example, in our litmus paper example, lemon juice has the active potential to turn blue litmus paper red, whereas blue litmus paper has the passive potential to be turned red by acidic liquids. When lemon juice is placed in contact with blue litmus paper, the active potential of lemon juice to turn blue litmus paper red, and the passive potential of blue litmus paper to be turned red by lemon juice, are both simultaneously actualized, and the blue litmus paper turns red.

of Zeus. In this case, the rough-hewn piece of marble is the material cause of the change of the marble into a statue of Zeus. But it is also fair to say that the rough-hewn piece of marble was potentially a statue of Zeus. Not all things have the same potential. A body of water does not have the potential to be sculpted into a statue of Zeus (unless it is frozen and the sculptor creates an ice sculpture). But the sculptor did not create the statue out of nothing. The sculptor merely actualized the potential already contained within the marble to become a statue of Zeus. In the case of Zeno's paradoxes, they almost all depend on a conception of a continuum as an infinite series of finite intervals. For example, in the case of the racetrack paradox, Zeno assumes that the racetrack cannot be traversed because it is an infinite series of finite intervals. But according to Aristotle, the racetrack is not actually divided into an infinite series of finite intervals. The racetrack is only potentially divided, and it can be divided as many times as we like, but it cannot actually be divided an infinite number of times.

What is the nature of a thing?

The nature (*physis*) of a thing is an internal principle (*arche*) of change or motion. For example, it is the nature of heavy objects made of the element of earth to fall towards the center of the earth. Each of the four elements seeks its natural level. If nothing external to them interfered with their motion, earth would settle to the bottom of the earth, with water at the next level above, followed by air, and then by fire, whose nature it is to rise. When something moves or changes according to its nature, it is not the subject of an external causal agent. Living things contain their own internal causal agent and are capable of initiating action themselves. The elements are not capable of initiating action, but they do resist movement that is contrary to their nature. When change or movement occurs in accordance with the nature of a thing, the same thing is both active agent and passive recipient.

What is actuality?

The English word "actuality" is used to translate two Greek words that Aristotle uses interchangeably: *energeia* (ἐνέργεια) and *entelechia* (ἐντελέχεια). The Greek word *energeia* is a noun that means "an act, a deed, or a work." This definition of *energeia* is in keeping with Aristotle's theory of substance or of what in general it means to be a thing: to be a thing is to act, to do something, to "work." Even static things that do not change are the end result of a change and are working to maintain their stasis by means of their actions. The word *entelechia* is a noun derived from the root word *telos* (τέλος), which means end, purpose, or goal, and the root word *exein* (ἔχειν), which means "to have, hold, or keep." The word *entelechia,* therefore, means "an end, purpose, or goal that is actively held or kept." In other words, an *entelechia* is an act, a deed, or a work that maintains an end, purpose, or goal. To be a thing is to actively work to achieve and maintain a final cause, which is its *telos.* The agent of a thing's action is its efficient cause. The type of thing it is working to achieve or maintain is its formal cause.

When a thing is part of a larger whole, its *telos* is its *function* (*ergon*) within the larger whole. For example, the function of the heart is to pump blood to the rest of the body. If the heart is cut out of the body, it ceases to be a heart, because it no longer functions to pump blood and has lost its defining *telos*. Not all ends are static states. An end can be an ongoing activity such as pumping blood or walking or seeing. For example, the function of the eye is the activity of seeing.

How is Aristotle's universe organized hierarchically in terms of form and matter?

Form and matter are relative terms. What is form at one level of Aristotle's universe is matter at another. For example, bricks are made of clay that has been fired in an oven. In this process, clay is the matter and bricks are the form. When we impress the form of bricks onto a particular piece of clay, we get this particular brick, which is a composite of form and matter. But we can take those bricks and build a house with them. In this process, the bricks are the matter and a house is the form. The end or purpose of the process of building a house is this particular house. The house becomes a home when someone inhabits it and makes it their home. In this process the house is the matter and the form is a home. The end or purpose of the process is to make this house a home. And

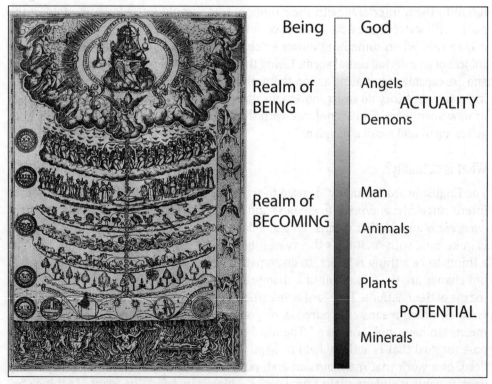

Aristotle's hierarchical theory of being is an important source of the medieval Christian idea of the Great Chain of Being, as seen in the diagram at left from Rhetorica Christiana by Fray Diego de Valades (1579). At right is an easier-to-follow diagram of the hierarchy.

so on. We can go on indefinitely, asking what the purpose of the home is, and what the purpose of the purpose of the home is, and so on. The end of each process in the hierarchy serves as matter for the purpose at the next higher level.

But Aristotle hates infinite series. There must be a finite limit to the hierarchy, a point at which we can go no higher. And that point is the prime mover, which Aristotle called *ho theos*, the god, and whom the medieval philosophers understood to be the God of Abraham. The prime mover is the ultimate purpose and highest good of the universe. In Cicero's Latin, Aristotle's god is the *summum bonum*. The prime mover does not serve as matter to any higher purpose because there is no higher purpose. The prime mover is pure form with no material component. The prime mover exists for itself, as its own purpose. As pure form, it cannot change because it has no untapped potential to actualize. There is nothing further for it to achieve, nothing more for it to be. It is already all it can be; indeed, it is all that can be, period. It is fully actualized. The analysis can proceed in the opposite direction. We can ask what the clay that we made the bricks out of is made of. The clay was made out of earth. Earth is one of the elements. And the elements are made out of prime matter. Just as the prime mover is pure form and is fully actualized, prime matter is pure matter without any form. It is pure potential that has not been actualized at all. In itself, it is nothing.

ARISTOTLE'S THEORY OF THE SOUL

What is the form of life?

The form of something is that which defines what it is. Since Aristotle defines life in terms of the power to perform biological functions, the form of life is the power to perform biological functions. A mere assemblage of material parts is not alive unless it has the power to perform biological functions. An eye, for example, is not alive unless it has the power to see. A stomach is not alive unless it has the power to digest food. Life is process, and the soul is the form of that process. Therefore, the soul, as the form of life, is nothing more and nothing less than the power to perform the biological functions of a living being, and the nature of a living thing is its soul.

What is a function?

A function (*érgon*, ἔργον) of something is what it is for, both its end or purpose (*telos*) and the deed, work, or activity involved in exercising that function. For example, the function of a knife is to cut. The function of a human being is to reason.

What is the soul of a plant?

The soul of a plant is its form, and its form is the power to perform the biological functions of a plant. The essential biological functions of a plant are nutrition, growth, and reproduction. Therefore, the soul of a plant is essentially the powers of nutrition, growth,

157

and reproduction. Now, since a thing or substance like a plant is a composite of form and matter, the soul and body of a plant, as form and matter, are components of a single entity. It is no more possible to separate the soul from the body of a plant than it is to separate the form of a seal from the wax upon which it is impressed. It is not possible to separate the soul of a plant from its body because it is not possible to separate the powers of a plant from its body. The powers of a plant exist only as powers of its body.

For example, the power of roots to draw water up from the ground cannot exist by itself apart from the roots which it is a power of. Thus, Aristotle avoids dualism. But he also avoids reductive materialism, because matter alone does not make something a living being. As the form of a living plant, it is the soul that gives the body of a plant the power to perform the functions of nutrition, growth, and reproduction. It is the soul that brings the body of the plant to life. When the soul of a plant is extinguished, all that's left is lifeless matter. Nor does all matter have the passive potential to receive the form of a living plant. A stone, for example, does not have the passive potential to receive the form of a living plant. Only organic matter that is composed of organs (such as roots, branches, and leaves) that are organized in an appropriate way (leaves are attached to branches, not to roots) has the passive potential to acquire the power to perform the biological functions of a living plant. The soul of a plant is, therefore, at the same time, the formal cause of the life of the plant, the efficient cause that impresses that form upon its body, and, as the power to perform the functions of a living plant, its end or purpose.

How do the Greek and Latin words for "soul" help us to understand Aristotle's conception of the soul?

The soul is the form of life and the power to perform the functions of a living being. The soul, then, is not a thing but a power that gives a body life. The ancient Greek word for soul was *psyche*, which was derived from a closely related word meaning "to breathe."

Therefore, the ancient Greek word for soul referred to a biological function that gave a body life. The Latin word for soul was *anima,* from which we get our words *animate* and *animator*, and according to Aristotle, the soul is an animator, a power that animates the body.

What is the soul of an animal?

The soul of an animal is the form of a living body that is itself composed of form and matter. Thus, the soul of an animal is the form of a form of matter. The living body of an animal has the same essential form as a plant—the powers of nutrition, growth, and reproduction—and for that reason it is known as the *vegetative soul*. The top-level form of an animal is the

Do animals like your pet dog have a soul? According to Aristotle, an animal has two souls: a vegetative soul and a sensitive soul.

power to perform the essential biological functions of an animal, which are the powers of sensation, appetite, and movement. The powers of sensation enable an animal to sense *pain* and *pleasure,* while an appetite for pleasure produces *desire.* The top-level form of an animal is known as the *sensitive soul.* Therefore, an animal has two souls: a vegetative soul and a sensitive soul.

Imagine what happens to an animal when it goes into a coma. It becomes a "vegetable," unable to move or sense anything. An animal can stay alive without a sensitive soul, but it will die if it loses its vegetative soul. The sensitive soul depends for its existence on the life of its body, since it is the form of that body. If the body dies, the sensitive soul ceases to exist. Just as a vegetative soul cannot exist without the matter of which it is the form, a sensitive soul cannot exist without the composite whole of a vegetative soul and matter, of which it is the form. For example, the powers of sensation cannot exist without living sense organs. In that sense, the sensitive soul is a more complex and higher level of functioning than the vegetative soul upon which it depends. All the functions of an animal's soul work together to serve the needs (the ends or purposes) of the whole animal: appetite and desire motivate an animal to move toward objects of sensation that may nourish it or enable it to reproduce.

What is the soul of a human being?

In Aristotle's philosophy, a human being is defined as a rational animal. This means that a human being is an animal with the form of rationality that differentiates it from other animals who are not rational. As an animal, a human being possesses both a sensitive soul and a vegetative soul. But as a rational animal, a human being also possesses the form of rationality, which is known as the *rational soul*. The rational soul is the mind or intellect—in Greek, *nous* (νοῦς). Like the vegetative and sensitive souls, the rational soul is a kind of power—in this case, the power to think and reason. Thus, a human being has three souls: the vegetative soul, the sensitive soul, and the rational soul.

Just as the vegetative soul and the sensitive soul work together to serve the needs of the whole animal, all three souls work together to serve the needs of a human being. The rational soul depends on sensation, without which there would be no source of knowledge. But thinking cannot be reduced to sensation. Sensation presents us with a series of particulars: this round-shaped splash of green, this burning sensation on my tongue, etc. Non-rational animals are incapable of going beyond particular sense-perceptions. But with the power of rational thought (*logos*), humans are able to remember a series of sense-perceptions and hold them in their imagination, and out of frequently repeated memories of the same thing they are able to conceive a universal concept (a form in the mind) that unites those sensations into one single experience. In other words, rational thought enables human beings to abstract universal forms out of particular sense-perceptions.

From the experience of many men, for example, the universal concept of man emerges. The basic function of the human mind, therefore, is to conceive universal forms. Only after these forms have been conceived by the mind can it then perform deductive, analytical reasoning upon them. Finally, it is only because humans have the unique capacity for rational thought that they can express those thoughts in declarative sentences of the form "*S* is *P*." That's why the Greek word *logos* means both rational thought and the expression of those thoughts in declarative sentences (sentences that are true or false and, if true, may convey knowledge). The power to conceive universal concepts precedes both deductive reasoning and linguistic expression.

What are the two parts of the mind or intellect?

According to Aristotle, the human mind is able to receive the forms, such as the form "man," from particular things, such as Socrates and Callias. In particular things, the forms exist in matter, as forms *of* matter. But when the mind receives a form from a particular thing, it does not also receive the matter of that thing. If the mind received the matter as well as the form, it would receive the particular thing itself. It would not be the form of man that entered the mind but the particular man Callias, which is absurd. But the mind is not just a passive vessel that receives the forms from particular things that are perceived by the senses. Just as the eye requires light to receive a visual image, the mind requires an active power to receive concepts. Aristotle called this active power the *active intellect* or *agent intellect*. It is the power to actively think and reason. Aristotle called the passive potential to receive the forms the *passive intellect*.

The process of conceiving universal concepts is not a simple process of impressing the forms found in particular things onto the mind. The mind must actively think about particular things in order to abstract the universal forms from them, since no particular thing is the same as its form. The number three, for example, can be found in three apples, three oranges, and three marbles, but it is not the same as any of these. To form the concept of the number three, the mind must actively sift through many particular examples of three things and identify the pattern that is common to them all. This requires an act of conceptualization performed by the agent intellect, not merely passive receptivity to the forms by the passive intellect.

What is the passive intellect?

The passive intellect is the capacity of the rational soul to receive the forms. But unlike vision, which is the power of the eye to receive visual forms, Aristotle denies that the passive intellect is the power of any organ of the body, such as the brain, to receive the forms. The passive intellect is not the form of the body or any of its organs because the passive intellect has the potential to receive any form, and the body and its organs do not. Sense organs are limited as to what forms they can receive because they themselves have form. For example, because an eye has the form of an eye and not an ear or a Geiger detector, it can only sense light and color, not sound or radiation. But the passive intellect does not have any form. It is nothing but the *potential* to receive form. It is not prime matter, but it is like prime matter insofar as it is pure potential without any actual form itself. It is therefore not limited as to what forms it can receive. It is like a completely blank slate that anything can be drawn upon. Because it has the potential to receive any form, it is subject to change as different forms are impressed upon it by the agent intellect. These changes of content in the passive intellect are what we experience as discursive reasoning, which is reasoning from one concept to another in a temporal sequence.

What is the active intellect?

The active intellect is the very *act* of thinking (*noesis*) itself, apart from the *content* of thought (*noema*, νόημα) or the series of forms that are contained in the passive intellect. The type of thinking referred to here is not the discursive reasoning that takes place in the passive intellect, but intellectual insight or intuition. As agent cause, the active intellect has the power to produce concepts by impressing forms upon the passive intellect. It is the opposite of the passive intellect, which is pure potential without any actual form itself. The active intellect is pure act, fully actualized, with no potential to be anything other than what it already is. Because matter is the potential to change, and the active intellect has no potential to change, the active intellect is pure form without any matter. This means that the active intellect is not only lacking any potential for change but that it is timeless. An act of thinking does not occur in time. It has no duration in time and is not preceded or followed in time by other acts of thinking.

Since no act of thinking can be distinguished as an *act* from any other act of thinking, there is only one act of thinking. However, the active intellect is a special kind of form because it is the agent by which all forms may be conceptualized. The active intellect is the form of forms or, more precisely, the form of the conceptualization of forms. It exists by itself on a higher ontological plane than the ordinary forms found in the passive intellect. The active intellect is similar to Plato's form of the Good, which is also the form of forms and exists on a higher ontological plane by itself. Just as Plato says that the Good is like the Sun whose light makes things grow (makes things "be") and be seen (be known), Aristotle says that the active intellect is like light that makes colors be seen. The things that Plato's Sun makes seen and the colors that Aristotle's light makes seen are the forms that Aristotle's active intellect makes known by impressing them upon the passive intellect.

Can the active intellect be known as a concept by the passive intellect?

Whether the active intellect can impress its own form onto the passive intellect and be known as a concept just like ordinary forms is an open question. Some ancient commentators believed that it could, whereas others believed that the active intellect, as God or the Good, was ultimately "beyond being" and ineffable. In any case, on its own ontological plane, there is only one form, the form of the active intellect, and it is not possible to differentiate it from any other form. On its own ontological plane, the active intellect is an indeterminate form, whereas the forms that reside in the passive intellect may be differentiated from one another and are therefore determinate. This would seem to preclude the possibility of conceptual knowledge of the active intellect.

Is the active intellect God?

This is a question that dogged both Christian and Islamic medieval interpreters of Aristotle for centuries. Some believed that since the active intellect has no determinate form to distinguish it from any other active intellect, there could only be one active intellect, and that active intellect is God, the prime and unmoved mover. Others could not reconcile their religious beliefs with the idea that a part of the human soul was identical to God. In any case, just as the passive intellect resembles prime matter, the active intellect resembles God, because God is an active intellect. In fact, God is nothing but an active intellect.

God does not have a material body, nor does God have a vegetative soul, a sensitive soul, or a passive intellect. Lacking a material substrate, God is pure form, eternal and timeless. Lacking a passive intellect, there is no content to God's thought except the act of thought itself. Hence, Aristotle declares that God is thought thinking thought. It is fitting, Aristotle

When it comes to the search for an immortal soul, do not look to the passive intellect, which only stores what is transient and temporary. According to Aristotle, we come closest to the divine by using our active intellect.

Is the rational soul immortal?

The passive intellect is not immortal because, as pure potential, it is subject to change. The active intellect does not change, but it has no content. So the rational soul is not immortal in the sense that we wish to be immortal, because the active intellect has no personal content, nothing that would make it "me."

says, that God should be thought thinking thought because thought is the noblest activity, the least onerous, and the most leisurely, because it is the only activity that an agent can engage in without moving. It is its own end, and it is contingent on nothing beyond itself. It is the ultimate "that for the sake of which." In all these ways, Aristotle's God resembles a mystic deeply engaged in contemplation with no determinate (finite, bounded, or contingent) object of consciousness.

ARISTOTLE'S ETHICS

What is Aristotelian ethics, and how does it differ from theory?

Aristotelian ethics is the study of social virtue and, more generally, excellence (*arête*) in personal character and in the actions that flow from our character. Aristotelian ethics is not a theoretical field of study but a practical one, insofar as we do not study ethics only for the sake of knowledge but to improve our character and the quality of our actions—in Aristotle's words, we study ethics "to become good." To do that we must, in addition to acquiring knowledge of universal principles, as we do in theoretical fields of study, make good practical judgments about the particular situations within which we act. However, practical judgments about particular situations can never be necessary and certain ("apodictic") because we can never know particular things in the sense of "know" that Aristotle means by the Greek word *episteme*. This is just as true in theoretical fields of study as it is in practical fields such as ethics. In physics, for example, we never obtain epistemic knowledge of particular physical things but only of the kinds or species (the universal "forms") to which they belong (for example, we know that the species of lemon is necessarily acidic, but a particular lemon is subject to changing contingencies and may not be).

The difference between theoretical and practical fields of study such as ethics is not that there is something unknowable about ethical principles. We can acquire knowledge of ethical principles just as well as we can acquire knowledge of the laws of physics. The difference is that in ethics, we seek not only to know universal principles of conduct but also to act in particular situations that cannot be known epistemically. For example, we may know that it is good to act with courage, but we can never know with certainty whether we should stand and fight in this particular situation. The decision to stand and fight requires a practical judgment about this particular situation. Thus, to act ethically we must not only acquire knowledge of universal ethical principles but also make good practical judgments about when and how those principles apply to particular situations.

What is *phronesis*?

Phronesis (φρόνησις) is a key concept in Aristotle's ethics. The Greek word *phronesis* was traditionally translated into the Latin word *prudentia*, from which we get our English word *prudence*. But because prudence has come to mean cautiousness, which has little to do with the original meaning of *phronesis*, the word *phronesis* is better translated as practical wisdom. *Phronesis* is the virtue or excellence of character that enables a person to make

What, exactly, is wisdom? An ethical person must also understand when it is practical and prudent to act.

good practical judgments about when and how universal ethical principles apply to particular situations. Since all other practical virtues depend upon good practical judgments, and since *phronesis* is the virtue of making good practical judgments, *phronesis* is a fundamental virtue upon which all the practical virtues depend and without which they would not even be virtues.

What is a practical syllogism?

A practical syllogism is a syllogism whose major premise is a universal ethical principle, whose minor premise is a practical judgment about a particular situation, and whose conclusion is an imperative to act. According to Aristotle, practical reasoning always takes the form of a practical syllogism because its purpose is not universal knowledge but action. An example of a practical syllogism would be the following:

• Major Premise: All men should temper their appetites and eat moderately.
• Minor Premise: I am a man.
• Conclusion: I should temper my appetite and eat moderately.

A practical syllogism therefore applies a universal ethical principle to a particular situation.

What is the process of ethical reasoning?

The process of ethical reasoning is essentially the same as the process of theoretical reasoning except that ethical reasoning does not end with episteme but takes the additional step of constructing a practical syllogism whose conclusion is an imperative to act. Just as with theoretical reasoning, the process of ethical reasoning begins with the experience of particular things, either one's own experiences or the experiences of others, and with reputable opinions about those experiences. Ethical reasoning of this kind begins already in childhood when our character is being formed.

Children are taught ethical principles by their elders, whom they trust and assume to be wise. They are presented with characters in real life and in art, myths, fables, and legends, who model good ethical behavior based on sound ethical principles. They experience the consequences of their own actions and draw appropriate conclusions from them. As children mature, they develop more sophisticated cognitive skills. If they are fortunate, they learn how to practice dialectics. They don't take the ethical principles they learned as children at face value. They question them and ask if they are really true. They draw out the logical consequences of their beliefs and identify ambiguities and inconsistencies. They collect their experiences and by a process of inductive reasoning, they intuit the common pattern—the form—that holds them all together. Out of this process they arrive at self-evident first principles that serve to logically ground their ethical opinions. Building on this secure foundation, they can then employ the deductive logic of the syllogism to construct a complete system of ethical knowledge. Armed with this elaborate set of ethical principles, they need only employ their practical judgment to construct a practical syllogism whose conclusion directs them to act.

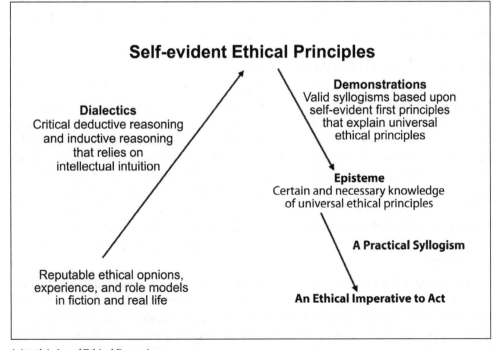

Aristotle's Arc of Ethical Reasoning.

What is virtue?

For Aristotle, virtue (*arête*) is more like strength and health than what we think of as something moral, because it is the power of a living being to function well. It is "good" only in the sense that it has the power to accomplish its end or purpose (*telos*), and unlike things that are moral, which may be moral without also being beautiful, what is virtuous in Aristotle's conception of the term is also by necessity beautiful because it has a well-ordered form. Under this conception of virtue, self-care can be virtuous, and so too can solitary thought, if it is done well. Indeed, anything that is done well is "virtuous." However, because humans are by nature social animals, most of the virtues are social virtues. And because humans generally do best within a well-governed *polis* or city-state, Aristotle regards the political virtues of citizenship and military service as second only to the intellectual virtues.

What is an intellectual virtue?

An intellectual virtue is a virtue or excellence (*arête*) of the rational soul—it is an act or activity (*energeia*) of the rational soul when it is functioning well. In other words, an intellectual virtue is an act of reasoning well. Aristotle identified at least three types of intellectual virtue. Theoretical wisdom (*sophia*) is the ability to engage in theoretical reasoning, which includes both the deductive logic of the syllogism and the intuition of first principles (*noesis*). Its end or purpose (*telos*) is to know. Practical wisdom (*phronesis*) is the ability to make good practical judgments about particular ethical situations. Its end or purpose is virtuous action motivated and determined by the appropriate emotion. Productive wisdom (*techne*) is the type of reasoning required in art and craftsmanship. Its end or purpose is to make excellent things.

What are the functions of a human being?

The functions of a human being are arranged in hierarchical order. At the bottom are the functions of the nutritive soul, which are nutrition or digestion, growth, and reproduction. These functions keep our body alive. At the next level are the functions of the sensitive soul, which are sensation, appetite, and movement or locomotion. The functions of the sensitive soul serve the needs of the nutritive soul and enable it to function well. For example, they provide food for our digestive system. Sensation enables us to sense pain and pleasure. The appetite to feel pleasure and to not feel pain produces desire and the emotions. Desire and the emotions motivate action and determine the choices we make. Actions are ranked hierarchically, with the political actions of citizenship and military service ranked above actions such as eating that humans share with animals.

At the top of the hierarchy are the functions of the rational soul, which are theoretical, practical, and productive reasoning. The functions of the rational soul serve the needs of the sensitive soul and enable it to function well. Emotions and actions that are mastered by practical reason—first and foremost the emotions and actions of citizenship and military service—are virtuous or excellent in a way that the emotions of non-

What is eudaimonia?

Eudaimonia is happiness, in the sense that we are happy when we get what we really need, but it is more than a pleasant state of mind. It is an objective condition. Eudaimonia is a life well lived, which means that we have functioned well or with excellence and virtue, and that we have achieved the goods (the end or *telos*) that according to human nature we need to reach our highest potential. Since some of those goods (such as the happiness of our children) may not be realized until after our death, there is an important sense in which it cannot be known if we have lived well until after our deaths, highlighting the difference between happiness as a state of mind and happiness as a life well lived.

rational animals cannot be: they exhibit the practical virtues. According to Aristotle, the rational soul is what sets humans apart from other animals, and it is our highest function. Of the three functions of the rational soul, Aristotle places theoretical reasoning above the other two because theoretical reasoning is something we do for its own sake, whereas practical reasoning is done for the sake of action, and productive reasoning is done for the sake of making something. Nonetheless, both practical reasoning and productive reasoning are important functions of a human being because they serve the needs of the sensitive soul and enable it to function well or with excellence (*arête*).

What is the best way of life that is likely to make us the most happy?

Aristotle considers several different ways of life that have been proposed to make us the most happy. The first is a life devoted to sensual pleasures. Aristotle dismisses this as a way of life suitable for cattle. The reason is that sensual pleasures satisfy the lowest functions of human life, the functions that we share with animals. He considers a life devoted to making money but dismisses that, too, because money is merely a means to an end, not an end in itself. A life devoted to making money would not in itself achieve any good or make us happy, unless of course we spent our money, but in that case, we would be devoted to some good beyond making money. Next, he considers a life devoted to honor. He has more respect for this way of life because it is devoted to the excellence of the higher functions of practical reasoning and action, and these bring happiness. However, he ultimately dismisses this, too, because honors are granted by others in ways that can be arbitrary and beyond our control.

Aristotle believes that the greatest and most stable and enduring happiness comes from reasoning and knowledge. Since humans are by nature rational animals, reasoning is our highest function and our ultimate good. It is when we reason that we are most like an immortal god and most happy. But it is important to point out that Aristotle is much more down to earth when it comes to happiness than his friend and teacher Plato. Although Aristotle agrees with Plato that our greatest happiness comes

What brings happiness to a person's life? Aristotle rejected the possibility that money or sensual pleasures do so. He believed that reasoning and knowledge bring happiness to rational humans, but he also acknowledged the importance of good family and friends.

from reasoning and knowledge, he recognizes that humans are embodied beings with lower needs, too, and that we need external goods such as friends, wealth, and political power to do noble deeds. He further says that "the man who is very ugly in appearance or ill-born or solitary and childless is not very likely to be happy, and perhaps a man would be still less likely if he had thoroughly bad children or friends or had lost good children or friends by death" (*Nicomachean Ethics*).

Are acts in themselves virtuous?

Acts are not in themselves virtuous. An act is virtuous only if the agent who performs the act is in a certain condition. The agent "must have knowledge, secondly he must choose the acts, and choose them for their own sakes, and thirdly his action must proceed from a firm and unchangeable character" (*Nicomachean Ethics* 2.4, 1105a31–34). Thus, it is not the act itself that is virtuous, but the agent's character, which disposes the agent to act in a virtuous way. For an act to be virtuous, the agent who performs the act must do so intentionally (knowingly), must choose the act, and must choose it for its own sake (not as the means to another end); and the act must proceed from a stable character trait, that is, a habit.

What is a *hexis* or, as it is often translated into English, a habit?

The Greek word *hexis* (ἕξις) is often translated as "habit," but that is not a perfect translation. *Hexis* is also translated as a "stable disposition, state, or condition, held in equilibrium." A habit is a stable component of character, a character trait. As Aristotle understands it, a habit is a learned ability or power of the sensitive soul to desire and act in a certain way in certain situations. It is not a mechanical reflex or a mindless routine, and it should not be confused with the conditioned responses of behaviorism. It is the power of an animate, sentient being to achieve and hold its end in a state of equilibrium, which it desires and which is the purpose or goal of its actions. A habit is therefore not a passive potential but an *active potential* that *when actualized* becomes an *entelechia*, that is, an act, deed, or work (an *ergon* or *function*) that actively holds or keeps (makes a home for) its end, purpose, or goal (its *telos*).

How can we understand habits in terms of the concept of nature and the four causes?

The nature of a thing is an internal principle (*arche*) of change that is essential to what that thing is, in other words, to its form. As an internal principle of change, the nature of a thing is the agent cause of a change that begins with that thing's innate potential or material cause for change and that ends with its final cause. But it is human nature to be able to learn habits, and once learned, a habit functions just like human nature. A habit is an internal principle of change that, once learned, is difficult to unlearn and becomes an enduring part of who someone is. Thus, we often call habits "second nature."

What is an emotion?

An emotion as Aristotle understands it is a type of desire. For example, lust is a desire for sexual pleasure. Love (*eros*) is a desire for the beloved. Fear is a desire to flee from harm and not feel pain. Courage is a desire to act in the face of danger. Social ambition is the desire for honor. Since desire is a function of the sensitive soul, and emotion is a type of desire, emotion, too, is a function of the sensitive soul. Our emotions determine how we choose to act and how we judge the choices and actions of others.

What is a practical virtue?

The sensitive soul has three functions: sensation, desire, and locomotion. A practical virtue is a virtue or excellence of the function (*ergon*) of desire, or emotion, which is a

---

What was the Greek word for ethics, and what did it mean?

The Greek word for ethics was *ta ethika* (τὰ ἠθικά), which was closely related to *ethikos* (ἠθικός), meaning ethical. Both words were constructed from the root *ethos* (ἠθος), which meant "character, habit, or custom." In Homer, the word *ethos* was used to mean "habitat, home, or accustomed place." The study of ethics as Aristotle understood it was primarily a study of the habits and customs of a person or people that constitute their character.

What is a good or virtuous habit?

A good or virtuous habit is one that is successful at achieving its end (its good or *telos*) and holding it in a state of equilibrium. To do that, a habit must produce the appropriate type of desire with an appropriate degree of intensity for a particular situation. But a habit is a learned ability or power of the sensitive soul, and types of desire are emotions. Therefore, a virtuous habit is a learned ability or power of the sensitive soul to produce the appropriate emotion with an appropriate degree of intensity for a particular situation. For example, if a habit causes you to be angry when you should feel proud, or to act like a buffoon when you should be witty, then it is not a virtuous habit but a vice. Virtuous habits will help you to achieve your end or purpose (*telos*) and get what you really need, as objectively determined by your nature. You might get what you desire if you have a bad habit, but you won't get what you really need, because if you have a bad habit, you will either desire the wrong thing or you will desire it either too much or too little. For example, if you are a glutton and your appetite is too great, you will become overweight and unhealthy. The appropriate appetite is not arbitrary but rather objectively determined by your nature.

type of desire. A practical virtue is therefore a virtue or excellence (*arête*) of the sensitive soul when it is functioning well with respect to the function of desire or emotion. But a function (*ergon*) is an act, deed, or work. And an act, deed, or work is virtuous only when it proceeds from a stable character trait or habit. Therefore, a practical virtue is an act, deed, or work (*entelechia*) of the sensitive soul that proceeds from an excellent character trait or virtuous habit. But a virtuous habit is a learned ability or power of the sensitive soul to produce the appropriate emotion with the appropriate degree of intensity for a particular situation. Therefore, a practical virtue can be defined as the appropriate emotion with the appropriate degree of intensity for a particular situation. Since our emotions determine how we choose to act, virtuous emotions lead to virtuous actions.

Aristotle identified a number of practical virtues: courage, temperance, generosity, munificence, healthy social ambition, pride, good temper, truthfulness in self-presentation, wittiness, friendliness, modesty, righteous indignation, and justice. Associated with each practical virtue are two vices, one in which the intensity of emotion is excessive, and the other in which the intensity of emotion is deficient. Reviewing Aristotle's list of practical virtues, we find that they are all derived from the virtues of an upstanding citizen of a typical Greek *polis* or city-state; and since, according to Aristotle, the greatest test of a citizen's virtue occurs on the battlefield, the virtues of citizenship are in their purest and most essential form the virtues of a warrior. The virtues of civilian citizenship are pale imitations of the virtues of a warrior, and the virtues of personal life and of the functions that we share with animals rank even lower.

How does the sensitive soul of a rational animal such as a human being learn the practical virtues?

The sensitive soul of a rational animal such as a human being is not capable of reasoning itself, but it can listen to and obey reason. It is by listening to and obeying practical reason (*phronesis*) that the sensitive soul learns the practical virtues. Children learn the practical virtues by listening to and obeying their wise elders, while educated adults can exercise their own capacity for practical reasoning. Practical reasoning masters our emotions and shapes our character traits into practical virtues, but they must be practiced to become stable habits. We learn our habits, Aristotle says, by doing; for example, "men become builders by building and lyreplayers by playing the lyre; so too we become just by doing just acts, self-mastered by doing self-mastered acts, courageous by doing courageous acts" (*Nicomachean Ethics*). To the extent that the sensitive soul listens to and obeys practical reason, it is rational, too, and the practical virtues are ranked by Aristotle as highly as practical reason itself in the hierarchy of human functions and real needs or ends (*telos*).

What is *akrasia*?

The Greek word *akrasia* (ἀκρασία) was in the past translated as incontinence. But today the word "incontinence" refers primarily to a loss of control over urination or defecation, and its use as a moral metaphor echoes the sixteenth-century German theologian Martin Luther's vision of the earth as a festering dump ruled by Satan. As Aristotle uses the word, *akrasia* is not a Manichean tug of war between the soul and the impure body but rather the failure of the sensitive part of the soul to listen to and obey the rational part of the soul. In particular, it is about the failure of desire to listen to and obey practical reason. Plato believed that it was impossible to do what you know is wrong. Desire always aims at what is perceived to be good. Therefore, if you know what is good, you must desire it. Relying on common sense, as he often did, Aristotle refuted that claim. We have all had experiences in which we knew what the right thing to do was, but we acted otherwise. For example, we knew we should have studied more for that exam, but we went out with our friends anyway. Aristotle explains this not in terms of desire overpowering reason, but in terms of desire disconnecting from reason. Although desire is directed by practical reason in a virtuous act, it is not always directed by reason. Desire can determine action independently of reason, and when it does so, we act in ways contrary to how we know we should act.

Is *akrasia* a struggle between desire and will?

Akrasia is not a struggle between desire and will, because Aristotle does not have a concept of will. The closest thing that Aristotle has to a concept of will is rational deliberation. We act most freely when we act on the basis of rational deliberation. But rational deliberation is not a motive force in the way that the will is conceived to be, and it cannot overpower desire. Desire for Aristotle remains the only motive force behind our actions. Practical reason (*phronesis*) is merely a wise, old sage (the *phronimos*) whom desire should consult. When desire does not consult practical reason, it becomes a passion (*pathos*), something that we passively suffer, rather than something that we freely choose to do. That's why Aristotle says in the *Nicomachean Ethics* that a life devoted to making ourselves feel good (pleasure), and not also to virtue and truth, is slavish and only fit for cattle. Animals act only on their feelings and have no capacity for practical reasoning.

Is a practical virtue the mean between the extremes of excess and deficiency?

Yes, but only in the sense that it lies between those two extremes. A practical virtue is not necessarily the arithmetical mean or average of two extremes. Where the mean falls between two extremes varies depending on the particular situation, and it is not necessarily at the midpoint. In some situations, it may be appropriate to be very, very angry. In other situations, it may be appropriate to be only moderately angry. In either case, the intensity of emotion must be neither more than it should be, nor less. But exactly how intense it must be cannot be calculated by averaging the intensities of each extreme. It can only be known by an act of practical judgment and will depend on the particular situation.

Aristotle's Practical Virtues

Emotion	Vice of Deficiency	Virtue of the Mean	Vice of Excess
fear (*phobos*) and confidence (*thrásos*)	cowardice (*deilos*)	courage (*andreia*)	reckless lack of fear or audacious confidence
desire for pleasure (*hēdonē*)	insensibility, puritanism, asceticism (*anaisthētos*)	temperance, self-mastery (*sōphrosunē*)	debauchery, being undisciplined or dissolute (*akolasia*)
desire to give	stinginess (*aneleutheria*)	generosity (*eleutheriotēs*)	prodigality (*asōtia*)
desire to donate large gifts for public benefit	pettiness (*mikroprepeia*)	munificence, tastefulness on a grand scale (*megaloprepeia*)	tastelessness (*apeirokalia*) or vulgarity (*banausia*)
desire for small honors (*timē*)	social apathy; no love of honor or social esteem (*aphilotimos*)	healthy social ambition; appropriate love of honor or social esteem	narcissism; excessive love of honor or social esteem (*philotimos*)
desire for large honors (*timē*)	undue humility, smallness of soul (*mikropsuchia*)	pride, magnanimity, greatness of soul (*megalopsuchia*)	vanity, vainglory (*chaunotēs*)

For Aristotle, a life devoted to only pursuing pleasure and not truth is a life fit only for cattle.

Aristotle's Practical Virtues

Emotion	Vice of Deficiency	Virtue of the Mean	Vice of Excess
anger; a painful desire for revenge for a slight or put-down (*orgē*)	meekness (*aorgēsia*)	healthy assertiveness, good temper, gentleness (*praotēs*)	the quality of being hotheaded or bad tempered (*orgilotēs*)
truth (*alēthēs*) in self-presentation	ironic self-deprecation (*eironia*)	truthfulness (*alētheia*) in self-presentation	braggadocio (*alazoneia*)
desire to amuse others	boorishness (*bōmolochos*)	wittiness (*eutrapelos*)	buffoonery (*bōmolochia*)
desire to please others	quarrelsome (*duseris*) and surly (*duskolos*)	friendliness (*philia*)	ingratiating; pleasing others (*areskos*) or flattering them (*kolax*)
shame	shamelessness (*anaischuntia*)	modesty (*aidōs*)	shyness or bashfulness (*kataplēxis*)
indignation	schadenfreude; rejoicing over another's calamities (*epichairekakia*)	righteous indignation (*nemesis*)	envy (*phthonos*)
desire to give or take	desire to take less and give more than is due	justice (*dikaiosyne*), desire to give and take what is due	greed; desire to take more and give less than is due (*pleonexia*)

Why did Aristotle's conception of practical virtue differ from the conception of virtue found in Christian morality?

Aristotle's conception of practical virtue was derived from the conception of virtue found in the upper classes of the ancient Greek *polis* or city-state. But the typical ancient Greek *polis* was a hierarchically ranked, male-dominated warrior culture based on the emotions of honor and shame. Ancient Greek culture underwent profound changes after Alexander the Great ended the autonomy of the ancient Greek *polis* and ushered in the Hellenistic age of empire. But Christianity would not exist for several more centuries, and its moral values would not be widely known or accepted until even later.

Consequently, Aristotle's conception of practical virtue was derived from the virtues of a hierarchically ranked, male-dominated warrior culture based on the emotions of honor and shame. The difference between Aristotle and the warrior culture in which he lived is that he was a philosopher, so he believed that reason should master the emotions and that the intellectual virtues stood at a higher rank than the practical virtues of warrior-citizens. Christian morality, on the other hand, was originally popular among the lower classes of Greco-Roman civilization, and its conception of virtue was generally in diametrical opposition to the conception of virtue found in the upper classes of the ancient Greek *polis*. Therefore, we should not be surprised that Aristotle's conception of practical virtue was quite different from the conception of virtue found in Christian morality.

What is Aristotle's virtue of good temper, and how does it differ from the Christian virtues having to do with anger?

Good temper, Aristotle says, is the mean with respect to the emotion of anger. By anger, Aristotle has in mind something more specific than what we understand when we use the English word "anger." In his book *Rhetoric*, Aristotle defines anger (*orgē*) as "a desire, accompanied by pain, for a perceived revenge, on account of a perceived slight on the part of people who are not fit to slight one or one's own." Good temper is the virtue of "the man who is angry at the right things and with the right people, and, further, as he ought, when he ought, and as long as he ought" (*Nicomachean Ethics*).

Aristotle says that the virtuous man is more likely to err in the direction of deficiency in regard to anger than to excess because the virtuous man "is not revengeful, but rather tends to make allowances." Indeed, the Greek word that we are translating as good temper, *praotēs*, means "calm, pleasing, or gentle." However, the virtuous man's tendency to err in the direction of deficiency regarding anger should not be confused with kindness or with the Christian virtue of patience. If the virtuous man tends to make allowances, it is out of a superabundance of strength, because he is too strong to be perturbed by insults from those beneath him, those who are not even fit to insult him. Aristotle does not counsel meekness, nor does he counsel us to turn the other cheek, as might the Christian moralist. On the contrary, the man who does not get angry at the things he should get angry about is a fool and is "unlikely to defend himself; and to en-

Aristotle says that the virtuous man is more likely to err in the direction of deficiency in regard to anger than to excess because the virtuous man "is not revengeful, but rather tends to make allowances."

dure being insulted and put up with insult to one's friends is slavish." The virtue of good temper occupies the mean between passive submission and excessive aggression. It is the virtue of healthy assertiveness.

What is Aristotle's virtue of temperance (*sōphrosunē*)?

The virtue of temperance (*sōphrosunē*) is the mean between too much and too little desire for the pleasures of our senses. Aristotle is particularly concerned about our desire for the pleasures of our sense of touch, which are the pleasures of food, drink, and sex, because we share our desire for these pleasures with nonrational animals. Coming from an irrational part of the sensitive soul that is not capable of listening to reason, our desire for the pleasures of food, drink, and sex can overwhelm our capacity for rational calculation and yield to excess. Our desire for the aesthetic pleasures of sight and hearing (such as music and the visual arts) poses no such danger because it does not stem from the irrational part of the sensitive soul that we share with animals.

Akolasia is the Greek word that Aristotle uses for the vice of excess desire for the pleasures of our senses. *Akolasia* is debauchery, the state or condition of being undisciplined or dissolute regarding our desire for the pleasures of the senses and, in particular, for the pleasures of food, drink, and sex. The vice of deficiency is *anaisthētos*, which is the etymological root of our word "anesthetic" (from *an-*, "without," and *aisthētos*, "sensible"), and means, literally, "insensible or without sensation." The person who suf-

Is Aristotle's virtue of temperance (*sōphrosunē*) moderation?

No, because the appropriate desire for the pleasures of food, drink, or sex may not be moderate in some situations. For example, it may be appropriate for Milo the wrestler to eat enormous amounts of food when he is training. The appropriate intensity of desire is not necessarily the middle point between two extremes. It is simply whatever is neither too much nor too little for a particular situation.

fers the vice of *anaisthētos* is incapable of sensing the pleasures of our senses and has no desire for them. Although Aristotle believed that we are at greater risk of suffering excess than deficient desire for the pleasures of our senses because he believed that the vice of excess is much more common, it is important to note that he believed that deficiency was also a vice.

How do Aristotle's ethical views about our desire for the pleasures of food, drink, and sex differ from those of Christian morality?

Lust is the sin of wanting to have sex for the purpose of enjoying sexual pleasure. Since the Middle Ages, the Church has taught that lust is a sin and that the only morally acceptable reason to have sex is to have children. For example, masturbation and sodomy are sinful because they are sexual activities we engage in for the purpose of enjoying sexual pleasure, not to have children. Sexual pleasure is not sinful, but it is merely incidental to sexual activity, not its rational purpose. Procreation is the rational purpose of sexual activity, because the natural function of our sexual organs is reproduction. Similarly, gluttony is the sin of wanting to eat for the purpose of enjoying the pleasure of eating, but the only morally acceptable reason to eat is to nourish the body. The pleasures of food are not sinful, but they are merely incidental to the activity of eating, not its rational purpose. Nutrition is the rational purpose of eating, because the natural function of our digestive organs is nourishment.

Aristotle would agree that it is wrong to desire pleasure for its own sake, because that would reduce us to the level of nonrational animals who are moved by the irrational part of the sensitive soul and have no capacity for practical reason. When our desire for food, drink, and sex is not directed by practical reason, it tends to become excessive, "for in an irrational being the desire for pleasure is insatiable … and if appetites are strong and violent they even expel the power of calculation" (*Nicomachean Ethics*). But there is a subtle difference between Aristotle and Christian morality on this point because for Aristotle the emphasis lies on reason, not on pleasure as such. What makes the excessive desire for pleasure a vice, for Aristotle, is that it is not directed by reason. The real vice for Aristotle is irrationalism, not indulging in our bodies. Indeed, according to Aristotle, an appropriate amount of bodily pleasure is necessary for a good life. For Christian morality, on the other hand, what makes the excessive desire for pleasure a vice is that we are indulging in our bodies instead of our souls. In that respect, Christian morality is closer to Plato than to Aristotle, because Plato, too, was a dualist who saw a moral struggle between the body and the soul.

What is the virtue of healthy social ambition?

The virtue of healthy social ambition is the mean between too little and too much desire for honor or social esteem. The person whose desire for honor or social esteem is excessive is a narcissist, that is, someone who views others as a mirror of themselves and whose self-esteem is entirely dependent on how others judge them. It is because of the vice of narcissism that Aristotle believed that honor was not the greatest good or ultimate purpose of human life. To love honor as the highest good would be to depend for your happiness on how others judge you and your actions. And that, Aristotle thought, would not be a very stable form of happiness, if it qualified as happiness at all.

Nonetheless, insufficient desire for honor or social esteem (*aphilotimos*) is also a vice, the vice of social apathy. Our word "apathy" is derived from the Greek word *apátheia* (ἀπάθεια), which has a different meaning than apathy because the root *páthos* (πᾰθοζ) of the word *apátheia* means both passion and suffering, and apathy is not a relief from suffering. Nor does apathy mean that one no longer suffers passion. But although the Greek word that our word "apathy" is derived from doesn't suit Aristotle's concept of *aphilotimos* very well, the modern meaning of the word "apathy" does. The modern concept of apathy became more widely used after World War I, when it was recognized as one of the effects of shell shock, or what we today would call posttraumatic stress disorder (PTSD). Soldiers who experienced the horrific conditions of trench warfare returned from the war disassociated from their own feelings, alienated from society, and indifferent to social judgments of their actions. This condition was known as apathy. According to both Plato and Aristotle, the love of honor (*philotimos*) is the primary virtue of soldiers, it is what gives them "spirit" (*thumos*), and when soldiers lose their love of honor they suffer the vice of *aphilotimos*. So, it is appropriate that we translate *aphilotimos* as "social apathy" in keeping with the historical use of the word "apathy" to describe the condition of soldiers returning from war who have become disassociated from their feelings (their *thumos*) and indifferent to social judgments of their actions.

What is the virtue of pride?

The virtue of pride, magnanimity, or greatness of soul (*megalopsuchia*) is the mean between too little and too much desire for large honors. The proud man deems himself worthy of great things and is truly worthy of them. Hence, he is "great souled" and possesses all the other virtues. Pride, Aristotle says in the *Nicomachean Ethics*, is "a sort of crown of the virtues," for it is not found without them, and it makes them greater by bestowing honor upon them. The vice of too little desire for large honors is undue humility or smallness of soul (*mikropsuchia*). The man who does not deem himself worthy of great things but is nonetheless worthy of them is "small souled" and unduly humble. Aristotle's opinion about pride is opposite to that of Christian morality, which condemns pride as a sin and lauds humility as a virtue. For Aristotle, it is undue humility that is a vice, not pride. The vice of too much desire for large honors is vanity or vainglory (*chaunotēs*). The man who deems himself worthy of great things but is not worthy of them is vain.

Who is the great-souled man?

The great-souled man is the man who possesses all the virtues to the highest degree and who knows it and rightfully thinks himself worthy of the greatest things. And since the greatest thing is honor, the great-souled man thinks himself worthy of the greatest honors (*Nicomachean Ethics*). But he is disdainful of honors bestowed by men because no honor they can bestow is

It is okay to have some pride, according to Aristotle; the key is not to be unjustly and overly proud. Just as bad, however, is to exercise too much humility, which Aristotle called being "small souled."

worthy of perfect virtue. He will be moderately pleased by great honors conferred by good men and accept them since they have nothing greater to give him. But he will despise honors bestowed by common people on trifling grounds. He is neither overjoyed by good fortune nor overpained by bad fortune because nothing, not even wealth or power or life itself, is as great as honor, and even that to him is not a very great thing. He does not take risks because there is little worth taking a risk for, but he will face great dangers without any thought for his life. He is generous towards others, but he is ashamed of receiving benefits because to give is a mark of superiority while to receive is a mark of inferiority. He is open and honest in his feelings because to conceal his feelings from others for fear of what they would think would be cowardly. He is prone to freely speaking what he truly believes "except when he speaks in irony to the vulgar." He has too much self-respect to be a flatterer. He is not much given to admiration or praise, but neither does he speak badly of others or hold a grudge, because few things are of great importance to him. Above all, he is a proud man, and he carries himself as such. He speaks with a deep voice and a level tone, and he walks with a slow, steady gait, "for the man who takes few things seriously is not likely to be hurried, nor the man who thinks nothing great to be excited."

ARISTOTLE'S CONCEPTS
OF LOVE AND FRIENDSHIP

What were some ancient concepts of love that were of ethical significance to Aristotle?

The Platonic concept of love as *eros* is a desire to be united with the beloved in beauty. It is primarily an aesthetic ideal, not a sexual one, though sexual love may be eroticized. However, Aristotle did not discuss *eros*. The Latin word *libido*, which we translate as lust, refers to a bodily desire for sexual pleasure with another person. Aristotle recognized this kind of love as an imperfect form of friendship. The Greek word *agapē* (ἀγάπη) was translated into the Latin *caritas*, from which we get the English word "charity," and is the basis for our moral concept of *altruism*. *Agapē* is the Christian concept of unconditional and universal love for everyone, regardless of merit. Aristotle had no such concept of love.

The Greek word *storgē* (στοργή) refers to the natural or instinctive love between a parent and child. Aristotle recognized *storgē* as a type of love, but since it is instinctual and devoid of choice, it is neither an expression of character nor a virtue. However, the natural love of a child for his or her father makes the child more receptive to the father's attempts to teach the child good, virtuous habits. The Greek word *philia* (φιλία) refers to the love between friends. Aristotle believed that friendship was a virtue or implied virtue. *Philia* is one of the necessary goods of life. Without friendship, Aristotle says, no one would choose to live.

How does the virtue of friendliness both resemble and differ from friendship?

Friendship is like friendliness insofar as it is a virtue or, Aristotle says, implies virtue. And the friendly man, with affection added, makes for a good friend. But the virtue of friendliness "differs from friendship in that it implies no passion or affection for one's associates; since it is not by reason of loving or hating that such a man takes everything in the right way, but by being a man of a certain kind. For he will behave alike towards those he knows and those he does not know" (*Nicomachean Ethics*). The friendly man chooses to please or pain others not because he loves them or hates them but because that is the honorable or expedient thing to do. Friends choose to please one another because they know and love one another.

What is friendship, and what are the three types of friendship?

Friendship is the relationship between two people who share a mutual and recognized love for one another as friends. But love is a feeling, and friendship is more than a feeling. Friendship is a state of character from which both feelings and acts of love spring. To love one another as friends (*philia*) means to have goodwill and confer benefits on one another of the same kind and for the same reasons.

There are three types of friendship corresponding to the three types of things that are loveable and desirable in another person: pleasure, utility, and good character. Friends who love one another for the pleasure they receive from each other give pleasure to one another in return. Friends who love one another because they are useful to each other make themselves useful to one another in return. And friends who love one another because they are good honor one another and perform virtuous actions in kind to preserve one another's virtue. Friendships of pleasure are based on love of the pleasure that friends provide for one another. Aristotle says that these types of friendship are common

Friendship, said Aristotle, is more than just a feeling because it is also a source of action and reciprocity.

among children and among bad adults whose ethical judgment and character never developed properly. For example, children become friends with their playmates because they enjoy playing together. Adults become friends with witty people because they enjoy their humor, and with people they find sexually attractive because they would enjoy having sex with them.

Friendships based on utility are common in business and commercial transactions, where friends are useful to one another. Only friendship based on a love of good character is true and perfect friendship, because those who love their friends for utility or pleasure do not love their friends for being who they are, and do not wish their friends well for their own sake, but love their friends because they are useful to them or provide them with some pleasure.

Friendships based on a love of good character last as long as each friend is good, and since goodness is an enduring thing, friendships based on a love of good character are the most enduring kind. They are also the most consistently pleasant because what is good without qualification is also pleasant without qualification. True and perfect friendships are rare, however, because good people are rare, and because it takes time for good people to get to know one another. Friendships based on pleasure or utility are common, but they are unstable and do not last long because what is pleasant or useful in one situation may not be in another.

How many true and perfect friends is it possible to have?

Not many. For good people, the perception of their own life and existence is pleasant because they perceive in themselves what is in itself good and most desirable, and they are supremely happy. But since they also perceive what is in itself good and most desirable in their friends, the perception of their friends' existence is pleasant to them, too. A

Why do we need friends?

Since humans are by nature social animals, friendship is one of the essential goods of human life. No man, Aristotle says, would choose to live without friends. But it is not just for pleasure and utility that we need friends. Good people need true and perfect friends for whom to do good deeds, because true happiness is found in virtuous action, and without friends who are deserving and good, there would be no one for whom to do good deeds. Contrary to the Christian ideal of *agapē*, Aristotle does not believe that good people should strive to love everyone unconditionally and without regard to merit. Aristotle believes that for good people to do good deeds for those who are not their friends, and with whom they do not share a mutual and recognized love, would be an injustice, not a virtue. Therefore, everyone needs true and perfect friends if they are to fully actualize their potential for virtuous action.

good person, therefore, wishes to perceive the life and existence of their friends, and they can do this only by living together and sharing in discussion and thought, for this is what living together means for a human being, "not, as in the case of cattle, feeding in the same place" (*Nicomachean Ethics*). Living together is required of friendship, and when friends are separated, their friendship becomes inactive. Sour people, Aristotle says, may bear goodwill toward one another and aid one another in need, but they are not friends because they do not spend their days together (live together) nor delight in each other. But since it is not possible to live with a large number of people, it is not possible to have a large number of true and perfect friends. It is possible, Aristotle says, to have many friends in the way proper to fellow citizens, "but one cannot have with many people the friendship based on virtue and on the character of our friends themselves, and we must be content if we find even a few such."

What does justice have to do with friendship?

Justice is giving and taking from others what is due, that is, what each party merits. But so is friendship. To love one another as friends means to have goodwill and confer benefits on one another of the same kind and for the same reasons. In friendships based on pleasure, friends give one another pleasure; they "get the same things from each other and delight in each other or in the same things" (*Nicomachean Ethics*). In friendships based on utility, friends are equally useful to one another. For example, in commercial transactions, friends exchange goods of equal value. If they didn't exchange goods of equal value, the exchange would be unjust, and they would no longer be friends. In friendships based on character, friends exchange benefits that are not necessarily equal in absolute terms, but that are equal in proportion to merit. In friendships based on character, each friend loves the other for who they are, and because they are good, not for what they get out of them. In that sense, no exchange occurs between friends of this kind. But in friendships based on character, each friend does good deeds for the other because they are good, and in proportion to their goodness.

The most important benefit that a person gets out of a friendship based on character is the opportunity to perform virtuous actions for their friend, not what they receive from their friend. But since each friend performs virtuous actions for the other friend in proportion to their goodness, a kind of reciprocal exchange does occur, and therefore, so does justice.

Is there a friendship that exists between parties who differ in virtue and function?

According to Aristotle, friendship is possible between parties who differ in virtue and function, such as between father and son, husband and wife, or king and subject. However, in these cases, the reasons that each party loves is different, and therefore, so is their love and friendship. "Each party, then, neither gets the same from the other, nor ought to seek it" (*Nicomachean Ethics*). "The better should be more loved than he loves, and so should the more useful, and similarly in each of the other cases."

There can still be justice in friendships of this kind if each party loves in proportion to the merit of the other party, because justice does not require absolute equality, but rather equality in proportion to merit. For example, it is not possible for children to give their parents life in return for the life that they received from them, but they can give them the honor that they deserve. But if the difference between the parties to a friendship is too great, the friendship will fail, because friendship functions best when there is equality in absolute terms, not merely equality in proportion to merit. That's why, Aristotle says, men who are much inferior to kings do not expect to be their friends. Nor do men expect the gods to be their friends.

ARISTOTLE'S
SOCIAL AND POLITICAL PHILOSOPHY

What is *koinōníā*?

Koinōníā (κοινωνία) is a Greek word that for Aristotle meant "community or friendly association." The word *koinōníā* appears numerous times in the Greek New Testament and is most often translated as "fellowship," although it is also translated, in order of decreasing frequency, as "contribution," "communion," "sharing," "participation," "communication," and "partnership." In the early Catholic Church, *koinōníā* referred to the sacrament of Holy Communion, in which members of the Church became one in the body of Christ.

What does friendship have to do with community?

A community (*koinōníā*) is by definition an association of people who have something in common that holds them together as one body. What they have in common, accord-

People who form community tend to do so when they have common goals to pursue.

ing to Aristotle, is some particular good or purpose (*telos*) that they pursue together but that varies from one community to another. For example, shipmates sail together. Soldiers fight together. And members of a bowling club bowl together. Similarly, friends have something in common that holds them together as if they were one person. A friend, Aristotle says, is another self, and the marks of friendship proceed from a man's relations to himself, since a friend: 1) wishes and does well for the sake of his friend; 2) wishes his friend to live for his sake; 3) lives with his friend; 4) has the same tastes as his friend; and 5) grieves and rejoices with his friend (*Nicomachean Ethics*).

Friends share a mutual and recognized love for one another as friends and confer benefits on one another of the same kind and for the same reasons. Thus, friends by definition pursue a common good together. But so do the members of every community. Therefore, the members of every community are friends. The nature of friendship and of justice—that is, the duties that friends have toward one another—will vary from one community to the next depending on each community's particular good or purpose: "Since the claims of parents and brothers, comrades and benefactors, are different, we ought to render to each that which is proper and suitable to each." But friendship and justice will be found in every community, because friendship, like community, is an association of people united by a common good or purpose. In fact, Aristotle says, members of every community address one another as friends, suggesting that friendship and justice are coextensive with community.

What does friendship and community have to do with the *polis* or city-state?

The polis or city-state is a political community. Like any community, the *polis* was originally formed, and continues to be maintained, for the common good of its members. The aim of lawgivers in the *polis* is the good of the community, and they call justice that **183** which serves the common good (*Nicomachean Ethics*). But whereas the other kinds of communities aim at some particular good—for example, sailors aim for profit in trade, comrades in arms aim for the gains of warfare, and some communities are formed for pleasure, such as religious guilds or dining clubs—the political community aims not at some temporary good but at what is good for the whole of life. All other kinds of communities, then, are parts of the political community, and the limited kinds of friendship given as examples correspond to the limited kinds of community from which they spring.

What are the six kinds of political constitution?

The six kinds of political constitution are based upon the three virtuous kinds of constitution and an equal number of corrupt versions of these. The three virtuous kinds of political constitution are monarchy, aristocracy, and timocracy or polity (*politeia*, πολιτεία). A monarchy is a political community ruled by one supremely good man, the king. An aristocracy is ruled by a few good men. And a timocracy or polity is ruled by many.

In theory, Aristotle considers monarchy to be the best of these and timocracy or polity to be the worst. However, since it is difficult to find one supremely good man, in practice Aristotle considers timocracy or polity to be the best. In a monarchy, the king is self-sufficient and surpasses his subjects in all good things. He therefore does not depend on his subjects to fulfill his needs but will look instead to fulfill their needs (*Nicomachean Ethics*). Monarchy is virtuous because it serves the common good, not the good of its ruler. In an aristocracy, a select few persons of good character rule. Together they are wiser than any one of them alone would be and even wiser than the sum of

What is *homonoia*?

The Greek word *homonoia* (ομόνοια) is closely related to the Greek word for harmony, *armonía* (αρμονία), and has been translated as "concord," "agreement," and "unanimity." While each of these translations captures an aspect of what *homonoia* means for Aristotle, none of them captures the whole meaning. *Homonoia* is political friendship (*politikē philia*), that is, friendship between citizens of a political community such as the Greek *polis* or city-state. It is a friendly relation between citizens who agree about what is in their common interest (their good or purpose), choose the same practical actions to achieve their common interest, and act together (*Nicomachean Ethics*). Bad men, Aristotle says, are not only incapable of political friendship but are also divided selves who suffer strife (*eris*, ἔρις) and discord within themselves. Bad men are not capable of *homonoia*, "any more than they can be friends, since they aim at getting more than their share of advantages, while in labor and public service they fall short of their share; and each man wishing for advantage to himself criticizes his neighbor and stands in his way; for if people do not watch carefully the commonweal is soon destroyed."

each. They, too, need nothing from their subjects and rule in the interest of their subjects, not their own.

A timocracy is rule by many honorable men, and since honor is a virtue that attaches especially to comrades in arms, a timocracy is rule by honorable comrades in arms. However, Aristotle's timocracy has a property qualification. In addition to being honorable comrades in arms, the rulers of a timocracy must possess a minimum amount of property. But if they do meet the property qualification, they are regarded as equal to all their comrades who meet the property qualification. Hence, most people, Aristotle says, call timocracy a polity. It, too, is virtuous because its rulers serve the common good, not their own personal interest, since they own property and are self-sufficient.

What are the three corrupt versions of the virtuous kinds of constitution?

The three corrupt versions of the virtuous kinds of constitution are tyranny, oligarchy, and democracy. Like a monarchy, a tyranny is ruled by one man, but instead of being ruled by a supremely good man, it is ruled by a supremely bad man. Monarchy becomes tyranny when the good king becomes bad and, instead of serving the common good, serves only his own perceived self-interest. Tyranny is the contrary of monarchy. If monarchy is the best kind of constitution, tyranny is the worst.

Like an aristocracy, an oligarchy is ruled by a few persons, but instead of being ruled by a few good persons, it is ruled by a few bad persons. Aristocracy becomes oligarchy when the aristocrats are corrupted by their wealth. Disregarding any other qualification, they distribute public office only to those who are wealthy and give to themselves what belongs to the commonweal.

Aristotle says that democracy is the least bad of the corrupt constitutions because it is only a slight deviation from a virtuous timocracy or polity. Both operate under the principle of majority rule. The difference is that whereas a timocracy grants the vote only to those who are honorable and possess a minimum amount of property, a democracy treats everyone equally and grants the vote to everyone—and since the majority of people are poor, a democracy is ruled by the poor. Though democracy is the least bad of the three corrupt kinds of constitution, it is still bad because the majority acts in its own perceived self-interest and robs from the rich instead of acting for the good of the whole community.

It might surprise many modern readers that Aristotle felt that democracies were one type of corrupt government. He felt democracies were bad because it made it possible for a misguided and selfish majority of citizens to act in their own interest and not the interests of all people.

Under which constitutions may friendship be found?

Since both friendship and justice are coextensive with community, there is no friendship, nor indeed genuine community (*koinōnía*), without justice. Thus, there is friendship and community in political communities based upon virtuous constitutions, but there is no friendship or community in states that are based upon corrupt constitutions. In monarchies, the friendship between the king and his subjects is like the friendship between a father and his son, because a king cares for his subjects like a father cares for his sons. The relationship between father and son is not equal, but it is just insofar as each loves the other in proportion to merit. In tyrannies such as Persia, Aristotle says, the rule of the father is tyrannical, because they treat their sons as slaves. In aristocracies, the friendship between rulers and ruled is like the friendship between husband and wife, because while the husband is generally superior in worth to his wife, he rules only in matters that he is competent to rule, while his wife rules in matters that she is competent to rule. Similarly, aristocrats are generally superior in worth to their subjects, but they rule only in matters that they are competent to rule. When their rule becomes based on power and wealth instead of merit, and extends to all matters regardless of competency, aristocracy becomes oligarchy. In the case of timocracies, the friendship between rulers is like the friendship between brothers because the rulers are equal to one another. But they are friends of their subjects, too, because they serve the common good of all. There is no justice in tyrannies because the tyrant has nothing in common with his subjects, and where there is no justice, there can be no friendship.

The relationship between the tyrant and his subjects is like the relationship between craftsmen and tool, soul and body, master and slave, or farmer and work-animal. There is no friendship, Aristotle says, "towards a horse or ox, nor to a slave *qua* slave. For there is nothing in common to the two parties; the slave is a living tool and the tool is a lifeless slave." There is, therefore, no friendship, justice, or community in tyrannies. However, although friendship is not possible with a slave *qua* slave, friendship with a slave *qua* man is possible, "for there seems to be some justice between any man and any other who can share in a system of law or be a party to an agreement" (*Nicomachean Ethics*). Democracy arises when the rulers are "weak and everyone has license to do as he pleases." Although democracy is a corrupt form of constitution and its citizens are little better than slaves without masters, friendship is possible to a limited degree because the citizens of a democracy are equal and have much in common.

Can there be friendship between different states?

Yes, there can. An alliance between Greek city-states (such as the Hellenic League) is a friendship of utility. However, friendship is not possible with or between barbarian (non-Greek) states because the people of those states do not live under virtuous constitutions. For example, friendship is not possible with a tyrant, who thinks only of himself. Nor is friendship possible with the tyrant's hapless subjects, who live like slaves and have never known either political friendship or justice. After the murder of the Persian emperor Darius III and the execution of Bessus, his assassin and would-be successor,

Alexander the Great tried to unite the upper echelons of Greek and Persian society under the Aristotelian principle of *homonoia*, or political friendship; but after Alexander's death, the Greek ruling class abandoned his attempt and failed to integrate the local population into their ranks.

Are pleasures good or bad?

Pleasures are not in themselves good or bad. Pleasures are good or bad only if the activities that are proper to them are worthy or not; and an activity is worthy or not depending on whether it is chosen by a person of good character or disposition. Bad people choose unworthy activities and pleasures; good people choose worthy activities and pleasures. So, it is not pleasures themselves that are good or bad but the activities that are proper to them and the character of the person who chooses those activities. "Now since activities differ in respect of goodness and badness, and some are worthy to be chosen, others to be avoided, and others neutral, so, too, are the pleasures; for to each activity there is a proper pleasure. The pleasure proper to a worthy activity is good and that proper to an unworthy activity bad" (*Nicomachean Ethics*).

Is pleasure the end or purpose of human life?

The end or purpose of human life is not pleasure but *eudaimonia*, which is activity in accordance with virtue or excellence, because happiness is desirable in itself, and only virtuous or excellent activity is desirable in itself. Pleasure is not *in itself* the end or purpose of human life but only *in activities* that are our end or purpose. Pleasure is bad if it is proper to an unworthy activity and neutral if, as in the case of amusement, it is not proper to any activity at all but is passively enjoyed. We do not live and exert ourselves in virtuous activity so that we can enjoy pleasant amusements. On the contrary, we enjoy pleasant amusements for rest and relaxation so that we can resume our activities in earnest.

What makes an activity worthy?

An activity is worthy if it serves a proper function or end of the agent who performs it, and it is more worthy if it serves a higher function than if it serves a lower function. Therefore, the pleasure that is proper to an activity is good if it serves a proper function or end of the agent who performs that activity, and it is better if it serves a higher function than if it serves a lower function. Since the function of sight, for example, is higher than the function of

Aristotle believed that the pleasure of an activity is good if it serves a proper function or end of the living being who performed it. The higher the function or end, the more worthy the activity and the better the pleasure. For example, the pleasure of scientific research is better than the pleasure of eating.

touch, which we share with non-rational animals, and the functions of hearing and smell are superior to the function of taste, the pleasures of sight, hearing, and smell are superior to the pleasures of touch and taste. And the pleasures of thought are superior to the pleasures of sight, hearing, and smell, because the function of thought is higher than the functions of sight, hearing, and smell (*Nicomachean Ethics*, 10.5, 1176a1–4).

Is true and perfect happiness found in practical activities?

No, it is not. Happiness is something we desire for its own sake and is found in leisure, but practical activities are pursued for ends beyond themselves. The practical virtues are exercised in their highest form in politics and warfare, but the pursuits of politics and war are not found in leisure, nor are they desired for their own sake. No one but the most bloodthirsty person desires war for its own sake. Nor does anyone engage in politics for its own sake; they do it to gain positions of authority, honor, or some other happiness distinct from political activity. "If then among practical pursuits displaying the virtues, politics and war stand out preeminent in nobility and grandeur, and yet they are unleisured, and directed to some further end, not chosen for their own sakes: whereas the activity of the intellect is felt to excel in serious worth, consisting as it does in contemplation, and to aim at no end beyond itself, and also to contain a pleasure peculiar to itself, and therefore augmenting its activity: and if accordingly the attributes of this activity are found to be self-sufficiency, leisuredness, such freedom from fatigue as is possible for man, and all the other attributes of blessedness: it follows that it is the activity of the intellect that constitutes complete human happiness" (*Nicomachean Ethics*).

In which activity is the truest and most perfect happiness found?

Since happiness is activity in accordance with virtue or excellence, and our best and most virtuous activity is found in the best and most virtuous part of ourselves, the truest and most perfect happiness is found in the virtuous and excellent activity of the best part of ourselves. But the best part of ourselves is the rational soul. For even beasts possess a sensitive soul. But the rational soul defines us as human beings and is our essential function. Therefore, the truest and most perfect happiness is found in the activity of thinking—not the thinking we do in the pursuit of knowledge, which we do for the sake of obtaining knowledge—but the thinking we do once knowledge is obtained, since that is the end or purpose of thinking. The contemplation of knowledge once it is obtained is our best and most virtuous activity and the most pleasant. "Happiness extends," Aristotle says, "just so far as contemplation does, and those to whom contemplation more fully belongs are more truly happy, not as a mere concomitant but in virtue of contemplation; for this is in itself precious. Happiness, therefore, must be some form of contemplation" (*Nicomachean Ethics*).

How can people be made good?

Having completed his study of ethics with his discussion of happiness, Aristotle turns to the question of how people can be made good, since that, after all, was the purpose of his study of ethics to begin with. He finds that there are three ways that people can be made good. They can be made good by nature, by habituation, and by teaching. By nature, he means that which is not a result of our own efforts but is "a result of some divine causes that are present in those who are truly fortunate." There is nothing we can do to change the way that nature forms our character. But we can work with what nature gives us as material for our own efforts. By habituation, Aristotle means learning by doing, that is, by practice. By teaching, Aristotle means instruction by means of rational argument and persuasion.

Aristotle is pessimistic about the prospects for improving humankind by means of rational argument and persuasion alone. He believes that too many people live by passion and will not listen to reason. However, if people are habituated and trained from youth on up to be good, then they will be more amenable to reason. A good man, Aristotle believes, will listen to reason. But it is difficult to habituate and train everyone to be good without the use of coercive authority, because being good is not pleasant to most people, especially when they are young, and their behavior is corrected only by pain, like a beast of burden. Therefore, Aristotle concludes, a system of laws, backed up by the compulsive power of the state, and proceeding from practical wisdom and reason,

One way to make people good is by teaching them how to do good things. This can be done by instruction but also through habituation—the practice of doing good.

is necessary to habituate and train people to be good and to live in accordance with reason and right order.

What is the state, and what is its ultimate end or purpose?

The state is the highest form of community, and its ultimate end or purpose is the highest good. The state is a community composed of more special communities that are devoted to lesser goods. The state is composed of villages, and villages are composed of households. The household is the fundamental economic unit of society. It consists of a man, who is the head of the household, his wife and children, and slaves. The household is based upon the two relations of husband and wife, and master and slave, both of which are natural and occur by nature. Its end or purpose is to produce material goods for its daily needs.

What are the three functions of the state that legislators must consider when framing a constitution?

Long before the Constitution of the United States divided the federal government into three branches, Aristotle recognized that there are three fundamental functions of the state that legislators must consider when framing a constitution. These are the functions of deliberation, execution, and adjudication. In the United States, the legislative branch of government performs the function of deliberation, the executive branch executes laws passed by the legislature, and the courts adjudicate differences of opinion about how to implement and interpret those laws.

According to Aristotle, the deliberative assembly is the supreme branch of government. It has the authority to make war or peace, form alliances with foreign states, pass laws, and, in accordance with the constitution, appoint citizens to offices in the other two branches of government. It is the function of the executive branch of government to administer the laws passed by the deliberative assembly. And, as in the case of the U.S. government, it is the function of the law courts to adjudicate differences of opinion about how to implement and interpret the laws.

There are many different ways that the state can be designed by a constitution to perform the functions of deliberation, execution, and adjudication, even within each of Aristotle's six fundamental types of constitution. For example, the deliberative assembly may be composed of all the citizens of the state, either at once or by turns; or of only those who meet a property qualification; or of a select few who have been elected to office by a majority of citizens. The number and type of offices in the executive branch and how citizens are appointed to them may differ from one constitution to another. And the courts can be designed in a number of different ways.

But the household is not self-sufficing, so in order to more fully provide for their needs, a group of households come together to form a village. But the village is not self-sufficing either, so in order to fully provide for their needs, a group of villages come together to form the state. The state is the smallest community that is self-sufficing. It is formed to provide for the material needs of its citizens, but its ultimate end or purpose is to make its citizens good and happy. The state is by nature prior to the individual because the individual is not self-sufficing and could not live without the state any more than a foot could live without the body to which it belongs. The state is a natural form of community and occurs by nature because the households of which it is composed are natural and occur by nature. Humans are by nature political because, alone among animals, it is their nature to engage in rational deliberation with one another about what is right and just.

Why did Aristotle believe that the state has a responsibility to educate its citizens, and how are they to be educated?

Like Plato, Aristotle believed that the state has a responsibility to educate its citizens because the ultimate end or purpose of the state is to make its citizens happy and good. Besides laws that correct bad behavior by punishing wrongdoers, the only way to make citizens good is to educate them from childhood on up. Education begins with the training of the body and its appetites, proceeds on to the moral habits, and ends with the development of the intellectual virtues. The purpose of education is to develop all of a citizen's powers for virtuous or excellent activity, culminating in the power to think and rule wisely, since that is a citizen's ultimate and highest function.

The first stage of education consists in gymnastics. Already before birth, the age and physical condition of parents is regulated to ensure that their children will be able to develop healthy physiques. Aristotle says that no deformed baby should live, but if the established customs of the state forbid infanticide and the population grows too large, then abortion should be practiced. Just as in Plato's educational system, young children not yet able to reason are trained to acquire good habits and character traits by being exposed to examples of outstanding virtue in art and real life. The people they associate with, the pictures and statues they see, the stories they are told, and the music they listen to are all carefully selected to train them to prefer virtue over vice. At the appropriate age, they will receive military training, but since war is only a means to peace, it is more important, Aristotle says, for citizens to acquire the virtues of peace. The training of the intellect is the final stage of education, since thought is a human being's highest function.

How much wealth did Aristotle think we needed to be happy?

Aristotle recognized that we need material goods or goods external to the soul in order to be happy, but we need them only as instruments to achieve happiness, not as ends in themselves, and we don't need so much wealth that we must become despots to acquire it. Possession of goods external to the soul does not in itself make us happy but is only a means to practice the virtues, which do make us happy. For example, we must possess a certain amount of wealth to be generous and munificent. Happiness is activity in accordance with virtue or excellence, and the truest and most perfect happiness is found in intellectual contemplation, which does not require the possession of great wealth.

What did Aristotle think about communism and private property?

Aristotle favored private property and opposed communism because, contrary to Plato, he thought that sharing all things in common would cause dissension and divide rather than unite society. Communism would only encourage freeloaders and cause arguments between individuals who felt that they were contributing more than their fair share to the commons or not getting enough in return. Long before modern economic theory, Aristotle recognized the tragedy of the commons in which selfish individuals neglect the commons or even damage it for their own personal gain.

What did Aristotle think about money?

Aristotle believed that the production of material goods by the household was natural and good because it was driven by the natural and limited need for food, shelter, and clothing. Similarly, barter is natural and good because it is driven by the natural and finite need for the material goods that are exchanged. However, the economy takes a dangerous turn when money is introduced as a convenient medium of exchange. With money appears retail trade, which is the art of producing wealth through the exchange of material goods for money. In retail trade, the pursuit of wealth is not limited by the natural and finite needs of the household, but is unlimited, since money is useful only for exchange, and the desire for exchange-value, unlike our natural needs, is unlimited. But the worst kind of exchange is the exchange of money not for material goods but for more money. Although Aristotle speaks only of usury, the logic of his argument implies that any exchange of money for the purpose of making more money—such as interest on loans but also including dividends and capital gains—is wrong. Aristotle says that of all the modes of exchange, the exchange of money for more money is the most unnatural and wrong. Since capital is by definition

Aristotle was against the ideals of communism. He also felt, however, that using money as a means of exchange was risky because that leads to producing goods for the sole purpose of getting money and wealth rather than just providing products needed to live.

money that is used to make more money, Aristotle was just as much a critic of capitalism as he was of communism.

Why does Aristotle believe that it is best for the city-state to have a large middle class?

According to Aristotle, there are always three economic classes in every state: the rich, the poor, and the middle class. However, except in some large city-states, the middle class is seldom large. In a city-state without a large middle class, either the rich predominate or the poor predominate. When the rich predominate, the city-state tends to take the form of an oligarchy. When the poor predominate, the city-state tends to take the form of a democracy. But the conflict between rich and poor makes both forms of city-state unstable and liable to revolution.

The rich and the poor fear and resent one another. The rich covet their wealth and fear that the poor will take it from them. The poor covet the wealth of the rich and look for every opportunity to take it from them. Both the rich and the poor are forever conspiring against one another. On the other hand, when a large middle class predominates, the city-state will take the form of a polity, which is the mean between oligarchy and democracy, and is the best practical form of the city-state. The rich and the poor will never conspire together to overthrow the middle class because they do not trust one another enough to cooperate. As a consequence, polity is the most stable form of city-state and the least liable to revolution.

In addition, a polity is better ruled than either an oligarchy or a democracy because the middle class is better able to rule and be ruled in turn than either the rich or the poor. The rich are spoiled by their power. They love to rule but they dislike being ruled, even by reason. They are neither willing nor able to submit to authority, even when they ought to. The poor, on the other hand, are wretched and weak, and lack honor. Poverty, Aristotle says, breeds vice, servility, and small-mindedness. The poor are incapable of rule. They do not know "how to command and must be ruled like slaves. Thus arises a city, not of freemen, but of masters and slaves, the one despising, the other envying; and nothing can be more fatal to friendship and good fellowship in states than this" (*Nicomachean Ethics*). Only the middle class knows how to both rule and be ruled in turn, and it is the most amenable to reason. Therefore, in practice, the best city-state is a polity ruled by a large middle class.

Why did Aristotle believe that slavery was natural and good?

There is nothing in Aristotle's philosophy that is more shocking to the modern ear than his views on slavery. For us moderns, there is hardly any social institution that is more abhorrent than slavery. It is the standard by which we judge nearly all other social injustices: a social practice is unjust to the degree to which it resembles slavery. But Aristotle not only condones slavery; he also believes that slavery is built into the very fabric of being. In his *Politics*, Aristotle says that there is no difficulty in establishing on the basis of both fact and reason that slavery is not a violation of nature, but that "from the hour of their birth, some are marked out for subjection, others for rule" (*Nicomachean Ethics*). The duality of ruler and subject is found not just in some human societies but also "in all things which form a composite whole." "Such a duality exists in living creatures, but not in them only; it originates in the constitution of the universe; even in things which have no life there is a ruling principle, as in a musical mode." What Aristotle is referring to is the duality of form and matter.

As we learned in Aristotle's physics, every physical being (not only living beings) is a composite of form and matter. In every physical being—that is, in every being that exists by nature—there is a formal component that acts and a material component that is acted upon. Now, in the opening pages of Aristotle's *Politics*, we read that form is a ruling principle and matter is the subject of that principle. In the case of living beings, the soul of a living being is the form of its material body. The soul of a living being is therefore the ruling principle of its body: a living being "consists of soul and body: and of these two, the one is by nature the ruler, and the other the subject."

There is a relationship between that which rules and that which is ruled in all natural things, but not all forms of rule are the same as the rule of master over slave. Aristotle draws a distinction between two types of rule that exist within a human being. The intellect rules the appetites with a constitutional and royal rule, which is the rule of free men and citizens. But the soul rules the body with a despotic rule, which is the rule of master over slave. It is natural and good, Aristotle believes, that the soul should rule the body, and

Aristotle said that the intellect rules over the appetites with a constitutional rule, but the soul rules over the body with a despotic rule.

that the intellect should rule the passions, in their respective ways. If they don't, illness and harm result. Indeed, wherever "there is such a difference as that between soul and body, or between men and animals (as in the case of those whose business is to use their body, and who can do nothing better), the lower sort are by nature slaves, and it is better for them as for all inferiors that they should be under the rule of a master. For he who can be, and therefore is, another's, and he who participates in rational principle enough to apprehend, but not to have, such a principle, is a slave by nature."

Does Aristotle's belief in slavery invalidate his entire philosophical system?

According to Aristotle, his belief in slavery is a logical and necessary consequence of his ontology (his theory about living and nonliving things). If slavery, then, is wrong, so too must his ontology be wrong. But his ontology is the foundation of his entire philosophical system. If his ontology is wrong, then so is his physics; if his physics is wrong, then so is his psychology; and if his psychology is wrong, then so is his ethics, politics, and economic theory. But Aristotle's system is saved by the fact that his belief in slavery is not a necessary and logical consequence of his ontology, as he claims it to be. Aristotle's ontology requires that all physical things are a composite of form and matter. Form is that which acts, and matter is that which is acted upon. But even if we concede that when form acts upon something it "rules" it (here, Aristotle is relying on the dual meaning of the Greek word *arche*, which means both principle and rule), Aristotle admits in the *Politics* that there is more than one form of rule, and not all forms of rule are despotic or like the rule of a master over a slave.

Constitutional rule suits free persons, not slaves. His only explanation for why some people are slaves is that some people are born that way. But he offers no explanation for why some people are born that way and others are not. It is just a brute fact in his mind, without explanation. Clearly, slavery is not a necessary consequence of the nature of living beings, because not all people are born slaves. Furthermore, there is a deep sense in which, according to Aristotle's ontology, every natural thing is a free and autonomous being, not a slave, because all natural things contain within themselves an internal principle of change, their "nature." Even a rock has an internal principle of change. It is not acted upon by the earth or by gravity (which Aristotle did not know anything about), but it moves itself toward the center of the earth according to its own internal principle of change. Aristotle's ontology is based on observations of living beings, and the one universal attribute of all living beings is that they possess an internal principle of change. They are self-regulating, self-organizing, autonomous beings. In other words, they are by nature *free*. They are precisely *not* slaves.

Given his objectionable comments about slavery and other issues, why would we want to read Aristotle?

Aristotle does not offer us merely a few facts or theories about this or that. He offers us a vast and yet remarkably coherent system of ideas that purport to explain *everything*.

He offers us a *world*. But, although Aristotle's philosophical system can be separated from his objectionable comments about slavery, there can be no denying the fact that his values and worldview are very different from our own. Why, then, would we want to read him?

First, Aristotle's philosophical system is one of the greatest intellectual achievements of all time. Breathtaking in its scope and logical rigor, it offers us a model for what philosophy looks like at its best. Our values and worldview may be different from his, but he bequeathed to us a vocabulary of philosophical concepts that still permeates both popular and academic thought. It can fairly be said that without a thorough knowledge of Aristotle, it is impossible to understand either the philosophers who came after him or the subsequent course of history in the West and beyond.

Second, we may want to read Aristotle precisely *because* he offers us a set of values and a worldview that is different from our own. We do not study philosophy to merely validate our own beliefs and make us feel better about ourselves. We study philosophy to challenge the underlying assumptions behind our values and worldview so that we may improve upon them. And to do that, there is nothing better than studying a philosopher whose values and worldview are different from our own. For that purpose, there is no better philosopher than Aristotle, because Aristotle presented the most comprehensive and coherent account of a world different from ours.

What is Hellenistic philosophy?

Hellenistic philosophy is any philosophy that was practiced in the Greek-speaking world during the Hellenistic period, which was the period between the death of Alexander the Great in 323 B.C.E. and the death of Cleopatra in 30 B.C.E. After his death in 323 B.C.E., Alexander's empire was divided into a number of smaller Greek states, stretching from Greece to as far east as the lands of modern-day Pakistan and Turkmenistan, and south to the lands of modern-day Egypt and the Middle East. Although Hellenistic philosophy was found everywhere in the Greek-speaking world, the greatest philosophical activity took place in the city of Athens in Greece, in the city of Pergamum at the western end of Asia Minor (modern-day Turkey), and in the city of Alexandria in Egypt, which was ruled by the Greek-speaking Ptolemies until Cleopatra's death and the Roman conquest in 30 B.C.E. By the end of the Hellenistic period, the Greeks had lost control over all the lands that Alexander conquered three hundred years earlier, including Greece itself. But Greek philosophy lived on under the auspices of the Roman Empire.

Which schools of philosophy were founded and flourished during the Hellenistic period?

Early in the Hellenistic period, Plato's Academy abandoned the Pythagorean metaphysics of the Old Academy and adopted Skepticism. And after exerting great influence over the initial development of Hellenistic philosophy, the Peripatetic school (Aristotle's school) went into decline, so much so that the ancient authorities believed that Aristotle's works had been lost for most of the period. The most historically important schools of philosophy in the Hellenistic period were the schools of Epicureanism, Stoicism, and Skepticism. Each of these was founded early in the Hellenistic period and survived for a couple of centuries after its end, into the early period of the Roman Empire.

In addition to these three major schools, there were several other schools founded during the Hellenistic period that are of lesser historical significance, including the Cyrenaics, the Cynics, and the Megarian school of dialectics (logic). Apart from their intrinsic interest, Cynicism and the Megarian school of dialectics (logic) are of some historical significance because of their influence on Stoicism. The Cyrenaics were hedonists like the Epicureans, but whereas the Epicureans founded a popular movement that survived for many centuries into the period of the Roman Empire, the Cyrenaics died out after only a few generations. At the end of the Hellenistic period, the philosophies of Plato and Aristotle both made a comeback, but Stoicism was integrated into interpretations of Plato and Aristotle, changing the way that they would be understood for the remainder of the ancient period and throughout the medieval period.

What do the Hellenistic schools of philosophy have in common?

Except for the Skeptics, who didn't believe anything, all Hellenistic schools of philosophy were materialists who believed that the only reality is the material world. All Hellenistic schools of philosophy rejected the idealism of Plato's theory of forms. Even the moderate idealism of Aristotle, according to which universals exist only in particulars, was rejected. Consequently, no school of Hellenistic philosophy was interested in the study of metaphysics in Aristotle's sense of the word as a study of things beyond physics and the material world of nature.

What kind of institution was a "school" of philosophy during the Hellenistic period?

A "school" of philosophy during the Hellenistic period was not a "school" in the modern sense of an institution in which classes are taught to students for a fee and degrees are granted; rather, it was a group of philosophers who shared a common set of philosophical principles and a common way of life. To study philosophy in the Hellenistic period meant not only reading books and attending lectures but also entering into a personal relationship with a mentor or teacher and with fellow philosophers.

The primary purpose of all schools of Hellenistic philosophy was to learn how to live well, and to do that it was necessary not only to read books and attend lectures, but to have personal contact with other individuals who were wise or who were at least engaged in the active pursuit of wisdom. That's why each of the Hellenistic schools of philosophy traced their intellectual lineage through a series of students and their teachers back to the founder of the school. All Hellenistic schools of philosophy except for the Epicureans claimed that they were the true heirs of Socrates and ultimately traced their lineage back to him.

With the exception of the Skeptics, whose primary concern was to show that the other schools, especially the Stoics, didn't know anything, all Hellenistic schools of philosophy were interested in the study of physics and biology, that is, in the study of the material world of nature. The only things to be known were what Aristotle called the "particulars": the things of the material world. And the only way to know those things was empirically, through our sense organs—not intellectually, by thought alone. The other common theme in all Hellenistic schools of philosophy was their focus on ethics, which they understood to be the study of how to live well. All other areas of philosophical inquiry were subordinate to ethics.

Did the Hellenistic philosophers study metaphysics?

Aristotle's "first philosophy" was the study of being *qua* being—that is, the study of what can be said about beings (the things that exist) just by virtue of the fact that they are beings (that they exist). But since, according to Aristotle, all physical things are subject to change, and since anything that changes is not fully actualized, that is, has not fully come to *be*, "first philosophy" is ultimately the study of something that exists beyond the physical world. For Plato, that something was the forms. For Aristotle, that something was God, the unmoved mover, who is fully actualized form, without any material component. Since Aristotle's "first philosophy" was ultimately the study of something beyond the physical world, and since the Greek root "meta" (μετά) means "beyond" or "after," the Hellenistic philosophers called Aristotle's first philosophy "metaphysics." But since the Hellenistic philosophers were materialists and didn't believe that anything existed other than the physical world, they rejected metaphysics. For the Hellenistic philosophers, the study of physics, that is, the study of physical things in the world, is the only legitimate study of being, that is, of the things that exist.

What happened to the writings of the Hellenistic philosophers?

Although the total number of papyrus scrolls written by Hellenistic philosophers probably numbered in the many thousands, very few survived the fall of the Roman Empire. We have only three letters written by Epicurus (the *Letters to Menoeceus, Pythocles, and Herodotus*); a collection of maxims by Epicurus; *The Hymn to Zeus,* written by the Stoic philosopher Cleanthes; and *De rerum natura* (*On the Nature of Things*), a long poem written by the first-century B.C.E. Roman Epicurean Lucretius. Not until the eighteenth century were some of the writings of another Epicurean, Philodemus (c. 110–c. 30 B.C.E.), recovered.

During the period of the Roman Empire, at the beginning of the Christian era, both pagans and Christians turned their attention away from the material world and towards the spirit. Christianity offered hope in the Kingdom of God—in heaven, not on earth. The pagans attempted to compete with the Christians by creating a new pagan religion based on their new interpretation of Plato and Aristotle, which we now call Neoplatonism. Neoplatonism, in turn, exerted a powerful influence over the development of Christian philosophy, beginning in the ancient period and continuing throughout the Middle

The three parts of Hellenistic philosophy were physics, logic, and ethics. Physics is the study of physical things in the world—which, according to the Stoics and Epicureans, are the only kind of things there are. Logic in this context refers not only to the study of formal logic but also more broadly to epistemology—that is, to the study of knowledge and what is the best way to get it. Since the Stoics and Epicureans were empiricists, they believed that the acquisition of knowledge begins with sense experience of the physical world. Empirical knowledge is perfected by subjecting our judgments about our sense experiences to rational examination, just as is done in science. Ethics in Hellenistic philosophy is the study of how to live well and be happy. According to an analogy used by the Stoics, the three parts of philosophy are like the three parts of a garden. The fence that surrounds and protects the garden is logic. The soil is physics, which provides knowledge of the world. And the fruit of that knowledge is ethics.

Ages, until the works of Aristotle were recovered in the twelfth century and began to directly influence Christian philosophy. Although Stoic ethics survived well into the period of the Roman Empire and may have influenced the development of both Christianity and pagan Neoplatonism, the Roman Stoics, let alone the Christians and Neoplatonists, had little interest in Stoic physics and only a passing interest in Stoic logic. Epicureanism, on the other hand, was universally and totally reviled because of its materialism and hedonism.

It is costly to preserve written texts. They must be stored and protected in libraries. Before the development of the printing press in the early modern period, they had to be copied by hand by highly trained scribes. If they weren't copied by hand, over time the material upon which they were written would decay and disintegrate, and the text would be lost. Even if the institutional resources to preserve the ancient texts of the Hellenistic period had existed during the Dark Ages following the fall of the Roman Empire, Christians would not have expended the effort to preserve them because the materialism of the Hellenistic philosophers seemed to them not only incorrect but heretical. There was also a language barrier to preserving ancient Greek texts of the Hellenistic philosophers because there was a lack of scribes who knew the Greek language in the Latin West.

What other sources of information do we have about the Hellenistic philosophers besides their original writings?

We know about them mostly through excerpts and commentaries on their works found in later writers. Greek Roman biographer Diogenes Laërtius (third century C.E.) is one of the best sources of information about Hellenistic philosophy. Cicero (106–43 B.C.E.) lived during the final years of the Hellenistic period and personally studied with both

Stoics and Academic Skeptics, so he had firsthand knowledge of Hellenistic philosophy. His dislike for Epicureanism and his embrace of the Socratic and Platonic traditions made him acceptable to later Christians. St. Augustine admired his rhetorical skills and his command of the Latin language. Consequently, a substantial body of his work survived, and he is considered one of our best sources of information about Hellenistic philosophy.

Stoicism was a popular school of philosophy among the Roman elite in the first two centuries of the Christian era. The most important Stoics of that period were Roman senator and consul Seneca (4 B.C.E.–65 C.E.), Emperor Marcus Aurelius (121–180 C.E.), and former Greek slave Epictetus (55–135 C.E.). These are also important sources of information about Stoicism in the Hellenistic period. The Skeptic Sextus Empiricus (c. 160–c. 210 C.E.) was both a philosopher and a physician. He is a source of information about Epicurus and is our best source of information about Skepticism in the Hellenistic period. Galen (130–200 C.E.) was also both a philosopher and a physician. An exceptionally large volume of his writings survive because his theories dominated medicine for thousands of years. Although Galen preferred Plato and Aristotle and was not sympathetic to the Hellenistic philosophers, information about Hellenistic philosophy can be gleaned from his writings if they are read with a critical eye. Similarly, information about Hellenistic philosophy can be gleaned from the unsympathetic writings of Philo and other Alexandrian Jews as well as the Alexandrian Church fathers Origen and Clement.

How did most of the writings of Epicurus survive?

According to Diogenes Laërtius, Epicurus wrote about 300 books. But little has survived. The *Letters to Menoeceus, Pythocles, and Herodotus*, and a collection of maxims known as the *Principal Doctrines* (Κύριαι Δόξαι), all survived because they were quoted in their entirety by Diogenes Laërtius in Book X of his *Lives and Opinions of Eminent Philosophers*. Although *Lives* was lost to the Latin West, the original Greek version survived in the Byzantine Empire (the Greek-speaking eastern half of the Roman Empire). Throughout late antiquity and the Middle Ages, the Byzantine Empire maintained diplomatic ties with, and at times even ruled, parts of southern Italy and Sicily. Due to these ties, a few ancient Greek texts became available in Sicily in the twelfth century.

Epicurus went against Platonism and founded his own school called "the Garden," which accepted both male and female students. Although a prolific author, only three of his letters survive to the present day.

In 1158 C.E. Henry Aristippus (c. 1105/10–1162 C.E.) returned to Sicily from a diplomatic mission with several ancient Greek texts given to him by Byzantine emperor Manuel I Comnenus. Among these was Ptolemy's *Almagest*. Other ancient Greek texts that were likely obtained by Henry from the Byzantine Empire and that were translated by him for the first time into Latin were Diogenes's *Lives*, Aristotle's *Meteorology*, and Plato's *Phaedo* and *Meno*. Henry was the archdeacon of Catania in Sicily and a member of the court of William I of Sicily, who ruled all of southern Italy and Sicily. In the late twelfth and thirteenth centuries, interest in the history of Greek philosophy had been aroused in the West by the translation of Aristotle into Latin. In the preface to his translations of the *Meno* and the *Phaedo*, Henry congratulates dignitaries in the Sicilian court for their interest in acquiring ancient Greek texts. He says that it was Maio, King William I's chief minister, and Hugh, the archbishop of Palermo, who asked him to translate Diogenes's *Lives*, and that the King himself asked him to translate the Greek church father Gregory of Nazianzus. However, a complete translation of Diogenes's *Lives* into Latin did not appear until the Renaissance.

Throughout the Middle Ages, Epicurus was known through a few fragmentary quotations that survived in other works, but he and the Epicureans were typically condemned as heretical and sinful lovers of carnal delights. In his poem the *Inferno*, Dante Alighieri (1265–1321 C.E.) consigned the Epicureans to the sixth circle of hell where they burned eternally for believing that the soul dies with the body.

What other writings of Epicurus and of Epicurean philosopher Philodemus have survived, and how?

Another brief collection of Epicurean maxims, the *Vatican Sayings*, was discovered in the Vatican Library in 1888. Believed to date to the fourteenth century, this collection of maxims contains many of the same maxims as the *Principal Doctrines*, and not all of them were written by Epicurus himself but by other Epicureans. A much greater collection of Epicurean writings was buried under thirty meters of volcanic ash when Mount Vesuvius erupted in 79 C.E. at the Villa of the Papyri in the seaside town of Herculaneum on the Gulf of Naples. The owner of the Villa was Caesar's father-in-law, Piso, and one of the wealthiest men in the Roman Empire. The Villa contained the largest collection of Roman and Greek sculptures ever found at one location. It was also host to Epicurean philosopher Philodemus and a large library of Epicurean writings.

The town of Herculaneum was rediscovered in 1709 when several statues of extraordinary beauty were found by farmers while digging a well. These and the discovery of other works of art at Herculaneum provoked the development of Neoclassicism in the late eighteenth century. The first excavation of the Villa of the Papyri did not begin until 1750 when about 1,800 papyrus scrolls that had been carbonized and preserved by the volcanic ash were discovered. Excavations have continued sporadically since the eighteenth century. Although reading the carbonized scrolls has always presented a great technical challenge, some of the writings of Philodemus were recovered, as well as a significant portion of Epicurus's great work, *On Nature*. Large parts of the Villa have not yet been excavated, so there may be more papyrus scrolls waiting to be found. New computerized X-ray techniques hold out the promise of being able to read them without rolling them out and damaging them.

The Villa of Papyri near Mount Vesuvius was one of the most luxurious homes of the first century C.E. It held a large collection of papyruses and many artworks, including statues and frescoes.

How was the work of Lucretius rediscovered?

Lucretius (c. 99–c. 55 B.C.E.) was a Roman aristocrat and Epicurean philosopher of the first century B.C.E. His book on Epicurean philosophy, *De rerum natura* (*On the Nature of Things*), was a masterpiece of Latin poetry, which influenced the great Latin poets Virgil and Horace in both style and substance. It contains most of what we know about the philosophy of Epicurus. The book was forgotten during the Middle Ages but somehow survived in a German monastery where in 1417 it was rediscovered by an Italian humanist scholar, Poggio Bracciolini (1380–1459). Poggio belonged to the second generation of Italian humanists, following Petrarch (1304–1374), who had brought renewed attention to the forgotten works of Cicero (106–43 B.C.E.) and the Roman historian Livy (59/64 B.C.E.–17 C.E.). Cicero was the single most important source of information in the Latin language about Hellenistic philosophy.

Poggio was a master of the Latin language who sought to revive the lost learning of classical Latin literature. Although he served as papal secretary to seven popes, he maintained ties with the very worldly Medici family and with Florentine humanists who were more interested in the *humanae litterae* (profane classical literature, the original basis for the "humanities") than in *divinae litterae* (biblical exegesis). Poggio was attracted to what he understood to be an Epicurean lifestyle devoted to pleasure. At the age of fifty-six, he left his mistress of many years and their fourteen children and married a noble Florentine woman who was just under eighteen years old, with whom he had another six children. In the spring of 1416, one year before he discovered the text of Lucretius in a monastery, he visited the German spa of Baden, where he found barely clothed men and women bathing together. He wrote to his friend and fellow humanist Niccoli (1364–1437) that he had discovered a felicitous school of Epicureans at the spa of Baden and compared it to the Garden of Eden, which he said "the Hebrews call the garden of pleasure."

What impact did the recovery of the writings of Epicurus and the Epicureans have on the modern world?

The writings of Epicurus and Lucretius had little immediate impact when they were first recovered by Italian humanists in the Renaissance. The name "Epicurus" still referred to an immoral lifestyle of pleasure seeking, not a respectable philosophy. When the great

Italian humanist Lorenzo Valla (c. 1407–1457) wrote about Epicurean philosophy, he did so through the device of a fictional dialogue between an Epicurean, a Stoic, and a Christian. Alone among medieval scholastics and Renaissance humanists, Valla tried to reconcile Epicurean hedonism with the Christian virtues of charity and beatitude.

Not until the sixteenth century did the essayist Montaigne (1533–1592) quote Lucretius at length. But even Montaigne did so because he admired the literary style of Lucretius's Latin poetry, not his philosophy. The real breakthrough for Epicurean philosophy came in the seventeenth century when French Catholic priest Pierre Gassendi (1592–1655), a proponent of early modern science, again tried to reconcile Christian and Epicurean philosophy. While he rejected the Epicurean view of the gods as detached and indifferent to human beings, as well as their belief that the soul dies with the body, he embraced their empiricism and the atomic theory of matter.

The modern scientific theory of the physical world is fundamentally at odds with Aristotle's theory of form and matter. In order to advance modern science, it was necessary to find an alternative to Aristotle, who had dominated the study of nature since the Middle Ages. Gassendi found that alternative in Epicurean empiricism and the atomic theory of matter. The first group of intellectuals in England to embrace Gassendi's Epicurean atomism was a circle of intellectuals that formed around Sir Charles Cavendish (c. 1594–1654), which included philosopher Thomas Hobbes (1588–1679) and mathematician John Pell (1611–1685). English physician and natural philosopher Walter Charleton (1619–1707) further adapted Gassendi's Epicurean philosophy to Christianity by arguing that the atomic theory of matter presupposes the existence of God. Consequently, in spite of the objections of the Cambridge Platonists, Gassendi's Epicurean philosophy became popular among early English scientists, including the members of the Invisible College.

The Invisible College was a circle of scientists that formed around Robert Boyle (1627–1691) and was a precursor to the Royal Society. Boyle was the founder of modern chemistry and a pioneer of the experimental scientific method. The Royal Society was the most distinguished professional scientific association in the history of early modern science. Like its predecessor the Invisible College, the Royal Society embraced Epicurean atomism and was dedicated to the experimental scientific method. Epicureanism subsequently influenced many prominent figures of the En-

Chemist, physicist, inventor, and philosopher Robert Boyle was influenced by Epicureanism. He was a founder of the scientific method and the field of chemistry.

lightenment and of the nineteenth century, including John Locke (1632–1704), Thomas Jefferson (1743–1826), Jeremy Bentham (1748–1832), and Karl Marx (1818–1883).

What happened to Aristotle's Peripatetic school of philosophy after he fled Athens in 323 B.C.E.?

After Alexander the Great's death in 323 B.C.E., Aristotle was forced to flee Athens due to anti-Macedonian sentiment in the city. Aristotle's longtime friend and research associate Theophrastus of Eresos (c. 371–c. 287 B.C.E.) became the scholarch or head of the Peripatetic school. Theophrastus retained that position for thirty-five years after Aristotle's death until his own death in 287 B.C.E. The Peripatetic school flourished during this period.

Theophrastus continued Aristotle's work in metaphysics, focusing on the problem of how the things apprehended by reason are related to the things apprehended by the senses. Since he believed that the only thing apprehended by reason alone was the prime mover, his concern was to explain how the prime mover, which is itself unmoved and eternal, can cause the material objects of sense to move. But more importantly for the subsequent history of Hellenistic philosophy, Theophrastus continued and indeed expanded the range of Aristotle's scientific study of nature. If Aristotle was the first to engage in a systematic, scientific study of animals, Theophrastus was the first to engage in a systematic, scientific study of plants.

After the death of Theophrastus, Strato of Lampsacus (c. 335–c. 269 B.C.E.) became the third scholarch of the Peripatetic school, a position he held until his own death in 269 B.C.E. Strato denied the need for a prime mover and abandoned the study of metaphysics. He believed that knowledge could be acquired only through scientific examination of natural events. Strato may have known Epicurus, who was an empiricist and a materialist. Like the Epicureans, Strato believed that the world is composed of tiny particles or atoms. In any case, he turned his attention exclusively to the material things apprehended by the senses. One of Strato's students in Alexandria, Aristarchus (c. 310–c. 230 B.C.E.), was the first to propose a heliocentric theory of the universe, contrary to Aristotle's geocentric theory. Hence, according to Cicero, Strato was known as a *phusikos* (φυσικός)—in English, a *physicist*—meaning he who studies "nature" (*physis;* φύσις). Strato replaced Aristotle's theory of the soul as the form of the body with the Stoic theory of the soul as *pneuma*, a material substance composed of fire and air. And he replaced Aristotle's teleological explanation of events in terms of purpose or function with purely mechanical causation. Cicero complained that Strato did not devote enough attention to ethics. In fact, Aristotle himself had given priority to theoretical knowledge over and above ethics. Out of forty-six works by Strato cited by Diogenes Laërtius, only a handful concern ethical topics. After Strato, Aristotle's Peripatetic school fell into decline and was not revived until the end of the Hellenistic period, when Aristotle's lecture notes and the works of Theophrastus were rediscovered and compiled by Andronicus, the eleventh scholarch of the Peripatetic school.

THE MUSEUM OF ALEXANDRIA

What was the museum of Alexandria?

The "museum" (Greek *musaeum* or *mouseion*, μουσεῖον) of Alexandria was not a collection of artifacts but a "temple to the muses," devoted to the study of Greek poetry and music, rhetoric and oratory, philosophy, mathematics, and science. It was more akin to a modern university than a museum. It included living space for scholars and scientists, an astronomical observatory, a medical school, dissection rooms, and the largest library in the ancient world. Modern estimates of the size of the library's collection range between a few tens of thousands to a few hundred thousand papyrus scrolls, or the equivalent of about 6,000 to 60,000 modern books. Most of the books were written by Greeks in the Greek language, but there was also a large collection of ancient Egyptian literature and books from other great civilizations as well.

An Egyptian priest named Manetho (*Manethōn,* Μανέθων) wrote a history of Egypt in the Greek language at the museum. The *Aegyptiaca* is a history of Egypt that still serves as an invaluable reference source for Egyptologists. According to the pseudepigraphic *Letter of Aristeas,* the Septuagint translation of the Old Testament from Hebrew into Greek was performed by seventy-two Jewish scholars at the museum under orders from Ptolemy II Philadelphus. Also found in the library was a history of Babylonia written in Greek by Chaldean priest and astrologist Berossus, of the early third century B.C.E. There were also works on Persia and Zoroastrianism and even Buddhist texts from the Kingdom of Ashoka (c. 268–232 B.C.E.), which had diplomatic ties with Ptolemy II Philadelphus.

What intellectual advancements were made at the museum of Alexandria?

The museum of Alexandria was the single greatest center of intellectual activity in the Hellenistic world. Zenodotus lived during the reign of the first two Ptolemies and was the first director of the Great Library of Alexandria. He was a grammarian and a literary scholar who established the foundations of literary criticism. He produced the first critical edition of Homer.

Callimachus (c. 305–c. 240 B.C.E.) was a poet and literary scholar at the museum who called himself a grammarian (*grammatikos*). His most important accomplishment was to invent library science. He wrote the *Pinakes* (πίνακεσ, or in English, "Tables"), the first library catalog and classification scheme, to serve as an index to the Great Library of Alexandria's collection. The *Pinakes*, or, more fully, *The Tables of Men Distinguished in Every Branch of Learning, and Their Works*, was the first attempt to categorize the accumulated knowledge of the civilized world by subject. In so doing, Callimachus created many of the divisions between intellectual fields of study that we still recognize today. His student Eratosthenes (c. 276–c. 194 B.C.E.) was a polymath and chief librarian of the library of Alexandria whose interests ranged from science to mathematics to literature. Eratosthenes studied with philosophers Aristo and Arcesilaus in

Athens, but he called himself a philologist (a *philologos* or lover of reason), not a philosopher. Today Eratosthenes is most famous for having accurately calculated the circumference of the earth.

Aristarchus of Samos (c. 310–c. 230 B.C.E.) was the first to propose a heliocentric theory of the solar system, and he also put the known planets in their correct order of distance from the sun. Herophilos (335–280 B.C.E.) and Erasistratus (c. 304–c. 250 B.C.E.) performed the first dissections of human bodies in the ancient Greek world at the museum and made great advances in medicine and anatomy. Euclid wrote the *Elements*, his textbook on geometry, which was widely used to teach mathematics until the early twentieth century.

What happened to the Great Library of Alexandria?

The Great Library of Alexandria flourished during the Hellenistic period but declined thereafter. As the number of scrolls owned by the library grew during the Hellenistic period, parts of the Great Library's collection were stored in the Serapeum of Alexandria and others in a warehouse close to the harbor. The Serapeum was the greatest temple in Alexandria, dedicated to the syncretic Greco-Egyptian god Serapis, who had been either created or refashioned by Ptolemy I Soter to reconcile the Greek and Egyptian populations of the city. According to some ancient reports, the Great Library was accidentally burned down by Caesar in 48 B.C.E. during the Siege of Alexandria in the Great Roman Civil War. While under siege in Alexandria, Caesar set fire to his own fleet

An ancient papyrus scroll from Euclid's *Elements of Geometry* dates between 75 and 125 C.E. It is astounding that this textbook was used by teachers as recently as the early twentieth century!

to block the harbor. According to some ancient reports, the fire spread to the Great Library itself, either partially or completely destroying it. According to other reports, the fire only spread to the warehouse that was located close to the harbor. In any case, modern scholars agree that a large number of scrolls survived the fire undamaged, and soon afterward attempts were made to replace some of those that were lost. But the library never regained the full glory that it had achieved during the Hellenistic period, when Alexandria was ruled by Greeks.

The Romans proved to be poor stewards of the Great Library of Alexandria, providing less support to it than the Ptolemies had and appointing directors to the library for political reasons instead of their professional qualifications. In the second century C.E., as the grain supply from Egypt became less important to the Romans, other cities, including Rome itself, replaced Alexandria as leading centers of learning. The quality of intellectual work at the museum declined until it apparently ended altogether. There are no historical records of scholars or scientists working in the museum of Alexandria after the 260s C.E. In 272 C.E., Roman emperor Aurelian burned down the quarter of the city that contained the Great Library and museum during his war to put down a rebellion led by the Palmyrene queen Zenobia that had swept most of the eastern Mediterranean. The Great Library and museum were almost certainly destroyed at this time, and if they weren't, they would have been destroyed when Roman emperor Diocletian laid siege to the city in 297 C.E.

However, that was not the end of libraries in Alexandria. The largest collection of books was contained in the Serapeum, which remained an important pagan temple and even contained classrooms where pagan philosophy was taught. By the third century C.E., pagan philosophy had become dominated by Neoplatonism, which was as much a religion as a philosophy. The goal of Neoplatonism was *henosis* (ἕνωσιζ), which meant unity with the divine. Plotinus (204/205–270 C.E.) had taught meditation as the means to achieve *henosis*, whereas Syrian Neoplatonist Iamblichus (c. 245–c. 325 C.E.) taught theurgy, the practice of religious and magical rituals. It was Iamblichean Neoplatonism that dominated the Serapeum in 391 C.E. when a Christian mob led by Pope Theophilus of Alexandria destroyed it, but by then it probably contained relatively few books. Neoplatonism continued to be taught in a tradition that identified with the original museum of Alexandria for centuries after the destruction of the Serapeum. Even the cruel murder of Hypatia in 415 C.E. by a Christian mob did not end the teaching of Neoplatonism in the eastern Mediterranean. The final destruction of pagan libraries in Alexandria came in 642 C.E. under orders from Caliph Omar, when a Muslim army conquered the city.

How did Aristotle influence the early development of philosophy and science in Alexandria?

The first Ptolemy who ruled Egypt, Ptolemy I Soter (c. 367–282 B.C.E.), was one of Alexander the Great's childhood friends, and together they had studied with Aristotle.

Thus, when Ptolemy established the mission of the museum, it reflected Aristotle's encyclopedic interests and unquenchable thirst for knowledge. The mission of the museum of Alexandria was to collect all the poetry, philosophy, and science of the ancient world and to study every facet of nature in the field and laboratory.

The second Ptolemy who ruled Egypt, Ptolemy II Philadelphus (308–246 B.C.E.), was said to have set the goal of acquiring 500,000 papyrus scrolls from throughout the eastern Mediterranean region. Every ship that entered the port of Alexandria was searched for books. When they were found, they were carefully copied by scribes before returning either the copy or the original to their owners. When Ptolemy I Soter founded the museum in Alexandria, he asked another student of Aristotle's, Theophrastus, to serve as its director. Although Theophrastus turned down the offer, he recommended his student Demetrius of Phaleron (c. 350–c. 280 B.C.E.), who accepted the position. Demetrius had been a distinguished orator and governor of Athens under Cassander, the Macedonian king and another one of Aristotle's students, until he was forced into exile by his political opponents following Cassander's death in 297 B.C.E.

According to Strabo (c. 64 B.C.E.–c. 24 C.E.), Demetrius used Aristotle's Lyceum as a model in the design and construction of the museum at Alexandria. There was a *peripatos* (covered walkway), a communal room for dining, and a collection of papyrus scrolls systematically organized into carefully designated categories as Aristotle may have organized the library at his school in Athens, the Lyceum. In fact, the Lyceum's library was one of the most important acquisitions of the library at Alexandria, perhaps forming the core of the collection. According to Athenaeus (c. 200 C.E.), the Lyceum's library was purchased by the second Ptolemy to rule Egypt, Ptolemy II Philadelphus (308–246 B.C.E.), from his tutor, Strato. According to Diogenes Laërtius, Demetrius wrote extensively on history, politics, poetry, and rhetoric, as Aristotle had, and there were categories devoted to these subjects in the library of Alexandria's classification scheme.

How did the Peripatetic philosopher Strato influence the development of science in Alexandria?

Strato (c. 335–c. 269 B.C.E.) further developed the empirical methods of Aristotle and Theophrastus and was the first to perform controlled experiments of the

A fresco preserved at the National University of Athens shows (left to right) Aristotle, Theophrastus, and a young Strato, who was their student and further developed their empirical methods.

physical world. His experiments with vacuums established the law of *horror vacui* (the principle that nature abhors a vacuum), which was the theoretical basis for the development of air and steam engines by the engineering school of Ctesibius (c. 270 B.C.E.). And his experiments with falling bodies demonstrated for the first time that the speed of falling bodies accelerates as they fall. Strato may have introduced the experimental method to the scientists who were working in Alexandria, some of whom were his students. He is known to have lived in Alexandria when he tutored Ptolemy II Philadelphus and to have advised him on the design of the museum where science was taught and practiced.

Among the colleagues and students in Alexandria who may have been influenced by Strato were anatomists Herophilos (335–280 B.C.E.) and Erasistratus (c. 304–c. 250 B.C.E.), astronomer Aristarchus (c. 310–c. 230 B.C.E.), and engineer Ctesibius. Strato carried Aristotle's empiricism to its logical conclusion. He eliminated the last vestige of Platonic idealism from Aristotle's philosophy and became a materialist. He believed that the world is composed of tiny particles or atoms and that the mechanical motion of these particles explained everything. Like Strato, the scientists who worked in Alexandria during the Hellenistic period were also materialists and explained physical events in purely mechanical terms without purpose or end (*telos*). The lungs, for example, were understood by Alexandrian scientists to operate in the same way as bellows. The heart was understood to operate like a water pump. Strato may have also laid the groundwork for scientific research in Alexandria by helping to introduce Aristotle's methods of logic and abstract conceptual reasoning.

The ancient Egyptians had a long tradition of medical practice stretching back thousands of years that included the use of surgery and drugs. They recognized the importance of cleanliness and consequently they had a lower rate of infection than European hospitals did until the twentieth century. And while Greek custom forbade dissection of the human body, it was a routine part of the embalming process in ancient Egypt. But the Egyptians had no understanding of how the internal organs of the body work or why cleanliness prevents infection. They understood illness in terms of dramatic stories about personal agents and their actions in the world. They believed that illness was caused by sin or by demonic supernatural forces, and therefore they treated it by performing religious rituals and practicing sympathetic magic. In general, they explained the world around them in concrete terms and failed to think abstractly. Consequently, they failed to develop an abstract theoretical understanding of medicine or biology.

Aristotle, on the other hand, developed methods of scientific reasoning based on the syllogism and the organization of kinds into genus and species that was particularly suitable for the study of biology. Although he did not dissect human bodies, Aristotle did dissect animals. He was a pioneer in the scientific study of animals and their anatomy, and some of his achievements were not surpassed until the nineteenth century. Aristotle's student Theophrastus was the founder of botany, the scientific study of plants, and was recognized as such by Carl Linnaeus (1707–1778), the "father of modern taxonomy." It is likely due to the influence of Strato and the Aristotelians that the scientists in Alexandria learned to think abstractly and develop scientific theories about the human body.

Where does the word "anatomy" come from, and what does it mean?

The English word "anatomy" comes from the Latin word *anatomia*, which in turn comes from the ancient Greek word *anatomē* (ἀνατομή). The ancient Greek word is composed of the root term *ana*, which meant "up," and the root terms *tomia* and *temnein*, which meant "cutting" and "to cut." Combining these root terms, we get "to cut up"—in other words, "to dissect." Anatomy is the scientific knowledge of the parts of the body learned by dissection.

How did scientists at the museum of Alexandria progress beyond both the Greek and Egyptian understanding of the human body?

Knowledge about the human body was limited in ancient Greece by the taboo against the dissection of human bodies. But no such taboo existed in ancient Egypt. The dead were routinely cut open and organs removed from their bodies to prepare them for mummification. In Egypt, the Ptolemies adopted many local customs, such as the marriage of siblings within the royal family, which those still living in Greece would have found to be abhorrent. Thus it was that for thirty or forty years during the tenure of Herophilos (335–280 B.C.E.) in Alexandria that the Ptolemies looked the other way while scientists performed dissections of human bodies. Not only did Greek scientists in Alexandria dissect the bodies of the dead, but according to later Roman physicians and Church fathers who assumed the worst about them, they even dissected the bodies of condemned criminals *before* they died.

Unlike the Egyptians who dissected the bodies of the dead for religious purposes, the Greeks dissected bodies to understand how they worked. The dissection of human bodies proved highly beneficial to the development of science in Alexandria. Scientists trained in Aristotelian forms of reasoning developed new theories about the lungs, the heart, the arteries and veins, the nervous system, and the brain. Most importantly, they developed new theories about the *pneuma* and how it circulates throughout the body. At the end of this brief period, the last human dissection was performed. They would not be performed again until the mid-sixteenth century.

What is *pneuma*?

*P*neuma (πνεῦμα) was the ancient Greek word for "breath," but because breath gives bodies life, it could also mean "spirit" or "soul." A body without breath loses its soul and is no longer alive. During the Hellenistic period, scientists in Alexandria theorized that *pneuma* circulated in both the blood vessels and the nerves of the body.

How did the development of the science of human anatomy in Alexandria alter the course of philosophy in the Hellenistic period?

Cutting the body open revealed that there was no spiritual entity inhabiting it but rather a mechanical system of tubes, pumps, and valves. Anatomical studies of the lungs and arteries offered a mechanical explanation for how *pneuma* nourishes and sustains the life of the body. Anatomical studies of the brain and nervous system offered a mechanical explanation for how the *pneuma* transmits sensations to the heart and brain and causes the body to move. These discoveries revolutionized the classical Greek understanding of the soul. Although Plato believed that the soul could survive the death of the body and Aristotle did not, they both believed that the soul was a fundamentally different sort of thing than the body. The discovery of the body's pneumatic system of nerves and blood vessels by scientists in Alexandria demonstrated to Hellenistic philosophers that *pneuma* is not fundamentally different from the body but is in fact an integral part of it. In this respect, the Hellenistic philosophers returned to the view of the Pre-Socratic Milesian scientist-philosopher Anaximenes, who equated soul (*psyche*), breath (*pneuma*), and air (*aer*, ἀήρ).

Who was Hippocrates?

Hippocrates (c. 460–c. 370 B.C.E.) was the "father of medicine" and the author of the "Hippocratic Oath," a set of ethical principles, including patient confidentiality and the promise to first do no harm, that physicians still swear by today. He was the first to believe that illness had a natural cause and the first to separate medicine as a scientific field of study from religion and magic.

Who was Praxagoras, and what did he do?

Praxagoras (born c. 340 B.C.E.) was an ancient Greek physician and medical scientist who taught medicine and human anatomy on the island of Cos. His father and grandfather were both physicians in the Hippocratic tradition. Praxagoras was the first physician in history to recognize the importance of the pulse as a vital sign. He studied Aristotle's theory of human anatomy and agreed with him that the

Called the "Father of Medicine," Hippocrates established the principle of patient confidentiality, believed that illness had a natural cause, and is known for the oath named after him to cause no harm to a patient.

mind was based in the heart, not in the brain. But he believed that the purpose of respiration was to replenish the body's *pneuma*, not to cool the inner heat produced by the body, as Aristotle believed. He also improved upon Aristotle's theory of the circulatory system by distinguishing, perhaps for the first time, between veins and arteries. Praxagoras believed that the veins carry blood but that the arteries carry *pneuma*—a view that dominated Greek medicine for over four centuries. Blood, he believed, is produced from digested food and distributed throughout the body by the veins, which originate in the liver, not the heart. However, his theory that breathing nourishes the arterial *pneuma* is close to the modern theory that the arteries carry oxygenated blood. Since the *pneuma* is the cause of motion in the body, Praxagoras believed that the arteries also serve the function that we now attribute to the motor nerves. He explained such disorders as epilepsy and paralysis as arising from cold phlegm that accumulates in the arteries and blocks the flow of *pneuma*.

Who was Herophilos, and what did he do?

Herophilos (c. 330–c. 260 B.C.E.) was born in the Greek town of Chalcedon in Asia Minor. At a young age, he relocated to Alexandria after completing his study of medicine and anatomy with Praxagoras on the island of Cos. Like his teacher Praxagoras, he was an empiricist and practiced the experimental method. He was the first scientist to perform dissections of the human body, and for a long time to come, the last. But in the brief span of about thirty or forty years when dissections were permitted in Alexandria, his anatomical studies and those of his colleagues yielded such a wealth of information about the human body that he is remembered today as the "father of anatomy." Anatomical dissections did not resume until the thirteenth century C.E., and the work of Herophilos was not surpassed until Vesalius (1514–1564) in the sixteenth century.

Herophilos wrote at least nine books. All were lost with the destruction of the Great Library at Alexandria, but he was quoted extensively by later physicians, including Galen (130–210 C.E.), most of whose writings were preserved. Herophilus discovered that the heart is the source of the pulse, not the blood vessels, as his teacher Praxagoras believed. He also realized that the nerves serve a different function from the blood vessels, and he even distinguished between motor and sensory nerves. He discovered that the brain, not the heart, is the center of the nervous system, the seat of thought, and the ruling part (the *hegemonikon*) of the soul. The brain's function is to produce sentience and motor impulses and to think and feel, not to cool the blood, as Aristotle believed. He traced the sinuses on the outer surface of the brain to their confluence in the *torcular Herophili*, which is named after him. He identified the ventricles of the brain and named the meninges (the dura mater, arachnoid, and pia mater). He also identified and distinguished the functions of the optic, oculomotor, trigeminal, facial, vestibulocochlear, and hypoglossal nerves. In addition to his anatomy of the nervous system, he also described the parts of the eye, reproductive organs, and the digestive system. He named the upper part of the small intestine the duodenum.

Who was Erasistratus, and what did he do?

Erasistratus of Ceos (c. 325–c. 250 B.C.E.) was a physician and medical scientist who dissected human bodies in Alexandria with his colleague Herophilos. He is known for most of the same anatomical theories that are attributed to Herophilos. However, Erasistratus was the first to explain how the heart's valves prevented blood from backing up and flowing in the wrong direction. He named the tricuspid valve. And while Herophilos distinguished between sensory and motor nerves, it was Erasistratus who traced the motor nerves to the cerebellum.

Before he arrived in Alexandria, Erasistratus served as physician to the court of Seleucus I Nicator, the Greek ruler of the Near East. Erasistratus came from a family of Greek physicians, and he was strongly influenced by the Aristotelians. He studied medicine at the school established by Praxagoras on the island of Cos with physicians Chrysippus of Cnidos and Metrodorus, who was the third husband of Aristotle's daughter Pythias. According to Diogenes Laërtius and Galen, Erasistratus also studied with Theophrastus, the second scholarch of Aristotle's Lyceum after Aristotle himself. But Erasistratus adopted his theory that the body is composed of tiny particles or atoms and his mechanical explanation of bodily functions from Strato of Lampsacus, who served as the third scholarch of Aristotle's Lyceum and as the private tutor of Ptolemy II Philadelphus.

Erasistratus used Strato's principle that nature abhors a vacuum (*horror vacui*) to explain how nutritious particles are absorbed from the blood. When microscopic spaces within the body are evacuated, nutritious particles are drawn through tiny pores in the walls of venous capillaries to fill the evacuated spaces by the principle that nature abhors a vacuum. The same principle explains how the lungs draw breath (*pneuma*) in from outside the body by expanding and opening up an empty space. *Pneuma* is then pumped by the heart from the lungs through the pulmonary vein and into the arteries. *Pneuma* that reaches the brain is transformed into psychic *pneuma*, which travels through the nerves, causing the mind to sense and feel and the muscles to move.

How did Erasistratus cure a broken heart?

When Seleucus I Nicator was an old man, he married a beautiful young woman named Stratonice. The king's eldest son, Antiochus, fell passionately in love with his stepmother, Stratonice, but suffered in silence knowing that he could not have her. According to a story told by many ancient sources, but also told about other famous physicians, Erasistratus cured Antiochus of his broken heart. None of the court's physicians could understand what was wrong with Antiochus until Erasistratus noticed that whenever Stratonice was close to Antiochus, he became warm, his skin changed color, and his pulse quickened. Erasistratus told the king that his son's illness was incurable because he was in love, but he could not have the woman he loved. When asked by the king who his son was in love with, Erasistratus lied and said that it was his own—Erasistratus's—wife. The king then asked Erasistratus to give up his wife to Antiochus so that he could be cured. Erasistratus responded by asking the king if he would give up his own wife if his son were in love with her. The king said he would most definitely, and when Erasistratus revealed

A 1774 painting by Jacques-Louis David showing Erasistratus curing Antiochus of a broken heart.

the truth, the king stuck by his word. Not only did the king allow his son to marry Stratonice, but he gave him dominion over several provinces of his empire.

THE STOIC THEORY OF THE COSMOS AND OF WHAT EXISTS

What is the Stoic theory of cosmic *pneuma*?

The Stoic theory of the cosmos was influenced by Heraclitus's notion of cosmic fire and by Plato's *Timaeus*. Although the Stoics were not Platonic idealists and did not believe in Plato's theory of the forms, they did embrace Plato's theory of the world soul and of a rational God (the "Demiurge") who crafts the universe. According to the Stoics, the cosmos is composed of two principles, one active and the other passive. The active principle is, as it was for Heraclitus, the *logos*, the principle of reason. The passive principle is the principle of *hyle* (ὕλη), the Greek word for passive matter or amorphous stuff. Stoic philosopher Chrysippus believed that *logos* pervades everything in the universe in the same way that a drop of wine can be blended into the entire ocean. The Stoic God is not therefore a transcendent God, like the Abrahamic God who exists outside of the world, but a pantheistic God.

The world, the Stoics believed, is a living, rational animal, and God is its soul. The world soul pervades everything in the universe, but the ruling part of the world soul (the *hegemonikon*) is located in the heavens. However, the word "soul" must be read with caution, because the Stoic God is not immaterial or spiritual. According to the Stoics, only physical bodies can cause anything to occur, because causation requires physical contact between a causal agent and its object. The cosmic soul is rather like the warm breath or *pneuma* that courses through our nerves and arteries. Just as *pneuma* gives the human body life, so does God as cosmic *pneuma* give the world life. The cosmic *pneuma* is a substance that the Stoics likened to fire because like fire, it is forever acting and effecting change. But unlike fire, it is not chaotic.

Like Plato's Demiurge, the cosmic *pneuma* is a craftsman who effects change in an ordered fashion according to a rational plan (in accordance with the *logos*, as Heraclitus had said). The Stoic God is therefore a providential God because everything happens according to His plan, even if mere mortals cannot comprehend it. And because everything happens according to God's plan and can happen in no other way, God is Fate. Periodically, the entire universe is consumed by the cosmic fire and then regenerated again out of it, in an eternal cycle of recurrence. The same sequence of events repeats eternally, in accordance with God's rational plan, which is Fate (*heimarmenē*) and Providence (*pronoia*). According to the Stoics, a wise and happy person accepts whatever comes and even learns to love fate (Latin *amor fati*) because they know that God's plan is for the best.

Why and how was Stoic philosophy influenced by the medical research of Praxagoras and the scientists at the museum of Alexandria?

The Stoics were materialists and empiricists. They believed that the only reality is the material world and that knowledge of that world comes only through sense experience. Therefore, they would have welcomed the results of scientific research and integrated those findings into their theories because scientific research is based on empirical facts. Such appears to be the case concerning anatomical research in Alexandria.

As scientific knowledge about *pneuma* improved during the Hellenistic period, Stoic theories about pneuma likewise improved. At the beginning of the period, Praxagoras believed that the mind is based in the heart, not the brain, and that it reaches out to the skin and sense organs through the arteries, which carry *pneuma*. Indeed, we find a similar theory of *pneuma* with early Greek Stoic philosopher Chrysippus (c. 279–c. 206 B.C.E.), who, like Praxagoras, believed that the mind is based in the heart. According to Galen (130–200 C.E.), who believed that the mind is based in the brain, Chrysippus cited Praxagoras and was presumably influenced by him. But later in the Hellenistic period, according to Epicurean philosopher Philodemus (c. 110–c. 30 B.C.E.), when the Stoic philosophers had time to digest the results of Alexandrian science, they believed that the mind was based in the brain, not the heart. In any case, the Stoic theory of *pneuma* parallels the theory of *pneuma* developed by Greek medical scientists.

What is the Stoic theory of *pneuma* in the human body?

Since cosmic *pneuma* permeates and orders everything in the universe, it must also permeate the human body. Therefore, what we call our soul or psychic *pneuma* is really just a small part of the cosmic *pneuma*—in other words, a small part of God, who is the soul of the world. One can think of it as a spark flung off the great cosmic fire. The Stoic theory of psychic *pneuma* parallels the theory of *pneuma* found in Praxagoras, Herophilos, and Erasistratus. For the Stoics as for these scientists, *pneuma* enters the body through the lungs, is pumped by the heart through the arteries and nerves, and passes through tiny pores into every part of the body. According to the Stoics, *pneuma* is an active and rational principle that imposes order on matter. The more complex that order is, the greater the "tension" (Greek *tonos*). The lowest level of tension is the "cohesion" (Greek *hexis*) that holds inanimate objects like stones or bones together. At the next higher level of tension is "nature" (Greek *physis*), which brings bodies to life. At an even higher level of tension is soul proper (*psyche*), which gives animals the powers of sensation and movement. Finally, at the highest level of tension is the human capacity for reason (the rational soul or *logike psyche*), which is housed in the ruling or commanding faculty of the soul, the *hegemonikon* (ἡγεμονικόν).

The early Greek Stoics, Zeno of Citium (c. 334–c. 262 B.C.E.) and Chrysippus (c. 279–c. 206 B.C.E.), both located the *hegemonikon* in the heart, not the brain. Since speech, cognition, and emotion are acts of the *hegemonikon*, they too are located in the heart. According to Chrysippus, the soul extends out like the tentacles of an octopus to all parts of the body, filling them with vital breath (*pneuma*), regulating and controlling the powers of nourishment and growth, reproduction, sensation and locomotion. Messages from the skin and sense organs are carried by *pneuma* through the body's network of arteries and nerves to the heart, where the *hegemonikon* "passes judgement like a king" on what the senses have reported. Some later Stoics adapted the theory to locate the *hegemonikon* in the brain, not the heart, as Herophilos and Erasistratus had done, but otherwise the theory remained the same.

What kind of things exist according to the Stoics?

The only kind of things that exist according to the Stoics are material things, that is, bodies extended and located in space. They believed that the universe is a solid sphere of matter—a plenum—without any empty spaces within it, and that it can be divided indefinitely into smaller parts. There are no atoms or indivisible units of matter according to the Stoics. Beyond the outer surface of this sphere, there lies only empty space or "void" (κενός), without end. In addition to bodies, the Stoics recognized a class of things that are incorporeal (ἀσώματα); these are time, place, void, and meaning or sense (the "sayables" or "things said"—in Greek, *lekta*, λεκτά). Incorporeal things have only a derivative mode of existence that is dependent upon bodies, which the Stoics called "subsistence," from the Greek *hypostasis* (ὑπόστασιζ). Like the Latin word *substantia* ("substance"), the Greek word *hypostasis* meant to "stand" (*statis*) "under" (*hypo*).

For the Stoics, there are two ways in which something can *be*. Both fall under the category of "something" (τί). Both are real, but only one "exists." The other merely "subsists." Subsistent beings (*hypostases*) are made real by being hypostasized (*hyphistasthai*). This distinction allowed the Stoics to deny that universals—the *lekta*, the "things said"—exist. Instead, they "subsist." The Stoics therefore turned Plato upside down. Whereas Plato believed that universals were what really existed, and that corporeal bodies were merely imitations or shadows of them, the Stoics believed that corporeal bodies were what really existed, and that universals merely subsisted in a condition that was dependent upon bodies. Plato had already distinguished between naming a subject and attaching a universal predicate to it, that is, saying (Greek *legein*) something about it. The Stoic *lekta* are acts of predication about corporeal bodies but not bodies themselves.

THE EPICUREAN THEORY OF PHYSICS AND OF WHAT EXISTS

What kind of things exist according to the Epicureans?

In addition to material things or bodies, the Epicureans also believed that empty space exists. The Epicureans were empiricists. Bodies are known to exist because we can perceive them. Empty space cannot be perceived, but the Epicureans claimed that it must exist to explain movement. If there were no empty space, there would be no place for a body to move into. The world would be like a giant jigsaw puzzle, with each part locked into place.

What was the Epicurean theory of atomic physics?

Epicurus (341–270 B.C.E.) was an atomist, similar to the Pre-Socratic philosophers Democritus (c. 460–c. 370 B.C.E.) and Leucippus (c. fifth-century B.C.E.). According to Epicurus, reality consists of matter and empty space—and in its foundations, nothing else. But matter is not continuous as it was for the Stoics and cannot be divided without limit.

Matter is made up of indivisible atoms. The Greek word *atomos* (ἄτομοζ) meant,

According to the Epicurean theory, matter exists and empty space exists, the latter existing because it has to in order to allow movement.

literally, "not (*a-*) divisible (*-tomos*)." Atoms are very small. Indeed, they are microscopic. But they are not mere points in a continuum. They are extended in three dimensions. Atoms have hard surfaces that are impenetrable, and the only way they can effect one another is by colliding into one another's surfaces, bouncing off one another, or getting entangled together. As they collide into one another, they form arrangements of atoms that we perceive as bodies. We do not directly perceive atoms because they are too small. But we infer the necessity of their existence from our perceptions of bodies, which are arrangements of many atoms. Bodies can change when atoms are added or taken away from them or when their constituent atoms are rearranged. But atoms themselves are indestructible and never change.

Atoms have mass or weight, and if unimpeded by other atoms, they fall downward. They have no color, taste, sound, temperature, or odor. They possess only the primary qualities of weight or mass, shape, size, location, and velocity. However, when they collide with our sense organs, we experience color, taste, sound, temperature, odor, and all the other secondary qualities belonging to bodies. Unlike Democritus, who believed that only the primary qualities are real and that the secondary qualities exist only "by convention," Epicurus was a consistent empiricist and maintained that secondary qualities were objectively real.

How did the Pre-Socratic philosopher Parmenides discredit the appearances?

According to the Pre-Socratic philosopher Parmenides, appearances are deceiving. There seem to be many things in the universe, and they seem to be changing. But in reality, there is only one thing in the universe, appropriately called the "One" or the "Monad," and it never changes. Parmenides argued that the concept of nothing (what is not) is inconceivable because as soon as you conceive of it, it becomes something (it is). Given that the concept of nothing is inconceivable, so is change and multiplicity. Change is inconceivable because for change to occur, something has to come to be that was nothing (that was not), or vice versa, something has to cease to be (to not be) that was. So it is impossible to conceive of change without conceiving of nothing (of what is not). But since it is impossible to conceive of nothing (of what is not), it is impossible to conceive of change. And since the ancient Greek philosophers assumed that reality is conceivable (because it exists in accordance with the *logos*), Parmenides concluded that reality does not change.

Similarly, multiplicity is not conceivable because it entails the concept of void or empty space, which is nothing. Parmenides argued that since nothing is inconceivable, there cannot be empty space between things, because empty space is nothing, and what cannot be conceived cannot *be*. But if there is no empty space between things, then all things would be conjoined. And if all things are conjoined, they would form one continuous whole (as opposed to separate and discrete parts). This may seem counterintuitive if you think that even if everything is conjoined, there would still be differences between different parts of the whole. But Parmenides assumed with other Pre-Socratic philosophers that everything is ultimately made of the same primary material. If you assume that, and also assume that everything is conjoined together, then the universe

What was the Epicurean theory of the universe?

The Epicurean universe is not exactly a "uni-verse" (from the Latin meaning "one turned") because it is not a unified whole. But it is all that is. The Epicurean universe is an infinite expanse of space that is only partly filled with an infinite number of atoms. The reason that there must be an infinite number of atoms is that if there were a finite number in an infinite space, the atoms would be so spread apart that they could never arrange themselves into bodies. But we know that there are bodies because we can perceive them.

Atoms come in a large but finite number of different sizes and shapes, but there is an infinite number of atoms of each different size and shape. There is an up and a down in the Epicurean universe. Although atoms have different weights, they all fall downward at an equal rate of speed in empty space unless impeded by other atoms, just as they do according to modern physics. Because they fall with an equal rate of speed, were it not for the "swerve," atoms would fall down in parallel with one another and never collide or become entangled with one another and arrange themselves into bodies. The "swerve" is a random fluctuation in the direction that atoms fall, sending them slightly off course so that they collide into one another and form bodies. Whole worlds (*cosmoi*) are formed this way, and according to the Epicureans, there is not just one but many such worlds, akin to our galaxies. The Epicurean universe is therefore a random, mechanistic affair with no place for Aristotle's teleology, Stoic providence, or divine intervention.

would be like a giant ball of clay in which each part is the same as any other, because they are all made of clay.

How did Epicurus save the appearances from Parmenides?

Epicurus denied that the concept of nothing could not be conceived. The concept of nothing can be conceived if it is conceived of as empty space. And because it can be conceived, it *is*, it *exists*. Epicurus agreed with Parmenides that what is something cannot become nothing, and what is nothing cannot become something. But the atoms that populate empty space are indestructible and unchanging. They neither come to be out of nothing nor do they perish and become nothing. They merely move from one location in space to another. As they move, they form different spatial arrangements with one another. And that is what we perceive as change. But that change is not a substantial change. Each atom is a monad, exactly like every other in its being or substance, because they are made of the same indistinguishable material. Neither are all things conjoined to form one continuous whole because, according to Epicurus's atomic theory, the parts of the universe are separated from one another by empty space. Therefore, by introducing the concept of empty space, Epicurus saved the appearance of both change and multiplicity.

THE EPICUREAN THEORY
OF KNOWLEDGE

How did Epicurus explain sensation?

According to Epicurus, the surface of material objects emits a thin film of atoms, called in Greek a *tupos* (τύποζ)—a complex word that carries many meanings, including a blow or pressing, a mark or an impression, a pattern, a model, or an image. From its source in a material object, a *tupos* travels toward our sense organs, where it impresses itself upon them and causes us to experience a sensory representation of the material object. There is no action at a distance in Epicurean physics. Because all material objects are composed of atoms, and no atom can affect another without directly touching its outer surface, all sense organs operate like the sense of touch.

Epicurus's explanation of eyesight is remarkably similar to the modern one. According to the modern explanation of eyesight, photons bounce off objects and travel toward the eye, where they impact the retina, causing us to experience an image of the object. Roman Epicurean Lucretius empirically confirmed the Epicurean theory of vision by explaining in the same way as the modern theory how the image in a mirror is reversed. The modern theory of hearing is slightly different, but in essence the same. In the modern theory, a material object (such as the vocal chords of a human being or a musical instrument) sets in motion a chain of causal events from one molecule of air to another until the molecules of air immediately in contact with the eardrum strike it and form an impression that causes us to hear a sound. The modern theory of smell is even more consistent with the Epicurean theory. According to the modern theory of smell, molecules are emitted from material objects and travel to our nose, where they lock into receptors that send a signal to our brain that causes us to smell an odor.

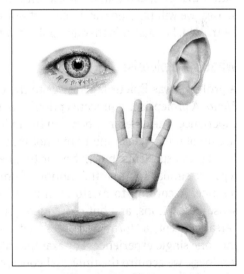

According to the Epicureans, what is the source of knowledge?

The Epicureans were empiricists. They believed that the senses are the source of all knowledge. This holds true not only for simple empirical facts like "the sun is shining" but also for abstract ideas like "the sum of the angles of a triangle equals 180 degrees" and "theft is wrong." Some truths are given immediately by the senses. Other truths can be reasoned from the senses. For example, we cannot sense empty space, but we know it must exist because

Epicureans believe that knowledge is only obtained by information received through a person's five senses.

221

we can sense the movement of bodies; if there were no empty space, there could not be any movement.

Can the senses ever be mistaken, according to Epicurus?

According to Epicurus, the senses never err. They always accurately report the impression of a thin film of atoms upon them. If we see something that isn't there, it's not because the senses are not accurately reporting a sense impression, but because we are misinterpreting that impression. In a classic example given by Lucretius, a square tower appears to be round when viewed from a distance. But that is not because our sense organs are not accurately reporting the impression left upon our eyes by the atoms that traveled from the tower to our eyes. It is because the arrangement of those atoms has become altered over the course of their trajectory from the tower to our eyes. Sensation, Epicurus believes, is like pain. You may be mistaken about the cause of your pain, but you cannot be mistaken about the fact that you do feel pain. Similarly, you may be mistaken about the object represented by a visual image, but you cannot be mistaken about the fact that you do see that image.

How can the senses be trusted if they sometimes mislead us?

The Epicureans acknowledge that the senses may sometimes mislead us. For example, a square tower may appear round when viewed from a distance. But this error does not prove that the senses cannot be trusted. The tower really does appear round when viewed from a distance. Our eyes do not err in reporting a round image. The error arises when we make the false judgment that the round image we see represents a round tower. If we walk closer to the tower to obtain a clear and direct perception of it, we will see that the tower is not round but square. So it is not sensation that errs but our judgment about our sensation that errs, and that error can only be corrected by sensation. If we don't trust our senses, we will have no way to correct our errors of judgment. The senses can therefore be trusted, because it is they and only they that can correct our false judgments.

What is a prolepsis?

A prolepsis was Epicurus's answer to the challenge to empiricism presented in Plato's *Meno*. A prolepsis is a preconception, that is, a concept that we possess prior to a given experience. The difference between the Epicurean concept of a prolepsis and both Plato's notion of innate ideas and Kant's notion of *a priori* concepts is that a prolepsis is prior to a given experience but not prior to all experience. The Epicurean concept of a prolepsis is similar to Aristotle's notion of universal concepts but with one important difference. According to Aristotle, humans have the capacity to remember a series of sense-perceptions, and out of frequently repeated memories of the same thing, a universal concept (a "form") emerges that unites those sense-perceptions and memories into one single experience. For example, after the experience of many particular acts of kindness, we acquire the universal concept of kindness.

According to Aristotle, universal concepts cannot be revised by further experience because though they arise out of experience, they are not reducible to experience. Their

What was one of the classic challenges to empiricism faced by Epicurus?

One of the classic challenges to empiricism faced by Epicurus comes from Plato's dialogue the *Meno*. The argument is based on the premise that it is necessary to know what you are looking for in order to find it. For example, if you are looking for a lost set of keys in a cluttered room, it is easier to find them if you have a clear picture of the keys in your mind as you search for them. Similarly, Socrates argues that it is impossible to find knowledge in our sense experience unless we already know what we are looking for. That knowledge may be latent until it is triggered by a sense experience and made explicit. Socrates says that it is forgotten until it is retrieved from memory in an act of learning. But if we did not have that knowledge prior to our experience, we would have no way of recognizing it in our sense experience when we found it. In fact, as Immanuel Kant (1724–1804) pointed out thousands of years later, our sense experience is shaped by concepts that we possess prior to our experience. Without those *a priori* concepts, we would have no coherent sense experience at all. Therefore, sense experience depends on knowledge that does not itself come from sense experience. This would appear to undermine the empiricist claim that all knowledge comes from sense experience.

truth is absolute and final. But for Epicurus, a prolepsis is only a rough and ready summation of many sense experiences. It can and indeed must be revised as we acquire more experience. However, a prolepsis does provide us with a preconception that allows us to identify and recognize things as particular examples of a type. For example, once we acquire the concept of kindness, we can identify a subway rider's giving up his seat to a person in need as an act of kindness. Our prolepsis may be revised by further experience, but that is no argument against it. In fact, just as we need our senses to correct our erroneous judgments about sensation, we need a prolepsis to acquire the experiences that will correct our prolepsis. Without a prolepsis, we would never be able to identify and recognize particular examples of a given type that would cause us to revise our prolepsis. For example, our preconception of kindness might help us to identify kind individuals who teach us more about the nature of kindness. Without our relatively crude concept of kindness, we would never be able to acquire the experience necessary to improve our concept.

EPICUREAN ETHICS

What are pain and pleasure, according to the Epicureans?

According to the Epicureans, pain and pleasure are sensations that we feel in our bodies. Since pain and pleasure are kinds of sensation, and since sensation is the source of knowledge, pain and pleasure are sources of knowledge. We know by sensing pleasure that it is intrinsically good and by sensing pain that it is intrinsically bad. We naturally avoid pain and seek pleasure in order to achieve happiness. Pain and pleasure, therefore, serve as guides to our choices and actions in the world. They are the source of our ethical knowledge about how to live well and achieve happiness (*eudaimonia*). The Epicureans were hedonists. They believed that the proper goal or end of our choices and actions is pleasure and the elimination of pain.

What are emotions, according to the Epicureans?

According to the Epicureans, emotions are sensations of pleasure and pain combined with their associated desires and aversions. For example, according to Epicurean philosopher Philodemus (c. 110–c. 30 B.C.E.), the emotion of anger is a certain kind of painful sensation accompanied by the "fierce desire to pursue and contend with the offending person, if one can." The Epicurean theory of emotion differs in an important way from the Stoic theory. According to the Stoics, an emotion is a cognitive judgment, a kind of intellectual act. But according to the Epicureans, an emotion is primarily a feeling or sensation. The sensation of pleasure or pain may be followed by a cognitive judgment about the cause of the sensation, which in turn is followed by a desire for or an aversion to the cause. A feeling of anger may be followed by the belief that it was Xenodorus who offended me and a desire to contend with him. But the cognitive judgment follows the feeling or sensation, not the reverse, because according to the Epicureans, the feeling or sensation is itself a source of ethical knowledge.

What kind of desires are there, according to the Epicureans?

The Epicureans divide desires into natural and unnatural desires and further divide natural desires into those that are necessary and those that are not. A natural desire is one that arises out of our nature. Examples include the desire for food, shelter, sex, and protection from bodily harm. But not all natural desires are necessary. For example, the desire for food is natural, but the desire for gourmet food is not necessary. Simple food is all that is necessary to sustain one's health. Desires that are neither natural nor necessary are "vain" and "empty" (κενóζ).

What are the two types of pleasure?

According to the Epicureans, the two types of pleasure are static and kinetic. Static pleasure is the pleasure of being in an unchanging condition free of pain or disturbances. There are two types of static pleasure. *Aponia* (ἀπονία) is the absence of pain. According to the Epicureans, it is

Emotions, according to Epicureans, are feelings of pleasure and pain associated with desires and aversions.

the greatest bodily pleasure. An example would be eating a simple but nutritious meal that satisfies your hunger and leaves you in a state of postprandial contentment. *Ataraxia* (ἀταραξία) is the absence of anxiety. It is the feeling of equanimity or tranquility that one has when not perturbed by fear or unfulfilled desires. It is the greatest pleasure possible.

Kinetic pleasures are the pleasures felt while performing an activity. The problem with kinetic pleasures, according to the Epicureans, is that they are always accompanied by unfulfilled desire, and unfulfilled desire is painful. As soon as the activity ends, so does the kinetic pleasure associated with it. The bodily pleasures of eating, drinking, and having sex are kinetic pleasures. Though pleasurable, they are accompanied by the painful sensations of hunger, thirst, and unquenched desire. Thus, while Epicureans are hedonists in the sense that they believe that pleasure is the greatest good, they are not sensualists, because they do not believe that the bodily pleasures are the greatest pleasures.

Which kind of desires lead to happiness and which to unhappiness?

Desires that are neither natural nor necessary lead to unhappiness. These desires are based on false beliefs and social convention rather than on nature. Examples include the desire for social recognition, status, money, and power. Because they are based on nothing real, Epicurus describes them as vain or empty (κενός). These desires can never be satisfied because they have no natural limit. The more you have, the more you want, leaving you forever unsatisfied. Natural desires arise out of the nature of who we are. They are based in something real. When these desires are satisfied, we feel pleasure, which is a real and immediate good. However, the greatest pleasure and the least pain is achieved by limiting our natural desires to those that are necessary. For example, simple but nutritious foods are preferable to gourmet foods because simple foods are easier to obtain and satisfy the same real needs. Should the opportunity to eat gourmet foods come along with no associated costs, then the Epicurean would choose to eat them. But in general, luxury items cause more pain than they are worth.

What did the Epicureans think about sex?

The Epicureans thought the same thing about sex that they thought about gourmet food. We have a natural desire for sex, but it is not necessary and we can live perfectly well without it. Because sex is a kinetic pleasure, it is mixed with pain. Moreover,

Hunger is one example of a natural desire that, when satisfied with food and drink, results in pleasure. Simple foods are better because they are easier to obtain to satisfy hunger; fancy, gourmet foods can sometimes cause pain because they require more effort to obtain.

it is costly, and its consequences are often unpleasant. But sex is an authentic pleasure because it is not based in empty opinion or artificial social convention but in our real nature as sexual beings. Whether an Epicurean chooses to have sex or not boils down to a matter of weighing the pleasure expected from the experience against the risk of pain. If the risk of pain can be reduced, then the Epicurean would be more likely to choose to have sex. For example, an Epicurean would be more likely to choose to have sex if there were means available to reduce the risk of disease and unwanted pregnancies.

However, from an Epicurean point of view, the greatest danger of having sex is psychological. The greatest danger of having sex is if we become attached to it and treat it as if it were not only a natural pleasure that we are sometimes fortunate to enjoy but as an absolute necessity as well. This is what happens when we fall passionately in love. We become obsessed with our beloved but are never satisfied because passionate love is like a mirage that is always just out of reach. Passionate love in the Epicurean view is not real. It is an artificial social construction, like myths or fairy tales. Besides disturbing our tranquility (*ataraxia*) with romantic fantasies and obsessive thoughts, passionate love threatens our self-sufficiency (*autarkeia*) by making us dependent on another person's desire. This is why Lucretius recommended having casual sex with multiple partners. By having sex with multiple partners, we can avoid falling in love with any one of them and retain what is most important to an Epicurean: *ataraxia* and *autarkeia*.

The Epicureans did not believe that human beings are monogamous by nature but by social convention. They felt the same way about marriage, even if it is polygamous. Marriage is a social convention. It is neither natural nor necessary. Epicurus himself did not marry or have children. However, some of his followers did. In order to maintain one's inner peace and tranquility, the Epicureans recognized that it is sometimes necessary to go along with prevailing social customs. In those circumstances, the Epicureans recommended marriage for the person who could keep a level head and not fall passionately in love.

What did Epicurus think about friendship?

If the Epicurean view of sex gives the impression that the Epicureans were cold, heartless monsters, then the Epicurean view of friendship (*philia*) may give the opposite impression. One of the principal doctrines of Epicurus states, "Of the things which wisdom provides for the blessedness of one's whole life, by far the greatest is the possession of friendship." According to Diogenes Laërtius, Epicurus wrote a letter to his friend Idomeneus on the last day of his life. In that letter, Epicurus told Idomeneus that in spite of suffering the most severe pain possible, he was having a "blissful day" because he was enjoying the memory of their past conversations. According to the Epicureans, psychological pleasure can be had not only from the present but also from memories of the past. Epicurus concludes his letter by asking Idomeneus, in keeping with his lifelong attitude toward him and toward philosophy, to watch over the children of another friend and fellow Epicurean, those of Metrodorus.

The *Letter to Idomeneus* testifies to the deep bonds of affection that existed between members of the Epicurean community. And what a community it was. For the Epicureans, philosophy was not a solitary pursuit but rather a conversation between friends who lived together communally. In 307/306 B.C.E., Epicurus established a community of philosophers just outside the city gates of Athens, close to Plato's Academy, in a house and a large walled garden that he privately owned. Hence, the school of Epicurus was called "the Garden" (κῆπος). There, removed from the disturbances of politics and city life, the Epicureans enjoyed simple pleasures, philosophical conversation with friends, peace, and tranquility. Unusual for their time, the Epicureans welcomed women and slaves into their community. The Epicurean way of life flourished for many centuries and was so appealing that Epicurean communities sprang up all over the Mediterranean, and every year on his birthday, the Epicureans celebrated Epicurus as their founding hero.

According to the Epicureans, is anger good?

The Epicurean position on anger lies midway between Aristotle's and the Stoics'. Aristotle believed that anger is an appropriate response to a wrongful offense and that to not react with anger would be a mark of weakness, not moral strength. "Revenge," Homer said in the *Iliad*, "is sweeter far than flowing honey," and according to Aristotle, anger is not only right but pleasurable, because it entails an anticipation of revenge. The Stoics, on the other hand, condemned anger as an irrational passion that leads to unhappiness and should always be extinguished. According to Epicurean philosopher Philodemus (c. 110–c. 30 B.C.E.), the emotion of anger is a certain kind of painful sensation accompanied by the "fierce desire to pursue and contend with the offending person, if one can."

In his work on anger, Philodemus distinguishes between natural anger and empty (κενόσ) anger. Natural anger is based in a natural desire to protect oneself from harm, whereas empty anger is based in an empty desire to inflict pain on the offending party for its own sake. Empty anger is sadistic. It is based in the empty belief that inflicting pain on the offending party is good in itself and pleasurable. Animals share with humans the capacity for natural anger. They may respond violently to those who threaten to harm them or their loved ones. But they are not sadistic or cruel. They do not respond violently because they believe that inflicting pain on those who harm them is good in itself and pleasurable. Empty anger is not natural and therefore cannot be necessary either. Therefore, on the Epicurean principle that desires that are neither natural nor necessary are bad, empty anger is bad. Because natural anger is painful, it is not a wholly good thing. However, because it is based in natural desires that come from human nature and do not rest on false or empty beliefs, it is not bad either. Natural anger is a necessary means to an end, not something to enjoy for its own sake. Since it is based in natural desires, it remains within fixed limits. It does not feed on itself and boil over into raging madness the way that empty anger does. The wise therefore maintain their peace and clarity of mind even when they are angry. The Epicurean philosopher is not subject to the intense rage that the heroes of Homer's epic poems suffer.

227

According to the Epicureans, should we act only for immediate pleasure, or should we also plan for the future?

The Epicureans believed that pleasure is the only thing that is in and of itself good. Everything else is merely a means to that end. We know that pleasure is good because we immediately sense that it is good—in other words, we know it is good because it feels good. But though all our knowledge begins with immediate sensation, it does not end there. Not everything we know is immediately sensed. Some knowledge is acquired by reasoning *from* immediate sensation. For example, we reason from the sight of smoke that there must be fire, and from the sight of fire that smoke will follow. As rational beings, we are capable of understanding the underlying causes of our experience, and by means of that knowledge we are able to anticipate the future. For example, we know that if we eat candy and don't brush our teeth, we will get cavities and experience pain. The Epicureans hold that a rational person will therefore aim to maximize pleasure and minimize pain over the entire course of their life, not just in the immediate moment. As a consequence, a rational person will sometimes forego pleasure or even endure pain in the present moment for the sake of future pleasure. This principle extends to our agreements or contracts with others. For example, a rational citizen will pay taxes and obey the law in order to enjoy the services and protection afforded by the state.

According to Epicurus, what is justice?

Positive law—the body of laws established by human government—is not the same thing as justice. Positive law is not necessarily or by definition just. Positive law may be unjust—but not, as Cicero and the natural law tradition say, because it violates a higher law, a universal "natural law" established by God or Reason. The only "law of nature," according to Epicurus, is a "pledge of reciprocal usefulness, that is, neither to harm one another nor being harmed" (Diogenes Laërtius, *Lives*, 10.139–154).

Justice, according to Epicurus, is an agreement or contract between two or more parties made for their mutual and reciprocal benefit. "Justice is not a thing in its own right, but exists in mutual dealings in whatever places there is a pact about neither harming one another nor being harmed." There is no justice or injustice between animals because they are unable to make contracts with one another. Nor is there any justice or injustice between nations or any other parties who

Just because something is a law does not necessarily mean it is just. Epicurus believed justice can be defined by a contract between two or more people that is made for mutual or reciprocal benefit.

> ## According to Epicurus, what is injustice, and why should you not commit unjust acts?
>
> Injustice is the violation of a contract between two or more parties made for their mutual and reciprocal benefit. Contrary to the Socrates of Plato's dialogues, Epicurus believes that there is nothing inherently wrong with injustice. The only reason that you should not violate a just contract is because you can never be sure that you will not be found out and punished. You will spend the rest of your life looking over your shoulder in fear of getting caught. That would disturb your inner peace and tranquility (*ataraxia*) and defeat whatever benefits you derived from cheating on the contract in the first place.

have not made a contract with one another. Justice is relative to the needs of those who contract with one another and is not the same for everyone everywhere. There are no eternal, universal, or objective principles of justice. What is just at one time or in one place may not be just at another time or in another place. If a contract turns out to not be mutually beneficial to all who agreed to its terms, then it was not a just contract to begin with. On the other hand, a contract can start out being just and become unjust when circumstances or other factors change.

THE EPICUREAN THEORY OF THE SOUL

What is the Epicurean theory of the soul?

According to the Epicureans, the only two types of real things are matter and empty space (void). The soul is capable of effecting and being affected by other things. But empty space is not capable of effecting or being affected by anything, because a thing can only effect another thing by touching it, and empty space cannot touch anything. Therefore, the soul must be a material thing, just like the body. And since matter is made up of atoms, the soul must be made up of atoms. The soul, Epicurus said, is made up of fine atoms distributed throughout the body that resemble breath with an admixture of heat. The very finest atoms of the soul account for the power of sensation. Thus, the Epicurean notion of the soul resembles the medical notion of *pneuma*, which is a mixture of air and fire, and which gives a body life and sensation.

According to the Epicureans, can the soul survive the death of the body?

The soul is just a part of the body, so when the body is destroyed, so is the soul. The soul cannot function without the body, just as the body cannot live without the soul. Without a body and sense organs, the soul cannot sense anything, including pleasure and pain.

What is an emergent property?

An emergent property is a property of a whole system that its parts or components on their own do not have. Emergent properties are not possessed by the parts of a system on their own, but they emerge from those parts when they combine and interact to form a whole system. For example, chemical molecules on their own do not have the property of life. But when the right chemicals are combined and interact to form an organic system, the property of life emerges from them.

How did the philosophy of Epicurus differ from the philosophy of Democritus?

According to Epicureans, the soul dies along with the body, so there is no existence after death.

Democritus (c. 460–c. 370 B.C.E.) said that the only real things are atoms. Everything else is mere fiction and arbitrary social convention. The Epicureans were atomists like Democritus. They believed that everything is composed of atoms. But they did not believe that everything other than atoms is mere fiction and arbitrary social convention. The Epicureans trusted their senses more than Democritus did. Our senses do not perceive atoms. They perceive bodies with a rich variety of qualities such as color, temperature, sound, taste, and odor. According to Democritus, bodies and their qualities are not real. But according to Epicurus, bodies and their qualities *are* real because they are composed of atoms. Although bodies and their qualities differ from their component atoms, they are based in and emerge from those atoms. Bodies and their qualities are "emergent" properties.

Are any of our actions free or voluntary, according to the Epicureans?

The soul is composed of atoms, and if the movement of those atoms were entirely determined by the force of other atoms striking them, none of our actions could be free or voluntary. But the Epicurean theory of physics is not entirely deterministic. According to the Epicureans, atoms randomly "swerve" off course—much like the "Brownian motion" of particles in a fluid that was discovered by Robert Brown in 1827—with the difference being that the Epicurean "swerve" is uncaused. Of course, the freedom of the soul cannot be reduced to the random fluctuations of its component atoms. Freedom means more than random, uncaused, or unpredictable motion. It means that we are the origin of our actions. The random motion of the soul's component atoms is only a necessary condition of our freedom. Without it, we could not be free. But it is not a sufficient condition. The freedom of the soul is an emergent property of its component atoms and cannot be reduced to their random motions.

THE EPICUREAN THEORY
OF RELIGION AND THE GODS

What did the Epicureans think about religion?

At the beginning of *On the Nature of Things,* Lucretius pays homage to Epicurus with the following words: "At a time when human life—before the eye of all—lay foully prostrate upon the Earth, crushed down under the weight of Religion, which showed its head from the quarters of heaven with hideous aspect, glowering down upon men, it was a man of Hellas who was the first to venture to lift up his mortal eyes, and stand up to Religion, face to face." Not frightened by stories of the gods or by thunder and lightning bolts sent down from the heavens, Epicurus was the first to unlock the secrets of nature. And "by his victory, the terror of religion is trampled underfoot, and we, in turn, are lifted to the stars."

EPICUREAN PSYCHIATRY

What is the purpose of philosophy, according to the Epicureans?

The purpose of philosophy, according to the Epicureans, is not to acquire knowledge for its own sake but to heal the human soul and alleviate suffering. In that respect, Epicurean philosophy is like many religions, whose purpose is also to heal the human soul

---

What was the Epicurean theory of the gods (theology)?

Although the Epicureans were no fans of religion, believing it to be little more than a collection of frightening superstitions, they were not atheists. They reasoned that since belief in the gods is nearly universal, there must be some empirical basis to it. And even if the gods exist only by social convention, it is better to believe in them, because to violate such a widespread social convention would be to invite controversy, and that would disturb one's inner peace and tranquility (*ataraxia*). On the other hand, to believe the frightening stories told about the gods would also disturb one's inner peace and tranquility.

To overcome this dilemma, the Epicureans resolved that the gods are material bodies composed of a very fine film of atoms. Because the atoms that they are composed of are so fine, they exist like ghosts or apparitions. They do not have the power to intervene in human affairs, nor are they effected by them in any way. They exist in an ethereal realm far above the earth, where they reside eternally in blessedness and peace, undisturbed by and unconcerned with the affairs of mortal beings on earth. The gods therefore exist, but they are nothing to be feared.

and alleviate suffering. The difference is that the Epicureans believe that the way to heal the human soul and alleviate suffering is to acquire knowledge. You cannot overcome suffering by fooling yourself with fanciful delusions, no matter how flattering or pleasant they may at first sight appear to be. You must face up to reality. So the purpose of philosophy, according to the Epicureans, is to heal our souls by feeding us a hefty dose of reality. Epicurean philosophy is a psychiatric medicine.

What is the *tetrapharmakos*?

The *tetrapharmakos* (τετραφάρμακοζ) is the fourfold Epicurean remedy for suffering and a formula for happiness. The root term *tetra* means "four," and *pharmakos* means "medicines." The four medicines

Happiness and freedom from anxiety is obtained through tetrapharmakos, the knowledge that death should not be feared, the gods should not be feared, pain can be endured, and pleasure can be obtained.

are the knowledge that (1) pleasure is easy to get; (2) pain is easily endured; (3) the gods are not to be feared; and (4) death is not to be feared. With this fourfold knowledge, you can achieve the greatest happiness, which is freedom from anxiety (*ataraxia*).

What is the first medicine of the *tetrapharmakos*?

Pleasure is easy to get. According to the Epicureans, the greatest pleasure is the absence of pain (*aponia*). Therefore, the pleasure of eating simple foods, such as bread and olives, when you are hungry is just as great as the pleasure of eating gourmet foods, because simple foods eliminate the pain of hunger just as well as gourmet foods. But simple foods are easy to get. Therefore, there is no reason to be anxious about obtaining them. The same holds for other bodily pains, such as thirst and cold. Water will satisfy thirst just as well as the finest wine. Simple shelter will protect you from the cold just as well as a mansion. Therefore, live simply, and you will be free of pain and anxiety.

What is the second medicine of the *tetrapharmakos*?

Pain is easy to endure. Pain is easy to endure because pain is either brief or chronic, and either mild or intense. But pain that is mild is easy to endure. And pain that is intense usually ends quickly, because pain that is both chronic and intense is rare. Therefore, pain is almost always easy to endure, either because it is mild or because it is short in duration. Therefore, there is no need to feel anxious about pain.

What is the third medicine of the *tetrapharmakos*?

The gods are not to be feared. The gods live perfect lives of everlasting bliss and tranquility in a realm apart from humans and are consequently unconcerned with us. They need and expect nothing from us. Nor are they prone to anger, because anger would disturb their tranquility. Therefore, there is no reason to feel anxious about what the gods may do to us.

What is the fourth medicine of the *tetrapharmakos*?

Death is not to be feared. The gods would not punish us after our death even if they could, because the gods are not concerned with us. But the gods cannot punish us after our death because the soul does not survive the death of the body. Therefore, death is not to be feared, because when we are alive, we are not dead, and when we are dead, we do not exist. Therefore, we will never experience death. Therefore, there is nothing to be feared.

THE CYRENAIC SCHOOL OF HEDONISM

What was the other school of hedonism in the Hellenistic period?

The other school of hedonism was the Cyrenaic school. The Cyrenaics originate with Aristippus (c. 435–c. 356 B.C.E.) who, like other members of his school, hailed from the Greek colony of Cyrene on the southern coast of the Mediterranean—hence the name of the school, "the Cyrenaics." In Athens, Aristippus became a student of Socrates, alongside Xenophon, Plato, and Antisthenes. But the Cyrenaic school didn't take off until a grandson of Aristippus, Aristippus the Younger, completed the development of

his grandfather's philosophy. Aristippus the Younger lived in the second half of the fourth century B.C.E., and in ancient literature he was often conflated with his grandfather. Aristippus the Younger had three students who each modified their teacher's philosophy in different ways. These were Anniceris (flourished c. 300 B.C.E.), Theodorus the Atheist (c. 340–c. 250 B.C.E.), and Hegesias (flourished in the third century B.C.E.).

The Cyrenaic school flourished for only a brief period of time. Whereas the moderate hedonism of the Epicureans was well received and survived into the period of the Roman Empire, the much more uncompromising hedonism of the Cyrenaics was never a good fit for either Greek or Roman culture. Consequently, the original

A pupil of Socrates, Aristippus founded the Cyrenaic school of philosophy. The Cyrenaics were a hedonistic school, holding that life is about seeking pleasure, although such pursuits should be tempered with self-control.

works of the Cyrenaics were not preserved, and we have only a few scattered anecdotes from secondary sources with which to piece together their philosophy.

What were the two main ethical principles taught by Aristippus?

Following Socrates, Aristippus asserted an ethic of self-control, freedom, and self-reliance. But he broke from Socrates in his estimation of the value of pleasure. In Xenophon's collection of Socratic dialogues, the *Memorabilia*, Xenophon recounts a dialogue between Socrates and Aristippus in which Socrates tried to persuade Aristippus that in order to maintain self-control, he must not pursue pleasure as the highest good. But Aristippus did not believe that the two ethical principles were incompatible. In one of several scandalous anecdotes that has survived, Aristippus is reported as saying to his students that the problem with whorehouses is not going into them but rather getting out. In other words, there is nothing wrong with pursuing pleasure. In fact, that is the purpose of life. But you must also be free and self-reliant, and to do that you must have self-control. Aristippus makes the same point in the statement that he is most remembered for: "I possess; I am not possessed."

How did the Cyrenaic conception of pleasure differ from that of the Epicureans?

According to the Epicureans, there is no neutral state between pleasure and pain, because the absence of pain is not only pleasurable but is also the greatest pleasure. The Epicureans believed that the absence of the pain of hunger or of lust that comes after eating a full meal or having an orgasm is a greater pleasure than the kinetic pleasures of eating or having sex. They believed that *ataraxia* is the absence of the psychological pain of anxiety and that it is the greatest pleasure of all. By contrast, the Cyrenaics believed that there is a neutral state between pain and pleasure and that the mere absence of pain is

---

What was the philosophy of hedonism taught by Aristippus the Younger?

Aristippus the Younger taught us to live in the present and enjoy the pleasures of the moment. Contrary to the Epicureans, Aristippus the Younger did not believe that pleasure was to be found in our memories of the past or anticipation of the future. In fact, according to his epistemology, all we can know is how things affect us now, in the present. We know that we feel good now or that we feel bad now, and that is how we know that present pleasures are good and that present pains are bad. Moreover, if we want to be free and self-reliant, we must be content with whatever pleasures the present brings us and not long for a future we do not have or cling to a past that is gone. We must have the self-control to walk out of the whorehouse. Otherwise, we will fail to achieve the inner peace and tranquility that was the highest goal of all Hellenistic philosophy: *ataraxia*.

not necessarily pleasurable. Furthermore, the prime examples of pleasure offered by the Cyrenaics are the sensuous pleasures of eating, drinking, and having sex. *Ataraxia,* in their view, is not merely the absence of anxiety but is a positive state that is achieved by enjoying whatever pleasures are readily available now, in the present moment.

What is the cradle argument for the hedonism of Aristippus the Younger?

Aristippus the Younger argued that immediate pleasure in the present moment is the highest good because it is natural for us to seek pleasure. According to the cradle argument, we know that it is natural to seek pleasure because even animals and young children who have not yet been influenced by social conventions seek pleasure. The cradle argument rests on the assumption that it is good for us to do what comes naturally and bad for us to live according to social conventions that are against our nature. The Cyrenaics believed that it is bad for us to do anything against our nature because in that case we would be working at cross purposes with ourselves and would fail to achieve the inner peace and tranquility (*ataraxia*) that all Hellenistic philosophers sought.

How did Anniceris modify Cyrenaic philosophy?

Anniceris modified Cyrenaic philosophy by expanding the sources of pleasure that he recognized beyond sensuous ones to include friendship, patriotism, and respect and gratitude for one's parents. According to Diogenes Laërtius, Anniceris believed that we should cherish friendship not as a means to an end (for example, as a means to gain political favors) but for the good feeling it gives us and for the sake of which we willingly endure hardships. However, it is not our friend's good feeling for which we endure hardships, but our own. Similarly, love of country does not serve instrumental purposes and may even cause us to endure hardships, but it is intrinsically pleasurable. According to Diogenes Laërtius, Anniceris believed that instruction is not enough to help us rise above social conventions and the opinions of the many. We must also correct our disposition by replacing bad habits instilled in us by social conditioning with good ones that bring us pleasure.

What were the beliefs of the Cyrenaic philosopher Theodorus the Atheist?

According to Diogenes Laërtius, Theodorus (c. 340–c. 250 B.C.E.) was a student of Anniceris and Dionysius the dialectician. He studied philosophy in Athens and served in the Ptolemaic court at Alexandria before retiring to his native Cyrene, which by then had become part of the Ptolemaic Empire. Wherever he went, he provoked outrage and in some instances was forced to flee.

As his name suggests, he was an atheist. But more than an atheist, he showed contempt for all social conventions. He believed that joy is the supreme good and that it is brought about by wisdom. Grief is the supreme evil and is brought about by foolishness. As a consequence, the wise do what brings them joy but not what brings them grief. Pleasure and pain are intermediate between joy and grief. Pleasure is a source of joy, and pain is a source of grief. Theodorus disagreed with Anniceris and believed that neither friendship nor love of country is a source of joy or pleasure. He believed that friendship does not exist. It does not exist between the unwise because as soon as their friends are no longer needed, the unwise end their friendship. It does not exist between the wise because the wise are self-sufficient and do not need friends. Nor is it advisable to risk one's life for one's country because to do so would be to throw wisdom away to benefit the unwise.

Like the Cynics, Theodorus followed nature, not social convention, and said that the world was his country. He believed that on occasion it is wise to commit theft, adultery, and sacrilege since none of them is against nature. They are wrong only according to social conventions that were invented to hold the foolish multitude together.

Who was Hegesias, and why was he known as the "Death Persuader"?

Hegesias (flourished third century B.C.E.) was the last of the three major Cyrenaic hedonists. Like Theodorus, he believed that friendship, and altruism more generally, does not exist, because all that we are interested in is our own pleasure. With the other Cyrenaics, he believed that pleasure is what makes life worth living. But, he observed, there is more pain in life than pleasure. Therefore, life is not worth living and you are better off dead. Due to his assessment that life is full of suffering, some scholars believe that Hegesias may have been influenced by the Buddhist doctrine that life is suffering (*dukkha*). But the Buddhists offered a remedy for suffering in their Four Noble Truths and in the Eightfold Path. Hegesias offered no remedy.

According to Cicero—who besides a brief reference by Diogenes Laërtius is our only source of information about Hegesias—Ptolemy II Philadelphus (285–246 B.C.E.) forbade Hegesias to teach in Alexandria because his students committed suicide—hence the name "Death Persuader." Other philosophers, including the Stoics, have argued that under exceptionally difficult circumstances, suicide is a reasonable option. But Hegesias is the only philosopher on record who argued that it is better to be dead and whose students were persuaded to commit suicide.

In the nineteenth century, Friedrich Nietzsche used Hegesias's argument against hedonism. According to Nietzsche, pleasure could not possibly be the purpose of life because there is more pain in life than pleasure. There must, therefore, be some other purpose. That appears to have been the conclusion arrived at by the Hellenistic philosophers, too, for with Hege-

Because he also felt that life was full of suffering, Hegesias might have been influenced by Buddhism. Unlike the Buddha, though, Hegesias offered no solutions to the problem of suffering.

236

> ## Why didn't Hegesias commit suicide like his students?
>
> The Cyrenaic theory of knowledge may have saved him from suicide. Since Hegesias lacked any causal understanding of how the world works, he could not predict the consequences of his actions. Not knowing what the consequences of his actions would be, he had no way to know if his actions would bring him pain or pleasure. All he knew was pain or pleasure in the immediate moment. But suicide is generally painful and unpleasant. People do not commit suicide because it is enjoyable but because they think it will end their pain. Since Hegesias had no way to know if suicide would end his pain, he could not with good reason choose to commit suicide. On the contrary, since suicide is generally painful and unpleasant, he had good reason not to commit suicide.

sias, the uncompromising hedonism of the Cyrenaic school comes to an end, done in by its own ruthless logic.

What was the Cyrenaic theory of knowledge?

According to the Cyrenaic philosophers, all we know is our immediate sensations. We know nothing about the nature of what causes our sensations. We know that smooth motions feel pleasurable to us and that rough motions feel painful. But we don't know anything about what causes those motions. Nor do we care, for all we care about is experiencing pleasure and avoiding pain.

How did the hedonistic philosophy of Hegesias come to resemble Epicurean hedonism?

Hegesias believed that there was little pleasure to be had in life, but at least he could minimize pain. According to Diogenes Laërtius, Hegesias believed that the "wise man will not have so much advantage over others in the choice of goods as in the avoidance of evils, making it his end to live without pain of body or mind." Thus, Cyrenaic hedonism, like Epicureanism, was reduced to the avoidance of pain, with little desire for joy or pleasure in a positive sense.

CYNICISM

Who were the Cynics?

The Cynics belonged to a school of philosophy that, like many other Hellenistic schools (with the notable exception of the Epicureans), was said to have descended in an unbroken line of teachers and students from Socrates. In his day, Antisthenes (c. 445–c. 365   **237**

B.C.E.) was the most well-known and respected student of Socrates, and his ethics laid the foundation for Cynicism.

Although modern historians are skeptical about it, the ancients believed that Antisthenes was the teacher of Diogenes of Sinope, the philosopher who first followed the mendicant lifestyle associated with the Cynics. Diogenes of Sinope (c. 404–323 B.C.E.) was the philosopher famous for his encounter with Alexander the Great, during which he asked the great man to get out of his sunlight. Crates of Thebes (c. 365–c. 285 B.C.E.) and his wife, Hipparchia of Maroneia (c. 350–280 B.C.E.), were in turn students of Diogenes. So too was Onesicritus (c. 360–c. 290 B.C.E.). Onesicritus accompanied Alexander the Great on his campaigns and met the Indian Gymnosophists—naked, ascetic philosophers whom he understood to be Cynics like himself. He was also the author of the story about Diogenes's encounter with Alexander the Great, a wonderful story that unfortunately modern historians believe was fictional. Metrocles of Maroneia (fl. c. 325 B.C.E.) was Hipparchia's brother and a student of her husband, Crates. Zeno of Citium, too, studied with Crates. Zeno was not a Cynic. He was the founder of Stoicism. But Stoicism adopted a great deal from Cynic ethics and traced its own lineage back through the Cynics to Socrates. Bion of Borysthenes (c. 325–c. 250 B.C.E.) studied at all the schools of philosophy in Athens but seems to have become a Cynic after studying with Crates. We do not know who Teles of Megara (fl. c. 235 B.C.E.) may have studied with, but he is an important source of information about the earlier Greek Cynics. Menippus (fl. third century B.C.E.) sharpened the Cynic wit into a type of satire that bears his name—Menippean satire—and that influenced the later Roman satirist Lucian (c. 125–c. 180 C.E.).

There were fewer Cynics in the first and second centuries B.C.E., but the philosophy enjoyed a revival under the Roman Empire. Demetrius the Cynic (fl. first century C.E.) was a close friend of Seneca's (c. 4 B.C.E.–65 C.E.), the extremely wealthy aristocrat and Stoic philosopher who served as a senator and later as advisor to Emperor Nero. In the first century C.E., there was a group of aristocratic Roman senators who opposed Nero's successor, Emperor Vespasian, on the basis of Cynic and Stoic philosophy. Cynic philosopher Dio Chrysostom (c. 40–c. 120 C.E.) was associated with this group, and for that reason he was exiled in 82 C.E. by Emperor Domitian. Dio wrote works opposing limits to free speech, arbitrary executions, and the confiscation of aristocratic property by kings or emperors. Cynicism did not completely fade from the scene until the late fourth century, and even then it left its mark on Christian ascetic traditions such as the mendicant Franciscan friars.

Who was Antisthenes?

Antisthenes (c. 445–c. 365 B.C.E.) was a close friend and student of Socrates and the teacher of Cynic philosopher Diogenes of Sinope (c. 404–323 B.C.E.). He is considered to have been either the founder of the school of Cynicism or its immediate predecessor. He appears in Xenophon's dialogues as a highly respected student of Socrates and in Plato's dialogues as one of the few who were present at Socrates's death. Unlike Socrates, he was a prolific writer—perhaps because he studied rhetoric with the Sophist Gorgias and developed a love for writing before becoming an ardent follower of Socrates—but little has survived. Antisthenes adopted the ethical teachings of Socrates but developed them in a more extreme form. Like Socrates, he believed that all that was necessary for happiness was virtue. But for him, virtue meant using reason to live a simple life in accordance with nature and steering clear of all the conventional markers of success such as wealth, family, power, status, and reputation. This could extend into open violation of the law as well as social convention, a practice that Socrates never recommended.

Antisthenes rejected pleasure as a tyrant more dangerous than madness and feared that it would rob him of his freedom, self-sufficiency, and independence. Consequently, he lived a life of severe poverty and self-imposed hardship. Like the Cynics after him, he carried a small

A student of Socrates, Antisthenes laid down the foundations for Cynicism.

pouch and a staff and wore only a thin blanket that served as a cloak. According to Diogenes Laërtius, he taught at the Cynosarges in Athens, a gymnasium for those like him who were born of foreign mothers, and attracted a following of poor students who adopted his mode of dress. He was known for his scathing wit, which he used to ridicule the opinions and social conventions of his fellow Athenians.

Which interpretation of Socrates most closely resembles Antisthenes?

Socrates (c. 470–399 B.C.E.) himself wrote nothing. We know of him and his philosophy only from the Socratic dialogues written by his students Plato (427–347 B.C.E.) and Xenophon (c. 431–354 B.C.E.). But the Socrates of Plato's dialogues is somewhat different from the Socrates of Xenophon's, and it is Xenophon's Socrates that most closely resembles Antisthenes.

The Socrates of Plato's dialogues is a master dialectician whose sharp intellect reveals the hidden contradictions and ambiguities in our common beliefs (*doxa*) and social conventions (*nomos*), leading to *aporia* (an impasse or paradox) in the early dialogues or to a vision of the forms in the middle dialogues. Although the Socrates of Plato's dialogues says that he knows nothing, he regards knowledge as the highest good and the source of virtue.

Like most Hellenistic philosophers, Antisthenes was a materialist. He rejected Plato's theory of the forms and felt that Plato had misrepresented Socrates. Antisthenes therefore emphasized the Socratic virtues over Platonic metaphysics.

The Socrates of Xenophon's dialogues is not so much an intellectual in pursuit of abstract knowledge as a paragon of practical virtue. Although many of the same virtues are found in the Socrates of both Plato and Xenophon's dialogues, in Xenophon there is a greater emphasis on the character of the man than on his ideas. Since all Hellenistic philosophers were materialists and were primarily interested in ethics, Xenophon's Socrates proved to be highly influential in the Hellenistic period.

Among the Socratic virtues that Antisthenes and the Cynics adopted as their own were the virtues of self-control and self-sufficiency. The Greek word for self-sufficiency was *autárkeia* (αὐτάρχεια) and it is from this word that we get the English word "autarky." Related to self-control and self-sufficiency was the virtue of indifference (*adiaphora*, ἀδιαφορία) to the external conditions of one's life. This virtue generated a toughness of character that made one capable of enduring pain and hardship (*ponos*, πόνοϛ). Greek heroes Odysseus and Heracles (Latin, *Hercules*) symbolized for Antisthenes and the Cynics the toughness of character that they sought to develop in themselves.

What was Cynicism?

Cynicism was more an ethic and a way of life than a theory. The Cynics lived like mendicant monks, homeless and begging for food on the streets, and were known for their biting remarks made to passersby. The Greek word for Cynic is related to the Greek word for dog, and the Cynics were thought to behave like dogs because they barked at strangers and shamelessly ate, had sex, and defecated in public.

The chief aim of Cynicism, as for all Hellenistic schools of philosophy, was happiness and a life well lived (*eudaimonia*). Like the other Hellenistic schools, the Cynics understood happiness as a state of mind in which one is free of negative emotions (*apatheia*) and disturbances that cause anxiety (*ataraxia*). But they had their own unique way of achieving happiness. Contrary to the hedonists, they did not believe that pleasure or the avoidance of pain brings happiness; instead, they believed it brings only mental disturbance. The Cynics held more strictly than any other Hellenistic school to the belief that only virtue is necessary and sufficient for happiness. Even the Stoics held a more moderate position, admitting pleasure as "indifferent," neither good nor bad in itself, but "preferred." For the Cynics, pleasure has no intrinsic relationship with happiness, and when pursued for its own sake, as if it were something good in itself, it always leads to unhappiness.

According to the Cynics, what is virtue?

Like Socrates himself, the Cynics believed that virtue is wisdom (*phronesis*, φρόνησιϛ) and that only wisdom brings lasting and durable happiness. The Cynic innovation was to introduce the concepts of *oikeíon* and *allotrion* into their discussion of wisdom. To be wise, the Cynics believed, is to know the difference between what belongs essentially

The painting *Diogenes Sitting in His Tub* (1860) by Jean-Léon Gérôme highlights the lifestyle of the Cynic, a homeless beggar.

to the self or is inherent to it, which they called in Greek *oikeíon* (οικείων), and what is external or foreign to the self, which they called in Greek *allotrion* (αλλοτριων). Unhappiness is caused by confusing what belongs to the self with what is external to it. The wise person knows that a long list of things that most people identify with are not *oikeíon*. These include social status, political power, reputation and fame, family, wealth, pleasure, health, and physical beauty. The belief that any of these things are inherent to the self leads inevitably to unhappiness, because that belief is false. But disabusing yourself of this false belief is not easy. It requires a rigorous course of disciplined exercise and training, which the Cynics called in Greek *áskēsis* (ἄσκησιζ), from which we get our English word "ascetic."

According to the Cynics, why does virtue bring lasting and durable happiness?

Virtue is wisdom (*phronesis*, φρόνησῖζ), and wisdom brings lasting and durable happiness because wisdom is unassailable. Antisthenes said, "Wisdom is a wall that cannot be breached, since no foreign force can ever break it down or betray it. This defense is furnished by one's own impregnable powers of rational thought" (Diogenes Laërtius, 6.13). It is these impregnable powers of rational thought and these powers alone that are *oikeion* or inherent to the self. All else is *allótrios* (ἀλλότριοζ) or foreign to the self and can be taken away from it.

241

What is the Cynic *áskēsis*?

The Cynic *áskēsis* is a rigorous course of ethical training or exercise by means of which the Cynics learned to live without anything that is *allótrios* or foreign to the self—or at least to live with the bare minimum required by nature. To learn to live without anything that is foreign to the self, the Cynics trained themselves to think independently of social opinion and to live according to the laws of nature instead of social custom. External goods were used only as needed, not for pleasure. By this means one could become free and self-sufficient (*autárkeia*), safe behind an impregnable wall from anxiety (*ataraxia*) and negative emotions (*apatheia*), and enduringly happy (*eudaimonia*). Because the laws of nature are rational and universal, whereas social opinion is arbitrary and custom is provincial, the Cynics regarded themselves not as citizens of the *polis* but as cosmopolitan citizens of the world (*kosmopolitês*).

What are some of the practices entailed in the Cynic *áskēsis*?

The Cynic *áskēsis* is a set of practices by which the Cynic learns to live without anything that is *allótrios* or foreign to the self. All these practices require painful effort and hard work (*ponos*, πόνοϛ). One such practice is to live a life of self-imposed poverty, or as it is sometimes called today, "voluntary simplicity." The Cynic learns to become independent of external goods by living with as few of them as nature requires. The Cynics wore only a thin blanket as a cloak, doubled over in winter for extra warmth, with no undergarments or shoes, and carried all their belongings in a small pouch. They slept in the doorways of public buildings, and they begged for food on the streets or picked wild vegetables. Their favorite meal was lentils. The Cynic learns to become independent of social goods by practicing shamelessness (*anaídeia*, αναίδεια).

The Cynics acted outrageously in public, "defacing the currency" (*nomisma*) by violating common social norms (*nomos*). When asked why he masturbated in public, the great Cynic philosopher Diogenes of Sinope replied, "If only it were so easy to soothe hunger by rubbing an empty belly." Diogenes masturbated in public not because it was pleasurable—though it may have been—but because it was natural. The fact that it was shameful only tested his resolve to live independently of social norms and without the rewards that come with obeying them.

The principle of *parrhēsía* (παρρησία) required the Cynic to speak freely, openly, frankly, and without reserve. The Cynics were known for their outrageous speech as much as for their outrageous behavior. One of the chief vices in Cynic ethics was *tuphos* (τύφοϛ), a Greek word that originally meant "smoke" or "vapor," but which in the hands of the Cynics meant "putting on airs," pretending to be something you are not in order to impress others and gain their approval. The Cynics strove to do the opposite: to speak frankly and act according to nature regardless of social opinion. To endure their self-imposed poverty, as well as the scorn that their outrageous speech and behavior provoked, the Cynics required the virtue of *karteria* (καρτερία), which meant "endurance," "perseverance," and "self-control." Centuries later, this Cynic virtue would evolve into the Christian virtue of patience. By means of all these ascetic practices, the Cynics developed *adiaphora* (ἀδιάφορα), by which they meant indifference to social opinion and the external conditions of life.

What is the *chreia*?

The *chreia* (χρεία) is the most common literary device used in ancient literature about the Cynics. A *chreia* is a brief anecdote—sometimes as short as a single sentence—used to tell a story about a character. The art of writing *chreiai* (plural of *chreia*) was part of the study of rhetoric, a cornerstone of ancient education. Most of what we know about the Cynics comes to us through the *chreiai*. Though not in general historically accurate, they often do an uncanny job of explaining Cynic philosophy.

What is the meaning of the *chreia* about Diogenes of Sinope and Alexander the Great?

The most famous *chreia* about Diogenes of Sinope was invented by the Cynic philosopher Onesicritus and was repeated countless times throughout the ages. According to this *chreia*, when asked by Alexander what he could do for him, Diogenes replied that he could get out of his sunlight. Alexander responded by saying that if he could be anyone, he would want to be Diogenes. Several key themes of Cynicism are encapsulated in this *chreia*. The reason that Alexander would like to be Diogenes rather than himself is that Diogenes is beholden to no one, not even the most powerful man in the world. Diogenes is more free and self-sufficient than Alexander because he needs nothing from anyone. Simple sunlight, which he gets for free from nature, is enough to satisfy him. Sunlight also represents the light of knowledge. By asking the most powerful man in the world to get out of his sunlight, Diogenes is saying that power, even when it is freely granted to you, obscures the truth. Therefore, the true philosopher rejects any offer of political position or power.

A 1534 Renaissance plate from Urbino, Italy, depicts Diogenes the Cynic reading while sitting in front of a tub. Alexander the Great approaches on horseback with three companions.

What did Diogenes and Alexander talk about after Diogenes asked Alexander to get out of his sunlight?

According to Letter 33 of the Cynic Epistles, which purport to have been written by Diogenes but were probably written by later Cynics, after Diogenes asked Alexander to get out of his sunlight, Alexander told Diogenes that he ought to have more respect for him since he could help raise him out of poverty. To this Diogenes replied, "What poverty?" He explained: "Poverty does not consist in the want of money, nor is begging to be deplored. Poverty consists in the desire to have everything, and through violent means if necessary—conditions that apply to you. Earth and springs are my allies in poverty, caves and animal fleece also. And not a single person is involved in war, on land or sea, because of it. We live our whole lives in peace and contentment." Diogenes goes on to criticize Alexander for not respecting Homer, who warned against *hubris* and taught the virtue of self-control.

What is the meaning of the *chreia* about Diogenes of Sinope and Plato?

Another *chreia*, this one from Diogenes Laërtius, tells the story of an encounter between Diogenes and Plato. When Plato came upon Diogenes washing lettuces, Plato said to him, "Had you paid court to Dionysius, you wouldn't now be washing lettuces," to which Diogenes replied, "If you had washed lettuces, you wouldn't have paid court to Dionysius." The story recalls Plato's visit to the court of Dionysius, the tyrant of Syracuse. In this *chreia,* Plato is saying that paying court to tyrants frees philosophers from hard labor and enables them to do philosophy. But for Diogenes, it is the ascetic practice of hard labor (*ponos*) that enables them to do philosophy, because in order to do philosophy, they must be self-sufficient (*autárkeia*) and free to speak their minds (*parrhēsía*). The point of this *chreia* is not just that being beholden to power corrupts the philosophical process but that in order to do philosophy, it is necessary to become so powerful yourself through ascetic practice that you no longer need those in power.

What was the meaning of the *chreia* about defacing the coins of Sinope?

Diogenes was the son of a banker named Hicesias, who minted coins for the treasury of his native Sinope (a colony settled by Greeks from Miletus on the southern shore of the Black Sea in Asia Minor). According to a famous *chreia* told by Diogenes Laërtius, either Diogenes of Sinope or his father defaced the coins. When they were caught, Diogenes was forced to flee Sinope, beginning his life as a wandering beggar. What is remarkable about this story is that defaced coins from the ancient city of Sinope have actually been found, suggesting that the story may be true. Defacing coins removes their monetary value, leaving only pieces of metal. The faces on the coins in this *chreia* have long been understood to represent conventional social values. Therefore, defacing the coins (*numismata*) represents removing conventional social values (*nomos*), leaving behind only a life lived according to nature. Chief among the conventional social values that Diogenes removed from his life was money.

What happened when Diogenes dined at the home of a very wealthy young man?

Letter 38 of the Cynic Epistles tells the story of the time that Diogenes dined at the home of a very wealthy young man. Every square inch of the hall in which he dined was covered with gold and fine paintings. When something got caught in his throat, Diogenes looked around the room and finding no better place to spit it out, he spit into the face of his wealthy host. Of course his host was offended and demanded an explanation, to which Diogenes responded, "You've finished every inch of this hall, but with no concern for your own self-improvement, you've made yourself the only place for spit to go." His host understood that Diogenes was referring to his lack of education; the next day he gave away his property, put on the Cynic cloak, and devoted the rest of his life to philosophy.

What did Diogenes think about marriage and children?

According to Letter 47 of the Cynic Epistles, Diogenes thought that marriage and children were more trouble than they were worth. He thought that if everyone were a philosopher, the human race would die out, and that would be no worse than if wasps or flies became extinct. But as it is, foolish people will continue to breed.

Who was Crates of Thebes?

Crates of Thebes (c. 365–c. 285 B.C.E.) was the most important student of Diogenes of Sinope and the teacher of Zeno of Citium (c. 334–c. 262 B.C.E.), the founder of Stoicism. Crates was born in the Greek city of Thebes to a wealthy family, but like the Buddha,

upon realizing that his wealth would not protect him from life's tragedies, he chose to give away his money and live the life of a Cynic philosopher. Crates was a physically unattractive man, but he showed such good will to the people of Athens that they opened their doors to him— hence his name "the door opener"—and welcomed him into their homes, where he would admonish them to heed the Cynic virtues. Crates summed up what philosophy meant to him when he said that what he got out of philosophy was a quart of beans and to depend on no one (*autárkeia*). As if to explain the implications of Cynic self-sufficiency further, the next quote from Crates that Diogenes Laërtius provides states that love is cured by hunger, and if not by hunger, then by time, and if not by time, there is always the yoke or bridle.

A wall painting at the Villa Farnesina, Museo delle Terme, in Rome depicts Crates of Thebes, a Stoic philosopher known as "the door opener."

How on earth did Crates ever get married?

It certainly wasn't due to his good looks, wealth, or gift for romance. Crates attracted the interest of a younger woman from an aristocratic family because of his philosophy and—even more surprisingly—his lifestyle. Hipparchia of Maroneia (c. 350–280 B.C.E.) fell in love with Crates and wished to marry him. Her parents were aghast, and at their urging Crates did all he could to persuade her that she should not marry him. Finally, when nothing else worked, he showed her that he had nothing to give her by taking off his clothes in front of her and saying, "Here is the man you wish to be your husband and here is all he owns. So consider your decision carefully, because you cannot be my wife unless you live the way I do." In spite of this characteristically Cynic stunt, Hipparchia chose to marry him and threatened her parents that she would commit suicide if they did not permit the marriage.

Shocking expectations of how a woman should behave in ancient Greek society, Hipparchia took up exactly the same dress and lifestyle as her husband. They lived in the stoas and porticoes of Athens, and according to one ancient source, they even gratified each other sexually in public, just as Diogenes had gratified himself. Crates accepted her as his equal, telling her in Letter 29 of the Cynic Epistles that "You are no weaker by nature, any more than bitches are weaker than male dogs." According to Letter 30 of the Cynic Epistles, when Hipparchia gave Crates a shirt that she made for him, he returned it, saying that she should not try to prove that she was a conventional wife, because he had married her for the sake of philosophy and to benefit humanity as a whole. Together, they had at least two children.

Who was Hipparchia of Maroneia?

Hipparchia of Maroneia (c. 350–280 B.C.E.) was the wife of Crates of Thebes and a Cynic philosopher in her own right who influenced the early Stoics. It is possible that she was introduced to philosophy at a young age by her brother Metrocles, who was a student of both Aristotle and Crates. She was one of very few women philosophers of ancient Greece, but unfortunately little record of her work has survived except for a few sayings and anecdotes found in later writers such as Diogenes Laërtius.

Hipparchia attended symposia (drinking parties where philosophy was discussed) that in ancient Greek society were normally reserved for men only. Diogenes Laërtius (*Lives* 6.98) tells a story about an encounter between Hipparchia and Theodorus the Atheist at one such symposium. Hipparchia challenged Theodorus with a clever argument whose conclusion was that it would not be wrong for Hipparchia to hit Theodorus. Theodorus responded by attempting to embarrass her by lifting up her cloak and exposing her. Of course, as a Cynic philosopher, she could not be embarrassed. Theodorus then resorted to quoting Euripides and asked her if she had abandoned a woman's work. She answered that yes, she had, and that she did not for one moment regret the time she spent improving her mind instead of working at the loom. By violating Greek social conventions that regulated the conduct of women, she was doing what Cynics had done

What was Dio Chrysostom's formula for happiness?

Dio Chrysostom (c. 40–c. 115 C.E.) was a Cynic philosopher of the early Roman Empire. His formula for happiness was the typical Cynic prescription to live a simple life according to nature. Artificial means of acquiring pleasure cause more trouble than they are worth. "The fact is, all man's ingenuity and advances in technology were at best mixed blessings" (*Oration* 6.28). The pursuit of pleasure by means of lawsuits, politics, or war is even more counterproductive. Living a simple life according to nature avoids the need for all of these. Great wealth and power are a curse. A king lives his life in perpetual fear of being murdered by his political rivals and is unable to enjoy anything. Only pleasures freely granted to us by nature (like the sunlight that Diogenes basked in) are worth enjoying. "Whatever cost a lot in terms of time, trouble and money, these things Diogenes rejected because, as he was able to show, they hurt whoever used them" (*Oration*).

since Diogenes of Sinope: defacing the common coin of social convention. But by marrying Crates, she did Diogenes one better, since she not only defaced the common coin of social convention but also the Cynic's own convention to not marry.

What did the Romans think about the Cynics?

At the end of the Hellenistic period, the Romans conquered the last remaining Greek dynasty, and the republic became an empire. The Romans were a practical people who were less interested in theory than the Greeks, but even in the increasingly decadent period of the empire, they admired the Cynic way of life because it exhibited the virtues of simplicity and austerity that they associated with the early republic.

The Stoic philosopher Seneca (c. 4 B.C.E.–65 C.E.), who served as both a senator and an advisor to emperors, described Demetrius the Cynic (fl. first century C.E.) as a "great man" and agreed with him that it is best to adhere to a simple set of a few philosophical principles so that they can be practiced continually until they become second nature. Seneca admired Demetrius's simple philosophy and austere way of life. But as a Roman, he could not appreciate the Cynic principle of shamelessness (*anaídeia*, αναίδεια) because honor was a fundamental principle of Roman society. Cicero, for example, admired the Greek Stoics, but he disliked the Cynics because they were shameless. He thought that no social order could exist without honor and shame. Other Romans, such as Seneca, admired the Cynics in spite of their principle of shamelessness and were willing to overlook it. In his discussion of Demetrius, Seneca made no mention of the Cynic principles of shamelessness, frankness, or freedom of speech (*parrhēsía*, παρρησία), or defacing the currency. Instead, he emphasized the virtues of painful effort and hard work (*ponos*, πόνος); endurance, perseverance, and self-control (*karteria*, καρτερία); and indifference (*adiaphora*, ἀδιάφορα) to the external conditions of life (but not to social opinion).

What did Emperor Julian think about the Cynics?

Although there were some important differences between the Cynic way of life and traditional Roman values, the Cynics were generally well tolerated by the Romans and continued to wander the empire until its collapse in the late fifth century C.E. In the fourth century C.E., Emperor Julian (331/332–363 C.E.) attempted to save the traditional pagan culture of Greco-Roman civilization by replacing Christianity with a mystical version of Plato's philosophy known since the nineteenth century as Neoplatonism. Like Seneca before him, Julian admired the Cynics. But whereas Seneca understood Cynicism as a proto-Stoic philosophy, Julian understood it as a kind of Platonism.

Emperor Julian (r. 361–363 C.E.) was the last non-Christian Roman leader. He promoted a mystical version of Neoplatonism as an alternative to Christianity in the empire.

In an amusing *chreia*, Julian tells the story about an incident in which Diogenes of Sinope scolded a young man who farted in public. "So, swine," Diogenes told the young man, "you've done nothing to deserve taking such liberties in public, and still you choose this large crowd to demonstrate your new-found contempt for what other people think?" Julian agrees with the Cynics that a philosopher should live according to reason, not social opinion, because we can only be happy if we live according to our nature, and it is our nature to reason. But we can do that only if we have developed our capacity for reason and used it to master our appetites and emotions. It is even worse, according to Julian, to obey our appetites and emotions than it is to obey social opinion. For the masses who have not developed their capacity for reason, it is better that they obey social opinion than that they do whatever gives them pleasure or feels good to them at the moment. Only philosophers who have developed their capacity for reason and mastered their appetites and emotions are entitled to disregard social opinion, speak frankly, and act without shame. But in any case, no one should fart in public. The masses should not fart in public because they should feel ashamed to do so. Philosophers should not fart in public because having developed their capacity for reason, they should know better.

Was Cynicism in the later years of the Roman Empire compatible with Christianity?

Julian (331/332–363 C.E.) was the last emperor who was not a Christian, and in 380 C.E. Christianity became the official state religion. But the Cynics survived another century until the fall of the Roman Empire, because they shared some common ethical principles with the Christians. Both the Cynics and the Christians were ascetics who believed that the most virtuous life is a simple life of self-imposed poverty. The mendicant monks of the Christian religion who achieved this ideal resembled the Cynics in their outward appearance and in their lifestyle. Asceticism requires patience, so both the Cynics and the Christians also believed that patience, or as the Cynics called it, *karteria*, was a virtue.

Another shared value that is closely related to both asceticism and patience was the Cynic principle of *ponos* (πόνος), which meant painful effort and hard work. And both Christians and Cynics agreed that it is wrong to pretend to be something that you are not in order to impress others. Where the Christians parted company with the Cynics was on the principle of shamelessness, just as Seneca did. Christians have always honored Seneca in art and literature because they shared his ethical principles. Dante placed Seneca in Limbo, far above the circle of hell, where he placed the Epicureans. The Christian attitude towards the Cynics was roughly the same as Seneca's. They admired the Cynics for the ethical principles and character traits that they shared with them while they overlooked the rest.

What did the postwar American counterculture have in common with the Cynics?

Stoicism has been an important part of Anglo-American Protestant culture since the eighteenth century. But the Stoics have much in common with the Cynics and trace their intellectual heritage back to them, so if Stoicism is a part of Anglo-American Protestant culture, then so is Cynicism.

The postwar American counterculture represented the Cynic side of Anglo-American Protestant culture as opposed to the more respectable Stoic side. Like the Cynics, the "hippies" became "enlightened" (they "tuned in, turned on," and became "hip" or "hep" to the truth). Like the Cynics, they "dropped out" of conventional society, went "back to nature," and lived a life of poverty or "voluntary simplicity." And like the Cynics, they spurned government, violence, war, and politics. They were citizens of the world and of nature, not of any city or nation-state. They rejected the family and had sex with whoever would consent to have sex with them. They even looked like Cynics: they let their hair grow long, walked barefoot, and dressed in rags. The one difference perhaps was that in spite of their generally ascetic lifestyle, the hippy ethic contained an element of hedonism. They believed that if it feels good, it is good. But even this can be reconciled with Cynicism by the fact that the Cynics, too, enjoyed simple pleasures, as long as they came easily and naturally. It was only the artificial pursuit of pleasure by means of technology, politics, violence, or war that they rejected.

THE MEGARIAN AND DIALECTICAL SCHOOLS OF PHILOSOPHY

What were the Megarian and Dialectical schools of philosophy known for?

The Megarian and Dialectical schools of philosophy were known for their work in logic and their influence on the development of Stoicism and Skepticism. The Megarian school of philosophy was another Hellenistic school of philosophy that traced its origins back to Socrates. The founder of the Megarian school was Euclides of Megara (c. 435–c. 365 B.C.E.), who was said to have been not only a student of Socrates but also one of the few who were present at his death. But Euclides also studied Eleatic metaphysics and logic. Euclides combined the Socratic concept of the Good with the Eleatic concept of the One to argue that the Good is the eternal and unchanging Being and that nothing else besides the Good exists. Ichthyas (fl. fourth century B.C.E.) was head of the Megarian school after Euclides, followed by Stilpo (c. 360–c. 280 B.C.E.).

Eubulides of Miletus and Clinomachus of Thurii (both fl. fourth century B.C.E.) were also students of Euclides. According to Diogenes Laërtius, Clinomachus founded a splinter group of Megarians known as the Dialectical school, which, like the original Megarian school, was known for its work in logic and dialectics. In fact, Clinomachus may have been the first to develop propositional logic. Philo the Dialectician and Diodorus Cronus (both fl. c. 300 B.C.E.) were members of the Dialectical school and were known for their work on propositional logic and for introducing modal logic (the logic of possibility and necessity) to Hellenistic philosophy. The logic of the Megarian and Dialectical schools can be found in both Stoicism and Skepticism. Pyrrho the Skeptic (c. 360–c. 270 B.C.E.) was said to have been a student of Stilpo; and Zeno of Citium, the founder of Stoicism, was said to have studied with Stilpo, Diodorus Cronus, and Philo the Dialectician.

Zeno of Citium (a city on the island of Cyprus) was the founder of Stoicism, a philosophy that built upon Cynicism and emphasized a life of virtue based on nature.

STOICISM

Who founded the school of Stoicism?

The school of Stoicism was founded in the early third century B.C.E. by Zeno of Citium (c. 334–c. 262 B.C.E.), and it took its name from the Stoa Poikilê or "Painted Porch" where Zeno and his students gathered. The Stoa Poikilê was a covered walkway or colonnade in the *agora* or marketplace of ancient Athens decorated with paintings of mythic and historic battles and other artworks seized in war. Thus, unlike the Epicureans, the Stoics positioned themselves at the center of civic life.

According to a charming story told by Diogenes Laërtius, Zeno was a wealthy merchant from Citium on the island of Cyprus. While on a voyage from Phoenicia to Piraeus, the port of Athens, to deliver a cargo of purple dye painstakingly extracted from sea snails, he became shipwrecked. Having lost everything he owned and left wandering the streets of Athens, he finally consulted the Oracle of Delphi for direction. The Oracle told him that he should color himself not with the color of dead snails but with the color of dead men. According to Diogenes, Zeno understood this to mean that he should study ancient authors, which he did. Back in Athens, he came upon a bookstore where he discovered Xenophon's *Memorabilia*. Pleased by the character of Socrates as he was described by Xenophon, Zeno asked the bookseller where he could find such men. At that very moment, Crates of Thebes happened to walk by, so the bookseller pointed to him and told Zeno to follow him. From that day on, according to Diogenes, Zeno became a devoted student of Crates and followed his strict Socratic ethics, though due to his modesty, Zeno never adopted the characteristic Cynic trait of shamelessness.

Besides Crates, Diogenes reports that Zeno studied with Stilpo, the head of the Megarian school, and with Xenocrates (396/395–314/313 B.C.E.) and Polemo (d. 270/269 B.C.E.), two successive heads of Plato's Academy. From Stilpo and other Megarians, the Stoics got the basis for their own study of logic. And from Plato's *Timaeus,* the Stoics acquired their belief in a providential god who designs and constructs the cosmos like a craftsman, according to a rational plan. Zeno of Citium was also inspired by Plato's *Republic* to write a book on the ideal society with the same title.

Who was Cleanthes?

Cleanthes of Assos (c. 330–c. 230 B.C.E.) was the second head (scholarch) of the Stoic school after Zeno of Citium. He was said to have studied with Crates of Thebes before becoming Zeno's student, and his ethics, like Zeno's, shares much in common with Cynicism. Originally a boxer, he

Cleanthes, Zeno's successor, who was also a student of Crates, shunned strong emotions as being destructive to self-control.

acquired the nickname "ass" because he exhibited the Cynic virtues of painful effort, hard work (*ponos*, πόνοζ), endurance, perseverance, and self-control (*karteria*, καρτερία). Cleanthes shunned pleasure (*hēdonē*) and the passions (*pathê*) of fear (*phobos*), strong desire or lust (*epithumia*), and distress (*lupē*) because they undermine self-control and are contrary to reason.

Cleanthes is best known for his poem "Hymn to Zeus" and for his contributions to Stoic physics, cosmology, and ethics. Cleanthes was a materialist who believed that only matter is real. Even the soul and the gods, he believed, are composed of matter. We know that the soul is material because qualities of the soul and the body are transmitted from parent to child by means of sexual reproduction. But he did not believe that the material world is lifeless or that it is composed of atoms engaged in random motion. He believed that the universe is animated by Zeus, who is a cosmic fire or thunderbolt, of which the Sun is only the most visible manifestation. He believed that Zeus as the cosmic fire is a rational ordering principle that permeates everything and gives all things their order, coherence, and being. The coherence of things in a whole is made possible by their *tonos,* or internal tension. In the human soul, tension is manifested as the quality of one's character. Those with a great deal of rational self-control can hold the disparate elements of their soul together in a coherent whole. Nothing happens by chance, according to Cleanthes, but by fate (*heimarmenē*). It is our duty to accept whatever fate brings us, because everything is determined by Zeus and happens for a reason.

Who was Epictetus?

Epictetus (55–135 C.E.) was a Greek Stoic philosopher who lived during the early period of the Roman Empire. Born in Asia Minor, he spent his childhood in Rome working as a slave for a secretary to Emperor Nero. While still a slave, he studied with Roman Stoic philosopher Musonius Rufus. Sometime after Nero's death in 68 C.E., Epictetus was freed from slavery and began his career teaching philosophy in Rome. When in 93 C.E. Emperor Domitian banished all philosophers from Rome, Epictetus fled to the Greek city of Nicopolis, where he established his own school of philosophy. One of his students was Arrian (c. 86–c. 160 C.E.), who recorded his philosophy in two works that have survived, the *Enchiridion* (or "Handbook") and the more complete *Discourses*. Although Epictetus was very much in the same tradition as the founding figures of ancient Greek Stoicism, Epictetus has most directly influenced how we think about Stoicism today, as represented for instance in the Serenity Prayer.

Who was Seneca?

Seneca (4 B.C.E.–65 C.E.) was the first of three famous Stoic philosophers who lived during the early period of the Roman Empire; the other two were Epictetus (55–135 C.E.) and Marcus Aurelius (121–180 C.E.). All three retained the fundamental principles of Stoicism that they inherited from the philosophers of the Hellenistic period, but they changed the emphasis by focusing more on the ethical question of how to live well and less on arcane

What is the meaning of the analogy of the dog and the cart?

The analogy of the dog and the cart is found in *The Refutations of All Heresies* by the third-century C.E. Christian theologian Hippolytus. According to Hippolytus, who given his hostility towards pagan philosophy may not be entirely reliable, the analogy of the dog and the cart was used by the early Greek Stoics to explain the nature of fate and our moral duty to follow it. In the analogy, a dog is tied to a cart. The dog has the freedom to choose whether to follow the cart willingly or not. If the dog chooses not to follow the cart willingly, it will be dragged along anyhow, by force. Therefore, it is wise for the dog to follow fate willingly, since fate will pull it along in the same way whether it chooses to follow willingly or not. It is an ethical imperative, according to the Stoics, to conform one's will to fate, since fate is the rational course of nature determined by Zeus. A hymn attributed to Cleanthes by the Roman-era Stoic Epictetus (*Enchiridion*) expresses the same idea: "Lead me, O Zeus, and you O Fate, to whatever place you have assigned me; I shall follow without reluctance, and if I am not willing to, because I have become a bad man, nevertheless I *will* follow."

problems in logic and the theory of knowledge. Of the three, Seneca was the only one to write philosophy in Latin rather than Greek. In addition to philosophical letters and essays, Seneca wrote tragedies and a political satire and was a gifted orator.

Seneca was born into an educated and aristocratic family from a Roman province of Spain. His father, Seneca the Elder (54 B.C.E.–c. 39 C.E.), wrote on Roman history and taught rhetoric in Rome; his nephew, whom he tutored, was the poet Lucan (39–65 C.E.). Seneca's aunt brought the young boy to Rome, where he studied with Stoic philosophers and became involved with politics at the highest levels. He fell in and out of favor with a series of emperors, including Caligula, Claudius, and Nero. Under Emperor Claudius, he was elected praetor, gathered a group of powerful friends around him, and served as tutor to the young Nero. When Claudius was assassinated in 54 C.E., Seneca and his friends became the *de facto* rulers of the Roman Empire until Nero matured into the role. In 65 C.E., Seneca's enemies accused him of having been involved with a plot to murder Nero. Nero ordered Seneca to commit suicide; he faced death with such fortitude and equanimity that his suicide became a popular subject of art and literature and inspired Christians throughout Western history.

Seneca was considered to have been the most Christian of the pagan philosophers and was even believed to have known and corresponded with St. Paul. Not until the fifteenth century was it discovered that a collection of letters between St. Paul and Seneca had been forged, probably in the fourth century C.E. In spite of this discovery, Seneca was so admired in the early modern age that his letters and essays served as a model for sermons and moral essays by the likes of John Calvin and Michel de Montaigne.

Why did Christians admire Seneca?

Christians admired Seneca the Younger (not to be confused with the Elder) both for the story of his death, which paralleled that of Jesus, and for his moral philosophy. Both Seneca and Aristotle defined anger as a painful desire for revenge. But whereas Aristotle believed that anger is an appropriate response to an insult or put-down, Seneca believed that anger is never an appropriate response to any harm done to us. Seneca taught that instead of seeking to retaliate against those who harm us, we ought to calmly seek justice for all. What is wrong is not what harms us personally but rather what is not in accordance with the rational order (*logos*) of the universe as established by an intelligent and providential God for the good of all. Therefore, Seneca, like Jesus, faced his execution calmly and without anger towards those who were responsible for his death.

Who was Marcus Aurelius?

Marcus Aurelius (121–180 C.E.) was a Stoic philosopher and the last of the so-called "five good emperors" of the Roman Empire. He was the son of Marcus Annius Verus III, who held the office of praetor, and Domitia Lucilla, who was heir to a huge fortune. After his father died, Marcus Aurelius was raised by his paternal grandfather, Marcus Annius Verus II, who held the office of consul in the Roman Senate and prepared his grandson to walk in his footsteps by providing him with the best possible education. The young Marcus studied Latin and Greek, grammar, and rhetoric, but he was especially interested in the writings of the Stoic philosopher Epictetus.

Marcus Aurelius served as consul several times before finally becoming emperor in 161 C.E. In 138 C.E., Emperor Hadrian selected the husband of Marcus Aurelius's pater-

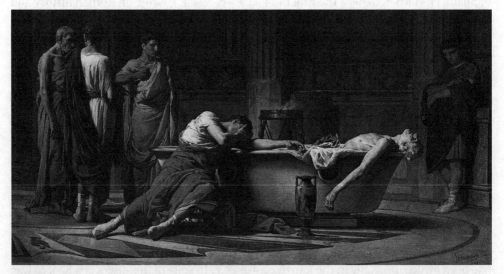

Manuel Domínguez Sánchez's *Death of Seneca* (*La Muerte de Séneca*, 1871). Seneca, while likely not guilty, was accused by Emperor Nero of plotting to have him killed. Nero therefore ordered Seneca to kill himself, which he did.

nal aunt, Aurelius Antoninus, as his successor, with the condition that he adopt Marcus Aurelius and Lucius Commodus. Following Hadrian's death in 138 C.E., Antoninus became emperor, and when Antoninus died in 161 C.E., Marcus Aurelius and his brother Lucius Commodus became co-emperors, until Lucius died in 169 C.E., leaving Marcus as the sole emperor.

Marcus Aurelius acquired a reputation as a particularly just and well-tempered ruler. However, he spent most of his time as emperor on military campaigns successfully fighting off the Parthians to the east and the barbarian hordes to the north. Indeed, Marcus Aurelius wrote his famous *Meditations* while on a military campaign against the Quadi, a Germanic tribe, according to a note appended to the work.

A statue of Marcus Aurelius can be viewed at the Capitoline Hill in Rome, Italy. Not only was he a Roman emperor, he was also a Stoic philosopher.

What is *Meditations* by Marcus Aurelius?

Meditations is a collection of notes that Marcus Aurelius wrote to himself (hence the alternate title, *To Himself*) in which he reflected on the ethical significance of his own thoughts and emotions. Though Marcus Aurelius did not introduce any new ideas to Stoicism, *Meditations* is one of the best sources of information that we have about Stoic philosophy. Written in an engaging style and with logical clarity, it is considered one of the great works of Western literature and philosophy. In his notes, Marcus Aurelius applied the principles he learned from his study of Epictetus and the ancient Greek Stoics to his own life.

From the ancient Greek Stoics, Marcus learned that the universe is an ever-changing but law-governed chain of cause and effect that is designed and constructed by the cosmic *pneuma*, which is the fiery breath and rational speech (*logos*) of a wise and providential god. Since the course of events in the universe is determined by a wise and providential god for the good of the whole, it is our duty to accept and even embrace our fate. But for Marcus this did not mean that we should remain passive in the face of our destiny and not act in the world. Marcus was not only a thinker but also a doer who fought and won many battles. We must act, Marcus believed, and we must act with the best intentions possible, but we must also be prepared to accept whatever happens as a result of our actions. From Epictetus, Marcus learned that it is up to us what we think and feel about what happens to us. We can accept our fate and gain some measure of inner peace and tranquility, or we can suffer the passions of fear, anger, grief, and irrational desire. We cannot control our fate. But we can control ourselves and our own judgments about what happens, because the self, as Marcus conceived it, is a "citadel," an impenetrable fortress that cannot be shaken by the events of the world.

Who was Chrysippus?

Chrysippus of Soli (c. 280–c. 207 B.C.E.) was the third head or scholarch of the Stoic school after the death of Cleanthes in about 230 B.C.E. Like Cleanthes, who developed the Cynic character traits of *ponos* and *karteria* by means of an *áskēsis* of disciplined exercise and training in the sport of boxing, Chrysippus developed those traits by means of an *áskēsis* in the sport of long-distance running. After his inherited fortune was seized by the king's treasury, Chrysippus moved to Athens where he studied with the Academic Skeptics Arcesilaus and Lacydes and developed his talent for logic and argument before becoming a student of Cleanthes. Chrysippus went on to surpass his teachers and become the greatest philosopher who lived between Aristotle (367–347 B.C.E.) and Plotinus (204/205–270 C.E.) and one of the greatest of all time.

Chrysippus wrote over 700 works on every possible subject and is credited with the development of propositional logic. Although only scattered fragments of his writings have survived, the history of Western philosophy would not have been the same without him. Chrysippus refashioned the philosophical works of Zeno and Cleanthes into a comprehensive logical system that made Stoicism the most important school of philosophy until the rise of Neoplatonism and an enduring influence on both Western philosophy and religion thereafter. Even Neoplatonism would not have been the same without Stoicism because, contrary to its name, Neoplatonism was not merely a revival of Platonism but was a philosophy that combined elements of Plato, Aristotle, and Stoicism.

STOIC LOGIC

According to Aristotle, why is logic not a part of philosophy proper?

According to Aristotle, logic is not a part of philosophy proper but is merely a tool for philosophers to use because Aristotle's logic is only about the form of arguments, not their content. For example, Aristotle's logic tells us that arguments of the form "All *A*s are *B*s, all *B*s are *C*s, therefore all *A*s are *C*s" are valid. But without filling in the *A*s, *B*s, and *C*s with content, we don't have even a claim to knowledge. "All cats are felines" is a claim to knowledge that is

The third philosopher to lead the Stoic school in Athens, Chrysippus believed that exercise such as boxing and running improved one's self-discipline.

either true or false, but "All *A*s are *B*s" is not. But philosophy consists of knowledge claims. Therefore, logic by itself is not philosophy.

What was the Stoic argument for the existence of God?

The Stoic argument for the existence of God was the intelligent design argument (also called the teleological argument or the argument from design). The Stoics derived their argument for the existence of God from Socrates, who used the same argument in Xenophon's dialogues. The argument from design begins with the observation that the world has a rational order. Because the world has a rational order, it could not have occurred by accident but must have been deliberately designed and constructed by a rational being. But the only rational being capable of designing and constructing the world would be God. Therefore, God exists. The argument relies on the same reasoning that you would use if you found a watch on a beach. If you found a watch on a beach, you would not assume that it was assembled by accident, but that it had been designed and constructed by an intelligent human being according to a rational plan.

What is the origin of Stoic logic?

The origin of Stoic logic lies in the Megarian and Dialectical schools of philosophy. Beginning with their founder Zeno of Citium, the Stoics were interested in the logic of the Megarian and Dialectical schools. The Megarians and Dialecticians were the first to work on a logic of propositions as opposed to the logic of terms developed by Aristotle. But it

Why did the Stoics disagree with Aristotle about the place of logic in philosophy?

The Stoics were materialists who believed that the study of the physical world is an essential part of philosophy, and because they believed that the physical world has a logical structure, they believed that logic is an essential part of philosophy, too. The Stoics believed that the logical structure of the physical world is evident to anyone who observes nature. Events do not occur in a random, chaotic fashion but rather according to logical rules of causation that determine what follows from what. Whereas Aristotle's logic is a logic of universal categories (e.g., "cats" and "animals") that determines what is a kind or species of what (e.g., cats are a kind of animal), Stoic logic is a logic of causation that determines what follows from what. A typical Stoic argument is "If it is day, it is light; it is day; therefore, it is light." This argument does not determine what is a kind or species of what but determines the causal relation between day and light: it is light because it is day. The Stoics believed that logic is a part of philosophy because, as a study of the physical world, philosophy is a study of causal relations, and causal relations are logical relations.

was Chrysippus who completed their work and who is credited with the development of propositional logic.

What are the differences between Aristotle's logic and Stoic logic?

Aristotle's logic is a logic of terms, whereas Stoic logic is a logic of propositions. Terms are either the subject or predicate of a categorical proposition. A categorical proposition asserts or denies that all or some members of one category (the subject term) are members of another category (the predicate term). By itself, a term has no truth value. Only when two terms are combined in a categorical proposition do you have a proposition that may convey knowledge and be true or false. For example, the term "cats" by itself means something, but it does not convey knowledge and is neither true nor false. In Aristotle's logic, terms are combined with the logical operators "all," "some," "is," and "is not" to form propositions. For example, combining the term "cats" with the term "animals" in the categorical proposition "all cats are animals" yields a proposition that conveys knowledge.

Aristotle's logic is a logic of categorical terms, because he did not believe that it was possible to acquire scientific knowledge about individuals but only about categories, kinds, or species of things—in other words, about the "forms." Stoic logic, on the other hand, is a logic of propositions. Propositions combine a subject and a predicate to form a complete declarative sentence that may convey knowledge and be true or false. Neither the subject nor the predicate of propositions in Stoic logic need be categorical terms, and in general they are not. Propositions are the elementary units of Stoic logic. They may be combined with the logical operators "if, then," "and," "or," and "not." For example, "it is day" is a proposition. Call it "p." "It is light" is a proposition, too. Call it "q." "If p, then q" is a proposition created by combining the propositions p and q with the logical operator "if, then." The Stoics recognized that arguments of the form "if p, then q; p; therefore q" are valid. In other words, if the premises "if p, then q" and "p" are both true, then the conclusion "q" must also be true.

What are the three parts of a meaningful statement?

According to the Stoic theory of language, any meaningful statement can be analyzed in three parts: the physical sound or mark made to indicate what is being said; the meaning or sense of what is said, which they called the *lektón* (sayable); and the physical thing that is ultimately referred to by what is being said. In modern linguistics, the physical mark or sound is the "signifier." The meaning or sense is the "signified." And the thing referred to is the "referent." The *lektón* is not a physical thing and does not exist in its own right. The *lektón* subsists only as something that can be said *about* physical things. For example, if I say "This is a tree," the signifiers are the actual sounds coming from my voice. The signified is the meaning or sense of what I am saying. The same meaning or sense can be conveyed in other languages using different words. For example, the same meaning or sense is conveyed by the English statement "This is a tree" as by the German statement "Das ist ein Baum." Finally, the physical thing ultimately referred to by what is being said in this example is this tree standing before me.

Though a *lektón* (plural *lekta*) can be any meaningful utterance, the Stoics were primarily interested in what they called *assertibles* (*axiomata*), which are propositions of the form "*S* is *P*." Propositions were of interest to the Stoics because only propositions convey knowledge and are either true or false. The science of logic is concerned not with signifiers as such but with the meaning or sense of what is said because it is the meaning or sense that determines the truth or falsity of a given statement.

What are the fundamental types of valid argument in propositional logic?

There are five fundamental types of valid argument in propositional logic that cannot be reduced to other argument types. Four of these have been given the Latin names *modus ponens*, *modus tollens*, *modus ponendo tollens*, and *modus tollendo ponens*. A fifth argument type is unnamed. The fifth type has the form "not both *p* and *q*; *p*; therefore, not *q*." *Modus ponens* has the form "if *p*, *q*; *p*; therefore, *q*." *Modus tollens* has the form "if *p*, *q*; not *q*; therefore, not *p*." *Modus ponendo tollens* has the form "either *p* or *q*; *p*; therefore, not *q*." And *modus tollendo ponens* has the form "either *p* or *q*; not *q*; therefore", *p*. None of the fundamental types of valid argument in propositional logic are necessarily composed of categorical propositions as the fundamental types of valid argument are according to Aristotle. That made propositional logic more amenable than Aristotle's logic to the study of particular things in the physical world and their causal relations to one another.

STOIC THEORY OF KNOWLEDGE

What is the difference between an impression and a belief?

An *impression* in Stoicism is a mere appearance or seeming to be something—for example, it appears or seems to be light. Impressions always take the form of propositions because they always assert something. A *belief* is an assent (*sunkatathesis*) to the assertion made by an impression, or a judgment that the assertion is true. For example, the belief that it is light is an assent to the assertion that it is light, or a judgment that the assertion "it is light" is true. A belief does not assert that something merely appears or seems to be the case, but that it *is* the case.

According to the Stoics, what is a true perception?

According to the Stoics, a true perception is an impression on the mind caused by the object of perception. So, for example, when you truly see the sun, it is because light radiates from the sun to your mind (which the Stoics believed was part of the body) and forms an impression upon it or alters it in some way. The word that the Stoics used for an impression was *phantasia*, which contains as one of its root terms the Greek word for light (*phōs*). Just as light shows not only itself but the object that it lights up, so too does a true impression show not only itself but also the object that caused the impression. According to the Stoics, an impression has the form of a proposition. For example, the impression of the sun has the form of the proposition "it is the sun." The impression of the sun is true if the proposition "it is the sun" is true. Just as light shows both itself and the object that it lights up, so too does a true proposition show both itself and the object referred to by the proposition—in this case, the sun.

How did the Stoics know if a perception is true?

Stoicism developed in part out of centuries of debate with the Skeptics, who did not believe that we could ever know anything or that we could ever be certain that we know what we think we know. In response to the Skeptics, the Stoics developed a theory to explain not only how we know but how we can be certain that we know what we think we know. The Stoics distinguished between two types of impressions. There are those that are caused by a real object in the physical world, and there are those that are not caused by a real object in the physical world.

Among those that are not caused by real objects in the physical world, there are two types. The first type are objects of our imagination, such as the characters in a novel. These are relatively innocuous because we know that they are not real. The second is more dangerous. These are the hallucinations and delusions of those who are mentally ill or whose sense organs are diseased. The Greek word that Chrysippus used for the first was *phantastikon*, and for the second, *phantasma*. Luckily for us, if we are healthy and our sense organs are working properly, our perceptions are generally reliable. When we see that it is light, it is because it really is light. But even among healthy perceptions Chrysippus distinguished between perceptions that we know for certain are true, and those that we do not know for certain are true. Impressions that we know for certain are true are called *cognitive impressions*. These are impressions that are so clear and distinct that they leave no room for doubt—for example, the impression that it is light when standing out in the noonday sun.

What is a cognitive impression?

The original Greek term used by the early Stoics for a cognitive impression was a *kataleptic phantasia* (φαντασία καταληπτική). Cicero translated the Greek word *katalepsis* into the Latin word *cognitio*, which is why a *kataleptic phantasia* is translated into English as a *cognitive impression*. But the original Greek word *katalepsis* (κατάληψζ) meant "grasping." A *kataleptic phantasia* was, therefore, an impression that you can grasp—in other words, one that you can hold firmly in your hands. What is held firmly is not only the impression but its object. I know that my perception of this book is a cognitive impression because I can reach out and hold the book firmly in my hands. Thus, while so many epistemological metaphors in ancient Greek philosophy refer to vision and light, the Stoic concept of a cognitive impression refers to manual dexterity and the sense of touch.

How did the Stoics understand causality?

The Stoics understood causality as a logical inference between two particular events. For example, the causal relation between fire and smoke (*F* causes *S*) is the logical in-

---

How did Zeno of Citium use his hand to explain what knowledge is?

According to Cicero, Zeno explained what knowledge is using his hand. Holding his hand open, he said that this represents a mere impression. The Skeptics believed that we cannot get beyond mere impressions. But the Stoics went much further. Holding his fingers together, Zeno said that this represents assent, or the belief that the impression is true. For example, if the impression is the proposition "it is day," then holding one's fingers together would represent the belief that it is day, based on the judgment that the proposition "it is day" is true. Then closing his fingers and making a fist, he said that this represents a cognitive impression. A cognitive impression is one that you can believe with certainty because it can, metaphorically, be grasped firmly in your hand. Finally, Zeno put his other hand over his fist and said this represents knowledge. The final step represents the integration of many cognitive impressions into a logically coherent system. One cognitive impression by itself does not make knowledge, any more than the axioms of geometry by themselves constitute the science of geometry, because the world according to the Stoics is a logically coherent system.

ference "if fire then smoke" (if F then S). Therefore, causal relations are not arbitrary or without rhyme or reason but are necessary and have a logical explanation. Cognitive impressions provide us with immediate and certain knowledge of causal relations. But since every event that occurs in the universe is causally related either directly or indirectly to every other event, one cognitive impression by itself does not constitute knowledge. The universe can only be understood as an integrated system, and our beliefs can only be judged as part of an integrated system, not in isolation from one another. That is why if we have one isolated experience in which we see something (such as smoke without fire) that does not fit with our other beliefs about the universe, we tend to dismiss it as a misperception, until enough of our beliefs are contradicted by our experiences that we must revise our entire system of beliefs about the universe.

According to the Stoics, how does knowledge improve our cognition?

Cognitive impressions depend on the observer and the knowledge that the observer brings to their experience. An expert observer with a large store of knowledge will have cognitive impressions that a naïve observer will not. For example, a mechanic might have the cognitive impression of a bad valve when hearing the same sound that a naïve observer believes is only an odd noise because the mechanic knows how engines work and the naïve observer does not.

Because cognitive impressions are not isolated truths but parts of a logically coherent system of knowledge, the more we know, the more cognitive impressions we are capable of having. Cognitive impressions are not, therefore, merely passive elements of knowledge, like bits of empirical data or facts, but cognitive skills that enable us to know and to learn. Cognitive impressions are not only elements of a kind of scientific knowledge that the Greeks called *epistēmē*, but elements of a productive knowledge or know-how that the Greeks called *technê*. *Technê* is the knowledge of how to make things, such as the things that are made in the fine arts and crafts; but in this case, *technê* is knowledge of how to "make" knowledge. The more cognitive impressions you have integrated into your system of knowledge, the more cognitive impressions you are capable of "making." Knowledge is therefore a virtuous circle: the more you know, the more you can learn and add to your store of knowledge.

Cognitive impressions can vary based on the observer's knowledge. For example, an experienced mechanic can detect an engine problem based on a noise that an ordinary observer would not be able to interpret.

What is the Stoic ideal of the sage?

The Stoic ideal of the sage (*sophos*, σοφός) is of a person who possesses supreme wisdom (*sophia*, σοφία), a paragon of virtue (*arête*) and integrity whose mind and character are composed of a logically coherent system of beliefs based upon a firm foundation of cognitive impressions. The sage is always consistent in his or her beliefs and actions and never suffers conflicting emotions. In Stoic terms, the mind (*hegemonikon*) of the sage has a very high level of tension (*tonos*) that holds its many parts together in a complex but unified whole. However, the mind of the sage is not only internally coherent but true, for the sage never errs or gives assent to false beliefs. The Stoics understood that few if any of us are ever likely to attain this ideal, but they believed that it is in principle attainable, because they believed that the world is logical, and therefore, it can in principle be completely and perfectly known. Although this faith in the rationality of the universe served primarily for the Stoics to inspire the ethical ideal of the sage, it also served to spur on scientific investigation in both the ancient and modern worlds.

According to the Stoics, what is wisdom?

Wisdom (*sophia,* σοφία), according to the Stoics, is an expertise in three interrelated types of excellence (*arête*), each of which is the subject of a different branch of philosophy. The three branches of philosophy required for wisdom are ethics, which is the study of excellence in behavior; physics, which is the study of excellence in nature; and logic, which is the study of excellence in reasoning. Wisdom is primarily an expertise in ethics, but since the Stoics hold that a good life is one lived in accordance with nature and its logical order, expertise in physics and logic are also required. Nature has a logical order because it is constructed that way by the fiery breath or *pneuma* of Zeus, which pervades everything. Nothing occurs by chance or without reason. Everything occurs as Zeus intended it to occur—not for its own sake, but for the larger good of the whole cosmos. A life lived in accordance with the natural order of things is a life of happiness (*eudaimonia*) and freedom from disturbance (*ataraxia*) because it is a life lived in harmony with the inexorable forces of nature and fate. Though ultimately everyone must live in accordance with nature and fate, only the wise know that nature and fate are good and freely give their assent to them.

THE STOIC THEORY OF THE SOUL OR PSYCHE

According to the Stoics, what is the human *psyche,* and what is its coordinating center?

According to the Stoics, the *psyche* is that which animates or gives life to the body. In humans and other animals, the *psyche* is composed of a small portion of cosmic *pneuma* that is breathed in through the lungs and pumped by the heart, where its coordinating center is located, to all parts of the body. The coordinating center of the human *psyche* is referred to by the Stoics as the *hegemonikon* ("that which leads"), because it is the ruling part of the *psyche*; but it may also be referred to as the *logike* (logical or rational) *psyche* or *nous* (mind), because this is where rational thought and emotion occur. The *hegemonikon* receives impressions from all parts of the body, judges and interprets them, and issues commands to act. It is misleading to translate the Stoic concept of *psyche* as "soul" because it is not a spiritual thing. *Psyche* is composed of *pneuma*, and *pneuma* is composed of material elements. The difference between *pneuma* and the body is not that one is material and the other is not, because they are both material, but that *pneuma* is composed of the active elements of fire and air, while the body is composed of the passive elements of water and earth. *Pneuma* is active in the sense that it designs and constructs things by imposing form on the passive elements of water and earth. The Stoic concept of *pneuma* is like our modern concept of DNA. It contains the information—or in Greek terms, the form—that shapes the way bodies develop.

For the Stoics, what are the two ways that the mind and its contents can be accounted for?

Although according to Stoic materialism the mind and its contents are material things that can be explained in strictly material terms, the Stoics allowed that the mind and its contents can also be described in what philosophers call "intentional" terms. Intentions are thoughts about something and can be expressed by propositions that say something about something. For example, it is possible to explain vision in strictly material terms as a causal process by which light passes through the eye and forms an impression on the *pneuma,* which is then pumped through the body's circulatory system to the heart where it is mechanically combined with sense impressions received from other sense or-

How did the Stoic account of the *psyche* differ from Plato's?

According to Plato, the *psyche* is divided into three parts: the reasoning part, the spirited part, and the appetites. Although Plato's ideal is for these parts to act in harmony with one another, as if they were one, because there are three parts it is possible for them to come into conflict with one another. For example, we might have an appetite for another slice of chocolate cake while our reason tells us that one is enough. Under the Platonic theory, psychological conflict, indecision, and doubt are explained in terms of a struggle between the different parts of the *psyche*. But according to the Stoics, the *psyche* is not divided into parts. The entire *psyche* of a healthy, mature adult is rational in the sense that it thinks in terms of propositional judgments of the form "*S* is *P*" and is capable of performing logical operations on those propositions. If a healthy, mature adult has irrational thoughts or acts in an irrational way, it is not because an irrational part of that person's *psyche* has overcome the rational part but because the rational part, which is the only part, has made a mistake or an incorrect judgment.

gans. But it is also possible to describe mental content in intentional terms. For example, a vision of light can be described in intentional terms as a thought (a "mental content") about seeing light, which may be expressed by the proposition "it is light." What is important to understand here is that for the Stoics, the material and intentional accounts are just two different ways of talking about the same thing, not two different types of thing. The Stoics were not mind-body dualists. There is only one type of thing, the material thing.

What kind of impression produces an impulse to act?

A hormetic impression (*phantasia hormetikê*) is an impression that in rational human beings produces an impulse (*hormê*) to act. Depending on a rational human being's knowledge and character as well as the nature of the object of an impression, the object of an impression may appear to be either good, bad, or indifferent. If the object of an impression appears to be good, then an impulse to act towards the object will be produced; if it appears to be bad, an impulse to withdraw from the object will be produced; and if it appears to be indifferent, then no impulse will be produced.

Due to their capacity to reason, humans are able to give or withdraw their assent from a hormetic impression, just as they are able to give or withdraw their assent from

The difference between an animal doing something and a human doing it is that animals are passively moved by hormetic impressions. So, is the cat stealing food in this photo doing something bad? No, this is not an evil act of stealing but simply an impulse. Humans, on the other hand, have the ability to act voluntarily on their own volition.

any impression. The Stoics reserve the word "act" for an impulse to move that follows upon an assent to a hormetic impression. Since animals lack the capacity to reason and, therefore, the capacity to give or withdraw their assent from hormetic impressions, animals cannot strictly speaking be said to "act." Instead, animals are passively moved by hormetic impressions. Rational human beings have the capacity for volition or voluntary action, but animals do not because animals cannot reflect upon their hormetic impressions and choose whether to act on them or not.

What kind of movements in the *pneuma* are produced by hormetic impressions?

Hormetic impressions produce involuntary movements in the *pneuma* of both animals and rational human beings regardless of whether an assent is given to those impressions. For example, both animals and rational human beings are startled by sudden, loud noises without reflecting on those noises and choosing whether it is appropriate to be startled. These involuntary movements of the *pneuma* are characterized by feelings or sensations in the skin and internal organs such as a pounding heart, sweaty palms, goosebumps, a wrenching stomach, shallow breathing, sexual arousal, or a blush. The Stoics attribute these feelings to movements in the *pneuma* such as contractions, expansions, and elevations. The Stoics associated different types of movement in the *pneuma* with different types of feelings.

What is the difference between mere feelings that follow upon hormetic impressions and an emotion?

An emotion is more than a mere feeling because it follows upon an assent to a hormetic impression. Both animals and rational human beings experience feelings in response to hormetic impressions, but only humans experience emotions because only humans are capable of reflecting on their hormetic impressions and giving or withdrawing assent from them. Roman Stoic Seneca applied this distinction to anger. If someone carelessly steps on my foot while waiting in line, I may feel anger; but only when I assent to the proposition that the feeling of anger is appropriate and perhaps act on it does that feeling become an emotion. Animals experience feelings and are moved by them, but they are incapable of experiencing emotions because they are incapable of entertaining propositions and giving or withdrawing assent from them. On the other hand, rational human beings experience mere feelings for only a fleeting moment before they give or withdraw assent from the underlying hormetic impressions that produced those feelings. The Stoics called a mere feeling in human beings a *propatheia* (προπάθεια) because it precedes (the Greek prefix *pro-* means the same as the English prefix *pre-*) an assent that would make it a human emotion. The Stoics concluded from these considerations that the psychic life of a rational human being is dominated by emotion, not mere feeling, and that emotion is morally significant, whereas mere feeling is not, because emotion entails choice and voluntary action, whereas mere feeling does not.

According to the Stoics, what are the two types of emotion?

The two types of emotion, according to the Stoics, are the *pathê* (singular *pathos*) and the *eupatheiai* (εὐπάθεια). The Greek word *pathos* (πάθος) means what one suffers or what is done to one, but it can also mean a strong feeling, passion, or emotion. In Stoicism, a *pathos* is an emotion that one suffers. The English word "passion" best captures the meaning of the Stoic *pathos* because a passion is a strong emotion that is "suffered" in the sense that it is difficult to control. The Stoics believed that the *pathê* are excessive impulses (*hormai pleonazousai*) because once they start, they are difficult to stop, and they always exceed reasonable bounds. According to the Stoics, in order to achieve happiness and live well (*eudaimonia*), it is necessary to eliminate the *pathê* and achieve a dispassionate condition called *apatheia* (the prefix *a-* means "not," so *apatheia* simply means "without pathê," not "apathy"). Though the condition of *apatheia* is without the *pathê*, it is not without emotion or action. The condition of *apatheia* is one of mental clarity in which a wise person experiences the *eupatheiai* and acts with full knowledge and deliberate intention. The *eupatheia* are good emotions (the prefix *eu-* means good) because they are produced by giving assent to true hormetic impressions—in other words, to impressions of objects that are really good or bad.

According to the Stoics, what are the beliefs and logical argument that an emotion is based upon?

According to the Stoics, an emotion is not a mere feeling in response to one's circumstances but is produced by an assent to a hormetic impression that is based upon a set of beliefs and a logical argument. According to the Stoics, an emotion presupposes that a certain type (or category) of object is either good or bad and that when a good or bad object of that type is either present or in prospect, a certain type (or category) of feeling and movement of the *pneuma* is appropriate. (The Stoics did not believe that objects in the distant past provoke feelings, because with time they lose their salience.) Given

---

How did Stoicism inspire modern cognitive psychotherapy?

The basis of modern cognitive psychotherapy is the insight that emotions are not mere feelings but are the product of our beliefs or cognitive judgments. According to modern cognitive psychotherapy, emotional problems are caused by false beliefs or cognitive distortions. We can therefore resolve our emotional problems by replacing our false beliefs with true ones and correcting our cognitive distortions. But this is exactly what the ancient Stoic philosophers recommended. Thus, it comes as no surprise that the founders of modern cognitive psychotherapy were inspired by Stoicism. Indeed, both Albert Ellis, who invented rational-emotive therapy, and Aaron Beck, who invented cognitive-behavioral therapy (CBT), have said that they were inspired by the ancient Stoic philosophers.

these categorical propositions, if the object of an impression is judged to be of a certain type and either present or in prospect, it follows that a certain type of feeling and movement of the *pneuma* is appropriate.

Finally, assenting to the hormetic impression that a certain type of feeling and movement of the *pneuma* is appropriate produces the emotion. For example, if I presuppose that wealth is a good thing and that when it is present it is appropriate to feel delighted, when I win the lottery and become wealthy, I will have the hormetic impression that it is appropriate for me to feel delighted. Assenting to this impression, I will feel the emotion of delight. All emotions are produced by logical arguments, but the premises and, therefore, the conclusions of those arguments may or may not be true. The *pathê* are produced by arguments that contain false premises and conclusions. The *eupatheiai*

Aaron Beck (1921–) is the father of cognitive therapy, which says that emotional problems can arise when one has false beliefs that don't match the truth, an idea that was stated long ago by the Stoics.

are produced by arguments that contain true premises and conclusions. That is why the wise enjoy only the *eupatheiai* while fools suffer the *pathê*.

According to the Stoics, what is the self and what is its sphere of control?

According to the Stoics, the human self or ego is the mind or *hegemonikon*, the control center of the *psyche*. Its chief capacity is the power to make cognitive judgments and to assert the truth or falsity of propositions. The mind has the capacity to judge whether the propositional content of an impression or mental image is true or false. For example, the propositional content of the sense impression of light is the proposition "it is light." When the mind receives a sense impression of light, it has the capacity to judge whether the proposition "it is light" is true or false. The mind also has the capacity to initiate action by judging that the propositional content of a hormetic impression is true. The Stoic self is like an impregnable fortress or citadel. It has complete and total control over anything that occurs within itself. The mind can assert that its own beliefs are true or false, and it can initiate action by asserting that an impulse (*hormê*) to act is correct. But it does not have any control over anything that occurs beyond its own self, including the consequences of its own actions.

STOIC ETHICS

What is the meaning and origin of the Serenity Prayer?

The Serenity Prayer was formulated in the twentieth century by Protestant theologian Reinhold Niebuhr (1892–1971) and has been adopted by many self-help groups today, including Alcoholics Anonymous. But its origin lies with Stoic philosopher Epictetus (55–135 C.E.), who began both his *Discourses* and the *Enchiridion* by distinguishing between what we can control (what is "up to us") and what we cannot control. What we can control are our own cognitive judgments, including our assent to hormetic impressions and our emotional impulses to act. Therefore, we should, according to Epictetus, focus our efforts on improving our own judgment and learn to accept everything else as part of the inevitable course of nature.

According to the Stoics, what is inherently good?

According to the Stoics, the only thing that is inherently good is wisdom, which is our own power to make rational judgments, and the only thing that is inherently bad is the absence of wisdom. Therefore, the Stoics held that wisdom, which is the chief virtue, is all that is necessary for happiness and a life well lived (*eudaimonia*). Nothing external to the self and its power to make rational judgments is inherently good or bad; in themselves, external things neither contribute to nor detract from happiness and a life well lived but are what the Stoics called *indifferents* (*adiaphora*). External things become good or bad only when they are used wisely or foolishly. The indifferents include nearly all the things that most people consider to be necessary for happiness and a life well lived, such as wealth, beauty, family, friends, reputation, health, and even life itself.

However, unlike the ascetic Cynics, who were strictly indifferent to external things, the Stoics distinguished between *preferred indifferents* (*proegmenon*) and *dispreferred indifferents* (*apoproegmenon*). Preferred indifferents are indifferents that, being in accord with nature, generally do contribute to a life well lived, if they are used wisely, whereas not being in accord with nature, dispreferred indifferents generally do not contribute to a life well lived. For example, wealth is a preferred indifferent that is good and that contributes to a life well lived if it is used wisely. It can easily turn bad, however, if used foolishly, for no good purpose. Death is a dispreferred indifferent, but in some cases the Stoics believed that it is wise to take your own life. For example, if a corrupt ruler demands that you commit wrongful acts, it may be wise to take your own life instead.

What is the Serenity Prayer?

God grant me the serenity to accept the things I cannot change, the courage to change the things I can, and the wisdom to know the difference.

What is the difference between the *pathê* and the *eupatheiai*?

A hormetic impression produces an impulse to act because it presents its object as being either beneficial and good, or harmful and bad, and therefore, as either desirable or repellant. The *pathê* are inappropriate emotions because they are produced by giving assent to hormetic impressions of external objects that are false. According to the Stoics, hormetic impressions of external objects are always false because external objects are indifferents. They are neither inherently beneficial and good nor harmful and bad. Therefore, in themselves, external objects are neither desirable nor repellant.

The *eupatheia* are appropriate (*kathēkonta*, καθήκοντα) emotions because they are produced by giving assent to hormetic impressions of wisdom and virtue, which are internal to the mind. Hormetic impressions of wisdom and virtue are always true because wisdom and virtue are inherently beneficial and good. Therefore, the *pathê* are inappropriate and detract from happiness and a life well lived, while the *euapatheia* are appropriate and contribute to happiness and a life well lived.

What are the different kinds of passion (*pathos*)?

The passions (*pathê*) may be divided into four categories depending on whether the object of the hormetic impression that produced them appears to be good or bad, and whether it appears to be present or in prospect. Hormetic impressions of objects that appear to be both good and present produce the passion of *hédoné* (ἡδονή), which may be translated as emotional pleasure, enjoyment, or delight. Hormetic impressions of objects that appear to be good and in prospect produce the passion of *epithumia* (ἐπιθυμία), which may be translated as excessive or irrational desire (*alogos orexis*). Hormetic impressions of objects that appear to be both bad and present produce the passion of *lupé* (λύπη), which may be translated as emotional pain or distress. Finally, hormetic impressions of objects that appear to be bad and in prospect produce the passion of fear (*phobos*, φόβοζ).

Within each of these categories there are many more specific kinds of passions that differ depending on the nature of their objects and how and by what means they appear to us. For example, within the category of irrational desire, we find both anger (*orgé*, ὀργή) and erotic passion (*éros*, ἔρωζ). Anger is a passionate desire to punish someone who appears to have unjustly harmed you or someone you care about. Erotic passion is a desire for sexual intercourse with someone who appears to be sexually attractive. Within the category of distress, we find grief and sorrow (*pénthos*,

One category of passion is distress. Grief falls into this category, as well as pity and envy.

πένθος), pity (*éleos*, ἔλεος), and envy (*phthonos*, φθόνος). Grief and sorrow are distress over another's death.

Pity is distress over another's undeserved suffering. And envy is distress over another's good fortune. Within the category of fear, we find fear of defeat (*agónia*, ἀγωνία) and fear of disgrace (*aischuné*, αἰσχύνη). Within the category of delight, we find schadenfreude or rejoicing over another's calamities (*epichairekakia*, ἐπιχαιρεκακία) and the pleasure that comes by means of being charmed, beguiled, or even bewitched in a deceptive way (*goēteia*, γοητεία). All the passions cause suffering because they require us to control their objects; but since they are external to the self, we cannot control them.

What are the different kinds of good emotions (*eupatheiai*)?

Contrary to the passions, which are produced by an assent to a hormetic impression of external objects, the good emotions (*eupatheiai*) are produced by an assent to a hormetic impression whose object is one's own wisdom and virtue. But although the good emotions are produced by an assent to a hormetic impression of one's own wisdom and virtue, which is internal to the self, they do not exclude acting with or upon external objects in the world, because many of the good emotions produce an impulse to act wisely and virtuously in the world.

Like the passions, the good emotions can be divided into categories depending on whether the object of the hormetic impression that produced them is good or bad and whether it is present or in prospect. The difference is that the object of the hormetic impressions that produce good emotions is one's own wisdom and virtue, not an external object, and there is no category of good emotions that is produced by a hormetic impression whose object is both bad and present. A good emotion is by definition a response to one's own wisdom and virtue, so its object is by definition good and can never be bad. That leaves only three categories of good emotion: *chara* (χαρά), often translated

What is the good emotion (*eupatheia*) of joy (*chara*)?

Assent to hormetic impressions of objects that are both good and present produce the *eupatheia* or good emotion of joy (*chara*, χαρά), which is a moral satisfaction with oneself and with the wisdom and virtue of the acts that one takes in the world. An example of joy is *térpsis* (τέρψἴς), which is the joy or gladness that comes from appreciating what your circumstances reveal about yourself. Stoic philosopher Epictetus (55–135 C.E.) said, "Circumstances don't make the man, they only reveal him to himself." Other examples of joy include *eufrosune* (εὐφροσύνη), which is the good cheer, joy, and mirth that comes from acting wisely; and *euthumia* (εὐθυμία), literally "good spirits," which, according to Stoic philosopher Seneca, is the joy that comes from believing in yourself and trusting that you are on the right path.

as "joy," for objects that are good and present; *boulesis* (βούλησιζ), often translated as "wish," for objects that are good and in prospect; and *eulabeia* (εὐλάβεια), often translated as "caution," for objects that are bad and in prospect.

What is the good emotion (*eupatheia*) of wish (*boulesis*)?

Assent to hormetic impressions of objects that are both good and in prospect produce the good emotion of *boulesis* (βούλησιζ), which is a wise and rational desire (*eulogos orexis*) with the confident expectation of achieving what is desired. The Stoic concept of *boulesis* was an early formulation of the concept of *will* (Latin *voluntas*) that would get further developed by Church father St. Augustine (354–430 C.E.) and others during the Roman Empire. Examples of *boulesis* include *eunoia* (εὔνοια), which is having good intentions for another for their own sake; *eumenia* (εὐμένεια), which is goodwill towards others; *aspasmos* (ἀσπασμός), which is a kind welcoming of other people; and *éros* (ἔρωζ), which as a *eupatheia* is a rational desire to form a friendship that may include sexual intercourse with someone whose beauty indicates good character and a natural aptitude for wisdom and virtue.

What is the good emotion (*eupatheia*) of caution (*eulabeia*)?

Assent to hormetic impressions of objects that are bad and in prospect produce the good emotion of *eulabeia* (εὐλάβεια), which for the Stoics meant a wise and prudent warning or caution against acting wrongly or unwisely in the future. Examples of *eulabeia* include *aidos* (αἰδώζ), which is caution against moral shame; and *hagneia* (ἁγνεία), which is commonly translated as "purity" or "chastity" and is derived from *hagnós* (ἁγνόζ), which meant pure or holy, but which for the Stoics meant caution against failing to perform religious duties.

According to the Stoics, what constitutes a person's character?

According to the Stoics, a person's character is constituted by the set of beliefs that they hold in their mind. Ultimately, all beliefs have ethical significance because according to the Stoics, the purpose of all knowledge is to act wisely. We do not seek knowledge for its own sake but in order to be happy and live well (*eudaimonia*). A person of good character holds beliefs that are not only true but logically interrelated to one another and consistent and that thereby form a coherent system. In physical terms, a person of good character has a high degree of "tension" (*tonos*), like a diamond that is held together by strong molecular bonds. In intentional terms, a person of good character has a high degree of integrity and consistency, resulting in a "smooth flow" of thoughts, emotions, and actions. A person of bad character holds beliefs that are false and logically inconsistent with one another. Due to their flabby lack of tension (*atonia*) and their lack of integrity and consistency, a person of bad character will experience a "fluttering" (*ptoia*) of the heart and soul, causing them to hold conflicting beliefs, suffer emotional conflict, and act in an erratic and inconsistent manner.

How does character determine our emotions and intentions to act in the world?

Our emotions and intentions to act in the world are produced by an assent to a hormetic impression that is a judgment that the propositional content of a hormetic impression is true. For example, the emotion of anger and the intention to punish are produced by an assent to the hormetic impression that it is appropriate to respond with anger to an undeserved offense and to punish the offender. In order to respond with anger to an offender, it is necessary to believe that an offense has occurred and to hold the belief that it is appropriate to re-

According to Seneca, only people of bad character hold grudges and become angry at perceived offenses.

spond to offenders with anger. The first belief is incidental in the sense that it is produced by the sense impression of a particular incident. The second belief is dispositional in the sense that it is not a response to a particular incident but, instead, is a preexisting belief that disposes one to respond to particular types of incidents in a certain way.

Dispositional beliefs depend on a person's character. According to Seneca and other Stoic philosophers, a person of good character does not hold the dispositional belief that it is appropriate to respond to an offender with anger, so they will not respond with anger to an offender. Only persons of bad character hold the false belief that it is appropriate to respond to an offender with anger and are disposed to respond to an undeserved offense with anger. Thus, it is not the offender who causes a person to respond with anger but the person's own character and dispositional beliefs.

How did Chrysippus explain how we can be responsible for our emotions and actions in a world in which everything is causally determined by everything else?

Chrysippus used the analogy of a rolling cylinder to explain how we can be responsible for our emotions and actions in a world in which everything is causally determined by everything else. Imagine pushing a cylinder on a flat surface. The movement of the cylinder is caused by pushing it, but the way the cylinder moves is determined by its shape. Pushing a cube might cause it to slide or tip over, but it will not cause it to roll. Pushing a cone will cause it to rotate around its apex in a circle. So, the movement of these objects is codetermined by both an external cause and the shape of the object itself. So too, according to Chrysippus, are our emotions and actions codetermined by both impressions that come from outside ourselves and by our own characters. The same impression will affect different people differently depending on their character, and in that respect, we are each responsible for our emotions and actions.

According to the Stoics, are we responsible for our own character?

Ultimately, the Stoics believed that we are responsible for our own character. The Stoics believed that we inherit character traits from our parents just as we inherit our physical appearance from them, because the seed of pneumatic material from which we develop comes from our parents and (like DNA) contains information that shapes how we develop. But the Stoics also believed that a person's character is constituted by the set of beliefs that they hold in their mind and that these beliefs change over the course of our lives as we give or withdraw assent from our impressions. Since it is "up to us" (*eph'hemin*) to give or withdraw assent from our impressions, it is "up to us" how our minds and character will develop beyond the traits we originally received from our parents. We are therefore ultimately responsible for our own character.

What are the different kinds of bad character traits?

A character trait (*hexis*, ἕξις) is a stable disposition to have a certain emotion and to act in a certain way in certain situations. It is based on the dispositional belief that it is appropriate to have a certain emotion and to act in a certain way because a certain kind of object is good or bad. A bad character trait is one that is based upon a dispositional belief of this kind that is false. A bad character trait predisposes a person to suffer the passions (*pathê*) or bad emotions and to act in ways that are not in accord with the natural order of the universe.

The Stoics identified four kinds of bad character traits based on four different ways in which the dispositional beliefs upon which they are based could be false. A *sickness*

According to the Stoics, are we free?

Although we are responsible for our emotions and intentions to act, we are not free in the sense of having a will that is free to choose anything regardless of whether it is good or bad. The Stoics conceived of freedom as the opposite of slavery. A slave is not free to do what they want. A slave must do what their master wants. To be free is to not be a slave. To be free is to be able to do what you want. But if you assent to false hormetic impressions, you will suffer contradictory emotions and intentions to act. You will not be able to do what you want, and therefore you will not be free because your wants will contradict one another. You will only be free in the sense of doing what you want if you assent to true hormetic impressions. But what is true is determined by the natural order of the universe, and you are not free to alter it to suit your wants. You are only free to conform your wants to it—to love what must according to the order of the universe happen anyhow (to love fate; in Latin, *amor fati*). According to the Stoics, we are free like the dog tied to a cart who is free to walk behind the cart willingly or by force, but who must follow the cart either way.

(*nosēma*; plural *nosēmata*) *of the mind* is based upon a false dispositional belief about the value of certain kinds of external objects. A sickness of the mind based upon the false dispositional belief that a certain kind of external object is intrinsically good is simply called a *nosēma*. A sickness of the mind based upon the false dispositional belief that a certain kind of external object is intrinsically bad is called a *proskopē* (plural *proskopai*) and is often translated into English as an "aversion." A *nosēma* is a disposition to suffer irrational desire for external objects that are not intrinsically good. A *proskopē* is a disposition to suffer fear of external objects that are not intrinsically bad. Sicknesses that occur in weak minds that suffer from a lack of tension (*atonia*) are called *arrōstēmata* (singular *arrōstēma*), which is usually translated as "infirmities." An infirmity is not an isolated error but indicates a deficiency in the structure of the entire belief system that constitutes a mind. The final category of bad character traits is the *euemptōsiai*, which is generally translated as the "proclivities." A proclivity is based upon the false dispositional belief that it is appropriate to have a certain emotion and to act in a certain way in a wide range of situations with different kinds of external objects. Thus, whereas the sicknesses are defined in terms of a specific kind of external object, a proclivity is defined by the passion or bad emotion that one is predisposed to suffer.

What are some examples of *nosēmata* (sicknesses of the mind)?

Examples of *nosēmata* given by the Stoics include love of money (*philarguria*), fame (*philodoxia*), women (*philogunia*), wine (*philoinia*), pleasure (*philēdonia*), and the body (*philosōmatia*). According to the Stoics, none of these things is worthy of love because they are not intrinsically or necessarily good. The only thing that we ought to love is wisdom (*philosophia*).

What are some examples of *proskopai* (aversions)?

Examples of *proskopai* (aversions) given by the Stoics include hatred of women (*misogunia*), humanity (*misanthrōpia*), and wine (*misoinia*). According to the Stoics, none of these things is worthy of hatred because they are not intrinsically or necessarily bad.

What are some examples of *arrōstēmata* (infirmities)?

Examples of *arrōstēmata* (infirmities) given by the Stoics include craziness for fame (*doxomania*), women (*gunaikomania*), food (*opsomania*), and birds (*ornithomania*). The difference between the

Stoics consider the love of money to be one example of a sickness of the mind.

275

arrōstēmata and the *nosēmata* is that the *arrōstēmata* indicate a sickness of the entire mind (mania) and not merely a mistaken belief about one kind of object.

What are some examples of *euemptōsiai* (proclivities)?

Examples of *euemptōsiai* (proclivities) given by the Stoics include being prone to anger (*orgilotēs*), envy (*phthoneria*), quarrels (*erides*), fear (*deilia*), pity (*eleēmosunē*), grief (*epilupia*), and wrath or boiling temper (*akrocholia*). All of these are irrational passions (*pathê*) or bad emotions because they are based on mistaken judgments about the value of a wide range of external objects.

How does character develop, according to the Stoics?

According to the Stoics, we are not born as merely empty receptacles; instead, we have innate propensities called the *aphormai* that are given to us by nature and provide an initial impulse (*hormê*) to develop our character. For example, since humans are by nature rational social animals, we are born with an innate orientation (*oikeiōsis*) toward others and a natural tendency to reason and engage in propositional speech (*logos*). Our innate orientation toward others and our natural tendency to reason provide an initial impulse for us to develop the social virtues, including the capacity to cooperate with one another, to recognize a common good and therefore to share common goals and intentions, and to act with fairness and justice for all. The *aphormai* are the seeds and the starting points of our development.

In order to complete our development, we must acquire practical knowledge from our experience, since character, according to the Stoics, is composed of beliefs, and beliefs are acquired only through experience. In an important respect, the *aphormai* are not only the starting point of our development but also its end (*telos*), the ultimate good to which all our actions aim, because, according to the Stoics, the end of human life is to live in accordance with nature, and since the *aphormai* are given to us by nature, by assenting to the *aphormai* and acting on them we are living in accordance with nature.

THE SOCIAL AND POLITICAL PHILOSOPHY OF THE STOICS

According to the Stoics, what is friendship?

Friendship (*philia*), according to the Stoics, is a community (*koinōníā*) of two or more people whose intentions are in concord (*homonoia*) with one another because they are united by a shared knowledge of the good (the ultimate goal or purpose of our acts). Since friendship requires a shared knowledge of the good, only those who are wise or who may become wise can become friends. A friendship between two mature adults can only occur between those who are already wise. But it is possible for a friendship to develop out of an erotic relationship between a mature adult and an adolescent who is not yet wise but whose beauty indicates that they have the potential to become wise. In an erotic relationship of this kind, a mature adult has a rational desire to form a friendship that may include sexual intercourse with an adolescent for the purpose of educating them and developing their aptitude for wisdom and virtue.

What did Cynic philosopher Diogenes of Sinope mean when he said that he was a citizen of the world?

According to Diogenes Laërtius (*Lives* 6.63), when Diogenes of Sinope (c. 404–323 B.C.E.) was asked where he came from, he answered, "I am a cosmopolitan," by which he meant that he was a citizen of the world or universe. The word "cosmopolitan" comes from the Greek word *kosmopolitês* (κοσμοπολίτησ), which is derived from the root terms *kosmos*, meaning "world" or "universe," and *politês*, meaning "citizen." What Diogenes of Sinope meant by saying that he was a cosmopolitan was that he was not a citizen of any *polis* unless the universe itself is considered a *polis,* because he lived according to nature—not according to the laws and customs of any *polis*. The Cynics believed that all one needs to be happy is virtue, and that virtue is living according to nature, not according to social convention, because the order of nature is rational and good, and social convention is not.

Who influenced Zeno of Citium in the design of his ideal city-state?

Zeno of Citium's philosophy of the ideal city-state was a response to Plato's *Republic* and an attempt to reform Plato's blueprint for an ideal city-state according to Cynic ethical ideals. Though Zeno of Citium (c. 334–c. 262 B.C.E.) was the founder of Stoicism and not a Cynic himself, he was deeply influenced by Cynicism. Zeno was a student of Cynic philosopher Crates of Thebes (c. 365–c. 285 B.C.E.), who was himself a student of Dio-

How did the Stoics conceive of the *polis,* or city-state?

Although large empires overshadowed the city-state in the Hellenistic period, the Stoics continued to think about politics in terms of the *polis* as the Greeks of the classical age had, and to use some of the same concepts that Aristotle in particular had used to understand it. Like Aristotle, the Stoics conceived of the city-state not merely as a government with jurisdiction over a given territory but as a community (*koinōníā*) of people who are united or in concord (*homonoia*) with one another in the pursuit of a common good, and who are therefore, by definition, friends. But since friendship requires a shared knowledge of the good, only the wise can be united with one another in a city-state. Those who are not wise are subject to strife (*eris*, ἔριζ) and discord, both within the city-state and within their own psyches.

277

genes of Sinope (c. 404–323 B.C.E.). So strong was the apparent Cynic influence on Zeno that according to the ancients, his book *The Republic*, in which he provided an account of the ideal city-state, was preceded by similar books of the same title by Crates and Diogenes.

But Zeno was also a student of Xenocrates (396/395–314/313 B.C.E.) and Polemo (d. 270/269 B.C.E.), two successive heads of Plato's Academy. Zeno's philosophy of the ideal city-state was intended as a Cynic response to Plato's *Republic,* but it was also modeled upon it and adopted some of the same principles. Like Plato, Zeno's overriding concern was with the internal sta-

Zeno's idea of a perfect city-state was basically that of a communist utopia in which all the citizens were friends sharing the same idea of the common good.

bility and concord of the city-state. This, he believed, could be achieved only if the citizens of his ideal city-state were friends and shared all things in common. Thus, like Plato's *Republic*, Zeno's ideal city-state was a communist utopia. But friendship is concord, and concord is shared knowledge of a common good. Those who do not share knowledge of a common good will find themselves in conflict about the affairs of life and cannot be friends. Therefore, in order to achieve concord and friendship, Zeno believed that all the citizens of the ideal city-state must be wise and share knowledge of a common good. Plato had a different view. According to Plato, only the philosopher-kings need be wise, so long as the lower classes know enough to follow their lead.

What are some other ways that Plato's ideal city-state differed from Zeno of Citium's?

First, Plato's ethical ideal was to live in accordance with principles that transcend nature and cannot be known through the senses. Zeno's ethical ideal, like the Cynics', was to live in accordance with nature, which can be known through the senses. Consequently, Zeno's ideal city-state was based on the laws of nature, conceived in opposition to social conventions, whereas Plato's was not. Second, Zeno's ideal city-state resembled Plato's "city of pigs," not the "city of luxury" that occupied most of Plato's *Republic*.

Plato's ideal city-state was designed not only for internal stability and concord but for military defense against foreign powers. Consequently, Plato's educational system included military training for the class of guardians. According to a manuscript of Philodemus (c. 110–c. 30 B.C.E.) found at Herculaneum, Zeno of Citium said that there was no use for military arms in his ideal city-state. All that Zeno's citizens need are a few simple foods they keep in their knapsack and virtue; and these, as a poem by Zeno's teacher Crates the Cynic states, are "not things apt to start wars or incite men to combat. Nor do the people of Pera [the ideal city-state] take up arms for money or fame" (Diogenes Laërtius, *Lives*).

What are some of the unconventional practices found in Zeno of Citium's ideal city-state?

Since Zeno's ideal city-state is based on the laws of nature rather than social convention, it allowed for many practices that violate common social norms and mores. For example, Zeno allows for cannibalism in his ideal city-state. He reasons that if a person loses a limb in an accident, or if a person dies, it is natural to treat the body as food and to eat it if you are hungry. Similarly, Zeno allows for incest. The institution of marriage does not exist in his ideal city-state. Everyone is free to have sex with anyone else, male or female, close relation or not, and regardless of social rank, as long as they mutually consent. Again, the principle is that it is natural and reasonable, and therefore wise, to have sex with someone that you are sexually attracted to, and that it is only arbitrary social convention that forbids sex between unmarried individuals, close relations, or those of different social ranks. Because sexual relations may occur between any two individuals, paternity is uncertain. Children were to be raised in common, as they were in Plato's *Republic*.

Likewise, all private wealth was to be abolished and held in common. Following Diogenes of Sinope, Zeno held that no money should be used by the citizens of his ideal city-state, since money has value only by social convention. Women and men should dress alike, engage in the same activities, and exercise together fully naked, since they are of the same human nature. The conventional institutions of the Greek *polis*—temples, law courts, and gymnasiums—were to be abolished. Likewise, Zeno regarded conventional Greek education to be useless.

What role did erotic friendship play in Zeno of Citium's ideal city-state?

Sexual relations between young men and adolescents was common in many highly militarized Greek city-states that required a loyal and effective fighting force. The best example of the military utility of male homosexuality was the Sacred Band of Thebes, which was the most effective unit of Theban warriors. But male homosexuality was common in many Greek city-states that, for the sake of an effective fighting force, separated men from women and devalued family life. Most notably in Sparta, which served as a model for both Zeno's communist utopia and Plato's, homosexuality was an integral part of a military culture that subordinated individual interests to group identity and the common good. As men aged out of military service and entered civilian society, they

Homosexuality was common in warrior states such as Sparta because it aided in creating an effective fighting force. Philosophers such as Zeno of Citium believed homosexuality helped foster group identity and contributed to the strength, concord, and unity of the city-state.

married and had children, but they retained the bonds they formed with other men during their military service, bonds that contributed to the strength, concord, and unity of the state long after the fighting was over.

Erotic friendship served a similar purpose in Zeno's ideal city-state, with a couple of important differences. First, erotic friendship did not serve any military purpose in Zeno's utopia, because he believed that there would be no need to fight wars. Second, since Zeno did not believe that there were important differences between the sexes, he probably allowed for erotic friendship between people of any sex, not just between males. But as in Sparta, erotic friendship served the purpose in Zeno's utopia of creating strong bonds between citizens that contributed to the concord and unity of the state. Also as in Sparta (and in Plato), erotic friendship served a pedagogical purpose, providing adolescents with dedicated teachers and mentors who could help them develop their natural aptitude for virtue or excellence (*arête*).

How did Chrysippus modify Zeno of Citium's philosophy of the ideal *polis* or city-state?

Zeno of Citium's ideal *polis* or city-state was, like Athens or Sparta or any other Greek city-state, a community of neighbors, that is, a community of people who live in close proximity and are acquainted with one another. Like Plato and Aristotle, Zeno thought about politics in terms of the historical Greek *polis*, which was not just a government but a community. What made a community good, according to Zeno, was its unity and concord, which was based on a shared knowledge of its common good.

Chrysippus modified Zeno's political philosophy by taking it to its logical conclusion. Since, according to the Stoics and their Cynic predecessors, there is only one good and it is the rational order (*logos*) of nature, or of the universe considered as a unified whole, it is not necessary for the citizens of the ideal *polis* to live in close proximity to one another. It is only necessary for them to share a common knowledge of the universal good. Therefore, according to Chrysippus, the ideal city-state was a cosmic city-state, and its citizens could live anywhere in the universe, so long as they shared a common knowledge of the good. Looked at another way, Chrysippus still considered the ideal city-state to be a community of neighbors, because they all lived in the same place—namely, the universe—and they all knew each other, because they were all alike in the only way that mattered to the Stoics: they were all rational social animals who shared the same knowledge of the same universal good.

How did Chrysippus's cosmic city-state differ from Zeno of Citium's ideal city-state?

Besides the fact that the citizens of the cosmic city-state need not live in close proximity to one another, what they share in common differs from what the citizens of Zeno's ideal city-state share in common. Zeno's ideal city-state is a communist utopia in which its citizens share everything in common, including property, sexual partners, and children. The citizens of Chrysippus's cosmic city-state do not share those sorts of things in common because they are not neighbors living in close proximity to one another, and they are not personally acquainted. All the citizens of Chrysippus's cosmic city-state share in common is knowledge of the moral rules of social behavior, that is, knowledge of justice and the proper treatment of others that makes it possible for them to live together as friends and in concord with one another. But these moral rules of social behavior extend across the entire universe. Therefore, those who recognize them are members of a community that extends across the entire universe and includes all rational social animals, wherever they may live—not only all rational humans, but the gods, too, who in their providential wisdom govern the cosmic city-state under the rule of law for the good of the whole universe.

How did the concept of natural law develop out of the Stoic idea of the cosmic city-state?

According to the Stoics, the universe is a cosmic city-state governed wisely by the gods according to the rules of right reason. Therefore, the universe has a rational order, and since the universe is a city-state, it has a rational social order. But the Stoics did not limit reason to the rules of logical inference, because logical inferences start from premises derived from cognitive impressions that are not themselves the product of logical inferences. For the Stoics, there is more to being rational than just knowing how to follow the rules of logical inference. To be rational is to know what is good and to act for a good reason or purpose (*telos*)—in other words, to be wise. Thus, the cosmic city-state has a rational social order not only in the sense that it has a causal structure that can be understood in terms of logical inferences but also in the sense that it has a good reason or purpose and is governed wisely by the gods. Hence, the rules of right reason by which the gods govern the universe are moral rules of social behavior.

The concept of natural law was originally derived by Cicero (106–43 B.C.E.) from the Stoic idea of the moral rules of social behavior embedded in the very nature of the universe. Natural law is the rational social order of the universe. Implicit in the concept of natural law is the thesis that the moral rules of social behavior are not arbitrary but are based in reason and the nature of the universe.

Did the Stoics after Zeno of Citium adopt the unconventional lifestyle of his ideal city-state?

No, they did not. In fact, they were probably embarrassed by it because it was often used by their critics against them. The Cynics embraced two distinct propositions, one positive and the other negative: (1) virtue is living in accordance with reason and the nature of the universe, and (2) social conventions are not natural and are not rational. Together, these two propositions explain Diogenes the Cynic's antinomianism, which means his antagonism to conventional social norms and his drop-out lifestyle. Following his teacher Crates the Cynic, Zeno of Citium, who was the founder of Stoicism, embraced both propositions, which is why the moral rules of social behavior in his ideal city-state were so unconventional. But most Stoics after Zeno seem to have made peace with conventional social life.

Writing in the third century C.E., Diogenes Laërtius (*Lives* 7.121) said that, according to the Stoics, it is wise to marry and have children, to honor established laws, and to engage in politics. Indeed, Seneca (4 B.C.E.–65 C.E.) was engaged in politics at the highest levels, while Marcus Aurelius (121–180 C.E.) was emperor. Neither dropped out of society. After Zeno, the Stoics believed that since humans are by nature social animals designed to live in politically organized communities, those who are wise will not only participate in society as it currently exists but are morally obligated to do so. Of course, they will aim to live in accordance with reason and the nature of the universe, and that will mean that their ideals will sometimes clash with existing social conventions. But they did not believe that the differences between their own ideals and existing social conventions were so great that they could not participate in society as it currently exists and contribute to its edification and improvement.

ACADEMIC SKEPTICISM

What happened to Plato's Academy after his death?

After Plato's death around 347 B.C.E., the position of scholarch or head of the Academy passed to Plato's nephew, Speusippus (c. 408–c. 339 B.C.E.), who held the post until his death. Xenocrates of Chalcedon (c. 396/5–314/3 B.C.E.) succeeded Speusippus and was scholarch from 339 B.C.E. until his death, followed by Polemon, who held the position until about 270 B.C.E. Finally, Crates of Athens, who was said to have been Polemon's *eromenos*, or boy-lover, was scholarch from 270 B.C.E. until about 265 B.C.E. Except for a few fragments, none of the writings of these philosophers have survived. We know about the philosophical theories of Speusippus and Xenocrates mostly from what Aristotle had to say about them, which may not be entirely reliable. And, of course, Aristotle had nothing to say about Polemon or Crates of

Speusippus, the son of Plato's sister, inherited the Academy after Plato's death and ran it for eight years.

Athens, because he was not alive when they were scholarchs of the Academy; therefore we know even less about them. However, all of these philosophers appear to have worked within the general framework of Plato's philosophy while modifying it in various ways or emphasizing different aspects of it.

Of most significance for the later development of Neoplatonic philosophy, Speusippus and Xenocrates carried on the metaphysical speculation about numbers that Plato had inherited from the Pythagoreans. There is evidence that the late Neoplatonic-Pythagorean philosopher Iamblichus (c. 245–c. 325 C.E.) may have read and been influenced by Speusippus. According to both Cicero (106–43 B.C.E.) and Skeptic philosopher Sextus Empiricus (c. 160–c. 210 C.E.), all of these scholarchs were "dogmatic" philosophers, which meant that they held positive opinions or claims to knowledge. From the point of view of Cicero and Sextus, the real revolution in the Academy occurred when Arcesilaus became scholarch in 265 B.C.E. and adopted Skepticism as the school's philosophy. This, according to Sextus, inaugurated a new period in the history of Plato's Academy, which he dubbed the "Middle Academy," in contrast to the dogmatic "Old Academy" that preceded it.

How could Skepticism have developed out of Plato's philosophy?

Plato did not write in straightforward prose but rather in the form of dialogues replete with irony and other figures of speech. Consequently, his dialogues yield to two fundamentally different interpretations. One interpretation emphasizes the theory of the forms. According to this interpretation, Plato was a dogmatist who believed that truth is absolute and can be known by the human mind. The other interpretation emphasizes the Socratic method, especially as it is found in the early dialogues. According to this interpretation, Plato was a Skeptic. Skepticism developed out of Plato's philosophy by

What does the Socrates portrayed in Plato's dialogues have in common with Academic Skepticism?

Academic Skepticism shares much in common with the Socrates portrayed in Plato's dialogues—especially with the Socrates portrayed in the early dialogues. Both employ a dialectical method of inquiry (*elenchus*) that inevitably comes to an impasse (*aporia*) and produces a state of puzzlement in which we are forced to suspend judgment (*epochê*). The dialectical method consists in making a series of opposing arguments. An argument is made supporting (or refuting) proposition "*P*." Then an argument is made supporting (or refuting) proposition "not-*P*." Since it is not possible for both *P* and not-*P* to be true (or false), we arrive at an impasse in which we must suspend judgment about whether *P* or not-*P* is true (or false). Like Socrates, the Academic Skeptics subject all claims to knowledge to this method, yielding a suspension of all knowledge claims (*akatalêpsia*).

pushing aside Plato's metaphysical speculations about the forms and embracing the Socratic method.

Did the Academic Skeptics claim to know that they knew nothing?

Socrates famously declared that he knew more than anyone else because at least he knew that he did not know anything, whereas everyone else thought that they knew something when they did not. But this claim entails a contradiction, because if Socrates did not know anything, then he would not know that he does not know anything. Expert logicians, the Academic Skeptics were aware of this paradox, and so they did not claim to know that they did not know anything. They merely suspended judgment and refrained from making any knowledge claims themselves while refuting their opponents' claims to knowledge. It is debatable whether Socrates was guilty

A Roman bust of Carneades, c. 150 B.C.E. Carneades was key in initiating a new era of Plato's Academy.

of contradicting himself either, or if his claim to know that he did not know anything was just another example of Socratic irony that was not intended to be taken at face value.

According to Sextus Empiricus, Carneades of Cyrene (213–128 B.C.E.) inaugurated yet another period in the history of Plato's Academy—the "New Academy"—when as scholarch he adopted a negative form of dogmatism by claiming to know that nothing can be known. But modern scholars do not believe that Carneades was a negative dogmatist. He did inaugurate a new period in the history of the Academy, but he did so by introducing the idea of a plausible belief, not by adopting negative dogmatism.

Which two schools of Hellenistic philosophy developed in opposition to one another?

Were it not for the Stoics, there would likely have been no Academic Skeptics because all of the Skeptics' arguments were directed against the Stoics. Conversely, were it not for the Academic Skeptics, Stoicism would have developed very differently, because the Stoics developed their philosophy in response to criticisms they received from the Skeptics.

What kind of knowledge were the Academics skeptical about?

The Academics were skeptical about the kind of knowledge that the Stoics proposed as their ideal. According to the Stoics, knowledge is a logically coherent system of beliefs that ultimately rests upon cognitive impressions (*kataleptic phantasia*). The Academic Skeptics did not question Stoic logic. In fact, they used Stoic logic in their skeptical arguments against claims to knowledge. But they did question the Stoic claim that it is possible to have a cognitive impression that accurately represents an object as it exists independent of its appearance to us. The Skeptics argued that none of our impressions are cognitive, that is, objective, and that none can be grasped with certainty, because there is always room for doubt. With that, the Skeptics undermined the Stoic conception of knowledge.

What was the difference between the Stoics and the Skeptics regarding the suspension of judgment?

According to the Stoics, a wise person will only assent to impressions that are known for certain to be true and, to avoid error, will suspend judgment whenever the truth of an impression is uncertain. The Skeptics agreed with the Stoics about the latter but either believed that certainty is not possible (the position of the so-called "negative dogmatists") or reported that they had not yet found it (the position of the Pyrrhonists). Therefore, the Skeptics suspended judgment about all their impressions, whereas the Stoics suspended judgment only when they could not grasp an impression with certainty.

How did the Skeptics think differently about the appearances (or *phenomena*) than other ancient Greek philosophers?

Beginning with the Pre-Socratics, what distinguished philosophy from ordinary thinking was that it questioned the immediate appearance of things. Philosophers wondered whether things appeared as they really were, or if the appearances could be better explained in terms of a reality that is not immediately apparent to the ordinary observer but that can be discerned by the rational mind. All ancient Greek philosophers offered an explanation of the phenomena that went beyond the immediate appearances themselves. They all claimed that the appearances are not what they appear to be but are manifestations of an underlying rational principle, the *arche*.

For the Milesian scientists, the *arche* was an element. For example, Thales said that all things come to be out of water. Anaximenes claimed that all things came to be out of air. According to Heraclitus, all things are fire and occur in accordance with the *logos*. According to Democritus, atoms are real, but what appears to us is not: "cold by custom, hot by custom; atoms and void in truth." According to Plato and his student Aristotle, the *arche* is something more abstract than either an element or atoms. They claimed that the appearances are to be explained in terms of forms or universal categories. But all Greek philosophers believed that there was a hidden *arche* behind the appearances that explained them, and that it was the duty of philosophers to discover what that *arche* was. The Skeptics stand out as the only school of Greek philosophy that refused to engage in this project to penetrate beyond the immediate appearance of things to an underlying reality. Instead of questioning the appearances, the Skeptics questioned the claims of their fellow philosophers to have discovered an underlying reality beyond the appearances.

What is the inactivity or *apraxia* objection to Skepticism?

The inactivity or *apraxia* objection to Skepticism is the charge that the suspension of all judgments about what is true or false, real or not real, would make it impossible to act in the world, or even to survive. According to a story relayed by Diogenes Laërtius (*Lives*) from Antigonus of Carystus (fl. third century B.C.E.), the Skeptic philosopher Pyrrho walked about in the world without holding any beliefs about what is true or false, real or not real, "taking everything as it came, whether it be wagons or precipices or dogs, and all such things, relying on his senses for nothing. He was kept alive by his acquaintances who followed him around...." If we suspend belief about the danger of walking off cliffs, then what would prevent us from doing so?

How did the *apraxia* objection pose a problem for the Stoics?

Although the *apraxia* objection was leveled against the Skeptics, not the Stoics, it posed a problem for the Stoics, too. According to the Stoics, we cannot act without assenting to a hormetic impression (a proposition that it is appropriate to act). But according to the Stoics, to ensure that they do not err, a wise person will only assent to cognitive impressions that are known with certainty to be true and will suspend judgment on any impression that is not certain. Therefore, according to the Stoics, a wise person will not act unless they have cognitive impressions about what they should do. A wise person is not completely paralyzed because, according to the Stoics, a wise person will act when they have a cognitive impression. And a perfect sage will always have a cognitive impression about what to do.

But what about those of us who are not perfect sages? What should we do in the frequent case in which we do not have cognitive impressions about what to do? How then should we act? The Stoic solution was to act on the best evidence or most reasonable (*eulogon*) impressions that we have without giving our full assent to them, since we do not know for certain that they are true. This is a lesser standard for action than what applies to the sage, but it is a greater standard than simply doing whatever feels good or appears to be appropriate.

What were the three main schools of Skepticism in the ancient world?

The three main schools of Skepticism in the ancient world were the Middle Academy, the New Academy, and the Pyrrhonists. The Middle Academy was founded by Arcesilaus (316/5–241/0 B.C.E.) in 265 B.C.E. The New Academy was founded by Carneades of Cyrene (213–128 B.C.E.) in 165 B.C.E. As Academic Skeptics in the latter part of the Hellenistic period made more and more concessions to the dogmatic philosophy of the Stoics, the Academic philosopher Aenesidemus (c. 80–c. 10 B.C.E.) called for a return to a pure form of Skepticism and founded his own school of philosophy modeled on the Skeptic philosopher Pyrrho of Elis (c. 360–c. 270 B.C.E.). The Pyrrhonists had their greatest spokesperson in the figure of Sextus Empiricus (c. 160–c. 210 C.E.), whose surviving works in addition to Cicero's are our richest source of information about Academic Skepticism in all its forms.

How can the different schools of Skepticism in the ancient world be distinguished from one another?

The different schools of Skepticism can be distinguished from one another by the kinds of belief they did or did not allow and by how they responded to the *apraxia* objection. Arcesilaus and the Middle Academy

Arcesilaus and Carneades were the founders of the Middle Academy and the New Academy, respectively, two schools of Skepticism.

may have allowed for assent to reasonable (*eulogon*) beliefs to address the *apraxia* objection. Carneades and the New Academy introduced the notion of *pithanón* (πιθανόν) beliefs into the Academy. *Pithanón* beliefs are not certain like cognitive impressions but are plausible, persuasive, or probable. Carneades may have allowed for assent to plausible beliefs to address the *apraxia* objection; Philo of Larissa (159/8–84/3 B.C.E.) certainly did. The Pyrrhonists addressed the *apraxia* objection by acting on the basis of what *appears* to be the case while suspending judgment on whether it really is.

How did Arcesilaus address the *apraxia* objection?

Arcesilaus founded the Middle Academy on the principle that a wise person will not assent to anything but a cognitive impression. Since he could not find any cognitive impressions, he suspended judgment on all knowledge claims. But in responding to the Stoic *apraxia* objection to Skepticism, he turned Stoicism against itself by adopting the Stoic solution to the *apraxia* objection. In cases where we do not have a cognitive impression of what to do, which as far as Arcesilaus could tell is every case, we should act on the most reasonable (*eulogon*) impressions that we have, without giving our full assent to them, since we do not know for certain that they are true. There is some question as to whether Arcesilaus actually believed this or if he was just using it as a dialectical argument against the Stoic *apraxia* objection.

Sextus Empiricus, who was perhaps the greatest Skeptic of them all, believed that Arcesilaus was not a pure Skeptic and that he did allow for reasonable beliefs, at least for the purpose of acting in the world: "Arcesilaus says that he who suspends judgment about everything regulates choices and avoidances and, generally, actions by reasonableness, and, proceeding according to this criterion, will act correctly [perform morally perfect actions]. For happiness arises because of prudence, and prudence resides in cor-

287

How did Carneades address the *apraxia* objection?

Carneades addressed the *apraxia* objection by introducing the principle of plausible (*pithanón*) belief into Skepticism. A plausible belief is one that is persuasive and probably true given the available evidence, but not certain. Like all Academic Skeptics, Carneades denied that we could ever be certain about anything, and since we cannot be certain, we should suspend judgment on our impressions. However, Carneades argued that for the purpose of taking action, we can overcome the *apraxia* objection by accepting or approving plausible beliefs, without giving our full assent to them. Therefore, Carneades used the principle of plausible belief to address the *apraxia* objection in the same way that Arcesilaus used the principle of reasonable belief to address it. Plausible beliefs, like reasonable ones, provide a rational criterion for practical action, but not a criterion for truth.

rect [morally perfect] actions, and a correct [morally perfect] action is that which, having been done, has a reasonable defense. Therefore, he who adheres to reasonableness will act correctly and will be happy" (*Adversus Mathematicos*).

According to Carneades, what are the three criteria of a plausible belief?

According to Carneades, the three criteria of a plausible belief are that it be plausible, uncontroverted, and tested. The degree of evidence that we require for our beliefs will depend on our practical circumstances. If the stakes are high and we have the time and resources to thoroughly investigate the matter, we will demand more evidence than if the reverse is the case. According to Sextus Empiricus, a plausible impression is one that appears to accurately represent its object and induces our assent, thereby establishing a plausible belief. An impression of an object can be more or less plausible depending on how clear in outline and distinct from other objects it is. For example, an impression of an object will be less clear and distinct if the object is small or far away or if our eyesight is poor (*Adversus Mathematicos*).

An impression that is both plausible and uncontroverted is more trustworthy than one that is merely plausible. An impression is uncontroverted if it is not contradicted by the other impressions that are associated with it. Sextus points out that impressions "are never isolated, but rather one depends on another like links in a chain." For example, an impression of a man is linked to impressions of his attributes and circumstances: "among the former are color, size, shape, movement, speech, dress, footwear, and all the rest; among the latter are the air, light, day, the heavens, earth, friends, and all the rest." Our initial impression of a man is uncontroverted when our impressions of his attributes and circumstances do not contradict our initial impression. "For that this man is Socrates we trust from the impression of all the customary characteristics belonging to him."

The most trustworthy impressions that warrant assent are ones that in addition to being plausible and uncontroverted are also well tested. An impression is well tested when it and its associated impressions are diligently examined and scrutinized. This entails an examination of the object of the impression, the medium through which the impression is received, and the subject who judges the impression. Is the object small? Is visibility poor due to atmospheric conditions? Is our eyesight poor? A specific example that Sextus gives is an impression of a coiled rope in a dark room that at first sight appears to be a snake. The initial impression of a snake is controverted by the impression that it does not move. Finally, testing the impression of a snake by prodding it with a stick reveals that it is in fact a rope, not a snake.

How did Carneades scandalize the Romans?

The Romans were expanding their control over Greece when they fined the Athenians the enormous sum of 500 talents for sacking the town of Oropus in 158 B.C.E. Desperate to lower the fine imposed upon them, in 155 B.C.E. the Athenians organized a delegation of three leading philosophers—Carneades, the Peripatetic Critolaus, and the Stoic Diogenes of Babylon—to go to Rome and plead their case. Notably, the Epicureans did not join the delegation because they believed that engaging in politics would disturb their tranquility (*ataraxia*). The delegation was successful in persuading the Romans to lower the fine on Athens.

But while they were in Rome, they both intrigued and scandalized the Romans. Diogenes of Babylon offended the Romans by declaring that Rome was not a real city. Carneades gave a speech that was attended by both common people and Roman dignitaries in which he argued in favor of justice. The next day, he gave another speech arguing against justice. According to Cicero, Carneades argued that since different communities have different laws, there is no natural law, and justice is an arbitrary social construction. By arguing both sides of the case, Carneades was using the dialectical method of argument not to persuade the audience one way or the other but to suspend belief. According to Plutarch, the Roman dignitaries who heard Carneades speak, however, including Cato the Elder, did not suspend belief. They believed that Carneades was a danger to the state and expelled him from Rome.

What were the two different ways in which Carneades was understood by the Skeptics who followed him in the Academy?

Carneades founded the New Academy by introducing the principle of plausible (*pithanón*) belief into Skepticism. However, he was understood in two different ways by the Skeptics who followed him in the Academy. His student Metrodorus of Stratonicea (fl. 110 B.C.E.) interpreted Carneades to mean that for practical purposes, it is rational to assent to noncognitive impressions, so long as they are plausible and we recognize that they may be false. This interpretation of Carneades was later developed to its logical conclusion by the last Skeptic scholarch of the Academy, Philo of Larissa (159/8–84/3   **289**

B.C.E.). Meanwhile, Carneades's student Clitomachus (187/6–110/9 B.C.E.), who became scholarch of the Academy following Carneades, interpreted Carneades as a radical Skeptic who suspended judgment on all impressions. Skeptics often used the method of dialectics to set equally strong arguments against one another, not to persuade us that either is true but to lead us to suspend judgment on both. According to Clitomachus, Carneades introduced the principle of plausible belief into Skepticism only as a dialectical argument against the Stoic *apraxia* objection, not because he believed that we should assent to plausible beliefs but to lead us to suspend judgment on both plausible beliefs and the *apraxia* objection.

How did Philo of Larissa become the last Academic Skeptic?

The principle of plausible belief was a slippery slope that ultimately led to dogmatism. Philo of Larissa (159/8–84/3 B.C.E.) began his career as a student of the radical Skeptic Clitomachus and was his successor as scholarch of the Academy. But later he adopted a moderate Skepticism that allowed for assent to plausible belief. Earlier theories of plausible belief had tried to distinguish between approving or accepting a plausible belief and assenting to it. A plausible belief was to serve as a criterion for action but not for truth. To act on a plausible belief was to act *as if* it were true without asserting that it *was in fact* true. But there is a fine line between acting *as if* a plausible belief is true and asserting that *it is* true, and that line was crossed by Philo of Larissa in his *Roman Books*.

As the title suggests, the *Roman Books* were written in Rome. During the Mithridatic wars against Roman rule that resulted in Sulla's siege of Athens and the destruction of the Academy, Philo fled Athens for Rome in 88 B.C.E. Philo's exodus to Rome marked not only the physical end of the Academy but also the greatest challenge to Academic Skepticism. In the *Roman Books*, Philo challenged the fundamental assumption of both Stoic and Skeptic epistemology that a wise and rational person will only assent to beliefs that are known with certainty to be true. Philo retained the Skeptic position that we do not possess any certain knowledge. But he allowed that it was rational to assent to plausible beliefs, not only for the purpose of acting in the world, but also to assert their truth. Plausible beliefs might be false. We do not know for certain that they are true. But they might be true. Therefore, contrary to the Skeptics, knowledge is possible.

According to all schools of Hellenistic philosophy, the purpose of philosophy is to live well, and to live well requires that one reason well. Therefore, it must be rational to assent to plausible beliefs, because without plausible beliefs one cannot live well—indeed, one cannot act at all. If it is only possible to live well if one reasons well, and if it is only possible to live well if one assents to plausible beliefs, then it must be rational to assent to plausible beliefs. This position represented such a break from Academic Skepticism that it opened a door for an entirely new approach to the theory of knowledge. That approach would be taken by Philo's renegade student Antiochus of Ascalon (c. 125–c. 68 B.C.E.), who called for a return to the dogmatic Old Academy and who believed that Aristotle and the Stoics, rather than the Skeptics, were the true heirs to Plato's legacy.

PYRRHONIST SKEPTICISM

Who was Aenesidemus, and what kind of Skepticism did he develop?

Aenesidemus (fl. first century B.C.E.) was born in Knossos on the island of Crete and studied at the Academy in Athens under Philo of Larissa. He decried the turn towards dogmatism that Philo had initiated and that Antiochus of Ascalon completed, and he complained that except for their refusal to recognize cognitive impressions, the Academics had become nothing more than "Stoics fighting with Stoics." In an attempt to restore Skepticism, he developed a radical form of that philosophy, which he attributed to Pyrrho but which was largely his own creation. None of his writings have survived, but we know that his principal work was titled *Pyrrhôneoi logoi* (πυρρώνειοι λόγοι) or *Pyrrhonist Discourses*. Pyrrhonism survived into the period of the Roman Empire until it found its greatest exponent in Sextus Empiricus (c. 160–c. 210 C.E.), but it went into decline with the rise of Christianity and Neoplatonism, neither of which had any use for Skepticism. Thereafter, Pyrrhonism lay forgotten until in the sixteenth century it was rediscovered and subsequently exerted a significant influence on the development of modern philosophy.

Was Pyrrho a Pyrrhonist?

No, Pyrrho of Elis (c. 360–c. 270 B.C.E.) was a Skeptic, but he was probably not a Pyrrhonist. Diogenes Laërtius (*Lives*) lists a long line of teachers and their students extending from Pyrrho to Aenesidemus (fl. first century B.C.E.), but there is no evidence that Pyrrho had any significant followers other than Timon of Phlius (c. 320 B.C.E.–c. 235 B.C.E.). Modern scholars do not believe that Aenesidemus was continuing a tradition begun by Pyrrho but that he merely used Pyrrho's name to separate his own school of Skepticism from the Academy. Pyrrho himself wrote nothing.

The most reliable information we have about his philosophy comes from a fragment written about what his student Timon said about it, and even that is not very reliable since it is found in the writings of the fourth century C.E. Christian theologian Eusebius, who was quoting Aristocles of Messene, a Peripatetic

Pyrrho of Elis was not, as one might assume, a Pyrrhonist, but merely a Skeptic.

philosopher who probably lived in the first century C.E. According to Aristocles, "Timon says that Pyrrho declares that things are equally indifferent and unmeasurable and undecidable, and that for this reason neither our senses nor our opinions tell the truth or lie; and so we ought not to put our trust in them but ought instead to be undogmatic and uncommitted and unswayed, saying of each and every thing that it no more is than is not, or both is and is not, or neither is nor is not" (*Preparatio Evangelica*). The passage is strangely reminiscent of the Buddhist philosopher Nagarjuna (c. 150–c. 250 C.E.), who also used the logical tetralemma ("that it no more is than is not, or both is and is not, or neither is nor is not") to deny that things have an inherent nature or essence. But it is not evidence that Pyrrho was a Pyrrhonist because, according to the passage, Pyrrho claimed to know at least two things: (1) that all things are indifferent and unmeasurable and undecidable, and that for this reason (2) nothing can be known. Therefore, Pyrrho was not a Skeptic in all things, as were the Pyrrhonists.

What is negative dogmatism?

Positive dogmatism is a positive claim to knowledge—a positive assertion of a belief or a claim to know that a belief is true. Negative dogmatism is a negative claim to knowledge—a negative assertion of a belief or a claim to know that a belief is not true. An example of negative dogmatism is the claim to know that you do not know (to know that your beliefs are not true). Another example of negative dogmatism would be to claim to know that the Stoics do not know (to know that Stoic beliefs are not true). Negative dogmatism was a concept introduced by Aenesidemus to further distance himself from Academic Skepticism, which he felt was not rigorous enough. Not only did Aenesidemus reject the positive dogmatism of Philo and Antiochus, but he also rejected the negative dogmatism of Carneades, who claimed to know that he did not know, and to know that the Stoics did not know. A true Skeptic, according to Aenesidemus, makes no claims to knowledge at all, whether positive or negative.

How did Aenesidemus achieve a suspension of judgment about whether our beliefs are true or false?

Aenesidemus used the dialectical method to achieve a suspension of judgment (*epochê*) about whether our beliefs are true or false. By setting equally strong but opposite argu-

How did Aenesidemus avoid both positive and negative dogmatism?

Aenesidemus avoided both positive and negative dogmatism by suspending judgment on all beliefs. In his view, Skepticism is not a denial of knowledge claims or a demonstration that our beliefs are wrong. Skepticism is a suspension of judgment about whether our beliefs are true or false.

ments against one another, the dialectical method produces a state of equipollence (*isostheneia*) that makes it impossible to judge which of the opposed arguments is correct. The only option that remains is to suspend judgment.

What are the ten modes?

The ten modes are ten ways of setting equally strong but opposite arguments against one another in such a way that they seem to conclude to suspension of judgment. Aenesidemus was the first to devise the ten modes, but the most extensive discussion of them can be found in a surviving text written by Sextus Empiricus (*Outlines of Pyrrhonism* 1.35–163). Each of the ten modes is based on the different ways that things appear depending on either differences in the subject who judges them or on differences in the circumstances of the object being judged, or on both. Since there is no way to determine which of the different appearances is correct, each of the ten modes seems to conclude to suspension of judgment about how the object being judged really is in its nature.

Physician and philosopher Sextus Empiricus was a Pyrrhonist. Many of his writings survive in modern times, offering scholars one of their best sources not only on Pyrrhonism but also on Hellenistic philosophy in general.

The ten modes can be divided into three categories. The first category of modes is based on differences in the subject who judges. The second category is based on differences in the circumstances of the object being judged. And the third category is based on differences in both the subject who judges and the circumstances of the object being judged. Among the modes is the mode of relativity; however, according to Sextus Empiricus, the mode of relativity is the most general category of modes and includes all other modes as special types since all ten modes are types of relativity. Thus, according to all ten modes of argument, everything that appears is relative to either the subject who judges or the circumstances of the object being judged, or both.

What is each mode, specifically?

The first mode is based on differences between the ways that different animals perceive things. For example, dogs can hear and smell things that human beings cannot. The second mode is based on differences between the ways that different human beings perceive things. The third mode is based on differences between the senses. For example, a picture drawn with perspective may appear to have depth to the eyes but is flat to the touch. The fourth mode is based on different states and dispositions of the subject who judges—for example, whether the subject who judges is drunk or sober, sane or mad, awake or asleep, in need or sated, and so on.

293

The fifth mode is based on differences of positions and distances and places of both the subject who judges and the object that is judged. For example, a tower appears round from a distance but square when seen close up. The sixth mode is based on the mixture or combination of external objects with one another and with parts of the subject who judges. Since objects always appear in a mixture or combination with other objects or parts of the subject who judges, we cannot know what those objects really are in their own nature. One example that Sextus Empiricus gives is our complexion: since the color of our skin appears different depending on the temperature of the air and lighting, we cannot know what the color of our skin is in its own nature but only what it appears to be in combination with other factors (*Outlines of Pyrrhonism*). The seventh mode is based on differences in the quantities and structures of objects. In a curious example, Sextus says that filings of goat's horn appear to be white but when combined to form a whole horn, they appear to be black.

The eighth mode is the mode of relativity. This mode requires us to suspend judgment about what things really are in their own nature since everything is relative to other things. The ninth mode is based on differences in frequency of occurrence. The example Sextus gives is the difference between comets and the sun. Because comets appear in the sky much less frequently than the sun, we find comets more astounding than the sun, even though the sun would be far more astounding if we were not so accustomed to it. The tenth mode is based on differences in customs, habits, laws, and myths. This mode, Sextus says, has particular application to ethics. Because different people in different cultures have different customs, habits, laws, and myths, ethics is relative to each culture, and it is necessary to suspend judgment about what is by nature right or wrong.

What are the five modes?

The five modes are five ways of arguing against dogmatic claims to knowledge in such a way that leads to suspension of judgment. According to Diogenes Laërtius (third century C.E.), the five modes were first devised by the Pyrrhonist philosopher Agrippa, who lived sometime after the death of Aenesidemus (fl. first century B.C.E.); but like the ten modes, the most extensive discussion of the five modes can be found in a surviving text written by Sextus Empiricus (*Outlines of Pyrrhonism*).

The first mode is the mode of disagreement. The second mode is the mode of infinite regress. The third mode is the mode of relativity. The fourth mode is the mode of hypothesis. And the fifth mode is the mode of circular reasoning. The first and the third modes essentially summarize the ten modes devised by Aenesidemus, since the ten modes are all based on the relativity of appearances and the undecided disagreement between them. The other three modes are ways of disputing that these disagreements have been decided in favor of one side of the disagreement or the other.

In the second mode, the skeptic argues that what is offered as proof of one side of the disagreement is itself in need of proof, and what is given in proof of that is in need

> ## What was the purpose of Pyrrhonist Skepticism and the suspension of judgment?
>
> The purpose of Pyrrhonist Skepticism, as it was for all Hellenistic schools of philosophy, was to be happy and live well (*eudaimonia*). But it seemed to the Pyrrhonists—as it did to the Stoics and the Epicureans—that happiness is a state of tranquility and freedom from disturbance (*ataraxia*). Therefore, the purpose of Pyrrhonist Skepticism was to achieve a state of *ataraxia*, and the way to do that, it seemed to them alone, was to suspend judgment about all our beliefs.

of proof, and so on ad infinitum. In other words, if a dogmatist offers Q as proof that P is true, then the skeptic will require proof of Q; and if the dogmatist offers R as proof of Q, then the skeptic will require proof of R; and so on, ad infinitum, without end. Note that the skeptic does not conclude that P cannot be proven, which would be a dogmatic claim. The only conclusion the skeptic draws is that P has not yet been proven. As to whether P can be proven or not, the skeptic suspends judgment, since the inquiry appears to be infinite, and in any case, it has not been completed.

Should the dogmatist try to escape the infinite regress of the second mode by claiming to have found a hypothesis that does not require further proof, the skeptic employs the fourth mode, in which the skeptic denies that the dogmatist's hypothesis does not require proof. The principle behind the fourth mode is that a party to a disagreement cannot win a dispute simply by claiming that they are right. They must give reasons. Should the dogmatist try to escape the infinite regress of the second mode by arguing that P is true because Q is true, and that Q is true because P is true, the skeptic employs the fifth mode by pointing out that the dogmatist's argument is circular and, therefore, invalid.

What are some famous anecdotes about Pyrrho's exceptional freedom from disturbance (*ataraxia*)?

Diogenes Laërtius provides several vivid anecdotes about Pyrrho's exceptional freedom from disturbance or *ataraxia*. According to one anecdote, Pyrrho was said to have "washed a piglet himself because he was indifferent to what he did." According to another, "he did not even frown" when undergoing surgery without anesthesia (*Lives*). Yet another tells of the time when Pyrrho's "fellow passengers on a ship were frightened by a storm. He, however, was calm and serene and, pointing to a little pig on the ship who was eating away, said that the wise man ought to repose in just such a state of freedom from disturbance." A final anecdote suggests that Pyrrho's *ataraxia* was due to his exceptional control over his judgment, but not over his natural impulses: "Once when a dog attacked him and he panicked, he replied to someone who blamed him for this that it was hard to shed one's humanity, but that one should struggle against circumstances, as much as possible in one's actions, but if not then at least in one's words."

Why did it seem to the Pyrrhonists that *ataraxia* could be achieved by suspending judgment about our beliefs?

According to Sextus Empiricus the goal of the skeptic is to achieve a state of freedom from disturbance with respect to matters of voluntary judgment or assent to impressions and also moderate states with respect to matters of compulsion or involuntary assent to impressions (*Outlines of Pyrrhonism*). According to the Pyrrhonists, our own beliefs or judgments about impressions cause us disturbance. By suspending our beliefs or judgments about impressions, we can free ourselves from the disturbance they cause. For example, someone who believes that something is honorable will be disturbed when they do not possess it and even when it is possessed will become overly elated and fear losing it. On the other hand, someone who suspends judgment about what is honorable or good by nature does not become disturbed when they do not possess them or become excessively elated or fear losing them when they do possess them.

With regard to matters of compulsion or involuntary assent to impressions, such as pain, we are disturbed not only by the pain itself but also by our beliefs about our pain—for example, by the belief that pain is bad. We do not have control over the pain itself, but we do have control over our beliefs about our pain. Sextus admits that even the Skeptic experiences pain and is troubled by it. But ordinary people are disturbed not just by the pain itself but also by their belief that pain is bad by nature. The Skeptic does not escape pain itself but by suspending judgment does escape the emotional disturbance caused by our beliefs about pain.

How did Socrates remain undisturbed in the face of death?

Plato's dialogue the *Apology* recounts the story of the trial of Socrates on charges of impiety and corrupting the youth of Athens. In his defense, Socrates tells the jury that he has never been anyone's teacher, nor did anyone ever learn anything from him. Young people gathered around him only because they enjoyed hearing him question those who think they are wise but are not. Socrates's genius is strictly negative. He can show that those who think they are wise do not know what they think they know, but he does not claim to know anything himself.

In the closing paragraphs of the dialogue, Socrates reflects upon death. In a remark that anticipates the Epicurean theory of death, he says that if death is like a dreamless sleep, then it is nothing to be feared. In a remark that anticipates the Stoics, who believed that virtue is all that is necessary for happiness, he tells the jury to "keep this one truth in mind, that a good man cannot be harmed either in life or in death." And in anticipation of the Skeptical use of the suspension of judgment to achieve freedom from disturbance, Socrates ends the dialogue by announcing that "the hour to part has come. I go to die, you go to live. Which of us goes to the better lot is known to no one, except the god."

How did the Pyrrhonists solve the problem posed to them by the *apraxia* objection?

The Pyrrhonists solved the problem posed to them by the *apraxia* objection by stating that they could act on the basis of appearances alone, without judging whether those ap-

The Death of Socrates (1787) by Jacques-Louis David. The philosopher was put to death for allegedly corrupting the youth of Athens.

pearances are real or true, and therefore without any beliefs. The Pyrrhonist argument against the *apraxia* objection—like so many other Pyrrhonist arguments—depended upon Stoic concepts and arguments that were turned around and used against them.

The appearances are impressions of things or states of affairs. According to the Stoics, an impression is not in itself a belief. An impression does not become a belief until the subject who receives the impression assents to it by judging that it is true. For example, the perception of light is an impression, but it is not a belief until the subject who sees the light assents to it by judging that the proposition "it is light" is true. According to both the Pyrrhonist Sextus Empiricus and the Stoics, we passively receive impressions, but we actively and voluntarily adopt beliefs by assenting to impressions and judging them to be true. Sextus Empiricus explains that since an impression is an involuntary state, we do not have a choice about whether to have it or not. Our only choice is to judge whether it really is what it appears to be or not. Suspending judgment about whether our impressions are what they appear to be or not still leaves us with impressions that can guide our everyday behavior in the world.

Sextus believes that our impressions provide us with four kinds of rules that guide everyday behavior: (1) those given by our natural impulses and faculties; (2) the compulsion to act according to our own habits; (3) traditional laws and customs; and (4) crafts or technical skills learned by doing (*Outlines of Pyrrhonism* 1.22–23). In each of these rules of everyday behavior, we are guided by an impression or appearance of what to do. Because we passively receive these impressions, we can receive guidance about what to do from them without actively or voluntarily assenting to them. In other words, we can act according to habit, custom, or natural impulse, without thinking and holding beliefs, let alone holding entire philosophical systems of knowledge like those that the Stoic sage claimed to possess.

What was wrong with the Pyrrhonist solution to the problem posed to them by the *apraxia* objection?

The *apraxia* objection posed a problem for the Pyrrhonists not just because it called into question how someone with no beliefs could avoid walking off cliffs, but also because it called into question how someone with no beliefs could engage in ethical actions. Sextus Empiricus solved the problem of how someone with no beliefs could avoid walking off cliffs. But he did not solve the problem of how someone with no beliefs could engage in ethical action.

According to the Stoics, ethical action is always initiated by the agent's assent to a hormetic impression (*phantasia hormetikê*), that is, the agent's judgment that it is appropriate to act. Therefore, without a belief—the belief that it is appropriate to act—there can be no ethical action. It is possible to act without thinking or holding any beliefs—such as when we act out of habit, custom, or natural impulse—but when we do so, our actions are not voluntarily chosen. But involuntary actions are not ethical because we can neither take credit nor be held responsible for actions that we have not chosen. Therefore, actions performed without beliefs are not ethical. Thus, it would appear that by suspending all beliefs, the Pyrrhonists could not engage in ethical action, thereby defeating the purpose of philosophy, which was not only to survive and move about in the world but to engage in ethical action.

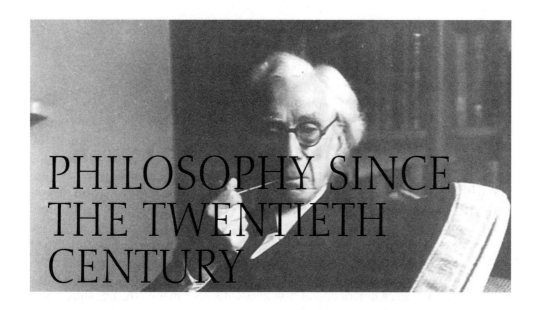

PHILOSOPHY SINCE THE TWENTIETH CENTURY

What happened to philosophy in the final years of the nineteenth century?

In the final years of the nineteenth century, philosophy became institutionalized in the modern research university. Prior to the development of the modern research university, many philosophers worked outside of a university. Even those who did work in a university did not generally work in departments specifically called "philosophy" departments. Many of the most famous historical figures whom we now take to be model philosophers were not known as philosophers in their lifetimes. David Hume (1711–1776), for example, who is so revered by academic philosophers today, worked as a librarian and was famous in his day for his history of England, not his books on philosophy. The conception of philosophy as a specialized academic discipline that could occupy a separate place in a bureaucratic organization apart from other specialized disciplines did not exist prior to the final years of the nineteenth century. However, in those years, the groundwork was laid for the schools of academic philosophy that would come to define what philosophy would be in the twentieth century.

How did higher education change in the nineteenth century?

The modern research university was invented in Germany in the nineteenth century, and like other ideas in education it spread from there to the United States. Nearly all Ivy League colleges in the United States were originally established to train ministers in the mainline Protestant denominations and were modeled on British universities. At the beginning of the nineteenth century, the undergraduate curriculum at these colleges was based on the liberal arts, which was a curriculum similar to what an ancient Greek or Roman may have studied, including instruction in the Greek and Latin languages. However, by the end of the nineteenth century, this classic model of education had been replaced by the modern research university.

What was the model of the modern research university?

The modern research university was based not on the study of the classic works of Greek and Roman literature and philosophy but rather on the scientific method. It is no coincidence that the modern research university developed while large-scale industrialization and urbanization were sweeping northwestern Europe and the United States. The modern research university was essentially a factory in which knowledge and the workers who produced that knowledge were mass produced. Knowledge was mass produced by the application of a reliable method—the scientific method. Knowledge workers were mass produced by training all students how to use the same standardized method. Such a system suited the needs of a large bureaucratic organization to manage many workers and to ensure quality control of the product of their labor. The important point to note here is that the modern research university did not merely impart students with knowledge but with a method by which knowledge could be produced. This ensured the large-scale production of new knowledge, not merely the transmission of old knowledge as the classic model of higher education had done.

How did the modern research university shape the development of philosophy in the late nineteenth and twentieth centuries?

Philosophy could not fully adopt the scientific method as its own because it was not suited to its subject matter. But since the purpose of the modern research university was to mass produce knowledge and the workers who produced that knowledge, it did need to adopt a method of some kind. Consequently, the most important schools of philosophy since the late nineteenth century have been defined not by their positive doctrines or beliefs but by the methods they employ. The recipient of a Ph.D. in philosophy is someone who has demonstrated mastery of a method of producing philosophic knowledge. Such an individual can go on to train others how to use the method they were taught and to produce new knowledge as an employee of the research university.

THE MAIN SCHOOLS OF PHILOSOPHY

What are the main schools of philosophy as it is practiced today in American colleges and universities?

The main schools of philosophy as it is practiced in American colleges and universities are analytic philosophy, Continental philosophy, and pragmatism. Analytic philosophy is by far the most popular school of philosophy in American colleges and universities. Continental philosophy represents the dissenting voice to the analytic establishment. Of these three, only pragmatism originated on American soil. But pragmatism is the smallest school of philosophy in American colleges and universities today, and it is important mostly due to its influence on the other two schools of philosophy. The three founding figures of pragmatism were Charles Peirce (1839–1914), William James (1842–1910),

300

and John Dewey (1859–1952). Analytic philosophy began in England and Vienna in the early twentieth century and became popular in the United States after World War II when American universities welcomed refugees from Europe. The founding figures of analytic philosophy were Gottlob Frege (1848–1925), Bertrand Russell (1872–1970), G. E. Moore (1873–1958), Ludwig Wittgenstein (1889–1951), and the Vienna Circle of Logical Positivists or Empiricists led by Moritz Schlick (1882–1936). Continental philosophy was developed by French and German philosophers in the twentieth century. It was imported at first into American departments of literature, and later into philosophy departments, beginning in the 1960s. The most important figures in Continental philosophy are Edmund Husserl (1859–1938), Martin Heidegger (1889–1976), Jacques Derrida (1930–2004), and Michel Foucault (1926–1984). Each of these schools of philosophy not only offers different answers to the perennial philosophical questions but also uses different methods in its practice of philosophy.

ANALYTIC PHILOSOPHY

Who was Bertrand Russell?

Besides being one of the founders of analytic philosophy and one of the most important logicians of the twentieth century, Bertrand Russell (1872–1970) was a leading peace activist. Though he was born into an aristocratic British family, he often found himself on the other side of the barricades from the establishment. Shortly before the start of World War I, Russell wrote, with Alfred North Whitehead (1861–1947), the *Principia Mathematica*, which was a landmark work in the history of logic that attempted to reduce mathematics to the rules of logic and set theory. However, his activism against British involvement in World War I led to the loss of his position at Trinity College, Cambridge, and his eventual imprisonment. In addition to being a pacifist, Russell was an atheist and an advocate of free love (sex without benefit of marriage). In 1927 he wrote his popular essay *Why I Am Not a Christian*. In 1940 an Irish Catholic judge in New York City ruled that he was morally unfit to teach philosophy at the City College of New York. In 1945 he wrote *A History of Western Philosophy*. After World War II, he campaigned for nuclear disarmament in partnership with Albert

One of the principal founders of analytic philosophy, Bertrand Russell was a logician, mathematician, social critic, and Nobel laureate.

Einstein and protested the Vietnam War with the French existentialist philosopher Jean-Paul Sartre (1905–1980).

Who was Ludwig Wittgenstein?

Ludwig Wittgenstein (1889–1951) was a student of Bertrand Russell's and a leading figure in analytic philosophy whose devoted followers made him into a virtual cult figure. Wittgenstein published only one short book in his lifetime, the *Tractatus Logico-Philosophicus* (Latin for "Logical Philosophical Treatise" or "Treatise on Logic and Philosophy"), an austere and enigmatic work composed of short numbered statements arranged in a hierarchical order. Philosophers still debate its meaning, but it had something to do with logic, language, and the limits of what can be said. Russell considered Wittgenstein to

A protégé of Bertrand Russell's, Ludwig Wittgenstein was considered by some to be a genius in the field of analytic philosophy.

be the most perfect example of a genius he had ever known. Indeed, even today a collection of his posthumously published manuscripts titled *Philosophical Investigations* (1953) is considered by many academic philosophers to be the most important work of philosophy in the twentieth century.

Wittgenstein was a tortured soul, and in spite of his charisma and his talent for playing the role of a genius, he could be a very difficult and unpleasant person. During one of his several hiatuses from his position at Trinity College, Cambridge, he taught in remote Austrian villages where he routinely hit children for making mistakes in mathematics. According to an account chronicled in the book *Wittgenstein's Poker* (2001) of a lecture given at Cambridge in 1946 by the philosopher of science Karl Popper (1902–1994), when Wittgenstein and Popper got into an argument about whether there were any real problems in philosophy or if philosophers merely misunderstood how language works, which was Wittgenstein's position, Wittgenstein picked up an iron poker from the fireplace and waved it about in a threatening manner. When Wittgenstein demanded an example of a moral rule, Popper answered "not to threaten visiting lecturers with pokers."

Wittgenstein's father, Karl, was a steel magnate in Vienna and one of the wealthiest men in the world, but he was a severe and demanding man who expected perfection from his children. Three of Wittgenstein's four brothers committed suicide, and Wittgenstein himself was throughout his life fraught with existential angst, which only added to his image of being exceptionally deep and intense. At a young age Wittgenstein, like his siblings, learned to play classical music to perfection on one of his family's seven grand pianos. In college he studied engineering, not philosophy or the humanities, and he retained an interest in engineering throughout his life. He served on the front lines in World War I and was awarded many honors for his courage and valor. During the war he wrote the *Tractatus* (1921). According to Bertrand Russell, he returned from the war a deeply spiritual and ascetic man. He gave away his vast fortune to his siblings and set out to lead a simple life as an elementary schoolteacher. What all these choices and accomplishments demonstrate is a capacity for severe discipline, a dominant trait in Wittgenstein's personality and one that he, like his father, expected to find in others.

What are the methods of analytic philosophy?

The main method utilized by analytic philosophers is logical analysis. This can take the form of either linguistic analysis or conceptual analysis. In linguistic analysis, one applies the tools of deductive logic to the analysis of words or sentences. In conceptual analysis, one applies the tools of deductive logic to the analysis of concepts or propositions. A proposition is a statement of the form "*S* is *P*," which makes the implicit claim that "*S* is *P*" is true. A proposition may be true or false. Since words are often used to express concepts and sentences are often used to express propositions, the two methods often boil down to the same thing in practice. However, there are other uses of language besides the expression of concepts or propositions, and in many cases, language does not express concepts or propositions without ambiguity or contradiction. It is the task of linguistic analysis to identify the nonpropositional uses of language and to remove the ambiguities and contradictions introduced by language into our expression of concepts and propositions so that a conceptual analysis can be performed on them. Conceptual analysis employs the tools of deductive logic to identify the essential meaning of concepts and to make fine distinctions between them. In its most rigorous form, logical

What do analytic philosophers have in common with one another?

Analytic philosophy has changed a great deal since its founding over a century ago. Logical positivism, in particular, was abandoned long ago. However, analytic philosophers still look to science as the most reliable if not the only source of knowledge. The philosopher's role, according to analytic philosophers, is not to discover scientific knowledge, since they are not scientists themselves, but to facilitate the scientific project by clarifying our use of language. They therefore share a common interest in science, the study of language, and logic. They are more often empiricists than rationalists, and they count important figures in the history of empiricism such as John Locke (1632–1704) and David Hume (1711–1776) among their predecessors. But analytic philosophers today don't agree about very much beyond these broad parameters. What they do share in common, however, is their style and method. It is by their style and method that one can most readily identify an analytic philosopher.

analysis entails reducing a series of statements in ordinary language that make an argument into abstract logical symbols, so that ambiguities can be eliminated, and the logical validity of that argument may be more easily assessed. In all cases, one is merely making clear what has already been said or known.

What is a simple example of logical analysis?

The sentence "All bachelors are unmarried" is an expression of a proposition of the form "*S* is *P*" where *S* is the concept "bachelors" and *P* is the concept "unmarried." A conceptual analysis of the concept "bachelors" reveals that the concept "bachelors" is composed of the concepts "male" and "unmarried" and that the proposition "All bachelors are unmarried" is true because the concept "bachelors" already contains within itself the concept "unmarried."

What is a more complex example of logical analysis?

Most of the analyses performed by philosophers are not as simple as the analysis of the concept of a bachelor. Take, for example, the concept of "action." How is the concept of action related to the concept of intention? How does action differ from behavior? Are actions necessarily voluntary? The concept of action is used in Immanuel Kant's categorical imperative, which states, in one of its formulations, "Act as if the maxim of your action were to become through your will a universal law of nature."

A clearer understanding of the concept of action might help us to better understand Kant's imperative. In general, analytic philosophers believe that we could solve many of our problems in philosophy if we applied their methods of analysis and became clearer about our use of language and concepts. But many uses of language and concepts are much more complex and difficult to analyze than the concept of a bachelor.

What is the problem with the sentence "The present king of France is bald"?

The problem with the sentence "The present king of France is bald" is that it appears to have the form "*S* is *P*." But sentences of the form "*S* is *P*" are either true or false. *S* is either *P* or it is not. According to the law of the excluded middle—a basic principle of logic—there is no third alternative. But the sentence "The

The statement "The king of France is bald" is neither true nor false because there is no king of France at the present time.

present king of France is bald" is neither true nor false because there is no present king of France.

How did Bertrand Russell solve the problem with the sentence "The present king of France is bald"?

Bertrand Russell solved the problem with the sentence "The present king of France is bald" by performing a linguistic analysis on it. According to his analysis, the sentence "The present king of France is bald" does not express a proposition of the form "S is P." A proposition must be either true or false. But "The present king of France is bald" is neither true nor false because there is no present king of France. The sentence "The present king of France is bald" is an example of what Russell called a "definite description." According to Russell's analysis, definite descriptions do not have the propositional form "S is P." Rather, definite descriptions, when appropriately analyzed, have the propositional form "There exists an individual that S, there is only one such individual, and that individual is P." When analyzed as a definite description, the sentence "The present king of France is bald" becomes "There exists an individual who is currently the king of France, there is only one such individual, and that individual is bald," and this sentence can be assigned a truth value. Since there is currently no king of France, the sentence is false, and the problem is solved.

CONTINENTAL PHILOSOPHY

What is Continental philosophy?

Continental philosophy is a school of philosophy that originated in Germany with Edmund Husserl's transcendental phenomenology but spread first to France, and then later to the United States. Today, Continental philosophy is no longer necessarily practiced in Continental Europe, nor is it limited to Husserl's phenomenology. The first challenge to Husserl's transcendental phenomenology came from his student Martin Heidegger, who advanced a new type of phenomenology that was both existentialist and hermeneutical. Following World War II, French philosophers, building upon both Heidegger's hermeneutics and Ferdinand de Saussure's

Edmund Gustav Albrecht Husserl was a German philosopher and founder of the discipline of phenomenology, which caught the imagination of Continental Europe in the early twentieth century.

(1857–1913) structuralist linguistics, developed various poststructuralist philosophies. In addition to Husserl, Heidegger, and the poststructuralists, the critical theorists are also generally categorized as Continental philosophers, not only for the trivial reason that many of them were German but also because they were influenced to a greater or lesser degree by the other Continental philosophers and also by Karl Marx (1818–1883). All the Continental philosophers share a common heritage in German Idealism, a philosophical movement of the early nineteenth century that included Immanuel Kant (1724–1804), Johann Gottlieb Fichte (1762–1814), Friedrich Wilhelm Joseph Schelling (1775–1854), Georg Wilhelm Friedrich Hegel (1770–1831), and Arthur Schopenhauer (1788–1860), and in German Romanticism, Søren Kierkegaard (1813–1855) and Friedrich Nietzsche (1844–1900).

Who was Martin Heidegger?

Martin Heidegger (1889–1976) was born to a poor family in the small, rural town of Messkirch in southwest Germany. His father was the sexton of the village church, and he was raised as a conservative Catholic. Unable to pay his own way, Heidegger studied theology at the University of Freiburg with the support of the Catholic Church and later switched to philosophy. His doctoral thesis on psychologism was influenced by contemporary interpretations of the medieval Catholic philosopher St. Thomas Aquinas and the

German Idealist Immanuel Kant (1724–1804). His habilitation thesis was on the medieval scholastic philosopher and theologian Duns Scotus (c. 1266–1308) and was influenced by Edmund Husserl (1859–1938). Between 1920 and 1923 Heidegger served as Husserl's personal assistant.

In 1927 Heidegger published *Being and Time*, which was a seminal text of Continental philosophy and one of the most important works of philosophy in the twentieth century. It was influenced by Aristotle's (384–322 B.C.E.) metaphysics, St. Augustine's (354–430 C.E.) philosophy of time, Kierkegaard's (1813–1855) existentialism, and Wilhelm Dilthey's (1833– 1911) hermeneutics. The book was dedicated to Husserl "in grateful respect and friendship" but departed from Husserl's philosophy in important ways.

German philosopher Martin Heidegger was a Continental philosopher concerned with existentialism, hermeneutics, and phenomenology. He has been controversial, however, because he supported the Nazi Party.

Many of Heidegger's students became important philosophers in their own right in the twentieth century, including Hans-

Georg Gadamer (1900–2002), who wrote on hermeneutics; Hannah Arendt (1906–1975), who had an affair and a lifelong friendship with Heidegger and who wrote on totalitarianism and the Holocaust; Leo Strauss (1899–1973), whose work inspired neoconservatives; and Herbert Marcuse (1898–1979), the Frankfurt School Marxist and father of the New Left. Arendt, Strauss, and Marcuse were all from Jewish families. During the 1920s, Heidegger was attracted to a political movement called revolutionary conservatism that served as a precursor to Nazism. In 1933 Heidegger became a member of the Nazi Party and was appointed rector of the University of Freiburg. Though he stepped down as rector of the university out of frustration that the Nazis had passed him over in favor of Alfred Rosenberg as their official philosopher, he remained a member of the Nazi Party until the war ended in 1945. He never apologized for his membership in the Nazi Party or for his support for the Nazis during the war. However, after the war he lumped the Nazis together with Americans and communists as modernists whose infatuation with technology threatened the future of civilization and of humanity's relation to "Being."

Throughout his life Heidegger, who loved the outdoors, spent a great deal of time writing philosophy in his small ski hut on the edge of the Black Forest. In 1934 Heidegger delivered a speech over the radio titled "Why Do I Stay in the Provinces?" in which he explained why he would not leave the Black Forest to teach in the modern city of Berlin. Heidegger believed that the Alemannic German Volk ("folk" or "people") of which he was a part were rooted in the soil of the Black Forest. In 2014 Heidegger's journals from the period 1931–1941 were finally published. These journals, called the *Black Notebooks,* revealed Heidegger's philosophical anti-Semitism, according to which Jews were responsible for modernity and its deracinating technology, which he opposed. From Heidegger's perspective, industrialized agriculture was morally equivalent to the Holocaust because they were both products of the same modern technological society that robs us of our destiny as a people and that uproots us from our heritage, from our language and culture, from our homeland, and from "Being." Before he died, Heideg-

What was the original method of phenomenological research in Continental philosophy?

Edmund Husserl (1859–1938), the founding figure of Continental philosophy, developed transcendental phenomenology as the primary method of philosophical research. He developed this method in the hope that generations of philosophers after him would use the phenomenological method to discover the essential or invariant and universal structures of "being" or of what "is." He believed that the phenomenological method would solve what he described as the crisis in the sciences. The crisis was that the sciences lacked a secure foundation and had lost their mooring in the immediate experience of the human subject, which Husserl called the "lifeworld."

ger asked a Catholic priest to bury him in the cemetery in Messkirch. When he died his wish was fulfilled, and his remains were returned to the soil from whence he came.

How did Heidegger change the phenomenological method?

Husserl's phenomenological method is still practiced by Continental philosophers, but it was challenged early on by Martin Heidegger (1889–1976), who shifted the focus away from the transcendental or universal subject of experience to the individual subject located in history, culture, and language. Heidegger did not regard language to be a transparent system of arbitrary labels for objects of experience that could be immediately intuited without language. He believed that there could be no experience of the world, and indeed nothing at all, without language. Thus, the problem of language occupied a central place in Heidegger's philosophy. This preoccupation with language continued with the poststructuralists, who adopted techniques of linguistics, and techniques of reading and the interpretation of texts, as their primary philosophical method. Consequently, Continental philosophy attracted the interest of departments of literature in the United States even more than it did departments of philosophy.

What is the phenomenological method?

At first glance, the phenomenological method looks like psychological introspection. In fact phenomenology does begin with introspection, but it doesn't end there. Husserl began by reflecting upon his own consciousness. However, upon doing this, he found that he was not only conscious of his mental acts. He was also conscious of the objects of those mental acts. It is the nature of consciousness that *I* am always conscious *of* some *object*. This property of consciousness is known as its "intentional" structure, and it is a universal feature of all consciousness. Consciousness always intends or "stretches towards" an object. When I believe, I believe something; when I love, I love something; when I imagine, I imagine something; when I desire, I desire something, etc. It was Franz Brentano (1838–1917) who first brought this property of consciousness to the attention of philosophers in nineteenth-century Germany. Husserl was one of his students, and intentionality served as the foundation for his own philosophy of consciousness. Due to the intentional structure of conscious-

The German philosopher Franz Brentano influenced such later thinkers as Sigmund Freud with his ideas about human consciousness.

308

ness, phenomenology is not only introspection in the sense of describing mental acts, but it is also a description of the objects of those mental acts.

What is the first step in the phenomenological method?

The first step in the phenomenological method is known as the phenomenological reduction or *epoché*. The word "epoché" as it is used in philosophy dates back to the ancient Greek Skeptic Pyrrho (360–270 B.C.E.), who used the word to mean a "suspension of judgment." In phenomenology, the *epoché* is the suspension of judgment about the existence of the external world or of any other claims about the objects of consciousness as they exist in themselves, apart from our consciousness of them. Husserl also refers to the *epoché* as a "bracketing" of consciousness. It's as if we place quotation marks around our experience. We examine our consciousness and its objects, but we do so as if we were quoting someone else. We do not affirm or deny the objective reality of our experience but merely describe it as it appears.

What is the second step in the phenomenological method?

The second step is the eidetic reduction. The eidetic reduction is the reduction of the objects of consciousness to their essences. The essence of something is what it must be to still be itself. The eidetic reduction is performed by examining variations of the object of consciousness. If an object continues to be itself after a given property of that object is altered, then that property is not essential to it. With each variation of the object, we further remove unnecessary properties until we reduce the object to its essence. The essence is the invariant residue of the eidetic reduction.

What are some examples of the eidetic reduction and their invariant residues?

An example of an invariant residue remaining after an eidetic reduction has been performed is the idea of a table. An eidetic reduction of a table requires us to examine variations of a table. Some variations of a table can still be recognized as tables. For example, we may recognize that tables of different colors are still tables. Some variations of the idea of a table may no longer be recognized as tables. For example, we may not recognize a piece of wood without legs as a table. We would then know that legs are essential

---

Doesn't the epoché leave behind only subjective experience?

It is a misunderstanding of the epoché to say that what remains after the epoché has been performed is only a subjective experience. The objects of consciousness and even our judgments about those objects remain. Since our experience generally includes judgments about the objective reality of the objects of consciousness, we describe those judgments too. But we do not affirm or deny those judgments in our description of the experience as we do in the experience itself.

to being a table. Another example would be sets of three things, such as three apples or three oranges. The invariant residue of the eidetic reduction performed on sets of three things is the number three. The number three is the one thing that all sets of three things have in common. It is the essence of sets of three things. Without the number three, a set would not be a set of three things.

What is the third step in the phenomenological method?

The third step is the transcendental reduction. The transcendental reduction extends the epoché and the eidetic reduction to the ego, the subject of consciousness. The transcendental reduction brackets out our judgments about the objective existence of the ego in the external world. We examine the ego only as a phenomenon of consciousness. Then we perform the eidetic reduction on it. The residue that remains from this reduction is the set of invariant or essential structures of consciousness itself. It is the transcendental ego that is identical across all acts of consciousness.

What are some examples of the transcendental reduction and their invariant residues?

An example of an invariant or essential structure of consciousness itself would be its intentional structure. No matter how many variations of consciousness we examine, we always find that consciousness has an intentional structure. Another example of an invariant or essential structure of consciousness would be attention. Attention radiates out from the ego. *I* attend to *this,* not *that.* Husserl called this the "ego's ray of attention." The field of attention is differentiated into a foreground, which is at the center of the ego's ray of attention, and a background, which surrounds the foreground and helps determine what appears. For example, depending on how we direct our attention to the duck-rabbit diagram, it appears as either a duck or a rabbit. Attention can be more or less diffuse, more or less focused. The degree of focus varies, but attention itself does not. Attention is a universal or invariant feature of consciousness.

What is existential phenomenology, and how does it differ from transcendental phenomenology?

Existential phenomenology rejects the notion of the transcendental ego or of transcendental structures of consciousness in general. Existential phenomenology insists that phenomenological investigation begins and ends with consciousness as it actually exists. Existence, however, is bound and limited in many respects. Existential consciousness is bound and limited

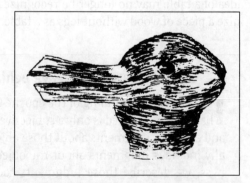

The duck-rabbit illusion in this illustration is an example of how human perception can view the same thing in more than one way.

by the body, and it experiences the world only through the body. Existential experience always occurs from a particular point of view or perspective, not from everywhere all at once. Existential consciousness is located in society and history, and it experiences the world only through its language and the culture that is transmitted to it through that language. There is no universal or god-like perspective. Existential consciousness is finite and temporal, bound by birth at one extreme and by death at the other.

What role does the body play in existential phenomenology?

Maurice Merleau-Ponty (1908–1961) was an existential phenomenologist who was particularly interested in describing perceptual experience. In his investigations, he discovered that the sentient body experienced from within, what he called the "lived body," is always implicated in our perception of objects external to our bodies. In other words, our perceptual experience of external objects is always bound up with our experience of our own bodies. Therefore, it's not possible to know external objects apart from one's own body, as they exist in themselves.

Consider the following examples. When I use a cane, my experience of the cane is so bound up with my experience of my body that I experience the cane as part of my body. I feel the concrete sidewalk at the tip of my cane as if I had touched it directly with my hand, because the cane feels like an extension of my arm. Similarly, once I become familiar with the car I am driving, it feels like an extension of my body. Even when I touch something directly with my hand, I do not feel the object by itself. I feel my hand touching the object. These examples illustrate how my experience of my body may be bound up with my perceptual experience of objects external to my body. Existential phenomenology always remains at the level of concrete embodied experience, because the object of perception can never be completely abstracted out of my body and its experience. In this sense, existential phenomenology is radically perspectival. We always perceive objects from our own perspective—that is, from the point of view of our own bodies. We never perceive objects as they are in themselves, apart from our perspective on them. By contrast, transcendental phenomenology claims to discover the essential nature of the objects (and the acts) of consciousness.

Strongly influenced by Husserl and Heidegger, Maurice Merleau-Ponty was a French phenomenological philosopher who was interested in the nature of perception.

What role does language play in existential phenomenology?

Just as we experience objects only through and in our bodies, we experience them only through and in language. To see what existential phenomenologists mean by this, consider the duck-rabbit diagram again. In transcendental phenomenology, one can switch between the duck and the rabbit by shifting one's attention. To see the duck, you focus on this part of the drawing. To see the rabbit, you focus on that part. But another way to switch between the duck and the rabbit is to utter the word "duck" to yourself if you want to see the duck, or utter the word "rabbit" if you want to see the rabbit. This is a simple example that illustrates a much more general point. How we narrate our lives, what we say about our experience, either silently to ourselves or to others, in writing or speech, determines what we experience. Existential phenomenologists therefore believe that experience is inseparable from linguistic acts. To understand those experiences, then, to give a proper phenomenological account of them, we must examine our narratives and other linguistic acts. To do this, existential phenomenologists have recruited age-old techniques of reading and interpretation of texts, including hermeneutics, which was originally developed as a tool for the interpretation of religious scriptures.

Is it possible, according to existential phenomenology, to obtain objective knowledge of the world?

The interpretation of linguistic acts can serve as a method of eidetic reduction. As we vary our interpretation of a linguistic act, the object of consciousness presented by that act will vary. We can then examine the variations to see which properties of the object vary and which do not. However, whereas essences are directly intuited in the method of transcendental phenomenology, nothing is directly intuited in existential phenomenology. All objects of consciousness are mediated by our bodies, by language, and by our history and culture. But if we can only know the object through linguistic acts, then how do we know if the variations we observe are variations of the object itself or only variations of our linguistic acts? Put another way, how do we know if language illuminates its object or constructs it?

What is the hermeneutical circle?

The hermeneutical circle refers to the iterative cycle of interpretations of a written text. Each successive interpretation of a text alters our understanding of the text and effects subsequent interpretations. So interpretation is an endless iterative cycle. More specifically, the hermeneutic circle may refer to the fact that in order to understand the text as a whole, it is necessary to understand its parts, but in order to understand the parts, it is necessary to understand their context in the whole. Again, there is an endless iterative cycle of interpretations. Thus, interpretation is not an instantaneous flash of insight but is an ongoing process. According to some hermeneutical thinkers, this is how history works. Human culture is essentially a body of texts. History, they claim, proceeds through successive waves of interpretation of those texts.

What role does the hermeneutical circle play in phenomenology?

In Edmund Husserl's phenomenology, the variations made manifest by the eidetic reduction are particular instances or parts of a series of phenomena that can be understood as parts of a unified whole because they share the same essence. In order to achieve knowledge of the essence (the whole), we must examine the variations (the parts). But in order to recognize which variations (the parts) share a common essence (the whole), we must have some understanding of what the essence is. Husserl recognized the circle in his phenomenological method. But for him it did not mean that phenomenological investigation is an endless iterative process, because he understood knowledge to be like sight, not like the interpretation of a text. The essence appears after an examination of its variations, but it does appear. Sight is direct and immediate. The object itself appears before you in Husserl's phenomenological intuition. In existential phenomenology, by contrast, we do not have direct and immediate intuition of essences. Experience is mediated by our bodies and by language, culture, and history, all of which constitute a "text" subject to interpretation. As a consequence, particularly for the phenomenologists who believed that consciousness is always mediated by language, the phenomenological method became more hermeneutical—more about the interpretation of language, culture, and history as texts—and less about first-person descriptions of consciousness.

What is deconstruction?

Deconstruction is a method of interpreting or "reading" a text that was devised by Jacques Derrida (1930–2004). Derrida was influenced in the development of his method by Heidegger's hermeneutical phenomenology (indeed the word "deconstruction" originates with Heidegger), and also by Talmudic hermeneutics, and by Ferdinand de Saussure's structuralist linguistics. Hence, deconstruction can be considered both poststructuralist and postphenomenological. Whereas according to some theories of the hermeneutical circle the process of interpretation converges after successive iterations on a stable meaning or interpretation of the text, according to Derrida the process of interpretation never does converge. Instead, the text is "deconstructed."

Jacques Derrida of France formulated the theory of deconstruction, a way of interpreting meaning behind text.

What did Derrida take from Saussure's linguistics?

Derrida took from Saussure's linguistics the idea that a text or indeed any linguistic act is composed of signs that only have meaning because of their differences to all other signs. If all the words in our language were the same, none would have any meaning. "Cat" has the meaning it does because it is not "dog" or "god" or any other word. For this reason, the meaning of the signs that compose a text can never be known until all other signs are known and interpreted, since the meaning of a sign is constituted by its differences to all other signs. Hence, the hermeneutical circle: No one sign can be interpreted until all signs are interpreted. And all signs cannot be interpreted until each one is interpreted. However, according to Derrida, the hermeneutical process can never end. The process of interpretation never converges on a stable meaning. As Derrida puts it, playing on the French word *différer*, which means both "to defer" and "to differ," because the meaning of a text is dependent on the difference between signs, meaning is always *deferred*. Meaning is never *present*.

What is the metaphysics of presence?

According to Derrida, the entire history of Western philosophy from Plato to Husserl is committed to the idea that meaning can present itself to us directly and without mediation, whether that be a perceptual object, a material object, or an ideal concept or essence. This commitment is at the root of what Derrida called "logocentrism" and the "metaphysics of presence." However, according to Derrida, we can never achieve direct and unmediated intuition of a meaning outside the text.

How does Derrida's method of deconstruction defeat the metaphysics of presence?

Derrida's method of deconstruction is meant to defeat the metaphysics of presence. It is a method of interpreting a text that shows how all texts ultimately self-destruct. Derrida's method begins by identifying the binary oppositions upon which a given text depends. According to Derrida, any text or system of signs depends upon the differences between signs, but the most elementary difference is that of binary opposition. In philosophical texts we find, for example, the following binary oppositions: good/bad, mind/body, subject/object, rational/emotional, presence/absence, signifier/signified, being/becoming, masculine/feminine, etc. Moreover, according to Derrida, binary oppositions are hierarchical. One member of the binary pair is always elevated above the other. However, this hierarchical relationship is never stable. Successive interpretations of the text show how the hierarchy can be inverted, and then inverted again. All texts are like the duck-rabbit diagram. Not only does our interpretation of the text never stabilize, but it alternates between binary oppositions, thus defeating the attempt to establish hierarchical relations in the text.

What is the value of deconstruction?

Deconstruction destructures the text. Depending on your perspective, deconstruction is either a nihilistic destruction of meaning or a liberation from hierarchical structures. In either case, one could argue, this is the condition of our times, the "post-modern condition."

What is the postmodern condition?

The "postmodern condition" is a term coined by the French philosopher Jean-François Lyotard (1924–1998) in his book *The Postmodern Condition: A Report on Knowledge* (1979). According to Lyotard, the postmodern condition is the condition that society has increasingly found itself in since the end of World War II, in which there has been a loss of faith in what Lyotard calls *grand* or *meta-narratives*. A *grand narrative* or *meta-narrative* is a narrative that claims universal truth and validity. In the absence of grand narratives, all that remain are *micronarratives,* whose truth and validity may be recognized by particular communities of people but which are not universally recognized. Lyotard was a director of the International College of Philosophy founded by Derrida. If Derrida attempted to deconstruct all the grand narratives of modern society, then Lyotard described what remained after they were gone. However, Lyotard clung to one universal ethical principle: that grand narratives must never override micronarratives. Human culture should consist of a diverse collection of microcultures, not a universal or cosmopolitan culture, and there should be no grand narrative to which these microcultures are subordinate. Since the time of Lyotard's book on postmodernism, post-colonial and social justice scholars have built upon his work and the work of other French poststructuralists by arguing that all the grand narratives of the past were constructed by white, heterosexual, cis-gendered men. Therefore, deconstructing the grand narratives of the past will usher in a new multicultural society in which formerly suppressed micronarratives and their associated communities will be liberated.

Who was Michel Foucault?

Michel Foucault (1926–1984) was a French philosopher who wrote about power in society and its relationship to knowledge. He came out of the Continental philosophical tradition and was influenced by Heidegger, Nietzsche, and structuralism. His theory of knowledge shared with other poststructuralist thinkers the conclusion that it is not possible to obtain objective knowledge of the world or of the human beings in it. According to Foucault, what purports to be objective knowledge is constructed by pervasive systems of power for the purpose of social control. Foucault was a leftist throughout his life. Like nearly all French intellectuals in the 1950s, he was a member of the Communist Party. Though he grew disillusioned by the Party, he re-

Objective knowledge is, according to French philosopher Michel Foucault, impossible to achieve because knowledge cannot be separated from the power structures of society.

mained engaged with left-wing causes throughout his life, among them penal reform, antiracist action, and gay liberation. Foucault himself was gay. He enjoyed sadomasochistic sex clubs in San Francisco and spoke highly of them. Unfortunately, he engaged in unprotected sex before the dangers of HIV were known and died of the virus in 1984. Foucault has influenced a wide range of academic disciplines in the humanities and social sciences. His theory of how power constructs narratives, or as he called it, "epistemic discourse," influenced postcolonial theory. He has also had a profound influence on gender theory, queer studies, and third-wave feminism. For example, he has influenced the important feminist philosopher and gender theorist Judith Butler (1956–).

What, according to Foucault, is the difference between power in the *ancien régime* and power in the modern world?

According to Foucault, power in the *ancien régime* (the period in French history between the late Middle Ages and the French Revolution in 1789) was fundamentally different from power in the modern world. In the *ancien régime*, power is centralized in the body of the king. In the *ancien régime,* it is the king and his power that is made known and visible. Thus, in the opening pages of *Discipline and Punish* (1975), Foucault describes the public execution in 1757 of Robert-François Damiens. In the *ancien régime*, executions were performed in public for the purpose of making the king's terrifying power known and visible to all. In modern society, on the other hand, it is not power that is made known and visible but those who are subject to power, and especially those who transgress social norms and boundaries (such as the mentally ill, homosexuals, or criminals). In modern society, social control depends on systems of knowledge (such as the social sciences) about those who are subject to power rather than those who wield power or power itself. According to Foucault, in modern society, power is not exercised by one or a few individuals at the top of a social hierarchy but is dispersed throughout society and its institutions. Power in modern society is exercised by the subjects of power themselves, who in doing so sustain the system of power that controls them.

To illustrate his theory of power in modern society, Foucault refers his readers to the Panopticon, a prison designed by the utilitarian philosopher Jeremy Bentham (1748–1832). The Panopticon is constructed in such a way that the guards in the central tower can see the prisoners, but the prisoners cannot see the guards or each other. Because the prisoners cannot see if they are being watched or not, they must behave at all times as if they were. Thus, they, in effect, police themselves and can even be recruited to police other prisoners. In such a system, it is the subjects of power who are made known and visible, not power itself. Nor is power concentrated in the hands of a few centralized authorities. There is hardly any difference between the guards and the prisoners, and power is dispersed throughout society.

According to Foucault, what is the relationship between knowledge and power?

According to Foucault, knowledge and power are merely two sides of the same coin. They function together, and neither could exist without the other. Knowledge—or what Fou-

316

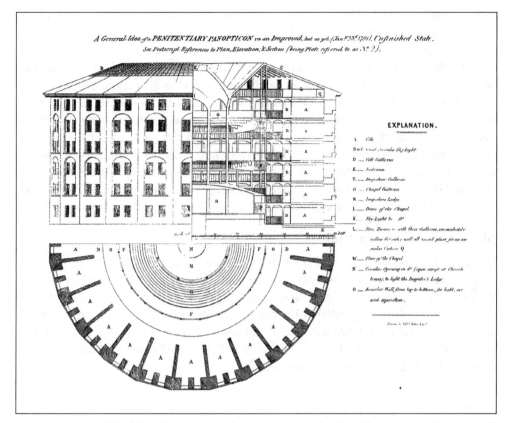

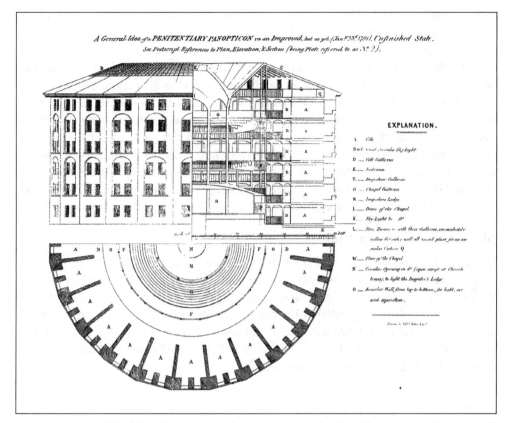

In the prison designed by philosopher Jeremy Bentham, prisoners are placed in cells in a circle on the outer wall, where they can always be seen by a guard but where they cannot see each other. This affects their behavior so that they actually police themselves because they do not know if they are being watched or not.

cault interchangeably calls "epistemic discourse"—both produces power and is constructed by it. Knowledge produces power by making it appear to be legitimate. Power produces knowledge by producing systems of epistemic discourse (statements that are asserted to be true). Systems of epistemic discourse—such as psychiatry, pedagogy, or theories of criminal justice or industrial management—are used to control the mentally ill, students, criminals, or workers. Institutions such as mental hospitals, schools, the criminal justice system, and the industrial workplace in turn produce systems of epistemic discourse that perpetuate their power. There is no knowledge outside of this system of power-knowledge. Because knowledge cannot exist apart from power, there is no objective knowledge. If we take knowledge to be statements that are not only asserted to be true but that are objectively true, then there is no knowledge at all according to Foucault.

What did Foucault and Chomsky argue about in 1971?

In a videotaped debate available today on YouTube, Michel Foucault and Noam Chomsky (1928–) argued about whether justice exists as a transcendent and universal ideal and whether it can be known apart from power. For Chomsky it was critical that justice exist as a transcendent and universal ideal that can in principle be known apart from power. Chomsky acknowledged that we may not in fact possess knowledge of such an ideal, but he argued that we can aspire to it and that we can at least obtain a better understanding of justice. Such a better understanding of justice is necessary, Chomsky believed, to create a better society. Foucault, however, denied that knowledge of an ideal justice, or even of a better justice, is possible or that it is necessary to create a better society. For Foucault, there is no transcendent or universal truth of any kind; there is only a competition between different systems of power-knowledge or epistemic discourse—what Lyotard called "micronarratives"—such as the class struggle between the proletariat and the bourgeoisie. Foucault, then, would agree with Thrasymachus, who boldly declared in Plato's *Republic* that justice is whatever those who seize power say it is.

What was Foucault's method?

Foucault's method of philosophical research was historical. In his early work, he called what he was doing an "archaeology of knowledge," but in his later work he adopted Nietzsche's term "genealogy," as if he were tracing lines of descent from ancient ancestors. Both metaphors suggest that Foucault was digging up the ancient roots of our contemporary systems of knowledge, or "epistemic discourse." Indeed, the final two books that Foucault completed before he died in 1984 were historical studies of sexual discourse in the ancient Greco-Roman world.

Glossary

active intellect or agent intellect—in Aristotle, the act of knowing (*noesis*) itself, apart from the content of knowledge (*noema*)

adiaphora—in Cynicism, indifference to the external conditions of one's life

aesthetics—the study of art and beauty

aísthisi—sensation or perception

akrasia—in Aristotle, the failure of desire to listen to and obey practical reason

allotrion—in Cynicism, what is external or foreign to the self

anaídeia—shamelessness; the Cynic learns to become independent of social goods by practicing shamelessness

analogía—analogy, proportion, or ratio

analogy—in Plato, an analogy shows how two things are related to one another in the same way as two other things, as in the formula, *a* is to *b* as *c* is to *d*; the prime example of an analogy in Plato is an equal proportion or ratio, as in the mathematical formula $a/b = c/d$

analytic philosophy—type of philosophy popular in Anglo-American universities since the twentieth century that is based on the method of logical analysis

apeiron—the unlimited; i.e., that without limits, ends, or boundaries; according to Anaximander, the *apeiron* is the source and origin of everything that exists

apodeixis—a demonstration or deductive argument whose conclusion is necessarily true

apodictic—logically demonstrable and therefore certain and necessarily true

aporia—an impasse or impassable situation, resulting in a state of perplexity, confusion, or puzzlement

apraxia objection—the charge that the suspension of judgment about all truth claims would lead to inaction

arche—(plural is archai) source, origin or beginning, and in the writings of the first philosophers, element or first principle; may also mean rule or ruler arête—virtue or excellence

aristocracy—from the ancient Greek word *aristokratía*, meaning rule by the best or most excellent

arithmetic mean (also known as average)—the sum of any sequence of numbers divided by the number of numbers in that sequence

áskēsis—in Cynicism, a rigorous course of disciplined exercise and training designed to build character

ataraxia—freedom from anxiety or disturbance

atoms—indivisible units of matter; in ancient Greek, *atomos*

autárkeia—self-sufficiency

aversions—(*proskopai*) in Stoicism, hatred of things external to the self that are not intrinsically bad

categorical statement—a statement that asserts or denies that all or some members of one category are members of another category

cognitive impression—in Stoicism, an impression that is known with certainty to be true; the ancient Greek word was *kataleptic phantasia*

cosmopolitanism—the belief that all the people of the world belong to one universal community

cosmos—an ordered world

decad—the perfect Pythagorean number of ten

declarative statement—a statement of the form S is P that asserts something which is either true or false

deconstruction—a method of interpreting texts devised by Jacques Derrida that subverts hierarchical structures and leaves the meaning of the text forever delayed or "deferred"

deductive logic—rules for reasoning from premises to a conclusion

democracy—rule by the people or by the many

dialectical logic—rules for reasoning between two opposed arguments

dialectics—in Plato, a philosophical dialogue by question and answer that seeks a mental or intellectual intuition (*noesis*) of excellence (*arête*) that can be expressed in a rational, verbal account (*logos*)

dianoia—discursive thought; in Plato, deductive reasoning in mathematics from premises to conclusions

doxa—belief or common opinion

dunamis—potentiality, what has the potential to exist, but which does not actually exist

elenchus—the Socratic method of dialectical reasoning that proceeds by question and answer and ends in a state of *aporia*

empiricism—a theory of knowledge according to which all knowledge comes from the senses

energeia—in Aristotle, actuality, what actually exists, an act, deed, or work, as opposed to potentiality, what potentially exists

entelechia—in Aristotle, an act, a deed, or a work that maintains an end, purpose, or goal

epistémē—knowledge in the truest sense

epistemic discourse—anything said or written that purports to be true and to convey knowledge

epistemology—a theory of knowledge that seeks to determine what knowledge is, whether we can obtain knowledge, and how we can obtain it

epoché—suspension of judgment

eros—the love of beauty

essence—the invariant attributes of a thing; the attributes a thing must have to be what it is

ethics—a theory about what is right and wrong, good and bad

eudaimonia—happiness or living well

eupatheia—in Stoicism, a good emotion produced by giving assent to a true hormetic impression (i.e., an impression that accurately presents its object as being either good or bad)

existentialism—a popular philosophy after World War II that focused on questions related to the existence of the individual, such as mortality and the ethical imperative to live authentically or true to oneself

existential phenomenology—a type of phenomenology that denies that it is possible to obtain knowledge that is not conditioned by one's own individual standpoint or perspective in the world

form—a Platonic form or idea is an ideal object of knowledge grasped by means of immediate intellectual intuition

geometric mean—the nth root of the product of any sequence of n numbers

geometric proportion—the equal ratio of every two successive numbers in a geometric sequence or progression

geometric sequence or progression—a sequence of numbers in which the ratio of every two successive numbers is equal

gymnosophists—the naked philosophers of ancient India

harmonic mean—twice the product of any two numbers divided by their sum, i.e., $2ab / (a + b)$

harmonic sequence—any sequence of numbers in which each number of the sequence is the harmonic mean of the number that came before it in the sequence and the one that follows it

hegemonikon—the ruling or commanding faculty of the soul; the rational mind; the Stoics identified the *hegemonikon* with the self or ego—in other words, the *hegemonikon* is who we are

henosis—unity with the divine, the goal of Neoplatonism

hermeneutical phenomenology—a type of phenomenology that uses the methods of hermeneutics to describe experience, as if experience itself were a text

hermeneutics—the theory of how to interpret written works or texts

hexis—a character trait

homonoia—concord, agreement, and unanimity; in Aristotle, political friendship (*politikē philia*), i.e., friendship between citizens of a political community such as the Greek *polis* or city-state

hormetic impression—(*phantasia hormetikê*) in Stoicism, an impression that produces an impulse (*hormê*) to act

idealism—the philosophy that holds that only ideas are real or knowable; the opposite of materialism

impression—in Hellenistic philosophy, a mere appearance or seeming to be something

indifferents—(*adiaphora*) in Stoicism, anything external to the self's own power of cognitive judgment; according to the Stoics, *indifferents* are neither inherently good nor bad

inductive logic—rules for reasoning from a finite set of cases to an additional case or to a universal claim (for example, reasoning from the observation of seven white swans to the claim that the eighth swan observed will be white or that all swans are white)

infirmities—(*arrōstēmata*) in Stoicism, a mania for things external to the self

intentionality—the structure of consciousness according to which I (the subject of consciousness) am always conscious *of* some *object*

karteria—in Cynicism, the virtue of endurance, perseverance, and self-control

kenòs—empty, vain, or futile; in Hellenistic philosophy, *kenòs* may also refer to the void or empty space

kinetic pleasure—in Epicurean philosophy, the pleasure felt while performing an activity

koinōníā—community or friendly association

lekta—in Stoicism, meaning or sense, the "sayables" or "things said"

logarithmic spiral—a spiral with a constant curvature

logic—rules for the best use of the human capacity to reason

logike psyche—the rational soul; the human capacity for reason; located in the *hegemonikon*, the ruling part of the soul.

322   **logos**—reason or a reasoned account

materialism—the belief that only matter and the material world are real

matter—the amorphous stuff that the physical universe is made out of; in ancient Greek, *hyle*

metaphysics—the study of reality; originally, in Aristotle, metaphysics referred to the study of things beyond the changing world of nature, such as God and the eternal attributes of being

methexis—an ancient Greek word that referred to the participation of the audience in the events on a theatrical stage but that in Plato was used as a metaphor to describe the relationship between the forms and physical things and events

mimesis—an ancient Greek word that meant imitation as on a theatrical stage but that in Plato was used as a metaphor to describe the relationship between the forms and physical things or events

mode—(*tròpos*) in Pyrrhonist Skepticism, a type of dialectical argument that leads to the suspension of judgment (*epoché*) regarding the truth or falsity of a proposition

morality—in philosophy, this term is usually used interchangeably with ethics

noema—the object of cognition; the content of what is known by the mind or intellect (*nous*)

noesis—cognition; the act of knowing by the mind or intellect (*nous*)

nous—mind or intellect

octave invariance—the property of the musical scale according to which the same notes repeat in every octave

oikeíon—in Cynicism, what belongs essentially to the self or is inherent to it

oligarchy—rule by a few wealthy families

ontology—theory of "being" or of what it is to "be" something; theory of the things that are

parrhēsía—in Cynicism, the principle of speaking freely, openly, frankly, and without reserve

particular—an actually existing individual thing, such as this pen in my hand, or my neighbor Tom

passive intellect—in Aristotle, the passive potential to receive the forms

pathos—(plural is *pathê*) in Stoicism, a bad emotion that one suffers

peripatetic philosophers—Aristotelian philosophers; the word "peripatetic" is from the Greek *peripatos*, meaning a covered walkway or a conversation had while walking because the Aristotelians talked about philosophy while walking under a covered walkway in their school, the Lyceum

phantasia—imagination

phenomena—(also transliterated as *phainomena*) appearances or what seem to be the case; *phenomenon* is the singular for one appearance

phenomenology—type of philosophy popular in universities since the second half of the twentieth century that is based on a systematic method of examining first person experience

philia—friendship

phronēsis—practical wisdom

physis—nature or the physical world; *physis* may also refer to what a thing is by nature (i.e., the nature of a thing); in Aristotle, a physical thing's internal principle of change

plausible belief—(pithanòn) in Academic Skepticism, a belief that is persuasive and probably true given the available evidence, but not certain

pneuma—"breath," but it could also connote "spirit" or "soul" because breath like spirit or soul is what gives things life

poiesis—making

polis—the city-state

ponos—in Cynicism and Stoicism, the virtue of painful effort and hard work

postmodernism—the loss of faith in grand or universal narratives and the consequent fragmentation and decentering of the culture

praxis—acting or doing

primary substance or being—in Aristotle, a particular thing; the subject of a declarative statement

prime matter—in Aristotle, pure potential without any actual form; the ultimate "stuff" of the universe

prime mover—in Aristotle, the prime mover is God; the prime mover is eternal and unchanging, the highest good, and the ultimate end or purpose of the universe; the prime mover is pure form, fully actualized, and has no unrealized potential or material component

proclivities—(euemptōsiai) in Stoicism, being prone to certain irrational passions or bad emotions

prolepsis—a preconception; in Epicurean philosophy, a concept that we possess prior to a given experience but that shapes our understanding of it

propatheia—in Stoicism, a mere feeling; an assent to a *propatheia* makes it an emotion

propensities—(aphormai) in Stoicism, innate tendencies to act in a certain way

proposition—the idea or truth claim expressed in a declarative sentence

propositional logic—the study of arguments constructed out of propositions and the connective terms "if, then," "and," "or," and "not"; for example, the argument, if *P* then *Q*, but not *Q*, therefore *P*

providence—God's foreknowledge of future events; in ancient Greek, *pronoia*

psyche—soul, though generally without the spiritual connotations that the English word has

psychologism—the reduction of logic to psychology with the claim that the rules of logic can be derived from a study of how our minds do in fact work; psychologism was rejected by the founders of both analytic philosophy and phenomenology

quadrivium—the Pythagorean curriculum made up of arithmetic, geometry, music, and astronomy

rationalism—a theory of knowledge according to which some knowledge comes from the mind, independent of the sense organs

romanticism—a philosophical movement opposed to the scientific and industrial revolutions that included a renewed appreciation of nature, emotional expression, and medieval society

scholasticism—philosophy of the late Middle Ages and Renaissance period based on a Catholic interpretation of Aristotle

secondary substance or being—in Aristotle, the essence of a thing; may be predicated of a particular thing in a declarative statement

sicknesses of the mind—(nosēmata) in Stoicism, love of things external to the self that are not inherently good

sophia—wisdom

sōphrosynē—temperance

static pleasure—in Epicurean philosophy, the pleasure of being in an unchanging condition free of pain or disturbances

structuralism—a method of philosophic inquiry that focuses on the structure or relationship between the parts of a system rather than the parts themselves or the history of the system

structuralist linguistics—a theory of linguistics according to which signs (units of language) have meaning only because of their structure or relationship to other signs

subsistence—in Stoicism, a derivative mode of being or existence, dependent on the existence of material bodies

syllogism—a deductive argument composed of categorical statements

symbolic logic—a type of deductive logic that prescribes rules for reasoning based on the form of arguments alone apart from their content, and that replaces meaningful statements in ordinary language with symbols

techne—knowledge of how to make something

telos—end, goal, or purpose

tension—the Stoic concept of a force that holds a complex system together as a unified whole; in ancient Greek, *tonos*

tetractys—a triangular configuration of ten dots that the Pythagoreans believed held all the secrets of the universe

tetrapharmakos—the fourfold Epicurean remedy for suffering

theoria—intellectual contemplation

timocracy—rule by those who are honorable

transcendental phenomenology—a type of phenomenology that seeks to describe the universal structures of consciousness

tyranny—rule by an unprincipled and undisciplined individual who seeks nothing but his own pleasure and total control over everyone else

universal—a category, species, type, or kind of thing to which many particular things may belong; for example, Lassie and Rover both belong to the category "dog"

utilitarianism—the ethical theory that the good is whatever produces the greatest happiness for the greatest number of persons

valid argument—a deductive argument whose conclusion must be true if its premises are true

void—empty space

Further Reading

ANALYTIC PHILOSOPHY

Austin, J. L. *How to Do Things with Words*. Cambridge: Harvard University Press, 1975.

Ayer, Alfred Jules. *Language, Truth and Logic*. New York: Dover Publications, 1952.

Collingwood, R. G. *An Essay on Philosophical Method*. Oxford: Oxford University Press, 1933.

Moore, G. E. *Philosophical Studies*. Cambridge, UK: Cambridge University Press, 2007.

Russell, Bertrand. *The Basic Writings of Bertrand Russell*. New York: Routledge, 2002.

Russell, Bertrand. *A History of Western Philosophy, and Its Connection with Political and Social Circumstances from the Earliest Times to the Present Day*. New York: Simon & Schuster, 1945.

Ryle, Gilbert. *Collected Essays 1929–1968: Collected Papers Volume 2*. London and New York: Routledge, 2009; Hutchinson, 1971.

Wittgenstein, Ludwig. *Philosophical Investigations: The English Text of the Third Edition*. Translated by G. E. M. Anscombe. New York: Macmillan Publishing Co., 1953.

Wittgenstein, Ludwig. *Tractatus Logico-Philosophicus*. Translated by D. F. Pears & B. F. McGuinness, with an introduction by Bertrand Russell. London & Henley: Routledge & Kegan Paul, 1961.

CONTINENTAL PHILOSOPHY

Foucault, Michel. *Discipline and Punish: The Birth of the Prison*. Translated by Alan Sheridan. New York: Vintage Books, 1979.

Foucault, Michel. *The History of Sexuality, Volume 1: An Introduction*. Translated by Robert Hurely. New York: Vintage Books, 1980.

Foucault, Michel. *The History of Sexuality, Volume 2: The Use of Pleasure*. Translated by Robert Hurley. New York: Vintage Books, 1986.

Foucault, Michel. *The History of Sexuality, Volume 3: The Care of the Self*. Translated by Robert Hurley. New York: Vintage Books, 1988.

Foucault, Michel. *Power/Knowledge: Selected Interviews and Other Writings 1972–1977*. Edited by Colin Gordon. New York: Pantheon Books, 1980.

Heidegger, Martin. *Being and Time*. Translated by John Macquarrie & Edward Robinson. New York: Harper & Row, 1962.

Heidegger, Martin. *Ponderings II–VI: Black Notebooks 1931–1938*. Translated by Richard Rojcewicz. Bloomington and Indianapolis: Indiana University Press, 2016.

Heidegger, Martin. *Ponderings VII–XI: Black Notebooks 1938–1939*. Translated by Richard Rojcewicz. Bloomington and Indianapolis: Indiana University Press, 2017.

Heidegger, Martin. *Ponderings XII–XV: Black Notebooks 1939–1941*. Translated by Richard Rojcewicz. Bloomington and Indianapolis: Indiana University Press, 2017.

Heidegger, Martin. *The Question Concerning Technology, and Other Essays*. Translated by William Lovitt. New York: Harper Torchbooks, 1977.

Heidegger, Martin. "Why Do I Stay in the Provinces?" Translated by Thomas Sheehan. In *Philosophical and Political Writings*, pp. 16–18, edited by Manfred Stassen. New York and London: Continuum, 2003.

Husserl, Edmund. *Cartesian Meditations: An Introduction to Phenomenology*. Translated by Dorion Cairns. The Hague, Netherlands: Martinus Nijhoff, 1977.

Husserl, Edmund. *Ideas Pertaining to a Pure Phenomenology and to a Phenomenological Philosophy, First Book: General Introduction to a Pure Phenomenology*. Translated by F. Kersten. The Hague, Netherlands: Martinus Nijhoff Publishers, 1983.

Ihde, Don. *Experimental Phenomenology: An Introduction*. New York: Paragon Books, 1979.

Ihde, Don. *Technology and the Lifeworld: From Garden to Earth*. Bloomington and Indianapolis: Indiana University Press, 1990.

Merleau-Ponty, Maurice. *Phenomenology of Perception*. Translated by Colin Smith. London and Henley: Routledge & Kegan Paul, 1962.

Saussure, Ferdinand de. *Course in General Linguistics*. Edited by Charles Bally and Albert Sechehaye with Albert Riedlinger. Translated by Wade Baskin. New York: McGraw-Hill Book Company, 1966; The Philosophical Library, Inc., 1959.

Sheridan, Alan. *Michel Foucault: The Will to Truth*. London and New York: Tavistock Publications, 1980.

ANCIENT GREEK PHILOSOPHY

Copleston, Frederick. *A History of Philosophy, Vol. 1: Greece and Rome from the Pre-Socratics to Plotinus*. New York: Image, 1993.

Jones, W. T. *The Classical Mind: A History of Western Philosophy*, Second Edition. New York: Harcourt Brace Jovanovich, 1970.

PHILOSOPHY BEFORE SOCRATES

Burnet, John. *Early Greek Philosophy*. Cleveland and New York: Meridian Books, the World Publishing Company, 1957; original edition 1892.

Kahn, Charles H. *The Art and Thought of Heraclitus: An Edition of the Fragments with Translation and Commentary*. Cambridge University Press, 1979.

Kahn, Charles H. *Pythagoras and the Pythagoreans: A Brief History*. Indianapolis and Cambridge: Hackett Publishing Company, Inc., 2001.

Wheelwright, Philip, Editor. *The Presocratics*. Indianapolis: Bobbs-Merrill Educational Publishing, 1960.

SOCRATES AND PLATO

Havelock, Eric. *Preface to Plato*. Cambridge and London: The Belknap Press of Harvard University Press, 1963.

Heelan, Patrick A. ìMusic as Basic Metaphor and Deep Structure in Plato and in Ancient Cultures,î in the *Journal of Social and Biological Structures*, Vol. 2, No. 4, pp. 279–291, 1979.

McClain, Ernest G. *The Myth of Invariance: The Origin of the Gods, Mathematics, and Music from the Rg Veda to Plato*. New York: N. Hays, 1976.

McClain, Ernest G. *The Pythagorean Plato: Prelude to the Song Itself*. Stony Brook, NY: N. Hays; Boulder, Colorado: Distributed by Great Eastern Book Co., 1977.

Plato. *Cratylus; Parmenides; Greater Hippias; Lesser Hippias*. Greek with English translations on facing pages by H. N. Fowler. Cambridge, MA: Harvard University Press; London: W. Heinemann, 1977; first published 1926.

Plato. *Five Dialogues: Euthyphro, Apology, Crito, Meno, Phaedo*. Translated by G. M. A. Grube. Indianapolis and Cambridge: Hackett Publishing Company, Inc., 1981.

Plato. *Gorgias*. Translated by Walter Hamilton. New York: Penguin Books, 1960.

Plato. *Phaedrus*. Translated with an Introduction by W. C. Helmbold and W. G. Rabinowitz. Indianapolis: The Library of Liberal Arts, Bobbs-Merrill Educational Publishing, 1956.

Plato. *Plato's Theory of Knowledge* (The *Theaetetus* and the *Sophist* of Plato). Translated by Francis M. Cornford. Indianapolis: The Library of Liberal Arts, Bobbs-Merrill Educational Publishing, 1957.

Plato. *The Republic*. Translated by Richard W. Sterling and William C. Scott. New York and London: W. W. Norton & Company, 1985.

Plato. *Symposium*. Translated by Benjamin Jowett. Indianapolis: Bobbs-Merrill Educational Publishing, 1948, 1956.

Plato. *Timaeus*. Translated by Francis M. Cornford. Indianapolis: Bobbs-Merrill Educational Publishing, 1959.

ARISTOTLE AND THE AGE OF ALEXANDER THE GREAT

Adler, Mortimer J. *Aristotle for Everybody: Difficult Thought Made Easy*. New York: Simon & Schuster, 1978.

Aristotle. *The Basic Works of Aristotle*. Edited and with an Introduction by Richard McKeon. New York: Random House, 1941.

Aristotle. *The Complete Works of Aristotle*, Volume 2. The Revised Oxford Translation, edited by Jonathan Barnes. Princeton: Princeton University Press, 1984.

Arrian. *The Campaigns of Alexander*. Translated by Aubrey De Selincourt. Revised, with a new introduction and notes, by J. R. Hamilton. London: Penguin Books, 1971.

Barnes, Jonathan. *Aristotle: A Very Short Introduction*. New York: Oxford University Press, 2000.

Beckwith, Christopher I. *Greek Buddha: Pyrrho's Encounter with Early Buddhism in Central Asia*. Princeton, NJ: Princeton University Press, 2015.

Gimbutas, Marija, Miriam Robbins Dexter, and Karlene Jones-Bley. *The Kurgan Culture and the Indo Europeanization of Europe: Selected Articles from 1952 to 1993*. Washington, DC: Institute for the Study of Man, 1997.

Kuzminski, Adrian. *Pyrrhonism: How the Ancient Greeks Reinvented Buddhism*. Lanham, MD: Lexington Books, Roman & Littlefield Publishers, 2008.

Plutarch. *The Age of Alexander: Ten Greek Lives: Artaxerxes, Pelopidas, Dion, Timoleon, Demosthenes, Phocion, Alexander, Eumenes, Demetrius, Pyrrhus*. Edited by Timothy E. Duff. Translated by Timothy E. Duff and Ian Scott-Kilvert. London: Penguin Books, 2012, 1973.

Plutarch. *The Life of Alexander the Great*. Translated by John Dryden. Edited by Arthur Hugh Clough. Introduction by Victor Davis Hanson. New York: The Modern Library, 2004.

Plutarch. *Moralia, Volume IV: Roman Questions. Greek Questions. Greek and Roman Parallel Stories. On the Fortune of the Romans. On the Fortune or the Virtue of Alexander. Were the Athenians More Famous in War or in Wisdom?* Translated by Frank Cole Babbitt. Cambridge, MA: Loeb Classical Library, Harvard University Press, 1936.

Robinson, Timothy A. *Aristotle in Outline*. Indianapolis and Cambridge: Hackett Publishing Company, Inc.: 1995.

Shields, Christopher. *Aristotle*, Second Edition. London and New York: Routledge, 2014.

Strabo. *The Geography of Strabo: An English Translation, with Introduction and Notes*. Translated by Duane W. Roller. Cambridge: Cambridge University Press, 2014.

HELLENISTIC PHILOSOPHY

Adamson, Peter. *Philosophy in the Hellenistic and Roman Worlds: A History of Philosophy without Any Gaps, Volume 2*. Oxford: Oxford University Press, 2015.

Cicero. *Cicero on the Emotions: Tusculan Disputations 3 and 4*. Translated by Margaret Graver. Chicago: University of Chicago Press, 2002.

Cicero. *On the Republic; and, On the Laws*. Translated by David Fott. Ithaca: Cornell University Press, 2014.

Diogenes Laertius. *Lives of Eminent Philosophers*, Volume 1, Books 1–5 (Loeb Classical Library No. 184). Translated with facing Greek text by R. D. Hicks. Cambridge: Harvard University Press, 1925.

Diogenes Laertius. *Lives of Eminent Philosophers*, Volume 2, Books 6–10 (Loeb Classical Library No. 185). Translated with facing Greek text by R. D. Hicks. Cambridge: Harvard University Press, 1925.

Dobbin, Robert, Editor and Translator. *The Cynic Philosophers from Diogenes to Julian.* Selections of ancient writings by and about Cynic philosophers. London: Penguin Books, 2012.

Epictetus. *Discourses and Selected Writings.* Translated by Robert Dobbin. London: Penguin Books, 2008.

Epictetus. *The Handbook (The Encheirideon).* Translated by Nicholas P. White. Indianapolis: Hackett Publishing Company, 1983.

Graver, Margaret. *Stoicism and Emotion.* Chicago and London: The University of Chicago Press, 2007.

Inwood, Brad, and L. P. Gerson, Translators. *Hellenistic Philosophy: Introductory Readings,* Second Edition. Selections of ancient writings by and about Hellenistic philosophers. Indianapolis and Cambridge: Hackett Publishing Company, 1997.

Lucretius. *The Nature of Things.* Translated by Alicia Stallings. New York: Penguin, 2007.

Marcus Aurelius. *Meditations.* A New Translation, with an Introduction by Gregory Hays. New York: Modern Library, 2002.

Schofield, Malcolm. *The Stoic Idea of the City.* With a new Foreword by Martha C. Nussbaum and a new epilogue by the author. Chicago and London: The University of Chicago Press, 1999. Original edition, Cambridge: Cambridge University Press, 1991.

Sellars, John. *Hellenistic Philosophy.* Oxford: Oxford University Press, 2018.

Seneca. *Anger, Mercy, Revenge.* (The Complete Works of Lucius Annaeus Seneca) Translated by Robert A. Kaster and Martha C. Nussbaum. Chicago: University of Chicago Press, 2010.

Seneca. *Dialogues and Essays.* A new translation by John Davie. Oxford, England: Oxford University Press, 2007.

Sextus Empiricus. *Outlines of Pyrrhonism.* Translated by R. G. Bury. Cambridge, MA, and London, England: The Loeb Classical Library, Harvard University Press, 1933.

Thonemann, Peter. *The Hellenistic Age.* Oxford, England: Oxford University Press, 2016.

Index

Note: (ill.) indicates photos and illustrations.

A

theory of physics and existence, 218 (ill.), 218–20
theory of the gods, 231
theory of the soul, 229–31
theory of the universe, 220

Epicurus
Hellenistic philosophy, 199, 201–3, 205, 218–23, 225–31
Pre-Socratic philosophy, 22
statue, 201 (ill.)

epilupia (grief), 276

Epirus [historical], 101, 104, 106

epistagapēmagapē (scientific knowledge), 163–64, 262. See also epistemology

epistemology. See also knowledge
basics of philosophy, 3–4
Hellenistic philosophy, 200, 234, 261–62, 290
philosophy of Aristotle and Alexander the Great, 130, 134, 136–37, 143, 147, 163–64
philosophy of Socrates and Plato, 64
philosophy since the twentieth century, 316–18

epithumia (lust), 252, 270. See also lust

epoché (suspension of judgment), 120–21, 283, 292, 309–10. See also suspension of judgment

Er, 70

Erasistratus of Ceos, 207, 210, 214, 215 (ill.), 217

Eratosthenes, 114–19, 116 (ill.), 206–7

Eratosthenes Teaching in Alexandria, 116 (ill.)

érgon (function), 156–57, 169–70. See also functionality

erides (quarrels), 276

eris (strife), 184, 277

eromenos (boylover), 282

éros (erotic passion), 68–69, 169, 179, 270

erotic friendship, 279–80

ether, element of, 14, 17, 20, 148–49

ethical reasoning, 164–65, 165 (ill.)

ethics
of Aristotle, 163–78
basics of philosophy, 3–4, 6–7
Epicurean, 223–29
Hellenistic philosophy, 199–200, 205, 212, 223–29, 234, 238–40, 242, 249, 251–53, 255, 263, 269–78, 294, 298
illustration, 165 (ill.)
philosophy of Aristotle and Alexander the Great, 98, 104, 115, 127, 131–32, 134, 163–80, 189, 195
philosophy of Socrates and Plato, 39–42, 64–67
philosophy since the twentieth century, 315
of Plato, 64–67
Pre-Socratic philosophy, 20, 22–23
of Socrates, 40–42
of the Stoics, 269–76

Ethiopia, 22

ethos (habit), 169. See also habit

Euboea Island, 130

Eubulides of Miletus, 250

Eubulus, 124–25

Euclid, 207

Euclidean geometry, 144

Euclides of Megara, 250

eudaimonia (well-lived life)
Hellenistic philosophy, 224, 240, 242, 263, 267, 269, 272, 295
philosophy of Aristotle and Alexander the Great, 167, 187

euemptōsiai (proclivities), 275–76

eufrosune (joy from wisdom), 271

eulabeia (caution), 272

eulogon (reasonable), 286–87

eulogos orexis (rational desire), 272

Eumenes, 109

eumenia (goodwill toward others), 272

eunoia (good intentions toward others), 272

eupatheiai (good emotions), 267–68, 270–72

Euphraeus of Orseus, 100

Euripides, 246

Europa, 101

Europe, 1, 44, 97, 107, 113, 300–301, 305

Eurydice, 100

Eurynoe, 100

Eusebius, 291

euthumia (joy from self-belief), 271

Euthydemus (Plato), 43

Euthyphro, 43–44

Euthyphro (Plato), 43

Euthyphro dilemma, 43–44

evolution, 12, 18–19

ex nihilo, creation, 54, 150, 154–55, 220

excellence, character. See *arête* (character excellence)

excess, vice of
Hellenistic philosophy, 267, 270, 296
philosophy of Aristotle and Alexander the Great, 170, 172–77
philosophy of Socrates and Plato, 66, 75, 77, 79
Pre-Socratic philosophy, 15, 23

exercise, importance of, 31, 77–80, 85–86, 191, 241, 256, 279

existence, Epicurean theory of, 218 (ill.), 218–20

existence, Stoic theory of, 216–18

existential phenomenology, 310–13

explanation, types of, 151–53, 158

F

farmers as part of an ideal society, 73–76, 74 (ill.), 83, 93–95, 186

fate, 216–17, 252–53, 255, 263, 274

Hellenistic philosophy, 199, 204, 207, 216–17, 228, 231–33, 251–52, 254–55, 257, 269, 281, 296
  philosophy of Aristotle and Alexander the Great, 102–3, 106–8, 110–12, 114, 117, 119, 124, 126, 131, 148, 150, 157, 162–63, 167, 182
  philosophy of Socrates and Plato, 40, 43–44, 60, 65–66, 70, 74, 76–78, 80–81
  philosophy since the twentieth century, 311, 314
  Pre-Socratic philosophy, 13–14, 19–20, 24, 27, 31
goagapēteia (deception), 271
goodness
  basics of philosophy, 3, 6–7
  Hellenistic philosophy, 224–25, 227–28, 234–35, 239–40, 245, 248–50, 254–55, 263, 265, 267–81, 286, 296
  philosophy of Aristotle and Alexander the Great, 97, 104, 108, 111, 113, 115–16, 131, 148, 157, 162–68, 170–87, 189–94
  philosophy of Socrates and Plato, 40, 44, 48–50, 55, 64–65, 67, 70–72, 75–78, 80–82, 88–89, 91, 94
  philosophy since the twentieth century, 314
  photo, 189 (ill.)
  Pre-Socratic philosophy, 20, 22–23, 33
Gorgias, 34–35, 239
Gorgias (Plato), 35, 71
Gospels, 94
Gothic architecture, 60
grand narrative, 315
Great Chain of Being, 156 (ill.)
Great Roman Civil War, 207
great-souled man, 177–78
Greco-Bactrian Kingdom, 124
Greece and Greeks
  Alexander the Great and philosophy of, 119–24
  basics of philosophy, 2, 6

Hellenistic philosophy, 197, 200–202, 206–8, 210–17, 219, 233, 238, 240, 244–48, 252–53, 255, 261–62, 277, 279–80, 285, 289
history of in the age of Aristotle and Alexander the Great, 99–110
map, 103 (ill.)
philosophy of Aristotle and Alexander the Great, 98–125, 127–28, 130–32, 170, 174, 182, 184, 186–87
philosophy of Socrates and Plato, 38–44, 46, 49, 54, 59, 62, 65, 67–69, 75, 77–78
philosophy since the twentieth century, 299–300, 309, 318
Pre-Socratic philosophy, 9–10, 13–14, 16–17, 19, 21, 24, 28–30, 33–34
Greek and Persian Empire, 105, 108–9
Gregory of Nazianzus, 202
guardians as part of an ideal society
  Hellenistic Age, 278
  illustration, 77 (ill.)
  philosophy of Aristotle and Alexander the Great, 113
  philosophy of Socrates and Plato, 75–79, 82–83, 85–86, 88, 93–95
Gulf of Naples, 202
gunaikomania (craziness for women), 275
Gygaea, 100
Gymnosophism, 22, 120–21, 238

H

habit
  Hellenistic philosophy, 235, 294, 297–98
  philosophy of Aristotle and Alexander the Great, 113, 119, 168–71, 179, 189–91
  photo, 189 (ill.)

Hadrian, Emperor, 115, 254–55
hagneia (purity), 272
hagnós (pure), 272
happiness
  Hellenistic philosophy, 200, 217, 224–25, 227, 232, 239–42, 247–48, 263, 267, 269–70, 272, 277, 288, 295–96
  philosophy of Aristotle and Alexander the Great, 115, 121, 131, 167–68, 177, 180–81, 187–89, 191–92
  philosophy of Socrates and Plato, 35, 41–42, 69–71, 73, 80, 84–85, 88, 91–95
  photos, 168 (ill.), 232 (ill.)
  Pre-Socratic philosophy, 22–23
haptic qualities of the elements, 149–51
harmonic mean, 59
harmonic sequence, 59
hate (strife), power of, 16–18, 80, 184
healthy social ambition, 170, 172, 177
hagapēdon (pleasure), 252, 270
hedone (pleasure). See also pleasure
hedonism
  Cyreniac school of, 233–37
  Hellenistic philosophy, 198, 200, 204, 224–25, 233–37, 240, 249
  philosophy of Aristotle and Alexander the Great, 104
  philosophy of Socrates and Plato, 90
  Pre-Socratic philosophy, 35
Hegel, Georg Wilhelm Friedrich, 2, 16, 306
hegemonikon (ruling part of soul), 213, 216–17, 263–64, 268
Hegesias, 233, 236–37
Heidegger, Martin, 37, 301, 305–8, 306 (ill.), 311, 313, 315
heimarmenagapē (fate), 216, 252. See also fate
Helios, 24

ontology. See also reality
philosophy of Aristotle and
Alexander the Great, 131–
32, 134, 144, 153, 161–
62, 194–95
Pre-Socratic philosophy, 25
Opis, 109, 116–17
opsomania (craziness for
food), 275
Oracle of Delphi, 15, 42, 102,
251
Oration (Dio Chrysostom),
247
Organon (Aristotle), 134, 137,
145–46, 153
orgagapē (desire for revenge),
173–74, 270
orgilotagapēs (hotheaded),
173, 276
Origen, 201
ornithomania (craziness for
birds), 275
Oropus [historical], 289
Orseus, 100
ousia (being), 138
Outlines of Pyrrhonism (Sextus Empiricus), 293–94,
296–97
Oxyartes, 109

P

paganism, 44, 114, 199–200,
208, 248, 253
pain
Hellenistic philosophy,
222–29, 232, 234–37,
240, 242, 247, 249, 252,
254, 270, 296
philosophy of Aristotle and
Alexander the Great, 112,
159, 166, 173–74, 189
philosophy of Socrates and
Plato, 68, 81, 83–84, 87,
91
Pakistan, 103 (ill.), 122, 197
Palermo [historical], 202
Palmyrene [historical], 208
Panopticon, 316, 317 (ill.)
paradoxes
Hellenistic philosophy,
239, 284

philosophy of Aristotle and
Alexander the Great, 153–
55
philosophy of Socrates and
Plato, 43, 50
Pre-Socratic philosophy,
14–16, 23, 25–28
Parmenides (Plato), 45, 48, 98,
135
Parmenides of Elea
bust, 25 (ill.)
Hellenistic philosophy,
219–20
philosophy of Aristotle and
Alexander the Great, 153–
54
philosophy of Socrates and
Plato, 49–50, 55, 81
Pre-Socratic philosophy,
18, 24–29
parrhagapēsía (freedom of
speech), 242, 244, 247
Parthians, the, 255
Parysatis II, 109, 122
passion
Hellenistic philosophy,
214, 226–27, 252, 255,
267, 270–71, 274–76
philosophy of Aristotle and
Alexander the Great, 102,
172, 177, 179, 189, 195
philosophy of Socrates and
Plato, 81, 84
photo, 270 (ill.)
passive intellect, 160–63
passive potential, 152, 154,
158, 160, 169
pathê (passions), 172, 177,
252, 267–68, 270, 274, 276
patience, 66, 174, 243, 249
Pausanias of Orestis [body-
guard of Philip II], 101, 106
Pausanius, King, 100
Pausanius [Greek historian],
101
pederasty, 67–68, 68 (ill.), 104
Peirce, Charles, 300
Peithon, 122
Pell, John, 204
Pella [historical], 122, 128
pénthos (sorrow), 270–71
Pera [historical], 278
perception
basics of philosophy, 4

Hellenistic philosophy,
218–20, 222, 230, 259–
62, 273, 293, 297
illustration, 310 (ill.)
philosophy of Aristotle and
Alexander the Great, 145–
47, 160, 171, 174, 180–
81, 185
philosophy of Socrates and
Plato, 48, 62–63, 88
philosophy since the twentieth century, 311–12,
314
Pre-Socratic philosophy, 34
Perdiccas [general of Alexander the Great], 109, 122
Perdiccas III [uncle of Alexander the Great], 100
Pergamon, Kingdom of, 122–
23, 133
Pergamum [historical], 197
Pericles, 19, 28
Perictione, 30, 38
Peripatetic philosophy
Hellenistic philosophy,
197, 205, 209, 289, 291
philosophy of Aristotle and
Alexander the Great, 98,
119, 129, 133–35
Persia and Persians
Hellenistic philosophy, 206
philosophy of Aristotle and
Alexander the Great, 100–
102, 104–10, 112–13,
115–20, 124–25, 128,
186–87
Pre-Socratic philosophy,
19, 22, 28–29
Persian and Greek Empire,
105, 108–9
Persian Empire, 101, 105–9,
113, 116, 120, 124–25, 128
Petrarch, 203
Phaedo (Plato), 84, 158, 202
Phaedrus (Plato), 69, 80
Phaenarete, 40
Phaestis, 130
phantasia (impression), 51,
259. See also impression
phantasia hormetikê
(hormetic impression), 265,
298. See also hormetic impression

348